THE AUTHOR OF THIS BOOK *was awarded in 1966 the* ALFRED A. KNOPF WESTERN HISTORY PRIZE *of five thousand dollars (exclusive of royalties) for the best-written manuscript in the field of western American history offered to the firm during the years 1964 and 1965. Mr. Knopf announced the prize at the October 1963 meeting of the Western History Association in Salt Lake City. It is offered biennially for a work that is* written with distinction *and in* which sound scholarship may be taken for granted.

AMERICA'S
WESTERN
FRONTIERS

AMERICA'S WESTERN FRONTIERS

THE EXPLORATION AND SETTLEMENT OF THE TRANS-MISSISSIPPI WEST

JOHN A. HAWGOOD

New York · Alfred·A·Knopf

1 9 6 7

THIS IS A BORZOI BOOK
PUBLISHED BY ALFRED A. KNOPF, INC.

First American Edition
© Copyright 1967 by John A. Hawgood

Distributed by Random House, Inc. Published in slightly different form
in Great Britain as *The American West* by Eyre & Spottiswoode Ltd.

Library of Congress Catalog Card Number: 66–19380

Manufactured in the United States of America

To RALPH H. GABRIEL, *who also said:*

"Go West! Young Man."

PREFACE

I WAS AT A ROCKY MOUNTAIN RENDEZVOUS. ON MY LEFT sat Kit Carson and on my right Mr. St. Vrain. We ate buffalo steak and elk meat washed down with "hailstones" of Taos "lightning." Green River knives lay on the table before us.

But it was September 22, 1963, and not the fall of 1833—when Céran St. Vrain and the Bent brothers had opened up their frontier fort on the Arkansas—and we were commemorating the one hundred seventeenth anniversary of the appointment of Charles Bent as the first United States Territorial Governor of freshly conquered New Mexico. The Kit Carson on my left was Kit Carson III, of Alamosa, New Mexico, the octogenarian grandson of the famous hunter and scout; and the Mr. St. Vrain on my right was Kent, the twelve-year-old great-grandnephew of Céran. This Mr. St. Vrain, while wielding his Green River knife like any Mountain Man, reminded us of which century we were in by ordering another Coca-Cola, while Kit Carson III and I buried our noses in the Mason jars in which had been mixed our second (or was it our third?) "hailstone."

In that place it was easy to imagine that it was a rendezvous in 1833 or 1843 and not one in 1963: The walls of the dining room were whitewashed adobe, just as Ruxton and Parkman had described them, and all around us at the table were people bearing such names as Bent and Charbonard, Autobees and Wootton.

Yet this was not the old Bent's Fort—long since decayed

(though soon to be restored) by the waters of the Arkansas—but a faithful, full-size replica of it, sedulously constructed of thousands of adobe bricks with wooden furniture made by craftsmen of Taos for amateur historians Sam and Betty Arnold, beside a red-rock outcrop where Ute Indians had sent up their smoke signals and "Folsom Man" had chipped away at his points, near Morrison, Colorado, on Bear Creek, just seventeen miles southwest of Denver.

To re-create the authentic atmosphere of the Old West, as Sam and Betty Arnold have achieved here, with their adobe walls and their Taos "lightning," their Father Martínez chairs, their Territorial Library in the watchtower, their Museum of the West and their unbounded enthusiasm, is one way of paying tribute to a formative era in the history of the United States and Canada. Another, and perhaps an even harder way, is to attempt to write a book within reasonable compass which can conjure up the West as it really was, and not as the dime novel, the Wild West show, the movies, and television have sometimes overdrawn it. It is this all but impossible task that is here being essayed.

To write about the West and not to have seen it is blasphemy. I have therefore sought to prepare myself for my task by visiting and revisiting as many historic places and sites, by following as many trails, and by talking with as many old-timers and latter-day *aficionados* as I possibly could during thirty years, and more than a score of crossings of the Continent of North America. Of course, had I been able to travel a century earlier—between 1829 and 1863 instead of between 1929 and 1963—I could actually have met Jedediah Smith and Davy Crockett, remembered the Alamo as an eye-witness, hurled hides over the cliff at Capistrano with Richard Henry Dana, sailed up the Sacramento with John Augustus Sutter, followed the Oregon Trail with Marcus and Narcissa Whitman, the Santa Fé Trail with Dr. Josiah Gregg and Susan Magoffin, the California Trail with Joseph Reddeford Walker—avoiding the Hastings Cutoff—and with Edwin Bryant. I could have ridden the Overland Stage with Mark Twain and perhaps rated a sentence or two in *Roughing It*. I could have met James Marshall in the California gold fields and "Old Pancake" Comstock on his "jumped" claims at Virginia City.

In 1829 the fur trade was in its heyday in the West: the first steamboats were nosing their way up western waters and getting stuck on sandbanks on the wide Missouri; Texas, California, and

New Mexico were still Mexican provinces; Black Hawk was still on the war path; Andrew Jackson was newly in the White House. There was not a single American settler in the entire Oregon country; there was no state of the Union, north or west of Missouri, and there would not be until 1846. The city of Chicago did not exist; San Francisco had neither name nor population. There was not a mile of railroad anywhere in the United States.

In 1863 the great transcontinental railroad surveys had been made, and the first road was to be completed six years later. The transcontinental telegraph (subject to interruption by Indian wire-parties!) was two years old and so was the Civil War. There were steamships and clipper ships around the Horn and up from the Isthmus to San Francisco (now a city of over 100,000 inhabitants). The border with Mexico ran exactly where it does today. The 49th parallel had been finally established as the boundary with Canada to Puget Sound, respected by both sides except for occasional Fenian raiders. The Emancipation Proclamation had been published in Washington and the Gettysburg Address delivered. It was a different and more solemn world from the unruly scenes at Jackson's first inaugural and the cider-barrel election of Tippecanoe and Tyler too, and the population of the United States had increased from under 13 million (in 1830) to over 31 million (in 1860).

Yet the frontier, much of it still unexplored, still dominated many aspects of American life. Horace Greeley was still there to say "Go West! Young Man." Frederick Jackson Turner was a two-year-old toddler in Portage, Wisconsin; Theodore Roosevelt was a sickly but pugnacious five-year-old in a Fauntleroy suit; Jim Bridger was still on the trail and so was Kit Carson; a young cavalry officer named George Custer, two years out of West Point, had just become the youngest brigadier general (at twenty-four) in the Union Army; much of the Indian Territory was still forbidden to white settlers; the much-hoped-for Homestead Act was only just passed and its effects on the development of the West as yet unrealized. Old-timers could still remember having met Daniel Boone . . .

Yes, in 1863 much of the Old West still remained and much of its history was still to be lived. By 1929 it was long since gone, though some of the children of the first settlers of the 1830's and 1840's were still around—and that year I met an old lady in Texas whose German-American immigrant husband had been hanged by Confederate night riders during the Civil War as a "Black Republican Abolitionist." In 1963 there are practically no survivors of those who opened up the frontiers and staked claims even in that last mad rush into the Cherokee Outlet of what is now Oklahoma on September 16, 1893. By an interesting historical coincidence Frederick Jackson Turner had delivered his paper on "The Significance of the Frontier in American History" at the Chicago Meeting of the American Historical Association on July 12, 1893, and had concluded by saying: "The frontier has gone and with its going has closed the first period of American history."

The frontier has gone—but the historian can re-create it. Seventy years after Turner spoke, a hundred years and more after the Overland Stage and the Pony Express crossed the trans-Mississippi West with then incredible rapidity and the messages of the transcontinental telegraph in no time at all, historians congregate annually by jet aircraft, by Thunderbird, by air-conditioned Cadillac, and by humbler jalopies, from the ends of the United States— and of the earth (the Turner thesis is studied today in Australia, India, and even Birmingham, England)—to attend meetings of the new Western History Association founded in Denver, Colorado, in 1962 (Denver was a few shacks about to be washed into Cherry Creek in 1862); assembling in Salt Lake City in 1963 (a century earlier the City of the Saints was still the half-built metropolis of the Mormon faith that Sir Richard F. Burton had just described, comparing it to Mecca in the early days of Islam); and to meet in 1964 at Oklahoma City (deep in the Cherokee Strip, Indian Territory, and unsettled until April 22, 1889; a community of 10,000 "Sooners" and "Boomers" the very next morning) and at Helena (in the 1860's the notorious "Last Chance Gulch" of the Montana gold rush, but now another state capital and site of one of the finest historical museums in the West) in 1965, and at the border gateway of *El Paso del Norte* in 1966. At each of these meetings the Old West was remade. Indeed, those who were at Denver in 1962 might prefer to say it experienced a second advent. Four hundred eager souls, most of them professionally dedicated to the re-incarnation and elucidation of the real American West, not the phony American West of the penny dreadful, the grade "B" movie, and the television "horse opera," met at Denver and rewarmed the campfires of Lewis and Clark and Manuel Lisa, of

Jedediah Smith and James Marshall, of Custer and Chief Joseph, and even of Teddy Roosevelt, Owen Wister, and Charles Lummis. Walter Prescott Webb was there in person. They decided to cherish their Western heritage in the pages of a new quarterly magazine. The Senior Senator for the State of Wyoming, himself stemming from the State University campus at Laramie, which houses the magnificent Coe Western History Collection in a new building of Rocky Mountain granite worthy of its theme, wished success to this new venture and its eager four hundred charter members in words that most admirably sum up their objectives and those of anyone who wishes to display the American West with all of its warts but none of its false fronts:

> There is no area of the country with a history more interesting and more distorted in the public mind than the American West. The struggles of the pioneer American to conquer the last Frontier have caught and retained the imagination of the public to such an extent that a veritable mythology has developed around the old West until dreams and reality have become all but indistinguishable. I would not deny Hollywood the income nor the public the re-creation of the myth of the "Wild West," but I believe that we also deserve a factual history on which we can build and maintain the richly deserved respect and admiration for the truly great feat of developing the West.

If that's the way your stick floats, Senator, you can have this child's vote "on the prairie."

JOHN A. HAWGOOD

Placer Hotel
Last Chance Gulch
Helena, Montana

OCTOBER *1965*

ACKNOWLEDGMENTS

T HE WRITER OF THIS BOOK IS INDEBTED TO EVERYBODY else who ever wrote or thought or talked about the West, and in many cases his debt is an unconscious one. But he is very conscious of the help and inspiration given him by such distinguished contemporary historians of the West whom he is privileged to number among his friends and mentors as Ray Billington, Oscar Winther, Tom Clark, and Ralph Gabriel. He has also sat at the feet of Frederick Logan Paxson, Joseph Schafer, Walter Prescott Webb, Frank Dobie, Pablo Martínez del Rio, and Robert Glass Cleland, now, alas, no longer around to receive his thanks. Those with whom he has explored the West and attempted to recapture its true atmosphere include Sam and Betty Arnold, John Bloom, Olwen Brogan, Jack Carroll, Merrill Burlingame, Lee Harlan, Robin Humphreys, Al Larson, Edgeley Todd, Kenneth Ross Toole, and Robert Utley. Many of his other excursions into and across the West have been as lone as those of Old Bill Williams, but in 1956 he took his son John, and in 1963 his daughter Anne, and in 1965 his son David with him and hopes that he has made them Western *aficionados*, too—or at least moderately tolerent of his enthusiasms.

Librarians and curators of manuscript collections in every part of the United States and also in Canada and Mexico have given the author advice and assistance. He cannot list them all, though he wishes to thank them collectively. He owes a very special and long-standing debt of gratitude to Leslie Bliss, Haidée Noya, Edwin

Carpenter, Erwin Morkisch, and their colleagues at the Huntington Library; George P. Hammond and his whole staff at the Bancroft Library; Agnes Wright Spring at the Colorado Historical Society; Dolores Renze at the State Archives in Denver; and Margaret Haford at the American Library in London.

The complete manuscript of this book was read for the author by Brian Hutton, of Birmingham, as well as by his British editor, John Bright-Holmes, and his American editor, Angus Cameron, greatly to its benefit, though the author remains fully responsible for any legal, technical, stylistic or other errors that it may still contain. It was John Bright-Holmes who in 1961 first suggested that he should write this book and who attended patiently its very slow delivery. He also secured the collaboration of William Bromage, a highly skilled cartographer. Valerie Hawgood has typed the manuscript—a task that must have been almost as hard in places as winning the West—correcting spelling and other mistakes with skill, patience, and celerity as she went along.

Illustrations were assembled by the author and the publisher from a wide field, and a special tour of Western art galleries and museums was made by the author in the autumn of 1965 to complete the selection of those printed in the book. The use of these pictures is acknowledged in the list of illustrations, but for special facilities the author and publishers also wish particularly to thank the officers of the Joslyn Art Gallery in Omaha, Nebraska; the Thomas Gilcrease Institute of American History and Art in Tulsa, Oklahoma; the Gertrude Vanderbilt Whitney Gallery of Western Art in Cody, Wyoming; the South-West Museum in Los Angeles; and the Smithsonian Institution in Washington, D. C.

Last—by no means least—the author's students in universities and colleges both in Britain and in America have had portions of this book inflicted upon them in lectures and seminars from time to time over the last three or four years. These they may still recognize in the printed version, though many changes have been made on the basis of how students have reacted in class, asked questions, written essays and answered examination papers. He thanks them one and all for having been such cheerful and friendly guinea pigs.

CONTENTS

(x v)

ILLUSTRATIONS

MAPS

Drawn especially for this book by W. H. BROMAGE

AMERICA'S
WESTERN
FRONTIERS

The Pre-Columbian

West

THE EARLIEST MAN ON THE AMERICAN CONTINENTS APPEARS to have been Homo sapiens. No remains of ape men (or near men) or "missing links" have been found in either North or South America, and, indeed, very few of any type of man who lived more than three thousand years ago. But artifacts that only man could have made or used, together with the bones of animals that were extinct fifteen to twenty thousand years ago, exist in profusion; and one human remain, that of "Tepexcan Man," discovered near Mexico City in 1947, appears to be at least fifteen thousand years old. Authentic older human remains may still be found, and a number of claims, as yet not generally accepted by the experts, would, if true, push man's tenure on the American continents back another five or ten thousand years, or, in the case concerning "Puebla Man," thirty thousand years. But Homo sapiens is believed to have existed on earth as long as a hundred thousand years; thus it is only within the last third, quarter, or fifth of this existence that he appears to have inhabited the Americas. For long ages after he had established himself in Europe, in Asia, and in Africa, the two Americas and all their rich flora and fauna remained unknown to man and unexploited by him.

Into these vast, empty continents it appears that man first made his way by the Bering Straits from Siberia to Alaska. Some early European settlers in North America, observing the Mongoloid features of the tribes they encountered there, imagined that they were getting near to China. It would have been more accurate to conclude that China had come halfway to meet them. The first "westward movement" was in fact a southeasterly one, and it took only two or three thousand years for man to spread all the way from Alaska to Tierra del Fuego and the stormy shores of Cape Horn. He remained at the hunting stage, a food gatherer rather than a food grower, for about another ten thousand years. Indeed in many places he never did proceed beyond the hunting stage; and the very earliest traces of agriculture that have been found are not more than about seven thousand years old. Metals first appear to have been worked at about the same time, but their use was not developed on anything like the scale of the Old World: early copper workings were not succeeded by an American bronze or iron age, and stone tools were in general use right up to—and indeed long after—the arrival of Columbus. Evidence of farming activities (for which the discovery of early milling stones, which may have been used to pound the wild grain, is not, but the finding of caches of primitive cultivated corn is, conclusive) is followed by traces of permanent village communities that grew corn and cotton, notably in the Valley of Mexico some four thousand years ago. Pottery does not seem to have come into use until a full millennium later; and the earliest receptacles and cooking pots of these farmers seem to have been closely woven watertight baskets, unsuitable of course for placing directly over a fire. Charles Lummis, in his book *Mesa, Canyon and Pueblo*, claims to have invented the name "Basketmakers" for these people, but this claim has been disputed. Still the name has stuck.

At this point it is perhaps necessary to refer, if only in passing, to the diffusionist school of thought, which presupposes that all New World cultures derive their essence from Old World origins, that the Mayan pyramids must derive somehow from the Egyptian. These theorists have claimed that the trunklike nose of the water god, carved all over the façades of some Mayan buildings—for example, the Palace of the Warriors at Chichén Itzá in Yucatan—is in reality an elephant's trunk, derived from either Africa or Asia, for the elephant is unknown to the Americas. Others have sought to demonstrate that American cotton was not indigenous but must have been imported from southern Asia; but nobody has been able to prove that maize, unknown to the Old World before the time of Columbus, is anything else than the Americas' greatest and most significant gift to agriculture (though the potato, the tomato, or the cacao and the tobacco plants would, according to some tastes, be claimants to the same honor). The diffusionists, however, have not been able to convince more than a small minority of serious scholars that their case is proved; for the general consensus of learned opinion is that man, coming late into the New World and already Homo sapiens but still in a savage state, without agriculture, without the ability to form permanent settlements, without any but the crudest tools (none of them metal), developed all of his pre-Columbian cultures and civilizations without any but the most fitful and accidental contacts with the Old World. He did not use the wheel, either for transportation or for shaping pottery (though wheeled toys have been found), and did not domesticate animals other than the dog and (only in the Andean region of South America) certain of the cameloids. The domestic cattle and fowl of the Old World were unknown. On the other hand, certain fruits, grains, and vegetable drugs entirely unknown to the Old World were widespread in the New by the time of Columbus. Alphabetic writing does not seem to have been used, but an elaborate system of glyphs was developed by the Olmecs and the Maya to facilitate dating and record keeping; the Aztecs and Mixtecs had a most expressive style of picture writing; and the Incas conveyed messages by a "shorthand" system of knotted cords, or *quipas*. Numerals were used, and elaborate mathematical calculations were performed. A sign for zero was invented, and a highly accurate calendar was worked out. This calendar is one of the finest achievements of the human—not merely of the Mesoamerican—mind, for it calculates the solar year even more accurately than does the Gregorian calendar, which we use today and which Britain and her American and other colonies so reluctantly adopted in the year 1753.

However, the most rapid and far-reaching advances from primitive origins through "archaic" beginnings to truly "high" cultures comparable to those of the Old World appear to have been concentrated in the two general areas of Mesoamerica and western South America from the high Andes to the Pacific coast. These areas today include parts of Mexico, Guatemala, the two Hondurases, and Costa Rica in North America and parts of Peru, Bolivia, and Ecuador, plus smaller areas of southern Columbia, northern Chile, and extreme western Brazil in South America. The cultural situation north of the present-day border between Mexico and the

United States was described not too inaccurately as early as 1851 by H. R. Schoolcraft: "The antiquities of the United States are the antiquities of barbarism and not of ancient civilization . . . whatever judgment may be formed respecting the ruins of Palenque, Cuzco, Yucatan and the Valley of Mexico."[1] Schoolcraft, understandably dazzled by the recent writings of John Lloyd Stephens[2] and William H. Prescott[3] and also influenced no doubt by the almost simultaneous publication of an eighth edition of the less scholarly but more vivid and popular work of the showman-artist George Catlin,[4] perhaps tended to paint too unrelieved a picture of barbarism north of the border. At that time, little was known about the pre-Columbian cultures of the American Southwest that had so recently become part of the United States. The great cliff-dwelling complex of Mesa Verde was still to be rediscovered. The "Horse Indians," who attracted perhaps the most admiring attention of mid-nineteenth-century anthropologists and artists, were of course a post-Columbian phenomenon, and their cultural importance had been greatly increased by their use and mastery of the lower half of the "Spanish centaur" and their adoption of some of the habits and devices—both good and bad—of the upper half.

The broader perspective of an additional hundred years of research and observation has placed the pre-Columbian Indians of the Southwest (and particularly of New Mexico and Arizona) on a slight eminence in the cultural scale in comparison with the other tribes and groups of the United States and Canada, but on nothing approaching the towering heights of the Maya or the Inca. In 1540, when these tribes were first encountered by the white men of Coronado's expedition—in the seven Zuñi pueblos, on the three Hopi mesas, at Acoma, and up and down the Rio Grande valley— they had reached a stage comparable to that of the Aztecs just before they began to raise Tenochtitlán out of the swamps of Lake Texcoco, or of the Incas just before their empire began to expand out of the valleys immediately surrounding Cuzco. The South-

1. *The Indian Tribes of the United States of America*, illus. by Seth Eastman (New York, 1851), I, v.

2. *Incidents of Travel in Central America, Chiapas and Yucatan*, 2 vols. (New York, 1843); both illus. by R. Catherwood.

3. *The Conquest of Mexico* (Boston, 1843) and *The Conquest of Peru* (Boston, 1847).

4. *Illustrations of the Manners, Customs and Condition of the North American Indians*, 2 vols. (8th edn.; London, 1851).

western tribes did not federate or unite, and no great conqueror arose among them. They practiced a subsistence agriculture with little trading beyond their immediate culture area. They had little knowledge of metals; they did not pursue the buffalo in the plains beyond their own mountains (though they did know something of

George Catlin sketching Indians.

the buffalo Indians); and their villages were of dried mud at best. They did not create the fabled cities of gold, paved with silver and studded with diamonds, of the Spanish imagination that had been inflamed by the loot of Montezuma and Atahualpa. Yet they were people of no mean achievement, and "barbarism" is too extreme a description for them. From an inhospitable environment they extracted all that they could to make life bearable and at times even good. The white man had something to learn from them, and their indigenous culture has eventually come to blossom rather than to fade under the impact of the *Anglo*—a rare phenomenon among the Indian tribes of North America.

Wherever else one looks among the tribes of the trans-Mississippi West (or even of the cis-Mississippi East, with which we are less directly concerned), it is impossible to match the cultural achievement of these Southwestern tribes. By the time of Columbus only they had approached the halfway point between barbarism and a truly florescent culture. Whether they ever could have built a Tenochtitlán or a Chichén Itzá, or accurately plotted the stars in their courses, or invented a sign for zero, or created an empire and a system of roads stretching from Oregon to Texas or from the Great Lakes to the Sea of California—all this remains unanswerable. Exploited by the white man, harassed by Indian horse-nomads on their borders, experiencing limited cultural interchange with middle America (and thus sharing virtually nothing of the Toltec heritage), they were never given the chance. In the little mesa village of Old Oraibi, probably the longest continuously occupied settlement in the present United States, the Hopi have tended for more than a thousand years to mark time rather than to be marked by it. They still conduct their pre-Columbian tribal ceremonies and speak their pre-Columbian tongue; they still hate the Spanish conquistadors and their handmaiden the Roman Catholic Church (which has never been allowed to rebuild a mission chapel on the mesa since its destruction in the seventeenth century); for their children they still whittle colorful *kachinas* (images of their many gods) from the roots of the cottonwood tree;[5] they still defang or mesmerize (they won't tell which) rattlesnakes for the snake dance, which the *Anglo* is permitted to witness in his thousands but not to photograph; they still catch live eagles (whether legal or not) on the Black Mesa over toward the distant Grand Canyon. They often send their children to high school and sometimes even to a university. They have trucks and electricity and radios. In Oraibi their schoolmaster is a gifted artist, and until recently their hotelkeeper was an author and musician who had

5. Down in the valleys below, a veritable Santa's workshop mass-produces inferior *kachinas* for the tourist trade.

once stayed away for twenty years and married an *Anglo* from Chicago. The Boeing jets and the DC 8's fly over them higher far than the eagle, but Old Oraibi remains Old Oraibi. Its people are free to make their way in the great world outside; but if they return to the pueblo on the mesa, they are subject to tribal law and must practice tribal ritual. When he returned to the mesa, White Bear, who once played with Fred Waring's Pennsylvanians, was expected to don his *kachina* costume with the rest and engage in an endless chant and shuffle until the rains came. He had to wear the striped regalia of a delight-maker and provide amusement to the assembled crowd. Back on the mesa he must shed his camera and his tape recorder, his hi-fi and his city suit; he must become once again —for an hour, a day, a week—a pre-Columbian Indian. Then back (if he wishes) to the fleshpots of Phoenix, Paris, or Peking.

The Hopi were never really reconquered by the Spaniards after the Great Pueblo revolt in 1680, and under the United States government they have been fortunate in that the reservation allotted them was the region of their ancestral mesas rather than some distant place of exile. Most of the other tribes have migrated or been shifted so far and so often that continuity with their pre-Columbian existence has been lost. Even where, like the Zuñi, they still remain where the Spaniards first found them, some of their most important pre-Columbian pueblos, like Hawikuh, have been abandoned and allowed to fall into ruin. A fate similar to that of Hawikuh has befallen Pecos, one of the greatest of the Rio Grande region's pueblos. Both Acoma and Taos have had to be rebuilt several times since the sixteenth century, and both suffered badly when taken by storm by the white men. Thus only on the three Hopi mesas—though even here a number of the villages are post-Columbian foundations—can the spirit of pre-Columbian Indian life in the American Southwest be said to have persisted without major dilution.

Elsewhere the achievements of the pre-Columbian cultures of the United States, how their peoples lived and thought, must be judged from archaeological evidence alone. This, unfortunately, is meager, although the low humidity of the American Southwest (like that of the Peruvian deserts) has helped to preserve many things (including textiles, basketwork, and even wood used in construction) that in more destructive climates would have disappeared completely. Only bones, metal and stone articles, and pottery would have remained for the archaeologist. Of these the metal articles (mostly jewelry and very rarely implements) were naturally most rare in communities still living in the Stone Age when Columbus came.

Significant cultural development may be said to have begun in North America between ten and twelve thousand years ago, when men fashioned rude weapons of stone and used them in hunting at places such as Folsom, in northeastern New Mexico. Little is known of these ancient inhabitants except that they used their "Folsom points" to some effect on the primitive bison and other animals of the time. Few human remains from this period have been found, and even the direct relationship of Folsom man to later Indian tribes is conjectural. The early Indian farmers of the "four corners" area of New Mexico, Arizona, Colorado, and Utah were already "Basketmakers"—the name by which their culture is usually designated—two thousand years ago. When they began to shelter in the caves of the area, they left more and more remnants behind for the archaeologist. They grew corn and squash and used the *metate*, or milling stone. They employed the throwing stick, or *atlatl*, but not the bow and arrow. They used cornhusks and reeds, strips of fur and animal skins, and dog hair (the dog seems to be the only animal they domesticated) for weaving into baskets, bags, sashes, and sandals. They stored their goods and sometimes buried their dead in stone-lined pits in the cave floors. Sea shells (obtained from afar by trade) and turquoise were used as adornment. It is unlikely that they built houses of any sort before about A.D. 450, the very time that the Maya were constructing their great temple-pyramids and ceremonial plazas.

From 450 to about 750 the more progressive of these Basketmakers, while sticking to their caves for shelter and protection, began to construct pit houses inside them of wood and dried mud, with stone foundations and hearths. These were small and mean, and much of their life—preparing food, cooking, curing hides, and so on—must still have been lived *al fresco*. These "modified" Basketmakers had pottery, in which they could cook, and used the bow and arrow, both undoubtedly borrowed from other peoples. Beans were grown and must rapidly have become a staple article of diet, as they have ever since remained in this area. Turkeys were domesticated, and the population seems to have increased considerably with the expanding means of subsistence.

By the end of the seventh century A.D. these people had spilled out of their cave dwellings and were living—at least during the warmer months and until the crops were harvested each year—in villages of pit houses near their fields in the valleys and on the mesas. From this fact it seems likely that it was a period of peaceful development relatively free from intertribal warfare or raids by nomads. By about A.D. 850 the farmer Basketmakers had become true villagers, and what is called "the Developmental Pueblo Period" had begun. They joined their houses together in terraces, thus exploiting the architectural economy of the "party wall," and made extensive use of adobe bricks, though still employing a wooden framework. These long, curving terraces—the foundations of which still exist in a number of places—were only one story high in this region, but the flat roofs—reached by wooden ladders—could have been used for drying, storage, sunbathing, or sleeping out. Pit houses were still built, but these were used less for living in than for ceremonial and recreational purposes, and were to evolve into the *kivas*—sometimes likened to primitive men's clubs —that are still a feature of the pueblos of the Southwest. In the course of time more and more stone was used in construction, and by about A.D. 1100 complete stone houses, mortised with adobe, were in common use. Pottery became more elaborate and decorated, whereas basketmaking appears to have been dying out. Cotton cloth was imported, for cotton could not be grown in the four-corners area, and there is no evidence that it could as yet have been woven locally.

The culminating phase of this society, what is collectively called the "Anasazi[6] culture," began around the middle of the eleventh century, and the period from 1100 to 1273 is therefore known as the "great Pueblo era." Larger and larger communities inhabited great communal structures, some containing hundreds of rooms and rising to five stories. Some were in river valleys, like Pueblo Bonito,[7] others in canyons, like Chaco, yet others on mesas or in caves in the cliffside, like Mesa Verde in the southwest corner of present-day Colorado. Their small *kivas* were supplemented by great *kivas*—sunken, roofed ceremonial halls or auditoriums—some

6. *Anasazi* is a Navajo word meaning "ancient ones."

7. Pueblo Bonito "could have sheltered 1200 inhabitants and it was the largest 'apartment house' in the world until a larger one was erected in New York in 1882."—H. M. Wormington: *Prehistoric Indians of the Southwest* (Denver, 1959), p. 86.

capable of holding hundreds of people, like that near the town of Aztec, New Mexico. By about 1300 defensive needs were driving the villagers off the mesa tops and back into the caves (where these existed), and such remarkable structures as the "Cliff Palace," with room for up to five hundred inhabitants, or "Spruce Tree House," holding up to two hundred, both at Mesa Verde, were constructed of timber, stone, and dried mud during the thirteenth century.

Ruins of the Cliff Palace, Mesa Verde National Park. Thirteenth century; the largest known cliff dwelling in the United States.

Then suddenly these were abandoned, partly because of the great drought from 1276 to 1299 and partly because of the increasing raids of the nomadic Navajo and Apache invaders. Forced to move, they went south and east, to become the ancestors of the modern Pueblo Indians of the Rio Grande valley.

During the period of cave dwelling all their arts and crafts had reached a cultural peak, and standards of comfort in these great caves were infinitely higher than those of the primitive Basketmakers thirteen centuries before. The Mesa Verde cultural area remained unknown to the Spaniards and throughout the Mexican and early American periods, until it was accidentally rediscovered by cowboys in search of straying stock in 1874, almost five hundred years since it had been evacuated. It is now one of the most impressive of all of the United States National Monuments, though still in a remote and sparsely settled area, far from any transcontinental highway.

The pueblos that the Spaniards first discovered, conquered, and found so disappointing were nearly all founded in or after the fourteenth century, like Zuñi and the great pueblo of Pecos. These belong to the "Regressive Pueblo" epoch following the great drought of 1276–99. The Hopi villages, though older, had not experienced the florescence of the "Great Pueblo" expansion. The evacuation of Mesa Verde and similar Great Pueblo sites is in some ways comparable (though their previous cultural achievement had been far less) to the remarkable migration of the Maya from their "Classical Period" (which used to be called "Old Empire") sites in Chiapas, Honduras, and Guatemala into hitherto much more thinly settled Yucatan, where they were said to experience a renaissance and a new florescence. It has been said of the Pueblo Indians of the American Southwest:

> The latter part of the thirteenth and the beginning of the fourteenth century was a period of great instability, migrations occurred and centres of population shifted. Once the shift had been made, however, important new communities developed in the drainage of the Little Colorado and the Rio Grande, and a renaissance began. It seems entirely possible that the Pueblo people might have achieved another remarkably high cultural stage had it not been for the arrival of the Spaniards in 1540. Even when other Europeans arrived in the Southwest, the native culture was far from being completely submerged, and while aboriginal progress was retarded, it was not entirely stopped.[8]

Beside the Anasazi, the Hohokam[9] culture of the Gila and Salt river valleys of south-central Arizona, although equally ancient

8. Wormington, pp. 107 ff.

9. *Hohokam* in the Pima language means "those who have vanished." For the Hohokam culture, see also Wormington, pp. 118–47.

and perhaps descended from the even more ancient Cochise people, is relatively unimportant. Irrigation by an extensive network of canals built between A.D. 600 and 1400 was its most significant achievement, for the multistory ruin known as Casa Grande (situated in their culture area near present-day Coolidge, Arizona) and similar structures, since completely destroyed, seem to have been the work of Pueblo (Anasazi) people moving into Hohokam territory around 1300. The Hohokam may have been the ancestors of the Pima and Papago encountered in this area by the Spaniards in the sixteenth and seventeenth centuries. The so-called "Mogollan" culture of the Upper Gila and Mimbres valleys of southwest New Mexico, even if truly distinct from the Anasazi and the Hohokam, produced nothing comparable to the giant pueblos of the one or the canal complex of the other, and in any case they had passed away by the middle of the twelfth century. The Sinaguas, a pre-Pueblo people who inhabited the Sunset Crater area in northern Arizona (where a major volcanic eruption occurred about A.D. 1066), also seem to have melted into the Hohokam and the Pueblo cultures and to have produced nothing distinctive. Even less is known as yet of the "Patayan" (or Yuman) culture of the lower Colorado valley on the borders of Arizona and the two Californias. When visited by Father Kino[1] in the year 1700, these people were still primitive agriculturalists, food gatherers, and hunters, barely higher in the cultural scale than the wretched California Indians encountered near San Francisco Bay in 1579 by Sir Francis Drake.

According to the census of 1850, the first taken by the United States government in the American Southwest, the Indian population of New Mexico—which then also included Arizona—numbered 92,130, or nearly one quarter of the 388,229 Indians enumerated in the whole of the United States.[2] The rest (apart from 32,231 in California and 22,733 in the Oregon Territory) were very widely scattered, and many of them were still nomadic. Thus the Indians of the Southwest were numerically as well as culturally by far the most important though by no means the most troublesome tribes (if the Apaches and the Comanches be excepted) encountered by the Spaniards in the seventeenth and eighteenth centuries, and by the Americans in the nineteenth century in their exploration and settlement of the West.

1. See Ch. ii, pp. 42–50.
2. Schoolcraft, p. 523.

CHAPTER I

Overland Exploration of North America (to 1800)

LTHOUGH COLUMBUS MAY BE SAID TO HAVE DISCOVERED the mainland of North America[1] (on his fourth and last voyage in 1502), his colonization and exploitation was entirely—and even then not very successfully—confined to the islands of the Caribbean. Although he vaguely realized that he had stumbled against a New World of colossal dimensions,[2] he did not know and could not imagine that the Pacific Ocean existed. It was the swashbuckling, absconding debtor Balboa who in 1513 "first gazed on the Pacific." Cortez himself was not to see the Pacific until his expedition to the Gulf of California—"the Sea of Cortez"—in 1535. Meanwhile, not only had his own spectacular conquest of Mexico taken place (1519–21), but Ponce de León had sailed twice (1512 and 1521) to Florida in his fruitless search for the fountain of perpetual youth, and Panfilo de Narváez (Cortez's old rival), with a grant from the king of Spain of all the Gulf Coast from Mexico to Florida, had led his six hundred men into the jaws of death in 1528. The four survivors of this ill-fated expedition, the worst disaster in all of Spain's exploration and colonization in North America until the Pueblo revolt of 1680, walked and begged their way, suffering unimag-

1. Though this long-standing claim has recently been challenged by the discovery of a fifteenth-century map, showing "Vinland," that recognizably outlines parts of the northeast coast of North America.

2. "Of this half part [of the world] Ptolemy had no knowledge. . . . Your highnesses have here another world [*otro mundo*]."—R. H. Major: *Select Letters of Columbus*, 2nd edn. (London, 1890), pp. 147–8.

inable hardships, right across from the final shipwreck off the Texas coast to western Mexico, via the inhospitable lower Rio Grande and Pecos river valleys, to return to Mexico City in 1536 and tell a wondrous tale. The leader of these four wanderers, Cabeza de Vaca, said that after eight years of wilderness living "I could not wear any clothing for some time, nor could we sleep anywhere else but on the ground."[3]

The travels of Cabeza de Vaca and his three companions, though one of the most remarkable human odysseys in history, was without plan or objective other than simply to survive and to

Buffalo as drawn by a sixteenth-century French artist from accounts brought back by explorers.

return to civilization. Until their final rescue they knew only vaguely where they were: "We resolved to go in search of the maize. We did not wish to follow the path where the cattle [buffalo] are, because it is towards the north and for us very circuitous, since we ever held it certain that going towards the sunset we must find what we desire. Thus we took our way, and traversed all the country until coming out at the South Sea [the

3. "The Narrative of Alvar Nuñez Cabeça de Vaca," tr. T. Buckingham Smith, in *Spanish Explorers in the Southern United States, 1528–1543*, ed. F. W. Hodge and T. H. Lewis (New York, 1907; repr. 1959), p. 120.

Pacific Ocean]."[4] In the exploration of North America the journey and the narrative of Cabeza are important mainly for having inspired the organization and influenced the routes of the two great expeditions led by Coronado and De Soto in 1540. Apart from Oñate's colonization of New Mexico, which began in 1598 and retraced nearly all of Coronado's route, besides following the Colorado from the San Juan all the way to the Gulf of California, these were the most significant—if not the most immediately fruitful—Spanish expeditions between those of Cortez and that of Portola and Father Serra into Alta California in 1769, which discovered San Francisco Bay and established the first outposts of Christian civilization in what is now the most populous state of the American Union.

Cabeza de Vaca's assessment of the riches of the lands he had traversed and the unvisited regions to the north about which he had heard was not very enthusiastic: "There is no blatant announcement of great mineral wealth—a mountain with scoria of iron, some small bags of mica, a quantity of galena with which the Indians painted their faces, a little turquoise, a few emeralds and a small silver bell was all."[5] Everybody seemed to think that Cabeza de Vaca was withholding vital information either to use on a new expedition led by himself or for the ear of the King and Emperor Charles I and V alone. He refused to serve under the viceroy, Mendoza, or under Coronado in Mexico, or under De Soto after his return to Spain. Says the Gentleman of Elvas, a Portuguese who accompanied De Soto to Forida in 1539 and who wrote the fullest and best account of his expedition: "Cabeza de Vaca . . . brought with him a written relation of adventures, which said in places: Here I have seen this; and the rest which I saw I leave to confer of with his Majesty . . . he and another [his companion Dorantes] had sworn not to divulge certain things which they had seen, lest someone might beg the government in advance of them, for which he had come to Spain; nevertheless he gave them to understand that it was the richest country in the world."[6] Whether he did so or not, that people were *prepared* to believe it richer than both Mexico and

4. Ibid., p. 105.

5. Hodge and Lewis, p. 8.

6. "The Narrative of the Expedition of Hernando de Soto, by the Gentleman of Elvas," tr. T. Buckingham Smith, in Hodge and Lewis, p. 136. (First pub. in Portuguese, 1557; first Eng. tr. Hakluyt, 1609.)

Peru was sufficient incentive. Grandees and gentlemen flocked to De Soto's banner, including even some of Cabeza de Vaca's own relatives. "He went for Governor to Rio de la Plata, but his kinsmen followed Soto," noted the Gentleman of Elvas, with some satisfaction: "Baltasar de Gallegos received the appointment of castellan, and took with him his wife. He sold houses, vineyards, a rent of wheat and ninety ajeiras of olive-field in the Xarafe by Seville."[7] The gold fever had assuredly seized upon the adventurous—though uxorious—Baltasar.

Although De Soto's expedition, after landing at Tampa Bay, Florida, discovered no great treasure of silver or gold, after which its members hungrily inquired everywhere they went, and although its leader himself was not to return from it, the expedition resulted in "our first geographical knowledge of the interior of the states of Florida, Georgia, North and South Carolina, Tennessee, Alabama, Mississippi, Arkansas, Texas and the Indian Territory [Oklahoma],"[8] and possibly also of Missouri and Louisiana. De Soto's were the first white men to see and traverse the Mississippi (which they named the River of the Holy Spirit and where De Soto himself found a watery grave) and the first to encounter the Cherokees, the Choctaws, the Chickasaws, and other important Indian tribes. The future cotton kingdom was their discovery.

The Narváez expedition had been all but wiped out, but better organization, wiser leadership, and greater luck brought over three hundred of De Soto's men safely if precariously back to Panuco, in northeastern Mexico, in 1543. When they finally reached Mexico City, they were greeted by Viceroy Mendoza much more warmly than were the leaders of the Coronado expedition, which Mendoza himself had sent out. At the time it was obviously thought that "the conquerors of Florida" had achieved more for Spain than had Coronado in Arizona, up and down the Rio Grande valley, in the buffalo plains, and on the Arkansas. Later appraisals would rank the two expeditions as equally important—and equally remarkable. Neither of them established new European colonies in North America or permanently subdued any Indian tribes. Neither discovered or blazed a viable route right across the mainland of North America, though they came very near to an accidental juncture on

7. Hodge and Lewis, p. 138.
8. Hodge and Lewis, p. 129.

the Brazos River in Texas, the upper reaches of which were most probably explored by Coronado and the lower reaches by De Soto's second and successor in command, Luys de Moscoso. But in the annals of geographical discovery both are of great significance.

Coronado started off from Compostela, in west-central Mexico, and traveled north over a thousand miles across mountains and

deserts to southern Arizona, then eastward nearly another thousand miles across what are now New Mexico and the panhandles of Texas and Oklahoma, most probably as far as eastern Kansas, and just possibly into Nebraska or Missouri. His were the first white men to see and live with the Pueblo Indians in their multi-storied apartment-house villages of adobe or dried mud, the first to see and describe the wonders of the Grand Canyon of Arizona, and the first to hunt the buffalo.

We know a great deal about the Coronado expedition, not only from letters and reports that Coronado himself sent back and from the records of the official inquiry into his conduct and leadership, but also from diaries and reminiscences of several other members of the party. The most famous of these is that of Pedro de Castañeda, a private soldier born in Castile and one of the earliest Spanish colonists in northern Mexico.

The Mexican border country and that part of southern Arizona through which Coronado and his three hundred Spanish gentlemen had passed with their retainers and more than a thousand Indian allies, driving large numbers of cattle and sheep before them to provide fresh meat for the expedition, was to remain virtually uninhabited, except by the fierce nomadic Apache Indians, until after the middle of the nineteenth century, when the Gadsden Purchase and the discovery of silver and other precious metals brought in the Americans and caused such tough towns as Tombstone to flourish briefly and violently and then to wither away to insignificance. Northward from the vicinity of Tombstone, Coronado's men journeyed on to their primary objective, the fabled "Seven Cities of Cíbola," round which travelers' tales had woven such a web of fantasy. These Seven Cities of gold and silver and turquoise turned out to be merely the seven Zuñi Indian pueblos, one of which, Hawikuh, they had to take by storm before the Indians would submit. The ruins of Hawikuh, which was destroyed and abandoned some years later, can still be inspected today, but the center of Zuñi life and ceremonial, including the famous Shàlaka dances with their giant human effigies, not unlike those of the carnival at Nice, has moved today some dozen miles eastward.

Oddly enough it was a native of Nice, on the Riviera in far-off Europe, who had led Coronado and his men to the so-called "Seven Cities of Gold." He was a Franciscan friar called Marcos, a veteran of the conquest and conversion of Peru, who, together with the Negro slave Estevan, one of the four survivors, with Cabeza de Vaca, of the Narváez expedition, had been sent out by Mendoza in 1539 on a pilot expedition. Estevan, proud of his reputation among the Indians as a medicine man, went ahead of the more prudent

Friar Marcos and was captured and killed by the Zuñi Indians at Hawikuh when his medicine at last failed and his demands for turquoises and women became too outrageous. Marcos, on hearing this bad news, had simply gazed on Hawikuh from a distant hill and then turned back to tell the tale of its riches, which he was able to imagine from seeing the fierce Arizona sun gilding the mud walls of the pueblo and possibly creating a mirage of silver paving in its plaza. When Coronado, taking a shame-faced Friar Marcos with him, discovered nothing but "a little crowded village looking as if it had been crumpled up all together . . . a village of about two hundred warriors . . . three or four stories high," Castañeda says that "such were the curses that some hurled at Friar Marcos that I pray God may protect him from them."[9] The friar was packed off back to Mexico in disgrace; but at least his life was spared, unlike that of another imparter of misinformation to the expedition.

This second "villain" was a Plains Indian whom Coronado found captive in the pueblo of Pecos, east of the Rio Grande. The captive undertook to guide Coronado across the plains beyond the mountains east of the Rio Grande to another great river in which there were, he claimed, "fishes as big as horses." He also said that "the lord of that country took his afternoon nap under a great tree on which were hung a large number of little gold bells, which put him to sleep as they swung in the air. . . . Everyone had their ordinary dishes made of wrought silver plate and their jugs and bowls of gold."[1] He called this eldorado the province of Quivira.

"The Turk," as the Spaniards called him, "because he looked like one"—he was probably a Pawnee Indian—was obviously an accomplished liar, and he may perhaps be designated as the inventor, though apparently not the patentee, of the Texas tall tale. Anyway, his tall tale took Coronado and his men, after wintering somewhat uneasily among the Pueblo Indians of the upper Rio Grande valley, off on another wild-goose chase even more spectacular and much more disappointing than their search for the "Seven Cities of Gold."

"The Turk" was later to confess that the Pueblo Indians had induced him to lead Coronado into the Great Plains in order that the expedition might get lost and perish. He almost succeeded.

After Coronado became convinced that "the Turk" was a

9. Hodge and Lewis, p. 300.
1. Hodge and Lewis, p. 314.

scoundrel, he sent the bulk of his force back to what is now New Mexico, and with thirty horsemen and half a dozen foot soldiers he himself turned northward "by the needle" (as Castañeda says) from the neighborhood of Lubbock, Texas, on the upper reaches of the Brazos River, and finally reached the Great Bend of the Arkansas River. But the province of Quivira contained only the straw-hut villages of the primitive Wichita Indians, and the only metal, precious or otherwise, that they saw was a copper plate around the neck of a chief. In disgust Coronado had "the Turk" strangled and after a few days turned back for the long forty-day trek to join his main force on the Rio Grande.[2] Of the buffalo plains as a whole Castañeda complained in a striking phrase that they consisted of "nothing but cows and sky." The whole life of the Plains Indians was dominated by the buffalo and based upon a buffalo economy. Another member of the expedition put it in this way:

> The Indians live or sustain themselves entirely from the buffalo, for they neither grow nor harvest corn. With the skins they build their houses; with the skins they clothe and shoe themselves; from the skins they make rope and also obtain wool. With the sinews they make thread, with which they sew their clothes and also their tents. From the bones they shape awls. The dung they use for firewood, since there is no other fuel in that land. The bladders they use as jugs and drinking containers. They sustain themselves on their meat, eating it slightly roasted and heated over the dung. Some they eat raw.[3]

Coronado sent out small parties of his men on a number of side expeditions, and several of these made discoveries at least as remarkable as those of the main party. One, under Tovar, visited the Hopi Indians on their mesas in central Arizona; another, led by Cardenas, pushed on northwestward from Cíbola past the Hopi

2. I have followed the route of Coronado to Quivira, crossing the Arkansas River at the point where he is supposed to have done so. The town of Great Bend I found to be hustling and modern, with ugly grain elevators and an aggressively new drive-in theater advertising a film about teen-age gang warfare in New York. The countryside there is dreary in the extreme, the great treeless plain stretching to the horizon and all the towns just like each other. Driving at sixty miles an hour it is tedious. Coronado's men, who sometimes didn't exceed six miles a day, must have found it unbearably dull. No wonder they went back and reported it to be incapable of settlement!

3. G. P. Winship: *The Journey of Coronado* (New York, 1922), p. 214.

mesas to the mighty canyon of the Colorado River, which they were the first white men to see. Gazing down the vistas of fantastically eroded and gorgeously colored pinnacles and stratified cliffs of the canyon, from the southern rim of a cleft in the earth's

View of the Grand Canyon. From Charles Lummis: *Some Strange Corners of Our Country* (1890).

surface more than a mile deep and in places more than ten miles to the northern rim, the Spaniards judged the river below to be "only six feet across, although the Indians said it was half a league wide." Three of them climbed down about a third of the way into the canyon—taking most of the day to do so—and, on returning, said that the river seemed very large from the place which they reached, while rocks which from the top had "seemed to be about as tall as a man" were found to be "bigger than the great tower of Seville," which is 275 feet high.

Coronado and his fellow Spaniards were the first Europeans and first white men to see all these things, now visited every year by many thousands of tourists. The buffalo are gone from the

Pueblo (Taos).

plains, but the great mountains and the great canyon of the Colorado remain just as they first found them. The villages of the Pueblo Indians are still almost exactly as they described them. Perhaps the most celebrated pueblo of all, that of Taos, seven thousand feet up in the mountains of northern New Mexico, near the source of the Rio Grande, was described by Coronado and Castañeda very much as D. H. Lawrence described it when he went to live there nearly four centuries later. It has obviously changed very little in external appearance.[4] Castañeda describes it

4. But beneath the surface perhaps the changes are much greater. I was there once for the fiesta and fair of San Geronimo (September 29 and 30), when the Indians of Taos perform their dawn races and autumn sunset dance, waving branches of the quaking aspen, the leaves of which have by then already turned golden, as they have for hundreds of years. One of the elders of the pueblo, hearing me speak, asked if I was English; and when I said I was, he requested me to wait a minute while he went away and brought back another younger man,

as "a large and powerful village . . . the river flowed through the middle of it. The natives crossed it by wooden bridges . . . at this village they saw the largest and finest hot rooms or estufas that there were in the whole country. . . . Hernando de Alvarado visited this village when he discovered Cicuye [Pecos]. The country is very high and very cold."[5]

After 1542 there was a lull in Spanish exploration. The sons and grandsons of the conquistadors were less adventurous and less impecunious than their fathers, and they had much to consolidate. The disappointments of the Coronado and De Soto expeditions had seemed to indicate that there was more wealth to be extracted from the mines and haciendas of the Mexico that Cortez had won than from fresh colonizing endeavors to the north. Though remaining ever vigilant in the face of intruders, French, British, or Dutch, Spain in America went on the defensive after the middle of the sixteenth century.

Yet although the conquistadors may be said to have overreached themselves at last, the original impetus died slowly. Men still talked wistfully about Quivira well into the seventeenth century and dreamed about the "Straits of Anian," providing a short cut to China, even longer. Many expeditions went out, but they were smaller, less confident, and often without government sponsorship. They helped to redefine the map of North America, though at times adding fresh misconceptions, like that of Father Antonio de la Ascensión, who in 1620 invented the island of Upper and Lower California when he chronicled Vizcaíno's seaborne expedition. By the end of the sixteenth century the Spaniards seem to have acquired their second wind: a new expedition on the grand scale was assembled by Juan de Oñate in 1598, with a contract to colonize what Coronado had seen but failed to conquer. The result was the subjection and settlement of the upper Rio Grande valley,

---

who told me haltingly—for the normal speech of the pueblo is still Spanish—that he had been in England during the war as a G.I. "I was in hospital at Huntingdon," he said. "Do you know Huntingdon?" I admitted that I had been there. "Then perhaps you know a girl friend I had there?" he asked. "Her name was Elsie Brown." Had I been a Spaniard, perhaps I should have been told: "Another Spaniard was here some time ago. His name was Captain Hernando de Alvarado. He was sent up from Pecos pueblo by his general, Don Francisco Vàsquez de Coronado. Perhaps you know them?"

5. Hodge and Lewis, pp. 340–1.

the country of the Pueblo Indians, and the most important Spanish achievement in North America during the seventeenth century.[6] Briefly lost in the Pueblo Revolt of 1680, New Mexico was firmly in Spanish hands again by 1693, though it remained a turbulent province even under Mexican and United States sovereignty as late as the nineteenth century.

Juan de Oñate, the *Adelantado*, or colonization contractor, for New Mexico, was not a conquistador adventuring out of Spain with a band of gold-hungry adventurers, though the blood of the conquistadors as well as that of the Aztec rulers mingled in his family, for he married a descendant both of Cortez and of Montezuma. This creole empire builder, born in Mexico and brought up in Zacatecas, prepared his expedition with great care, and after two years of delays caused by official red tape and by machinations of his rivals he started off for the Rio Grande early in 1598 with 400 men, 130 families, and over 7,000 animals. They passed the "Great River" at the Pass of the North on May 4, reaching the pueblo of Santo Domingo on July 7; and in August he was joined by the slower units of his caravan at his headquarters near there, which he had named San Juan. A church was built and the submission of the various pueblo communities peaceably secured. The colony of New Mexico was in being. It was to prosper, with only minor setbacks, for over three quarters of a century. By that time, despite the magnitude and the triumphs of the Pueblo Revolt of 1680, Christian civilization had been too firmly established in the province to be permanently eradicated.

With justifiable pride and pardonable exaggerations Oñate reported his success in a long letter to the count of Monterey, the viceroy of New Spain, on March 2, 1599. The tone of this letter contrasts vividly with the melancholy confessions of frustration and failure sent sixty years before from that same region to Viceroy Mendoza by Coronado (who had sought only gold and other portable treasures):

> Greatly to His [God's] advantage and that of his royal Majesty, they have acquired a possession so good that none other of his Majesty in these Indies excels it. . . . There must be in this province and in the others above mentioned, to make a conservative

6. See Paul Horgan: *Great River* (New York, 1957), Vol. I., *passim.*

estimate, seventy thousand Indians, settled after our custom, house adjoining house with square plazas. They have no streets, and in the pueblos, which contain many plazas or wards, one goes from one plaza to the other through alleys. They are of two and three stories, of an *estado* [the height of a man] and a half or an *estado* and a third each, which latter is not so common; and some houses are of four, five, six, and seven stories. Even whole pueblos dress in very highly colored cotton *mantas*, white or black, and some of thread—very good clothes. Others wear buffalo hides, of which there is a great abundance. They have most excellent wool, of whose value I am sending a small example.

It is a land abounding in flesh of buffalo, goats with hideous horns, and turkeys; and in Mohoce there is game of all kinds. There are many wild and ferocious beasts, lions, bears, wolves, tigers, *penicas*, ferrets, porcupines, and other animals, whose hides they tan and use. Towards the west there are bees and very white honey, of which I am sending a sample. Besides, there are vegetables, a great abundance of the best and greatest salines in the world, and a very great many kinds of very rich ores, as I stated above. Some discovered near here do not appear so, although we have hardly begun to see anything of the much there is to be seen. There are very fine grape vines, rivers, forests of many oaks, and some cork trees, fruits, melons, grapes, watermelons, Castilian plums, *capuli*, pine-nuts, acorns, ground-nuts, and *coralejo*, which is a delicious fruit, and other wild fruits. There are many and very good fish in this Rio del Norte, and in others. From the ores here are made all the colors which we use, and they are very fine.

The people are in general very comely; their color is like those of that land, and they are much like them in manner and dress, in their grinding, in their food, dancing, singing, and many other things, except in their languages, which are many, and different from those there. Their religion consists in worshipping idols, of which they have many; and in their temples, after their own manner, they worship them with fire, painted reeds, feathers, and universal offering of almost everything they get, such as small animals, birds, vegetables, etc. In their government they are free, for although they have some petty captains, they obey them badly and in very few things.

We have seen other nations such as the Querechos, or herds-

Indian architecture of the lower Mississippi valley. Drawn by A. de Batz,
June 22, 1732.

men, who live in tents of tanned hides, among the buffalo. The
Apaches, of whom we have also seen some, are innumerable.[7]

The further expeditions that Oñate proposed to send out from
New Mexico would, he thought, make him even more famous than

7. Eng. tr. in H. E. Bolton, ed.: *Spanish Exploration in the Southwest,*
1542–1706 (New York, 1908; repr. 1959), pp. 212–22. Orig. Spanish in Pacheco
and Cardenas: *Colección de Documentos Inéditos,* XVI, 302–15.

Cortez: "I should never cease were I to recount all of the many things that occur to me. I can only say that, with God's help, I shall see them all, and give new worlds, new, peaceful, and grand, to his Majesty, greater than the good Marquis gave to him, although he did so much."

We do not today utter the name Juan de Oñate, governor, *Adelantado*, and captain general of the province of New Mexico, in the same breath as Hernando Cortez, marquis of the Valley of

Acoma Indian Pueblo, and Spanish mesa-top Mission San Esteban Rey, New Mexico. The church was built in 1629.

Oaxaca, captain general of New Spain and of the coasts to the South; but in the short time remaining to him (until 1608) he saw a great deal more of the American West and Southwest than the actual Rio Grande valley area that he colonized. In 1601 he led an expedition toward the east, across the buffalo plains as far as the vicinity of Wichita, Kansas, and another in 1604, even more enterprising, to Lower California by land, forcing his way down the Colorado River and along the Gila to the head of the Gulf of California; and he sent his captain of the guard, Marcos Farfan, out from Zuñi in 1599 to rediscover the silver mines on or near the Big Sandy River in Arizona, which Espejo's expedition had found in 1583. Apart from these mines (which he did not exploit) and the pearls of the South Sea, or Pacific, Ocean (which he talked about a great deal but did not amass), Oñate, unlike the early conquistadors, was primarily interested in the lands he visited as possible agricultural and ranching settlements. Instead of dismissing the buffalo plains and the Kansas prairies as "nothing but cows and sky," he depicts them as a land flowing with milk and honey.

> We remained here for one day in this pleasant spot surrounded on all sides by fields of maize and crops of the Indians. The stalks of the maize were as high as that of New Spain and in many places even higher. The land was so rich that, having harvested the maize, a new growth of a span in height had sprung up over a large portion of the same ground, without any cultivation or labor other than the removal of the weeds and the making of holes where they planted the maize. There were many beans, some gourds, and, between the fields, some plum trees. The crops were not irrigated but dependent on the rains, which, as we noted, must be very regular in that land, because in the month of October it rained as it does in August in New Spain. It was thought certain that it had a warm climate, for the people we saw went about naked, although they wore skins. Like the other settled Indians they utilize cattle in large numbers. It is incredible how many there are in that land.[8]

He speaks of "the fertility of the soil, of its many people, of the wealth of the innumerable cattle, so much beyond number that they alone would suffice to enrich thousands of men with suet, tallow and hides; of the suitableness of the land for founding many important settlements, fortunately possessing all materials necessary for the purpose." A Kansas Pacific Railroad land agent could hardly have done better.

Oñate also vividly describes the villages and mode of life of the Plains Indians, little realizing that these tribes were on the eve of a great revolution that would make them infinitely more mobile, resourceful, and formidable than the relatively peaceful people he, and before him Coronado, had encountered. In the year 1600, as Oñate noted, the Plains Indians followed the buffalo on foot, and their only means of transportation was the dog *travois*. By 1700

8. Bolton, pp. 261–3.

they had the horse, and in the nineteenth century they proved infinitely harder to subdue and displace from their hunting grounds than would have been the case in the seventeenth. But Oñate and his men only came and saw and rode away.

The Spaniards, after a false start in 1540 and one enforced retreat in 1680, finally established a flourishing colony in New Mexico, but comparable efforts in Texas met with almost complete failure. It was left to immigrants from the United States and Europe to establish the first prosperous colonies there as late as the 1820's, 1830's, and 1840's. Yet Texas, first seen by Cabeza de Vaca and his fellow castaways and first partially explored by De Soto and Coronado, was of the utmost strategic importance to Spain in

America and was recognized as such from the sixteenth century on.

Farther east a French attempt to colonize Florida with a party of Huguenots sent out by Admiral Coligny had led to the prompt establishment of the first permanent Spanish settlement, at Saint Augustine, in 1565, after Admiral Pedro Menéndez de Avilés had sacked the French fort at the mouth of the St. Johns River and slaughtered its garrison. It was also the threat of French rivalry in Texas, rather than any independent desire to colonize that region, that first caused the Spaniards to establish outposts there. During the sixty years after the "Memorial" in which Father Benavides had in 1630 called attention to the possible ambitions of the English and the Flemings in Texas and Louisiana, a number of Spanish expeditions had crossed the Pecos eastward and the Rio Grande northward, but they all returned without leaving settlers or missionaries behind. The country, though fertile, was rendered highly inhospitable by unfriendly Indians. Captain Juan Domìnguez de Mendoza, who reached the Nueces River in 1684, found the Apaches hostile all the way. A significant passage in his report reads: "The hostile Apaches stole nine animals, seven from the Jumana Indians, and the others, a horse and a mule, from the chief and Ensign Diego de Luna, respectively. Because of carelessness these animals joined those of the Indians. It was not possible to follow them because of the great advantage which they had."[9] But it was neither troublesome Indians nor the cure of souls that led Alonzo de León on five separate expeditions into Texas between 1686 and 1690, each one probing more deeply than the last, to establish Spain's first real settlements there. It was the ominous news of a landing by a French party at or near Matagorda Bay in 1684 that really brought the Spaniards into Texas. La Salle, whose tragic story has been told so unforgettably by Francis Parkman,[1] had traveled from New France down the Mississippi all the way to its mouth in 1682 and claimed for his king, Louis XIV, "possession of this Country of Louisiana . . . from the mouth of the great River St. Louis on the eastern side, otherwise called Ohio . . . as also along the River

9. Bolton, p. 335.

1. *Discovery of the Great West* (Boston, 1869); 11th edn. extensively revised and retitled *La Salle and the Discovery of the Great West* (Boston, 1879). Repr. with introductory essay by John A. Hawgood (London, 1962; New York, 1963).

Colbert, or Mississippi, and rivers which discharge themselves therein, from its source . . . as far as the mouth at the sea or Gulf of Mexico."[2] To consolidate and exploit this claim La Salle had returned to France and outfitted a new expedition, which sailed for the Gulf of Mexico in 1684 but missed the mouth of the Mississippi, where he had intended to establish a colony, and finally landed in Texas at Matagorda Bay. The colonists he left behind in Texas when he departed on his ill-fated attempt to return to New France by land were all massacred or captured by the Indians. The few survivors were located by De León, whose fifth expedition, in 1690, established two missions under Father Massanet on or near the Nueces River. Although abandoned in 1693, these were the first Spanish settlements in what is now the state of Texas. The Spaniards continued intermittently to patrol the Texas coasts from the sea, but not until another quarter century had passed did they make a fresh attempt to colonize it by land.

Once again French colonial ambition and enterprise provided the spur. The French had finally established themselves—and the colony of Louisiana—at the mouth of the Mississippi River in 1699, and in 1714 a French trader, St. Denis, journeyed with great daring right across Texas, from the Red River at Nachitoches to the Spanish post of San Juan Bautista on the Rio Grande. His reception was mixed, but his arrival stirred the Spanish authorities to establish six missions along the route that St. Denis—who obligingly guided them back along it—had followed, and in 1718 to found the settlement of San Antonio, which was to remain the most considerable Spanish establishment in Texas for the whole century that still remained to Spain in America. Spain and France were at last face to face on their North American frontiers. Southeastern Texas could now be firmly settled, and by 1770 the province of Neuva Santander established there had six thousand inhabitants. Farther north and east the French continued to challenge Spanish power from the mouth of the Mississippi until, in 1762, Louisiana was transferred to the Spanish crown. The wild nomadic Indians of the plains, now completely masters of the horse, turned out to be more durable and more formidable. A mission and a presidio on the San Saba River, requested by the Apaches, was liquidated by the

2. Eng. tr. from Jacques de la Metaire: "The Narrative of the Expedition of M. de La Salle," in *Historical Collections of Louisiana and Florida*, ed. B. F. French (New York, 1875), pp. 18–19.

Comanches in 1759. This seems to have taken the heart out of the Spaniards, and in 1772 the Texan frontier was officially withdrawn, as a result of the Rubi Report of 1767.[3] Everything north of a line of fifteen new presidios was to be given back "to nature and the Indians" with the exception of one or two strong outposts, and the Apaches were, as far as possible, to be exterminated. The mission period in Texas ended almost before it had properly begun. The only good Indian now was a dead and not a converted one. But the Apaches were not exterminated, and their resistance to the white man was to continue until long after Spanish power disappeared from Texas in 1821. It may indeed be said to have survived, with Geronimo, almost into the twentieth century.

3. See H. E. Bolton: *Texas in the Middle Eighteenth Century* (Berkeley, 1915), pp. 89–91; and W. P. Webb: *The Great Plains* (New York, 1931; repr. 1962), p. 129 ff.

CHAPTER II

Imperialism on the

Pacific (to 1800)

I F TEXAS WAS SPAIN'S WORST REBUFF IN HER NORTHWARD AD-
vance out of Mexico, California was her most remarkable
success, all the more so because this success was belated
and almost unexpected. Apart from the most tenuous of
landfalls up and down her coasts the Spaniards left Upper California
severely alone for nearly two and a half centuries after Cortez's
first tentative probing in the direction of that "island"[1] where a
fabled "monstrous regiment of women" rivaled the realm of the

1. In May 1535 Cortez landed at what is now Puerta de la Paz, on the west
shore of the sea that had been named after him, and he (or his men) named it
California. He believed it to be the very island of Garcí Ordoñez de Montalvo's
romantic novel *Las Sergas de Esplandián* (1510): "On the right hand of the Indies
is an island called California, very close to the Terrestrial Paradise, and it was
peopled by Black Women without any man among them, for they lived in the
fashion of Amazonia. They were of strong and hardy bodies, of ardent courage
and of great strength. Their island was the mightiest in the World, with its steep
cliffs and rocky shores. Their arms were all of gold and so was the harness of the
wild beasts which they tamed and rode. For in the whole island there was no
metal but gold . . ." (tr. Stephen Clissold, in *The Seven Cities of Cíbola* [Lon-
don, 1961], p. 80). That Hernando Cortez had long known this romantic story is
proved from his instruction issued to his kinsman Francisco Cortez in 1524 urging
him to further exploration of the Pacific shores "because I am informed that down
the coast . . . there are many provinces thickly inhabited by people and containing, it is believed, great riches, and that in these parts of it there is one which is
inhabited by women, with no men, who procreate in the way in which the ancient
histories ascribe to the Amazons and because, by learning the truth regarding this
and whatever else there is on the said coast, God our lord and their Majesties will
be greatly served" (Pacheco and Cardenas, XXVI, 153; tr. in H. E. Bolton:
Spanish Exploration in the Southwest, p. 3, n. 1).

Amazons of ancient times. Then in the year 1769, when their American empire had barely another fifty years to run, the Spaniards, once again responding to a foreign threat rather than to a desire for new territory, began, at the port, presidio, and mission of San Diego, the establishment of a colony that was to prove in the long run more prosperous and more profitable (but not to them) than Mexico and Peru combined, and where the mythical wealth of the Seven Cities of Cíbola, of the kingdom of Quivira, and of El Dorado, combined, would be found in reality.

The California story will have to be told in this work in several installments.[2] Here no more than its modest beginnings need be traced. By the year 1800 California contained only a few widely scattered groups of white inhabitants, numbering not more than a few hundred persons altogether; but they held the coastal areas as far north as San Francisco Bay and dominated the thousands of Indians who lived there.

It is not precisely known how large the Indian population of California was before the coming of the white man, but estimates run as high as one hundred to one hundred fifty thousand. These Indians, of many different tribes and speaking many different languages, were Stone Age savages. They lived by hunting and food gathering and did not practice agriculture. Acorns and shellfish were among the principal items of their meager diet. They painted their faces and their bodies, and when they wore clothes at all, they dressed themselves in animal skins. The climate was kind to them and nature bountiful, if only they had known better how to make use of her gifts.

Ulloa, sent out by Cortez in 1539, had sailed all round the shores of the Gulf of California and up the Pacific shore of Lower California, thereby demonstrating (though few men at first accepted this fact) that it was a peninsula and not part of an island; and Alarçon, in 1540, had explored enough of the lower Colorado River to prove that it was not the opening of the mythical straits of Anian. In 1542 Cabrillo's expedition, still in search of the straits of Anian, coasted all the way up the Pacific shores of the two Californias, discovering San Diego Bay, Santa Monica Bay,[3] and Point

2. See Chap. iv, pp. 115–26; Chap. v, pp. 152–59, and Chap. xii, pp. 403–8.

3. Prophetically christened *Bahia de los Fumes*, owing to the smog caused by the many camp and signal fires of the Indians on its shores.

Conception (but missing Monterey Bay, Half Moon Bay, and the Golden Gate by standing out too far from the shore) on its way up to latitude 42° N, approximately at the mouth of the Rogue River, in southern Oregon, where it turned back. This was a remarkable achievement for two tiny vessels, poorly built and badly outfitted, underprovisioned and manned by conscripts and natives.[4] In the course of the voyage Cabrillo died on the island of Juan Rodriguez (now San Miguel Island) in the Santa Barbara Channel group. His lieutenant, Ferello, completed the expedition, which lasted nine months.

The diary of the Cabrillo expedition was not available to Francis Drake when he took the *Golden Hind* up the coast of California nearly three decades later; indeed, Drake did not even know whether or not Spain had ever taken formal possession of Upper California. He was therefore able to claim—and Hakluyt to repeat—in all sincerity that "the Spaniards hitherto had never been in this part of the country, neither did ever discover the land by many degrees, to the southwards of this place."[5] There is this to be said for this claim: Cabrillo's ships made no landfall north of Point Conception; and his formal claim to California in the name of Spain was made as far south as the site of the modern city of Ventura. If his expedition did find what was afterward named Drake's Bay, it certainly did not land there or at any point nearer than three hundred miles to the south. In 1579, therefore, it was literally *terra incognita* on which Drake landed, when "on the 5. day of June, being in 43. degrees toward the pole Arctic we found the air so cold, that our men, being grievously pinched with the same, complained of the extremity thereof . . . we thought it best for that time to seek the land, and did so, finding it not mountainous, but low plain land, till we came within 38. degrees towards the line. In

4. See G. Davidson in Geographical Society of the Pacific *Transactions and Proceedings*, Second Series, IV (1907); and idem: "An Examination of some of the Early Voyages of Discovery and Exploration on the Northwest Coast of America, from 1539 to 1603," *Report of the Superintendent of the U. S. Coast and Geodetic Survey for 1880* (Washington, D.C.), pp. 160–241. Davidson was able to identify "with practical certainty" (says Bolton) some seventy of the points mentioned by the diary of the expedition, which was not published in Spanish until 1857, in English until 1879.

5. "The Famous Voyage of Sir Francis Drake into the South Sea, and therehence about the Whole Globe of the earth, begun in the yeere of our Lord, 1577," in Richard Hakluyt: *Divers Voyages* (1st edn., London, 1582), III, 730–42.

which height it pleased God to send us into a fair and good bay, with a good wind to enter the same."[6]

Though Bolton claims that "to the student of ethnology the

Sir Francis Drake's Bay, or Jack's Harbour. From F. Soulé: *Annals of San Francisco* (1856).

diary of the Cabrillo expedition is of great interest as the record of the first contact of white men with the Indians of California above latitude 30°,"[7] Drake's observation of the Indians he encountered north of San Francisco Bay in the summer of 1579 was more detailed by far.[8] Unlike the Spaniards and Portuguese of Cabrillo's fleet, he did not content himself merely with claiming for his sovereign the land he had reached, but he persuaded himself that this land had been freely offered to him by the chieftains of the

6. Hakluyt, loc. cit.

7. *Spanish Exploration*, p. 12.

8. As recorded in Hakluyt and later amplified in Fletcher's *The World Encompassed*.

(3 8)

tribes who welcomed him to its shores. Neither knowing nor probably caring whether this was California or not, or whether it was part of the mainland or an island (Hakluyt, in his 1582 map, showed it as the latter), Drake conveniently interpreted the sign language and the gifts of the friendly and subservient Indian leaders as acts of submission to the English crown and, naming the land Nova Albion, "set up a monument of our being there, as also of her Majesties right and title to the same, upon a fair great post."[9]

The naming of Nova Albion[1] and the setting up of Drake's plate of brass[2] in the year 1579 came on the eve of England's era of overseas settlement. Six years later the Roanoke experiment in colonization began off the coast of "Virginia" (actually North

9. Hakluyt, loc. cit.

1. "Our general called this country Nova Albion, and that for two causes; the one in respect of the white banks and cliffs, which lie toward the sea; and the other because it might have some affinity with our country in name, which sometime was so called" (Hakluyt, loc. cit.). The name long remained a close rival to Cortez's choice of "California" to describe this region and very soon appeared upon maps, sometimes alongside the other (as in Hondius's *Vera totius expeditionis nauticae Description D. Franci* of 1595, in which Upper California is "Nova Albion" and Lower California is "California") and sometimes to its exclusion (as in Van Sype's *Le Voyage curieux faict autour du monde par Francais Draek, Admiral D'Engleterre* of 1581, in which "Nova Albio" appears directly to the north of and in larger letters than "Nova Hispanie" and in much larger ones than "Nova France"). The name "Nova" or "New Albion," indeed, continued to be used occasionally on British and French maps right up to the nineteenth century, though Father Kino did not use it in his celebrated maps of 1705 and 1710, nor, for obvious reasons, did other mapmakers in the service of Spain. Richard Hakluyt, in his revised Latin edition (1587) of Peter Martyr's *De Orbe Novo* (1534), had neatly solved the problem by inserting NOVA ALBION in large capital letters on the mainland and simply putting "Puncta California" in capitals and small letters against the extreme southern tip of the peninsula, making it appear a geographical description rather than a territorial claim, though he had heard about Cabrillo's voyage by that date.

2. In the year 1937, three hundred and forty-eight years later, Dr. Herbert E. Bolton announced the rediscovery of the original plate of brass by a young man called Beryle Shinn, while picnicking on a hill near Greenbrae, Marin County, just north of San Francisco Bay. The eminent director of the Bancroft Library, after exhaustive tests, satisfied himself and many other authorities concerning the plate's authenticity. If it is not genuine, then it is one of the finest historical fakes of all time, worthy of the genius of a Van Megeren. A photograph of a replica of the plate, which now reposes in the Bancroft Library at Berkeley, is reproduced on p. 40, courtesy of the Drake Navigators' Guild. An Elizabeth I sixpenny piece has been placed in the jagged hole in the plate. See H. E. Bolton, ed.: *Drake's Plate of Brass: Evidence of his Visit to California in 1579*, California Historical Society Special Publication No. 13 (San Francisco, Calif., 1937) and Colin G. Fink and E. P. Polushkin: *Drake's Plate of Brass Vindicated* (ibid., No. 14, 1938).

Carolina). Had Drake been an empire builder rather than an empire looter, or had the journey to Nova Albion by sea been shorter and less hazardous, who knows but that Britain's first plantation in the New World might have been on the West rather than on the East Coast of North America. The friendly natives, the rich soil, and the abundant game of Nova Albion would have made a "starving time" less likely than in Virginia or New England, and much of

Drake's "plate of brass." Elizabeth I sixpence is inserted in jagged hole (1579; rediscovered 1933).

the subsequent course of North America's history would have been different. What the Spanish response to such a challenge would have been is not hard to imagine, but whether it could have been effective is doubtful. Though thoroughly alarmed by the appearance of Drake in the Pacific and quickly hearing about his journey up the coast of California, Spain did nothing serious about effecting even a token occupation of that coast. Indeed, it was rather the need for a safe port of call for the Manila galleon than the desire to save California from the English that produced, over half a century after Cabrillo, Spain's next serious coastal survey of that area; and though the port was found, no permanent settlement anywhere resulted from Vizcaíno's expedition of 1602.

In 1595 a single-vessel expedition sent across the Pacific under Cermeño had rediscovered Drake's Bay, only to be shipwrecked there. At that time Sebastián Vizcaíno, a veteran of the Manila trade, was unsuccessfully attempting to plant a colony on the inner side of Lower California, but in 1599 the Council of the Indies commissioned him to re-explore the Pacific, or outer side, of the peninsula and to continue northward as far as he could. By contrast with Cabrillo's little cockleshells, this was a well-equipped expedition of three ships; the chief pilot had been with Cermeño at Drake's Bay, so presumably he knew what to avoid; a trained cosmographer, Father Ascensión (who also had once been a pilot), was also taken along. Visiting San Diego Bay and going through the Santa Barbara Channel (to each of the islands of which they gave their modern names), Vizcaíno's fleet sailed into Monterey Bay on December 15, 1602, thus discovering not only a good harbor for the Manila galleon but also the future capital (under both Spain and Mexico) of the two Californias. Christmas was spent ashore at this lovely if not oversafe bay: "We found ourselves to be in the best port that could be desired, for besides being sheltered from all the winds,[3] it has many pines for masts and yards, and live oaks and white oaks, and water in great quantity all near the shore. The climate is fertile, with a climate and soil like that of Castile; there is much wild game . . . and many game birds. . . . The land is thickly populated with numberless Indians. . . . They appeared to be a gentle and peaceable people."[4]

From Monterey, two of the ships sailed to about 42° and 43° respectively, their crews imagining for a time that buffeting storms were carrying them right into the straits of Anian; but they turned back past Cape Mendocino (40° 27′ N) and returned separately, in sore distress, to Mexico. Neither had made a single landfall north

3. The bay is in fact little protected from northwesterly storms, and that coast has been the scene of many shipwrecks since Vizcaíno's day. In 1845, for example, the *Star of the West*, out of Liverpool with iron bedsteads and bales of cloth, piled herself upon Point Pinos, providing a rich harvest to the beachcombers of the tiny village of Carmel.

4. "The Diary of Sebastian Vizcaíno, set down by Diego de Santander, Chief Scrivener, Mexico, 8th December 1603," in Bolton: *Spanish Exploration*, Ch. xiv, pp. 91–2. This bay must have appeared to the Spaniards, who went on to explore the Carmel River as well, to be very near indeed to the "Terrestrial Paradise." All they could find to complain of was the cold, for on New Year's Day, 1603, it snowed and "the hole from which we were taking water was frozen over more than a palm in thickness" (ibid., Ch. xv, p. 93).

of Monterey. Once again the Golden Gate was not observed. Although no settlers were left behind in California, Father Ascensión subsequently drew up a report[5] in which he stressed its suitability for settlement and described in detail methods toward this end. Somewhat deluded by his conviction (reached some years after the expedition returned) that the Californias constituted a great island separated from the mainland of North America by a "Mediterranean Sea," Father Ascensión nevertheless made recommendations that were, in effect, to be followed over a century and a half later in the actual colonization of Upper California by Spain. "If it should seem lost to his Majesty he can command that his Spaniards go by land to settle, some at the port of San Diego . . . and others at the Port of Monterey . . . for to endeavour to go by sea to settle there will be a very great and difficult task, on account of the head winds that prevail along the coast, because of the great difficulty of sailing there, as I have seen and experienced."[6]

The persistent delusion that California was an island was finally shattered only at the beginning of the eighteenth century by the explorations and writings of one of the most remarkable men ever to have worked and dwelt near that "rim of Christendom." This was Father Eusebio Kino (originally Kuehn), born near Trent in the south Tirol, and educated at Freiburg and Ingolstadt universities, a frustrated missionary to the Far East who was sent instead to Mexico by the Order of Jesus. After a brief spell in Lower California he went to the land of the Pima Indians, on the mainland of northwest Mexico, in 1687 and spent the rest of a most fruitful life there, dying in 1711 at one of the missions he had founded in what is now Sonora. Herbert E. Bolton, Kino's biographer and the rediscoverer, editor, and translator of his principal work,[7] says of the missionary's achievements:

In his day Father Kino was the principal personage in his field. It was he who created Pimería Alta as a Spanish province and inspired the occupation of Lower California. Had life and strength been

5. Dated Mexico, Oct. 12, 1620, in Bolton: *Spanish Exploration*, pp. 104–34.
6. Bolton: *Spanish Exploration*, p. 132.
7. *"Favores Celestiales de Jesus y de Maria SS^{ma} del Gloriosissimo Apostol de las Yndias,"* ed. and tr. H. E. Bolton: *Kino's Historical Memoir of Pimería Alta*, 2 vols., (Cleveland, 1919). Bolton's scholarly biography of Kino, *Rim of Christendom* (1936), supplemented his shorter and more popular *The Padre on Horseback* (Chicago, 1932; repr. 1963), an absorbing biographical sketch.

spared him to push with his wonted zeal and skill his projects for conversion and conquest in Alta California, six decades would not have elapsed, perhaps, before his dreams were realized, and then by the Franciscans, after his own order had been expelled from Spanish

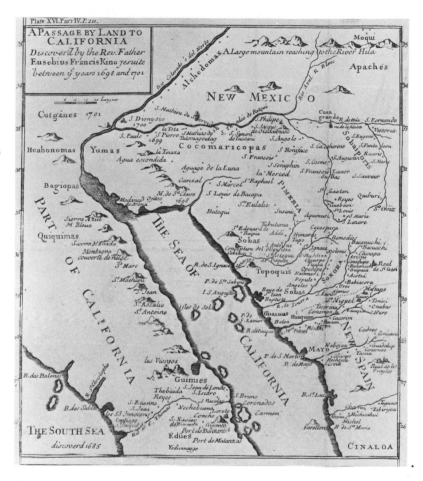

The Kino map of 1704—"A Passage by Land to California." English version, from *Philosophical Transactions of the Royal Society* (London, 1721).

America. He not only created Pimería Alta, but he first made known its geography. His map is the earliest extant showing the Gila, the Colorado, and southern Arizona, on the basis of actual exploration. His letters, diaries, and map, and his recently rediscovered History are indispensable sources for knowledge of the development of geographical ideas concerning California and for the early history of the region south of the Gila on both sides of the Gulf.[8]

The title itself of Kino's famous map, *Passage par Terre à la Californie*,[9] first published in Paris in 1705, contains a flat denial of Father Ascensión's theories. This map had been produced at the pressing request of the Rector of the College of Vera Cruz, who had written: "My Father Eusevio Kino, from Spain write persons to whom I cannot excuse myself, asking an exact account of the provinces which your Reverence has discovered, to what degrees of latitude and longitude they extend, the disposition of the nations, what rivers and land they comprise, especially those which slope to California from South and North, and whether California is an island or a peninsula . . . for they write me that upon this matter there is now much controversy in Madrid, with a variety of opinions. If everything can be shown on a map, so much the better."[1]

The charm and vigor of *Favores Celestiales* cannot be conveyed by summaries and short quotations. As J. B. Brebner says: "The thing to do is to read the records of Kino's dozens of itinerant missions, along the map he made of the dry broken mountain masses and the little fertile, irrigated valleys between the Altar and the Gila rivers (Pimería Alta). They recapture the inimitable enthusiasm and courage of the man."[2] This exceedingly muscular Christian, who saw no visions and has never been claimed to have performed a miracle, stated:

In these twenty-one years up to the present time, I have made . . . more than forty expeditions to the north, west, northwest and southwest, of fifty, eighty, one hundred, two hundred and more leagues, sometimes accompanied by other fathers, but most of the time with only my servants and with the [Indian] governors . . . of different rancherias or incipient pueblos from here and from the interior. To the north and northeast I have travelled on different

8. Bolton: *Spanish Exploration*, pp. 429–30.

9. Reproduced on page 43. A later Kino map (dated 1710) has recently been discovered, and published by Ernest J. Burrus, S.J., in *Kino and the Cartography of Northwestern New Spain* (Tucson, 1965).

1. Bolton: *Spanish Exploration*, p. 436.

2. *The Explorers of North America 1492–1806* (London, 1933; repr. New York, 1955), pp. 340–1.

occasions more than one hundred and thirty leagues to Casa Grande, which is a building of the ancients of Montesuma who set out from those lands when they went to found the City of Mexico."[3]

Some of these journeys were thus in the country of the dread Apaches, for whom Father Kino had very little use. Unless caught very young and promptly removed from Apacheria, they neither could be nor would stay converted. He thought it would be "very advantageous . . . to restrain the enemies of this province of Sonora, the Hocomes and Apaches," and on one occasion he reported with very obvious approval that he "found Captain Coro [a Christianized Pima Indian chief] with his people . . . dancing over the scalps of some hostile Hocomes whom he had killed a little while before."[4] Kino was always very careful to defend his faithful Pimas to the Spanish authorities against accusations of horse stealing. It was those Apaches again, he would explain.

Father Kino was also careful, wherever possible, to secure independent witnesses to his discoveries. On one occasion (in 1706, when he was sixty-two years old) he lugged an unfortunate Franciscan, Father Manuel de la Oxela, who had "come from Guadalaxara to these provinces of Sonora . . . to ask alms," all the way to the head of the Gulf of California, "far enough to plainly sight the land route to [Lower] California from the very high hill of Santa Clara"—which he forced Father Manuel to climb—"traversing in going and returning more than two hundred and fifty leagues."[5] Only after Kino made the Franciscan give him a "sworn certificate" to the effect that "California has a continental connection with the mainland of New Spain" did he let him return, foot- and saddle-sore, to Guadalajara, probably resolved never again to poach on the preserves of this doughty Jesuit.

Kino's geographical understanding, though at times exuberant (especially where the possibilities of exploiting his own discoveries were concerned), was very advanced for his day. "And here," he writes,[6] "I answer the question asked me in the letter of the Father Rector Juan Hurtasum [of the College of Vera Cruz] as to whether some rivers run into the North Sea or all empty into the

3. *Favores Celestiales*, Part V, Book 2, as tr. in Bolton: *Spanish Exploration*, p. 443.

4. Ibid., p. 446.

5. Ibid., Part V, Book 1 (Bolton, p. 435).

6. Ibid., Part V, Book 2 (Bolton, p. 450).

Sea of California by saying that this Colorado River, which is the Rio de Norte of the Ancients, carries so much water, it must be that it comes from a high and remote land . . . therefore the other rivers of the land of fifty-two degrees latitude [the Colorado actually rises at about 43° 20′ N] probably have their slope toward the Sea of the North, where Husson [Hudson] wintered." Kino thus deduced the existence of an Arctic Ocean drainage system in North America. His twenty-five-page treatise "A Cosmographical Proof that California is not an Island but a Peninsula" has been lost and was never printed; nor was *Favores Celestiales* published in his own day, but his map, separately published, ran through many editions and turned up in 1721 in the *Philosophical Transactions* of the Royal Society of London. Nevertheless British cartographers[7] continued to show Lower California as an island and Upper California as Nova Albion.

Kino, who was normally a tolerant and broad-minded man, could not abide that heretic Francis Drake, but less because he sacked the Spanish Main, singed the king of Spain's beard, and defeated the Armada than because—according to Kino—his views on the subject of California as an island and on the location of the Strait of Anian were unsound: "Although Drake, in order to carry his point that California was an island, would feign another strait of Anian with another much-talked-of sea of the North over here above California and that he had turned back from his navigation, yet it is all false."[8] In another place Kino says: "Drake is very much in error in his fabulous demarkation, in which he very wrongly depicts California as an island."[9] Nothing is said about the error of Father Ascensión, no heretic, but a Carmelite monk.

If Father Kino had no visions, he dreamed dreams; and his dream of the future,[1] written in 1710, the year before his death, is a remarkable declaration of faith, giving a cosmic view of western North America's position and importance such as few men in his day could have achieved:

> By promoting the new conversions of this extensive Pimería, with the favor of Heaven we shall be able shortly to enter upon the

7. Like Moll, in his map publ. 1727.
8. *Favores Celestiales*, Part V, Book 3 (Bolton, pp. 454–5).
9. Ibid., Part V, Book 2 (Bolton, pp. 444–5).
1. Ibid., Part V, Book 3 (Bolton, pp. 452–5).

reduction and conversion of the neighboring Apachería, which lies to the north and northeast of us, and extends northwest to the very large Colorado River, or Rio del Norte, above the thirty-fifth, thirty-sixth, and thirty-seventh degrees of latitude and beyond, for we know that it flows from northeast to southwest and issues about ten leagues west of the province of Moqui; for, we having sent messages to those natives up the Colorado River, already they invite us to enter to see them, and already they give us certain reports that soon, in imitation of the rest over here, they will become reduced to our friendship and to the desire of receiving our holy Catholic faith.

By way of the same Apachería, which is in thirty-two degrees latitude, we shall be able, with the divine grace, to enter to trade with New Mexico and with its nearest provinces, Moqui and Zuñi, for on an average it is not more than forty of fifty leagues, which is the distance at thirty-four degrees latitude, where live our already well-subdued and domestic Pimas Sobaiporis of San Fernando, the most remote, at the junction of the rivers Hila and San Joseph de Terrenate, or de Quiburi; at latitude thirty-six degrees, where are the provinces of Moqui and Zuñi; and as far as thirty-seven degrees, in which is found the Villa of Santa Fé of New Mexico; for we have also certain reports that before the revolt of New Mexico the Spaniards of those provinces used to come by way of Apachería to these our most remote Pimas Sobaiporis to barter hatchets, cloth, sackcloth, blankets, *chomite*, knives, etc., for maize.

With the promotion of these new conversions not only will the Christian settlements already formed, new and old, have more protection, and be defended by them, as has been suggested, but at the same time a way will be opened to many other new conquests and new conversions, in many other more remote new lands and nations of this still somewhat unknown North America: as for example, to the northward, to the Gran Teguayo; to the northwest, to the Gran Quibira; and to the west, to California Alta, of this our same latitude of thirty-four, thirty-five, thirty-six degrees, and farther, and to its opposite coast and the South Sea; and to its great Bay of the Eleven Thousand Virgins, to the famous port of Monte Rey, which is in neighboring and fertile lands (and a royal *cédula* came to Sebastian Biscaino that he should go to colonize it), and to the very renowned Cape Mendocino.

At the same time, after having entered to Moqui and New Mexico, to the northwest and the east, it will be possible to have communication with New France, and with the new conquests, conversions, and missions which at present they are making with their glorious and apostolic journeys from east to west. And if we enter to the north and northeast, and afterwards turn to the east, it will be possible to open a way to Europe from these new conquests and conversions of this North America where we are, only half as long as the road which we now have and are accustomed to travel, by way of the City of Mexico and the Port of Vera Cruz; for if the one road is much more than two thousand leagues, the other will be little more than a thousand.

Just as to the northeast and east of this North America we shall be able to have a shorter road to Europe, in the same way we shall be able to have by the northwest and the west a convenient land route to Asia, and to Great Tartary and to Great China, since to the westward of Cape Mendocino and connected therewith follows the land of Jesso; afterwards comes the land which they call Tierra de la Compañia (may our Lord grant that some day it may be of the Company of Jesus and converted to our holy Catholic faith) and the land nearest to Japan; and afterward the narrow Strait of Anian, which is no more than ten or twelve leagues across, and has the convenience of an island in the middle by which to pass to Great Tartary, and from there to Great China. . . .

Another great advantage of much value to both Majesties will be that these new conversions and this province of Sonora and all the kingdom of Nueva Biscaia, by way of the Rio Grande, or Hila, which is that of El Tison, and by the land route to California will be able to provide a port of call to the China ship, and trade with her, and succor with fresh food persons sick with the very painful disease of scurvy which she is accustomed to bring with her, originating from their salt, dry, and stale food, and all with very great advantages and gains for all, obviating the very long and costly transportation of many of their goods from these latitudes above thirty degrees to the port of Acapulco and from Acapulco to Mexico, and to these provinces of Nueva Biscaya, etc. And this port of call, with all due deference to the navigators of the China ship, it appears, might be at the Bay of Todos Santos, or at the famous neighboring port of San Diego of the opposite coast, which are at about the same latitude (though a little below) as the passage by land to California, that is, at thirty-five degrees.

· · ·

The realistic Kino concludes Book 3 with a valedictory protest against the mythmakers: "If we continue with the promotion and advancement of these new conversions we shall be able to continue to make correct maps of this North America, the greater part of which has hitherto been unknown, or practically unknown, for some ancients blot the map with so many such errors and with such unreal grandeurs and feigned riches as a crowned king whom they

Mission San Xavier del Bac. Founded by Father Kino, now on Papago Indian Reservation near Tucson, Arizona.

carry on chairs of gold, with walled cities, lakes of quicksilver, of gold, of amber and of corals."

How can all this nonsense be compared with Kino's own actual achievements, which he goes on to describe in Book 4? Besides "the salvation of so many souls in the very fertile and pleasant lands and valleys of these new conquests and conversions," there are already "very rich and abundant fields, plantings and crops of wheat, maize, frijoles, chick-peas, beans, lentils . . . vineyards . . . reed brakes of sweet cane . . . many Castilian fruit-trees, all sorts of garden stuff . . . Castilian roses, white lilies . . . very good timber for all kinds of building . . . plentiful ranches," and—as a sop to the old Adam—"many good veins of mineral lands bearing gold and silver; and in the neighborhood and even in sight of these new missions and new conversions some very good mining camps." Thus God and Mammon could continue to coexist.

By the year 1711 Kino and his fellow workers had advanced the frontier of Spain and of Christendom significantly, but not very extensively, up through northwestern Mexico into what is now southern Arizona. He was in every sense, therefore, one of the true founders of the civilization of the American West. The traveler who today circles for a landing at the Municipal Airport of Tucson, Arizona, catches a slanting view of the mission of San Xavier del Bac, founded by Father Kino in the year 1692, though today's mission church was rebuilt in 1783 on the ruins of the original one, destroyed in the great Pima uprising of 1750. The Papago Indians, long since converted to Christianity, live on their reservation around the mission and attend its school, now run by the Franciscan fathers who succeeded the Jesuits there when the Order to which Kino had belonged was dissolved.

The direction in which Father Ascensión in 1620, and Father Kino in 1710, had pointed was not to be followed by Spanish colonists and empire builders until 1769. Lower California, the conversion of which had also been Kino's ardent desire, proved extremely hard to settle, even in the eighteenth century. By 1768 the Jesuits had established fourteen scattered missions there, as far as 20° N. These too were inherited by the Franciscans and later handed over to the Dominicans. It was a barren and inhospitable peninsula then; today, nearly two hundred years later, it is sparsely populated, lacks a proper transportation network, and is mainly of interest only to fishermen. But it served as a base for the final settlement of Upper California; and, but for the Jesuits' endeavors there and the publicity they gave to them,[2] the securing of a foothold might have been considerably more delayed. For after the Pima rebellion of 1751 and a series of subsequent Indian troubles in Pimería Alta, the approach by land toward San Diego had to be from Lower California.

The Spanish colonization of Upper California is one of the best documented and most frequently retold stories in the history of western America. Only its most salient features need be repeated here. The stimulus, once more, was the fear of foreigners getting

2. Father A. M. Burriel: *Noticia de la California* (Madrid, 1757) was immediately tr. into Eng. as *A Natural and Civil History of California* (London, 1759). It dealt only with the peninsula.

there first. The Russians were already active in Alaska; the English had returned to Pacific waters and had captured the Manila galleon in 1742; it was thought that both powers had designs on California. The man who blueprinted their circumvention was José Gálvez, appointed *Visitador General* of new Spain in 1765 by that exceptionally energetic Spanish Bourbon, Carlos III. In 1769 Gálvez sent out expeditions by land and by sea to rendezvous at San Diego Bay. Starting out from Velicatá, in Lower California, the first overland expedition, under Fernando Rivera and Father Crespi, reached San Diego without undue difficulty on May 14; and the second, under Gaspar de Portolá and Father Junípero Serra, after greater hardships, for the dry season had commenced, on July 1. Portolá, a really tough character, was off again on July 14 in search of Monterey Bay. Following approximately the course of the still tortuous California State Highway 1, it took him until October 18 to find Monterey, and then he did not recognize it from the landward side as the same harbor that Vizcaíno and Father Concepción had described and the Manila galleons had occasionally visited. So he pushed on northward and stumbled upon a much greater discovery—San Francisco Bay—first seeing it from its southern, shallow end, near the site of present-day San José. Only in May 1770 was Monterey first properly identified and settled. "I proceeded to erect a fort to occupy and defend the port from the atrocities of the Russians," reported Portolá somewhat melodramatically.[3]

Meanwhile, a presidio and a Franciscan mission had been founded at San Diego, and during the summer of 1770 Father Serra established the Mission of San Carlos Borromeo at the mouth of the Carmel River near Monterey, making it the headquarters of the missions of Upper California. Here he remained until he died in 1784, establishing new missions and bringing Christianity and some civilization to thousands of Indians along the five hundred miles of coast and, in some of the inland valleys, all the way from San Diego to San Francisco Bay. By the time of Serra's death[4] the colonization

3. See H. E. Bolton, ed.: *Historical Memoirs of New California by Fray Francisco Palóu, O.F.M.*, 4 vols. (Berkeley, 1926), for the Portolá diary and other accounts of this expedition.

4. Father Serra, unlike Father Kino, is now well on his way to sainthood. Copies of the supporting documentation assiduously collected at the Santa Barbara mission by Father Maynard Geiger, O.F.M., are now being examined in Rome. The year 1969 is an obvious target for the beatification, at least, of Father Serra, as

of Upper California, with the Franciscan mission as its main instrument, was an accomplished fact and a resounding success.

The overland route was rendered safer, quicker, and more
comfortable before the mid 1770's by the pioneering work of Juan
Bautista de Anza, commandant at Tubac, and Father Francisco
Garces, who in 1774 set out from San Xavier del Bac, in Pimería
Alta (now at last repacified), past the other Kino missions of
northern Sonora, to Sonoita, to the Gila River and the lower Colorado, finally to burst through the Sierras into the Santa Ana River
valley and emerge, to everybody's surprise, at the recently founded
Mission of San Gabriel, some twenty miles east of the center of
present-day Los Angeles. The next year Anza led a larger expedition, complete with civilian colonists, to San Francisco Bay.[5] In
1776 the Mission of San Francis of Assisi (or Dolores) was built in
what is now downtown San Francisco. It still stands, having survived the fires of the 1850's and the great earthquake and fire of
1906, which destroyed many more modern buildings.

By the late eighteenth century Spain was short of manpower
as well as wealth. Her resources in the Indies as well as in Europe
were stretched to the utmost. Luckily for her, the way in which
she colonized Upper California, her empire's last successful fling in
the New World, was the most economical possible. A few able
officers and administrators, a few devoted Franciscan fathers, a few
companies of soldiers, and several hundred colonists were all that
she needed. She could not have provided more. The three institutions of presidio, mission, and pueblo were used to pacify and
convert the Indians and to set them to work. There was nothing
spectacular about this technique of colonization; it made nobody
rich quickly, and the settlements grew quite slowly; but it worked.
Two years after Father Serra's death, and after Anza had departed
to govern New Mexico, a French exploring and scientific expedition led by Comte de la Pérouse visited several of the Spanish
establishments in Upper California, and described the colony in its
report. Said La Pérouse:

A lieutenant-colonel who resides at Monterey is governor of the
two Californias. His domain is more than eight hundred leagues in

---

it will mark the bicentennial of his arrival in Alta California and his establishment
of the first mission there.

5. See H. E. Bolton, ed.: *Anza's California Expeditions*, 5 vols. (Berkeley,
1930).

extent, but his true subordinates are 282 cavalrymen who must form the garrison of five little forts and furnish squads of four or five men at each of the twenty-five missions or parishes established in Old and New California. So small a force controls about fifty thousand Indians roving over this vast part of America, of whom about ten thousand have embraced Christianity. . . . New California, in spite of its great distance from Mexico, seems to me to possess infinitely more advantages. . . . But not until 1770 [sic] did the Franciscans establish the first mission here. There are now ten of them, in which

California Indians at Mission San José de Guadalupe, 1806. Drawn by artist of the Rezanov Expedition.

they count 5,143 Indian converts. . . . New California, in spite of its fertility, does not yet have a single agricultural settler [*habitant*]. A few soldiers married to Indian women living in the forts or scattered out as squads of guards at the different missions are the only representatives of Spain in this part of America. California is no less attractive than Virginia on the other side of the continent, except that it is farther from Europe. Proximity to Asia should make up for that. . . .[6]

6. *Voyage de J. F. Gallup de la Pérouse autour du Monde* (Paris, 1797). The translation used is that made by Professor John W. Caughey for his

La Pérouse's description of life at the Carmel mission as it was in 1786 could have applied to most of the other nine missions established at that time, except perhaps the newly founded one at Santa Barbara,[7] opened, as he noted, on September 3 of that year:

The fathers from Mission San Carlos, two leagues from Monterey, came to the presidio. They were as obliging to us as were the officers of the fort and the two frigates. They invited us to go and dine with them and promised to help us know in detail the regime of their missions, the mode of life of the Indians, their arts, their new customs, and in general all that could interest the curiosity of travelers. We accepted with pleasure these offers which we would have hesitated to solicit. It was arranged that we should set off the next morning. M. Fages wished to accompany us, and he took the responsibility of providing us horses. After crossing a small plain covered with bands of cattle and in which were only a few trees to protect these animals from the rain or too great heat, we climbed some hills and heard the sound of several bells which announced our arrival. The priest had been notified by a rider sent ahead by the governor.

We were received as the lords of the parish making their first entrance into their lands. The president of the missions, wearing his cope and sprinkler in hand, awaited us at the door of the church, which was illuminated as for the greatest feast day. He conducted us to the foot of the high altar, where he intoned the *Te Deum* in thanks for the success of our voyage.

Before entering the church we had crossed a plaza where Indians of both sexes were ranged in line. Their expressions revealed no astonishment and left us to doubt that we were the subject of their conversation during the rest of the day. The church is a regular fort, although covered with thatch. It is dedicated to St. Charles and ornamented with reasonably good pictures, copies of Italian originals. There is a picture of hell, in which the painter

contribution to *Problems in American History*, ed. R. W. Leopold and A. S. Link (New York, 1952), pp. 6–16, and also used in Caughey's anthology (with Laree Caughey) *California Heritage* (San Francisco, 1962), pp. 77–82. Repr. here with his permission. An earlier Eng. tr. publ. London, 1799.

7. The history of this mission has been told in engaging detail by Father Maynard Geiger, O.F.M.: *Mission Santa Barbara, 1782–1965* (Santa Barbara, 1965). The year 1782 was that of the building of the Santa Barbara Presidio, which preceded the mission itself by four years.

seems to have shared the imagination of Calot. As it is absolutely necessary to make a strong impression on the minds of the new converts I am persuaded that such a picture has never been more useful in any country and that it would be impossible for a Protestant cult which proscribes images and almost all the other ceremonies of our church to make any progress among this people. I doubt that the picture of paradise, which is opposite to that of hell, produces on them an equally good effect. The quietude that it represents and that sweet satisfaction of those who surround the throne of the Supreme Being are ideas too sublime for lowly humans. But rewards must be shown beside punishments, and it is a rigorous requirement to permit no change in the nature of the delights which the Catholic religion promises.

On leaving the church we passed the same file of Indians; they had not left their post during the *Te Deum*. The children were a little apart and formed in groups before the house of the missionaries, which faces the church, together with the storerooms. On the right is the Indian village, consisting of about fifty huts which lodge the 740 persons of both sexes, children included, who make up Mission San Carlos, or of Monterey.

These huts are the most miserable that one could find anywhere. They are round, six feet in diameter by four in height. Sticks of the size of an arm, fixed in the ground and coming together in an arch at the top, are the framework. Eight or ten bundles of straw badly arranged on these sticks more or less protect the occupants from the wind or rain. When the weather is fair, these huts are left half uncovered. The only precaution is to have two or three bundles of straw in reserve.

The exhortations of the missionaries have never been able to change the general architecture of the two Californias. The Indians say that they like the open air, that it is better to set fire to your house whenever you are eaten up by too many fleas, and to be able to build another in less than two hours. The wild Indians, who change camp frequently, like the hunting Indians, have another good reason. . . .

The monks, by their answers to our questions, left us ignorant of nothing about the regime, which is a sort of religious community, for no other name can be given to the rules that they have established. They are the temporal as well as the spiritual rulers; the products of the land are entrusted to their control.

There are seven hours work a day, two hours of prayer, and four or five on Sundays and feast days which are consecrated entirely to repose and divine worship. Corporal punishment is inflicted on Indians of both sexes who neglect the exercises of piety, and several sins which in Europe are punished only by divine justice are here punished with irons or the stocks. To revert to the comparison with the religious communities, the moment that a neophyte has been baptised it is as though he had pronounced eternal vows. If he runs away to return to the home of his relatives in the rancherías [the wild villages], he is asked three times to return and if he refuses

Mission San Carlos Borromeo at Carmel, California. From F. Soulé: *Annals of San Francisco* (1856).

the missionaries call on the authority of the governor to send soldiers to take him from the bosom of his family and bring him back to the mission where he is condemned to receive a certain number of lashes. These people have so little courage that they never offer any resistance to three or four soldiers who in this fashion violate so obviously their rights, and the custom against which reason protests so strongly is maintained because the theologians have decided that they cannot conscientiously administer baptism lightly, and the government serves as a sort of godfather, aiding their perseverance. . . .

We wished to witness the distribution that is made at each meal, and as all the days are the same in this religious order, in tracing the history of one of these days, the reader will have that of the entire year.

The Indians, as also the missionaries, rise with the sun. They go to prayers and mass, which lasts an hour. During that time there is being prepared in the middle of the plaza, in three great kettles, out of barley which has been roasted before being ground, that kind of gruel which the Indians call *atole*, of which they are most fond, although it is not seasoned with butter or salt and would be for us a most insipid meal.

Each hut sends to get the ration for all its people in a bark vase [an urn-shaped basket]. There is no confusion or disorder, and when the caldrons are empty, they distribute the scrapings to the children who have best learned the catechism lessons. The meal lasts three quarters of an hour, after which they all go to their work. Some go to till the land with oxen, others work in the garden, each according to the needs of the community and always under the supervision of one or two of the religious.

The women are only charged with the care of their households and of their children and to roast and grind the grains. This operation is most laborious and tedious, because they have no other means but to crush the grain on a stone with a pestle. M. de Langle, observing this operation, presented his mill to the missionaries. It would be difficult to render them a greater service. With it four women can do the work of a hundred. It will release time for spinning wool and for weaving rough cloth. But thus far the padres, more occupied with heavenly than worldly interests, have neglected to introduce even the most useful arts. They are so ascetic themselves, that they have not a single chamber with heat, although the winter here is sometimes rigorous. The greatest anchorites never practiced a more edifying life. (Note: Father Fermín de Lasuén, president of the missions of New California, is one of the most estimable and respected men I have ever met. His gentleness, charity, and love for the Indians are beyond expression.)

At noon the bells announce dinner. The Indians leave their work and send for their ration in the same basket as for breakfast. This second stew is thicker than the first, having wheat, corn, peas, and beans added to it. The Indians call it *pozole*. They go back to work from two o'clock to four or five. They then go to evening prayers, which last about an hour, and then follows another ration of *atole* like that at breakfast. These three distributions subsist a large number of Indians. Perhaps we should adopt this most economical soup in our years of famine. Some seasoning could be added to it. The whole science of this cuisine is in roasting the grain before grinding it. As the Indian women have no pottery or metal vessels for this operation, they do it with basketry trays over glowing coals. They turn the trays with such dexterity and quickness that they manage to puff and crack the grains without singeing the tray, though it is most combustible. The best roasted coffee does not approach the perfection of toasting that the Indians know how to give their grain. It is distributed [for roasting] every morning, and the least irregularity with the issue is punished with the lash, but it is rare that anyone exposes herself to such punishment.

These punishments are administered by Indian magistrates called *caciques*. In each mission there are three, chosen by the people from those whom the missionaries have not excluded. To give a fair idea of the office we should say that these caciques, like the heads of the quarters, are passive instruments carrying out the wishes of their superiors, and their principal functions are to serve as beadles in the church and to maintain order and rectitude there. The women are never whipped in public but in a closed room far enough removed so that their cries will not by any chance rouse a compassion which might lead the men to revolt. The latter, on the contrary, are exposed to the view of all their fellows so that their punishment may serve as an example. They usually beg for mercy; the executor then reduces the force of the blows, but the number is always irrevocably fixed.

The rewards are small distributions of grain, which they make into small biscuits cooked on the coals. On great feast days the ration is beef. Many eat it raw, especially the fat, which to them is as delicious as excellent butter or the best cheese. They skin the animals with dispatch, and if they are fat, they are like crows croaking their pleasure and devouring immediately the parts of which they are most fond.

They are often allowed to hunt and fish, and on their return they customarily give the missionaries a present of fish or game, proportioning the amount to what is necessary, increasing it if they know that guests are visiting their superiors. At their huts the women raise some chickens, giving the eggs to their children. These chickens belong to the Indians, as do their clothes and the other small things of the household and the chase. No instances of thievery have ever occurred among them, although their doors consist only of a bundle of straw placed across the entrance when all the occupants are away.

These customs may seem patriarchal to some of our readers. They will not consider that any of these dwellings had any object to tempt the cupidity of the neighbors. The Indians' nourishment is assured; they have no other need but to give birth to other beings who must be as stupid as they.

The men at the missions have made a greater sacrifice to Christianity than the women, because polygamy was permitted and it was the usage to marry all the sisters of a family. The women, on the contrary, have acquired the advantage of receiving exclusively the favors of one man. . . .

The missionaries have constituted themselves as guardians of female virtue. An hour after supper, they lock up all those whose husbands are absent and all the girls over nine years of age, and until morning keep them under the surveillance of matrons. Even these precautions are not always sufficient. We saw men in the stocks and women in irons for having eluded the vigilance of these female arguses for whom two eyes were not enough.

The converted Indians have kept all the old usages that their new religion does not prohibit: the same huts, the same games, the same costumes. The richest consists of a cloak of otter skins which covers the loins and reaches to the knees. The lazier have only a scrap of cloth which the mission has furnished to cover their nakedness and a small mantle of rabbitskin covering their shoulders and reaching only to the waist. The rest of the body is absolutely bare, even the head, although some have straw hats, very neatly plaited.

The women's garb is a cloak of poorly tanned deerskin. Those at the mission are in the habit of making a corselet with sleeves. It is their only garment except a small apron of rushes and a deerskin skirt which covers the loins and reaches to the knee. The young girls under nine wear only a simple girdle and the boys go naked.

Captain Vancouver came to Monterey in the 1790's and a Russian scientific expedition to San Francisco Bay a decade later; their descriptions of these places were very similar to that of La Pérouse. The missions of Alta California, which grew in number to twenty-one, continued to thrive until the 1830's, when their secularization by the Mexican government soon brought this first, pastoral, and (for the Spaniards living there, at least) almost idyllic phase of the country's history to an end.

No other new colony was founded by Spain in the eighteenth century. Louisiana came to her ready-made in 1762, ceded by a France exhausted from the Seven Years' War. She was to lose it again to Napoleon Bonaparte in 1801; though she regained Florida from Britain in 1783. New Mexico she retained but did not extend (despite the heroic explorations of Fathers Garces and Escalante in the 1770's). Texas she almost lost. In the newly opening territory west of the Missouri she proved less enterprising than the British, the French, or the Americans.[8] Her star of empire had almost set.

8. See Ch. iii.

CHAPTER III

Exploring and Exploiting the Louisiana Purchase: Lewis and Clark, Pike and Long

HE AMERICANS, WHO WERE TO BE THE ULTIMATE INHERitors of the whole of that great region, still did not have sovereignty over one inch of the trans-Mississippi West in the year 1800; nor by that date had they played any significant part in its exploration. This had been the work of Frenchmen, Spaniards, and British and French Canadians. Though the little *Columbia* of the American Captain Gray had carried the stars and stripes of his new nation ahead of the flag of any other country into the mouth of that great river of the West which now bears his ship's name, it was the Spaniard Francisco de Ulloa who had found the mouth of the Colorado and circumnavigated the Gulf of California, or the "Sea of Cortez." Another Spaniard, De Soto, was the first white man to find the "River of the Holy Spirit" (the Mississippi); and a Frenchman, La Salle, was the first to traverse it from its upper reaches west of the Great Lakes to its delta on the Gulf of Mexico and to rename it the Colbert. De Soto and Coronado respectively had explored the lower and the upper Arkansas River valley and had come within about three hundred miles of each other—and of spanning the continent. Though, as the old Confederate Army song tells us, "the first white man through the Cumberland Gap was Doctor Walker, an English chap" (he went through in 1750), this was still a long way east of the Mississippi, and so was Daniel Boone's party, which began the colonization of Kentucky and Tennessee through that same gap in 1775 (a year before the Declaration of Independence); but as early as 1739 two intrepid Frenchmen, the Mallet brothers, had pioneered

Interior of a Mandan chief's hut, 1833, by Karl Bodmer.

the route up the Platte River, far west of the mountains, which later became the well-beaten Santa Fe Trail. They had returned to French Louisiana by way of the Canadian River, the name that it has since borne to commemorate their exploit and to puzzle many students of geography; for though it flows from its source in New Mexico through Oklahoma and the panhandle of Texas to its confluence with the Arkansas, it is still "the river of the Canadians" Pierre and Paul Mallet.[1]

Nor were Americans the first to cross the wide Missouri—the

1. J. B. Thorborn, in *Chronicles of Oklahoma*, VI:2 (June 1922), 181-5. See also Brebner, op. cit., p. 287.

ACROSS CANADA
BY LAND TO THE PACIFIC
1672 – 1793

St Simon & Albanel 1672
Kelsey 1690-1692
Hendaye 1755
Hearne 1770
 1771-1772
Pond 1778
Mackenzie 1789 & 1792-93

ST. SIMON &
ALBANEL 1672

KELSEY
1690-92

HEARNE 1770

HEARNE
1771-72

POND
1773

HENDAYE
1755

MACKENZIE 1789

1792-93

only river that had shown real promise of leading to a practicable route to the far Pacific Ocean or to the fabulous "Northwest Passage" to Asia. One day in 1673 Joliet and Marquette had crossed its mouth where it empties into the Mississippi and had been told by local Indians that California was not very far away. And La Vérendrye and his sons, in addition to their explorations in Canada as far west as Manitoba, had struck overland across the prairies of what are now Minnesota and the Dakotas to the upper Missouri and traded with the Mandan villages, where for so long men were to believe that the "Welsh Indians" of Prince Modoc's "migration" dwelt.[2] In 1743 they had even reached the Bad Lands and seen (but not traversed) the Black Hills of South Dakota. Some would even claim that what they saw were the most easterly peaks of the Rockies.[3]

Last and by no means least, the first man to travel overland from the Middle Western settlements all the way to the Pacific Ocean was not an American but a Scots Canadian, Alexander Mackenzie. Part of the way had been blazed for him by such men as Anthony Henday, Samuel Hearne, Jonathan Carver, Alexander Henry, and Peter Pond. Mackenzie reached Puget Sound, on the Pacific shore of North America, via the Fraser River "from Canada, by land, the 22nd July, 1793" (as he commemorated his achievement in an inscription on a rock at the Sound), beating Lewis and Clark by more than a decade.

Indeed it was Mackenzie's *Voyage from Montreal through the Continent of North America* (London, 1801) that inspired Thomas Jefferson, then president of the United States, to organize the Lewis and Clark expedition. This was by no means the earliest attempt of this first American imperialist to put his countrymen to the forefront in the opening up of the trans-Mississippi West; and within a decade he had so far succeeded in this endeavor that American explorers had taken their place on at least an equal

2. Much nonsense has been written about Prince Modoc (or Modog) and the Welsh Indians. For a critical analysis of the legend, see David Williams: "John Evans' Strange Journey; Part I: The Welsh Indians," *American Historical Review*, LIV (Jan. 1949), 277–95. Jefferson wrote to Lewis about Evans's map of the upper Missouri on Jan. 13 and 22, 1804; see *The Original Journals of Lewis and Clark*, ed. R. G. Thwaites (New York, 1904), VII, 291–2.

3. *Journals and Letters of La Vérendrye and His Sons*, ed. and tr. L. J. Burpee (Toronto: Champlain Society; 1927), and A. S. Morton, in *Canadian Historical Review*, IX:4 (Dec. 1928). See also Brebner, pp. 300 ff.

footing with the others. In the nineteenth century they dominated the exploration and exploitation of the region.

Earlier in the eighteenth century Bishop Berkeley in his celebrated poem had used the world "empire" quite innocuously in "Westward the Course of Empire takes its way," while Jedediah Morse, in his *American Geography* (1789), spoke more purposefully of "the American Empire which will eventually comprehend

Offering of the Mandan Indians, by Karl Bodmer.

millions of souls west of the Mississippi." Jefferson and, even more so, his disciple John Quincy Adams believed in the expansion of the American people (though not necessarily of the sovereignty of the United States under the Constitution of 1787) throughout the American continent, and they were among the first to strike a note that was to be banged very hard indeed in the age of "manifest destiny" by coiners of such phrases as "Fifty-four-forty or Fight."

From a very early date Thomas Jefferson had been interested in American expansion westward beyond the limits of the thirteen colonies. A boy of seven when Dr. Walker became "the first white man through the Cumberland Gap" (not so very far from Jefferson's birthplace at Shadwell, in upstate Virginia), he was a man of thirty-two when Daniel Boone led his party of emigrants through the Gap into Kentucky in 1775 in defiance of the British Royal Proclamation of 1763; and at thirty-three, partially inspired by such events, he drafted the Declaration of Independence, which contains a protest against the hated Proclamation line, a barrier that was attacked with equal vehemence both for its injustice and for its impracticability by Edmund Burke in Parliament at Westminster. In 1785, while minister to France, Jefferson sent John Paul Jones to spy out the plans of Comte de la Pérouse, then preparing his circumnavigation of the globe,[4] and soon afterward he dispatched John Ledyard (formerly a corporal of Marines in the Royal Navy under Captain Cook but now a loyal American) across Siberia to nose out a land route from the Pacific to the Atlantic. "Wrong Way Ledyard" almost reached Kamchatka before Catherine the Great sent him back under escort to the Polish border. "Thus failed the first attempt to explore the western part of our northern continent," wrote Jefferson many years later.[5] He meant, of course, the first American attempt.

Jefferson went on trying. In the early 1790's, while Secretary of State, he was encouraging George Rogers Clark to explore beyond the Mississippi border and the French scientist Andre Michaux (who was to be assisted by a young protégé of Jefferson's, Lieutenant Meriwether Lewis) to make an expedition up the Missouri and over the Continental Divide to the Pacific, ostensibly under the patronage of the American Philosophical Society of Philadelphia. In April 1793 Michaux was instructed to find "the shortest and most convenient route of communication between the United States and the Pacific Ocean within the temperate latitudes"; unknown to both Jefferson and Michaux, however, Captain Gray had already discovered the mouth of the Columbia River from the sea, and Mackenzie was well on his way overland to Puget Sound. Thus Jefferson, Michaux, and the unfortunate George Rogers Clark (no longer supported by his French backers) were

4. *The Jefferson Papers*, ed. J. P. Boyd, VIII, 373 ff.

5. In his "Memoir of Meriwether Lewis," in *The History of the Lewis and Clark Expedition*, ed. E. Coues, 4 vols. (New York, 1893), I, xviii–xix. See also *Jefferson Papers*, X, 220–2, 315–16, 548–9, and XI, 216–18, 637–9; and Richard Van Alstyne: *The Rising American Empire* (Oxford, 1960), pp. 79–80, whose citation of the above references is here acknowledged.

left at the post, and neither projected expedition ever even crossed the Mississippi.

"Jefferson finally realised his dream in the celebrated Lewis and Clark expedition (1804–06), but the expedition was twenty years behind its schedule according to his way of thinking," says Van Alstyne.[6] Early in 1801 Jefferson learned through his agents the momentous news that France had regained sovereignty over

Missouri River at Council Bluffs, by F. Piercy. From H. J. Warre: *Sketches in North America* (London, 1849).

Louisiana. This huge territory, comprising more than a third of the area of what is now the continental United States (excluding Alaska), had been handed over to Spain in 1762 by its French founders. Spain in her years of decline, with her dwindling resources stretched to the utmost elsewhere, had done little to develop it even under the relatively enterprising King Carlos III and

6. *The Rising American Empire*, p. 80. This book, a refreshingly unorthodox and nonjingoist treatment of the subject, is not afraid to call a spade a spade and an empire an empire. Compare Norman Graebner's equally original *Empire on the Pacific* (New York, 1955).

the more energetic governors he appointed, but she did cling tenaciously to the strategic settlement of New Orleans—a city that
retained much of its French character; also, while she failed to keep
the Americans from establishing their boundary on the Mississippi
down to latitude 31° in 1783, she did bottle them off from any part
of the Gulf of Mexico by regaining Florida from Great Britain in

Village of mandan Indian. with earth covered Wigwams

Mandan village, by George Catlin.

that same year. But as the Americans pushed westward into Kentucky and Tennessee, down the Ohio River on their flatboats to
colonize the Ohio, Indiana, and Illinois territories north and west of
the river, and along the Natchez Trace to open up new cotton and
trading country beyond the Carolinas and Georgia, they found the
Mississippi River becoming ever more important to them as an
artery of trade and commerce. Spain's various attempts to keep the
Americans from trading down the Mississippi to the Gulf had
never been overly effective and were brought to a temporary halt
by the terms of Pinckney's treaty of 1794. Now, less than a decade
later, New Orleans and the river's mouth, in addition to the huge
hinterland, were transferred back from the effete hands of Spain
into the ruthlessly ambitious control of the young general Bona-

parte, just returned from his misadventures on the Nile in search of newer worlds to conquer and recently established under the thin disguise of "First Consul" as absolute dictator of a reinvigorated France, a France more powerful than she had been since the middle years of Louis XIV. The prospect for the infant United States was alarming. Bonaparte was known to intend sending an army to the Mississippi Valley, and an expedition to the island of Santo Domingo—which could act as a stepping-stone—was already in being. He might easily reconquer Canada and then push his empire to the Rocky Mountains and even beyond. Had not La Pérouse surveyed the shores of the Pacific and the posthumous report of his voyage been published by the Convention? The expansion of the United States might thus easily be strangled in infancy.

Despite his great love for France, which had not been materially shaken by the plots of Citizen Genêt, and the cooling of the alliance with that country in the 1790's, Jefferson fully recognized the menace she constituted to the future of the United States. If necessary, an alliance with the Great Britain of George III must be sought in order to counteract this menace. Jefferson resorted at first to psychological warfare. That he might be forced to seek a close alliance with Great Britian was "leaked" through the Franco-American gunpowder manufacturer Dupont de Nemours to government circles in Paris. When Napoleon Bonaparte read Jefferson's "confidential" opinion—"The day that France takes possession of New Orleans . . . seals the union of two nations who in conjunction can maintain exclusive possession of the ocean. From that moment we must marry ourselves to the British fleet and nation"—he must have been strengthened in his already half-formed resolve to cut his losses in the New World, as he had already done in the Levant, and concentrate on the sufficiently formidable task of becoming master of Europe. His lightning *volte-face* when he offered Louisiana to the American plenipotentiaries Livingston and Monroe through his ministers Talleyrand and Barbé-Marbois resulted in the transfer of the great territory to the United States for a mere $15 million. When asked to define the limits of this cession, Talleyrand simply said: "You have a noble bargain; make the most that you can of it."[7] Jefferson did exactly that.

7. See B. Hermann: *The Louisiana Purchase* (Washington, D. C.: Gov. Printing Office; 1898) for details, documentation, and maps of the Purchase.

On "the 8 Frimaire of the Year XII of the Republic" (November 30, 1803) the city of New Orleans was formally handed over by France to her "loyal and faithful ally" (so ran the proclamation), the United States of America. News traveled more slowly to the upper Mississippi, and it was not until March 9, 1804, that St. Louis was transferred. By that time Meriwether Lewis and William Clark had already reached that frontier outpost, and they witnessed the ceremony which meant that the first year of their explorations would now be on American soil. On May 14, 1804, they set off from St. Louis up the Missouri Valley. By August 3 they reached and named Council Bluffs, because there they went into council with the dangerous and incalculable Sioux Indians, whose hunting grounds they would have to traverse. They were at the villages of the friendlier and more settled Mandans in time to go into winter quarters among them. They set out again in April 1805, and it was not until November of that year that they reached their goal, the shore of the Pacific Ocean.

Driving one day during the summer of 1955 from Chicago to California, I halted about noon at a historical spot, known as Three Forks, a few miles west of Bozeman, Montana. Almost exactly 150 years earlier Meriwether Lewis and William Clark reached this same place. The scene they observed on that summer day in the year 1805 could have been little different from the one I saw a century and a half later. A wide plain surrounded by rolling and lightly wooded hills stretched to the horizon, with not a human habitation in sight. Where the three moderate-sized streams came together to make the one big river, there were sand bars; and below their point of confluence stood low bluffs of bare rock. On the narrow V-shaped spit of land between the Madison and the Gallatin rivers I found the three historical markers put up by the state of Montana. The center one bore this inscription:

WHERE THE MISSOURI BEGINS

The Lewis and Clark Expedition, leaving St. Louis . . . May 14, 1804, traveling by boats up the Missouri River into unexplored country, reached here July 27, 1805. They had arrived at their first objective, fulfilling a vital function of their mission. . . . Caution is taken to preserve this part of the area just as nature carved it, the way it must have been when Lewis and Clark first saw it. . . .

I sat down on the bank and searched in my copy of the *Journals* for the words in which the explorers themselves had described the scene. William Clark had written:

LET NO MAN DESTROY IT.

Lewis and Clark and Sacagawea, by Charlie Russell. Heroic bronze statue photographed near Three Forks, Montana.

A fine morning. We proceeded on a few miles to the three forks of the Missouri. Those three forks are nearly of a size; the North fork appears to have the most water and must be considered as the one best calculated for us to ascend.

And Meriwether Lewis commented:

Both Captain Clark and myself corresponded in opinion with respect to the impropriety of calling either of these streams the Missouri, and accordingly agreed to name them after the President of the United States and the Secretaries of the Treasury and State, having previously named one river in honour of the Secretaries of War and Navy. In pursuance of this resolution we called the South West fork Jefferson's River, in honour of that illustrious personage Thomas Jefferson (*the author of our enterprise*). The Middle fork we called Madison's River in honour of James Madison, and the South East fork we called Gallitin's River in honour of Albert Gallitin. The two first are 90 yards wide and the last is 70 yards.

Every American schoolgirl has heard of the young Shoshone Indian squaw Sacagawea—meaning "birdwoman"—who accompanied the Lewis and Clark expedition from April 1805 until its return to comparative civilization nearly eighteen months later, and of her husband, the French-Canadian interpreter Toussaint Charbonneau, and her baby boy, Baptiste, who was born a little before the expedition started off from its winter quarters in North Dakota. More monuments have been raised in the United States to Sacagawea than to any other woman, American or foreign. She has become an American folk heroine of major importance, rivaling if not outshining such figures as Virginia Dare, Pocahontas, Barbara Frietchie, and Calamity Jane. It has even been claimed that if Sacagawea had not accompanied the expedition, it could not have succeeded. Yet at the time she was only a girl of eighteen, bought out of slavery by Charbonneau from an Indian tribe that had captured her some five years earlier in an attack on a party of her own people in the vicinity of these same Three Forks of the Missouri. Lewis refers briefly to her capture in his *Journal* entry dated Sunday, July 28, 1805:

Our present camp is precisely on the spot that the Snake Indians were encamped, at the time the Minnetares of the Knife River first came into sight of them five years since. From hence they retreated about three miles up Jefferson's river and concealed themselves in the woods. The Minnetares pursued, attacked them, killed 4 men, 4 women, a number of boys, and made prisoners of all the females and four boys. Sah-cah-jar-we-ah, our Indian woman, was one of the female prisoners taken at that time; tho' I cannot discover that she shews any emotion of sorrow in recollecting this event, or of joy in being restored to her native country; if she has enough to eat and a few trinkets to wear I believe she would be perfectly content anywhere.

Sacagawea seems to have returned with her husband to the upper Missouri valley and to have died of a fever at Fort Manuel

Minataree Village with earth covered Wigwams

Minataree village, by George Catlin.

Lisa, on the Yellowstone River, at the age of twenty-five in the year 1812. Desperate attempts (including the promotion of a bill before Congress) have been made to identify Sacagawea with an Indian woman who lived to the great age of ninety-seven, and who was buried in 1884 on the Shoshone Indian Reservation in the Wind River valley of Wyoming. (I was shown her alleged grave when I camped nearby.) Even more zealous romantics have manu-factured a love affair between her and William Clark, but there's not a shred of evidence to support this. Bernard De Voto[8] speaks scornfully of how the Lewis and Clark expedition has been pro-moted into "the Sacagawea expedition" in which they and their command "were privileged to assist"; but in fact Lewis and Clark and their men were interesting enough in themselves to make em-broidery quite unnecessary.

8. *The Journals of Lewis and Clark*, ed. Bernard De Voto (New York, 1953; London, 1954), from which these extracts are taken.

William Clark, born in Virginia and brought up in Kentucky, was the more experienced frontiersman. At the age of thirty-three he was a striking figure with flaming red hair, and everywhere he went he was accompanied by his faithful Negro slave York and his Labrador retriever Scammon. York became a legend on the Upper Missouri, and many a kinky-haired papoose appeared up and down the river as testimony to his extraordinary popularity among the squaws. After the expedition returned, Clark settled down in St. Louis, first as superintendent of Indian affairs, then as territorial governor of Missouri. He died in 1838.

Meriwether Lewis, also a gentleman of Virginia, had attended the College of William and Mary. His family were neighbors of Thomas Jefferson in Albemarle County, and in the year 1801 President Jefferson invited his young friend and protégé (who was then a captain in the Army, serving on the Michigan frontier at Detroit) to come to Washington as his private secretary. It was while filling that office and residing at the recently completed White House that Lewis was entrusted by the president with the leadership of the expedition to the West. Lewis's claim to fame rests almost entirely upon the success and the achievements of that expedition, for he was not long to survive its return to civilization. Appointed governor of the Louisiana Territory by Jefferson in 1807, he died in October 1809 in somewhat mysterious circumstances, either having been murdered by thieves or (as Jefferson always believed) having killed himself in a fit of depression.[9]

Lewis was only thirty-five years old when he died, and his early death lends special interest and poignancy to the somewhat optimistic entry that he made in his *Journal* on August 18, 1805, his birthday, when the expedition was crossing the Continental Divide from the Salmon River into the Bitterroot Valley. That evening, in a rather more philosophical mood than usual, he wrote:

This day I completed my thirty-first year, and conceived that I had in all human probability now existed about half the period which I am to remain in this Sublunary world. I reflected that I had done but little, very little, indeed, to further the happiness of the human race or to advance the information of the succeeding generation. I viewed with regret the many hours I have spent in indolence, and

9. See Jefferson's "Memorial to Meriwether Lewis," in Coues (ed.), op. cit., Vol. I.

now sorely feel the want of that information which those hours would have given me had they been judiciously expended. But since they are past and cannot be recalled, I dash from me the gloomy thought, and resolve in future, to redouble my exertions and at least endeavour to promote those two primary objects of human existence, by giving them the aid of that portion of talents which nature and fortune have bestowed on me; or in future, to live for *mankind*, as I have heretofore lived for myself.

The expedition had spent a long, cold, and relatively inactive winter (1804–05) in log cabins surrounded by a stockade at the Mandan Indian villages near the present site of the city of Bismarck, North Dakota; and Lewis and Clark had no intention of spending another winter on the long journey to the shores of the Pacific. Unfortunately, when they reached the Three Forks of the Missouri in July 1805, more than a year after they first set out west and with nearly a thousand miles still to go, they made a decision that jeopardized the success of their whole venture. Having to choose which of the three rivers they should follow to its source on the Continental Divide, they selected the most westerly of them, which they had named the Jefferson. This led them into some of the most difficult country of their journey, a jungle of towering peaks, rushing torrents, and deep forests, interspersed with bare uplands devoid of pasture for the horses purchased from the Snake Indians to use when forced to abandon their boats and strike overland. Lewis, not unmindful of the dramatic significance of passing the watershed from the Atlantic to the Pacific river systems —they were the first white men to cross the fabulous Continental Divide in this part of North America—wrote in his diary on August 12, 1805:

At the distance of 4 miles further the road took us to the most distant fountain of the waters of the Mighty Missouri in search of which we have spent so many toilsome days and restless nights. This far I had accomplished one of those great objects on which my mind has been unalterably fixed for many years. Judge, then, of the pleasure I felt in allaying my thirst with this pure and ice-cold water which issues from the base of a low mountain or hill of a gentle ascent for half a mile. The mountains are high on either hand and leave this gap at the head of this rivulet through which the road passes. Here I halted a few minutes and rested myself. Two miles below McNeal had exultingly stood with a foot on each side of this little rivulet and thanked his god that he had lived to bestride the mighty and heretofore deemed endless Missouri. After refreshing ourselves we proceeded on to the top of the dividing ridge from which I discovered immense ranges of high mountains still to the West of us with their tops partially covered with snow. I now descended the mountain about three-quarters of a mile which I found much steeper than on the opposite side, to a handsome bold running creek of cold clear water. Here I first tasted the water of the great Columbia river.

Misled by inaccurate maps and by even more inaccurate Indian tales, the party spent over fifty days getting through this terrible stretch of the headwaters of the Jefferson River and the upper reaches of the westward-flowing Salmon River—aptly named by the fur traders of the following generation "the river of no return." When they finally came down the long Bitterroot Valley out of this mountain wilderness into the small plain of Missoula, which they thankfully called Traveler's Rest, it was already September. The ability of Sacagawea to interpret for them and the skill of new and friendlier Snake Indian guides now took them much more rapidly over the Lolo Pass and—waterborne once again—down the Clearwater River valley to its junction with the Snake River. Here at a point now appropriately called Lewiston they were within a few days' travel of the mighty Columbia River, which was to lead them directly down to the Pacific. William Clark described his first sight of this spot on October 10, 1805:

> The country about the forks is an open plain on either side. I can observe at a distance on the lower larboard side a high ridge of thinly timbered country. The water of the South fork is a greenish blue, the north as clear as crystal. Immediately in the point is an Indian cabin and in the South fork a small island we came to on the starboard side below with a view to make some lunar observations; the night proved cloudy and we were disappointed. The Indians came down all the courses of this river on each side on horses to view us as we were descending. Worthy of remark that not one stick of timber on the river near the forks and but a few trees for a great distance up the River we descended. I think Lewis's River is about 250 yards wide, the Koos Koos Ke River about 150 yards wide and the river below the forks about 300 yards wide.

Lewiston, Idaho, today is a flourishing city of some 15,000 inhabitants, the center of a prosperous lumbering and agricultural region. Two great modern bridges span the Clearwater (Lewis's) River and the Snake River (the Koos Koos Ke), leading across to the much smaller city of Clarkston, Washington, both of them links in the Lewis-Clark Highway.[1]

Despite a heartbreaking series of rapids and portages to be negotiated in the fresh canoes they had been forced to construct when they handed over their horses for safekeeping to the Indians of Idaho, Lewis and Clark did manage to reach what they called "Cape Disappointment at the Entrance of the Columbia River into the Great South Sea or Pacific Ocean" on November 19, 1805, and their mission seemed to be accomplished. So wide was the Columbia River in its final stretches, so high were the waves and so strong the tides on its shores, that the explorers had imagined they were already in sight of the ocean almost a fortnight before they actually reached the river's mouth. On November 7, 1805, Clark had written in his diary: "Ocean in view! O! The joy!" and described it already as "this great Pacific Ocean which we have been so long anxious to see." It was the end—or nearly the end—of the long journey about which Lewis had philosophized in characteristic fashion seven months earlier on the day they had left their first winter quarters at Fort Mandan:

Our vessels consisted of six small canoes, and two large perogues. This little fleet altho' not quite so respectable as those of Columbus or Captain Cook, were still viewed by us with as much pleasure as those deservedly famed adventurers ever beheld theirs; and I dare say with quite as much anxiety for their safety and preservation. We were now about to penetrate a country at least two thousand miles in width, on which the foot of civilized man had never trodden; the good or evil it had in store for us was for experiment yet to determine, and these little vessels contained every article by which we were to expect to subsist or defend ourselves. However, as the state of mind in which we are, generally gives the coloring to events, when the imagination is suffered to wander into futurity, the picture which now presented itself to me was a most pleasing one.

1. The memory of the explorers is indeed kept green in every possible way in these twin cites that bear their names. You can sleep at the Lewis and Clark Motel, fill up with gas at the Lewis and Clark Garage, and eat at the Lewis and Clark Cafeteria.

Entertaining as I do, the most confident hope of succeeding in a voyage which had formed a darling project of mine for the last ten years, I could not but esteem this moment of my departure as among the most happy of my life.

They had chosen a bad season to sample the weather of the Pacific Northwest for the first time. On November 15 Clark complained: "The rainy weather continued without a longer intermission than two hours at a time: from the 5th in the morning until the 16th is *eleven* days rain, and the most disagreeable time I have experienced . . . where I can neither get out to hunt, return to a better situation, or proceed on: in this situation have we been for six days past." But drenched to the skin as they were every day, with their tents leaking and all their bedding and equipment soaked, Lewis and Clark soon set their party to work, and they themselves carefully reconnoitered the surrounding country for a suitable place to go again into winter quarters. By December 7 they had found a reasonably sheltered site a little way back from the coast. Clark was relieved to withdraw from the stormy shore, where "the sea which is immediately in front roars like a repeated rolling thunder and have roared in that way ever since our arrival in its boarders, which is now 24 days since we arrived in sight of the great Western Ocean." And he adds plaintively: "I can't call it Pacific, as since I have seen it it has been the reverse." Many a voyager both before and since his time has felt the same about it.

The month being December, it was now too late in the season to turn back up the Columbia River. In addition they still had hopes that the relief ship half-promised them by Thomas Jefferson might one fine—or, more likely, wet—day come sailing round via Cape Horn. They inquired searchingly of the local Indians concerning any white men who might be in the habit of visiting the mouth of the Columbia River, and they were given a garbled list of names of ships' captains and descriptions of their vessels. On January 9, 1806, Lewis recorded: "The persons who usually visit the entrance of this river for the purpose of traffic or hunting I believe are either English or Americans. The Indians inform us that they speak the same language with ourselves and give us proofs of their veracity by repeating many words of English, as musket, powder, shot, knife, file, damned rascal, son of a bitch. . . ." (Equally tangible evidence was provided by the name "J. Bowman" tattooed on the arm of one of the Chinook squaws who visited their camp.)

At the mouth of the Columbia River, Lewis and Clark and their little party of twenty-nine white men, one black man, one red-skinned woman, one half-breed baby, and a dog, set up their second winter quarters. They had achieved the main objective of their mission, but it was to be nearly another year before they were back on the Mississippi at St. Louis. The journey back east to St. Louis and to Washington, D. C., was to be as hazardous as the way west, if not so tedious. They had already learned much that was new, and they had reinforced a claim that was eventually to give a great northwestern empire to the United States.

Poring over their maps and notes in their quarters at Fort Clatsop, on the Pacific coast, during the winter of 1805, they decided even before they started off again early in 1806 to divide their party into two groups when they reached Traveler's Rest. One (under Lewis) would travel overland by what is now known as the Great Blackfoot Valley by a short cut to the Falls of the Missouri; the other (under Clark) would return to the Jefferson River and Three Forks, but then portage across what is now the Bozeman Pass to the upper Yellowstone valley and use that river as a return route to the Missouri. The rendezvous was to be at the mouth of the Yellowstone.[2]

But before they were to traverse this better way back, Lewis and Clark had much to do and even more to think about. As defined by Thomas Jefferson, theirs was to be a scientific, fact-finding, and specimen-gathering expedition as well as a voyage of exploration. From their first winter quarters on the middle Missouri they had already sent back a mass of notes and trophies, including such items as "the tail of a mule deer, a weasel and three squirrels from the Rocky Mountains . . . the skin of a yellow bear . . . one tin box containing insects, mice, etc. . . . one buffalo robe

2. I have traveled over most of their return routes in one direction or the other—up the Blackfoot River, over the Bozeman Pass, down the Yellowstone—and visited most of the landmarks they described. Sometimes, of course, the country is almost unrecognizable from their descriptions: at and below the Great Falls of the Missouri, for instance, where the scars of industry and the backing up of the river waters caused by Fort Peck Dam have imposed a new pattern on the landscape. But elsewhere, as at the spot where Lewis camped on a little hill above the Clearwater stream near its confluence with the Blackwater at Greenough, Montana, almost everything remains exactly as it must have been in July 1806. The National Park Service hopes to be able to preserve certain undeveloped parts of the Lewis and Clark route as a wilderness area.

A Piekann (Piegan) Indian, August 1833, by Karl Bodmer.

painted by a Mandan man representing a battle fought 8 years since by the Sioux and the Recaras [Arikaras] against the Mandans," and even three cages containing "a living burrowing squirrel of the prairies," "living magpies," and "a living hen of the prairie." Even before Lewis and Clark could return to civilization, the indefatigable Jefferson had issued a sort of interim report on their expedition in the shape of a message to Congress,[3] drawing extensively on this material. But the fruits of the winter's labors at Fort Clatsop had to be brought back with them, and the number of specimens and artifacts they could carry over the snows of the Continental Divide, even in the interests of science (and for Thomas Jefferson and the American Philosophical Society of Philadelphia), was strictly limited by logistic considerations. They did not do so badly,[4] but "male and female antelope, with their skeletons . . . horns of the mountain ram, or *big horn*," could not be included.

Jefferson had enjoined the two captains to acquire what knowledge they could of "the state of morality, religion and information" among the Red Indian tribes they encountered. They did their best, but their ethnological researches were sometimes a cause of embarrassment to them. On their way west they had been forced to put up with the avarice, bad manners, and hostility of the Teton Sioux; on the way back Lewis and three of his men nearly came to grief trying to make friends with a Blackfoot war party, and while in winter quarters at Fort Clatsop they were plagued by the unwelcome presence of a very persistent and importunate band of Chinooks, a people for whom both had the profoundest contempt. Clark's *Journal* entry for November 21, 1805, reads:

An old woman and wife to a Chief of the Chinooks came and made a camp near ours. She brought with her 6 young squaws (*her daughters and nieces*) I believe for the purpose of gratifying the passions of the men of our party and receiving for those indulgences such small presents as she (the old woman) thought proper to accept of. The women of the Chinook nation have handsome faces, low and badly made, with large legs and thighs which are generally swelled by a stoppage of the circulation in the feet (which are small) by

3. *Message from the President of the United States Communicating Discoveries Made in Exploring the Missouri, Red River and Washita by Captains Lewis and Clark, Doctor Sibley and Mr. Dunbar; with a Statistical Account of the Countries Adjacent. February 19, 1806* (Washington, D. C., 1806).

4. *Pace* W. P. Webb, who in *The Great Plains* (Boston, 1931; repr. New York, 1962), pp. 145–6, is at his grouchiest in his none too generous tribute to Lewis and Clark: "Why a man of Jefferson's philosophical and scientific turn of mind should have been unable to select more capable men for the enterprise, keen observers with trained minds, it is hard to understand . . . of course, the fact remains that the expedition succeeded in its main objective. It went to its destination and returned, and this success tends to obscure the imperfections of the reports."

many strands of beads or curious strings which are drawn tight around the leg above the ankle.

Despite this rather unflattering portrait of the Chinook squaws, the prudent captains took no chances with human nature: "We gave to the men, each a piece of ribbon to bestow on their favorite lasses, this plan to save valuable articles."

On March 15, 1806, the same group of Indians reappeared. Lewis reported their second advent with some asperity: "We were visited this afternoon by Delashelwilt, a Chinook Chief, his wife and six women of his nation which the old bawd his wife had brought for market. This was the same party that had communicated the venereal to so many of our party in November last, and of which they have finally recovered. I therefore gave the men a particular charge with respect to them which they promised me to observe." Two days later he was able to comment, with obvious satisfaction: "Notwithstanding every effort of their winning graces the men have preserved their constancy to the vow of celibacy which they made on this occasion to Captain Clark and myself." Even when the members of the expedition finally departed from Fort Clatsop on March 23, 1806, this persistent group of Indians pursued them up the Columbia River in canoes. "Soon after we set out from Fort Clatsop," wrote Clark, "we were met by Delashelwilt and his old bawd and his six girls. They had a canoe, a sea-otter skin, dried fish and hats for sale. We purchased a sea-otter skin and proceeded on." Apparently no other articles of commerce were offered or accepted before this singular floating emporium of millinery and vice disappeared from their ken and from history.

The solicitude shown by Lewis and Clark for the moral and physical well-being of their men on this occasion is typical of them and helps to account for the fact that of those of their party who left the Mandan villages on their way west in 1805—thirty men, one woman and a baby, and a dog—all returned safely to civilization in 1806. The only death on the whole expedition had occurred during the summer of 1804, when Sergeant Floyd died of what has since been diagnosed as a ruptured appendix. Of the thirty men who constituted the permanent party, all came through their various ills and mishaps safely if somewhat precariously. When Private Whitehouse had a fever, Lewis bled him with a penknife. "I had no other instrument with which to perform this operation," he wrote. "However it answered very well." When Sacagawea's baby son was ill, Lewis was equal to the occasion. On May 24, 1806, he wrote: "The child was very restless last night; its jaw and the back of its neck are much more swollen than they were yesterday though his fever has abated considerably. We gave it a dose of cream of tartar and applied a fresh poultice of onions." The child survived.[5]

Soon after starting on their return journey by boat up the Columbia River the party explored the entrance to a large tributary which they had missed on the way down because it was masked by an island. This they called the Multnomah River, and though the Indian name is still used locally today and has been given to one of the leading hotels of Portland, Oregon, the river is now known as the Willamette. William Clark and his seven men, who paddled into its waters on April 2, 1806, were the first Americans at the sites of Fort Vancouver and Portland, and the first precursors of the countless thousands of their countrymen and of immigrants who have since come over the Oregon Trail to the Great Northwest through the gorges of the Columbia River known as the Dalles. Clark described the scene at the mouth of the Multnomah: "Multnomah discharges itself in the Columbia on the South-East and may justly be said to be a quarter the size of that noble river. . . . From the entrance of this river, I can plainly see Mt. Jefferson which is high and covered with snow, South-East, Mt. Hood East, Mt. St. Helians [Mount St. Helens] and a high humped mountain to the East of Mt. St. Helians."[6]

On the journey home the party was sadly embarrassed in its relations with the Indians it encountered by its lack of articles for gifts and trade, for almost everything of this sort had been used up before they left Fort Clatsop. Sacagawea had sacrificed her best string of beads in exchange for a specially fine sea-otter skin that

5. See p. 275. Baptiste Charbonneau in his thirties and forties was often at Bent's Fort. He was taken to Europe by one of his noble patrons, the duke of Württemberg. Everybody seems to have liked and respected him.

6. On a fine day the traveler who nowadays arrives at Portland by air sees all four of these peaks—Mt. Adams and Mt. St. Helens to the north of the Columbia River, and Mt. Hood and Mt. Jefferson to the south—as well as many others in the impressive Cascade Range. Mount Hood, with its symmetrical snow-covered cone, is an unforgettable sight in the dawn or sunset glow, and one wishes that the more poetically minded Lewis rather than the matter-of-fact Clark had described it in the *Journals*.

the captains ardently desired to take home with them. By March
1806 Lewis computed: "Two handkerchiefs would now contain
all the small articles of merchandise which we possess; the balance
of the stock consists of 6 blue robes, one scarlet, one uniform
artillerist's coat and hat, five robes made of our large flag, and a
few old clothes trimmed with ribbon. On this stock we have
wholly to depend for the purchase of horses and such portion of
our subsistence from the Indians as it will be in our powers to
obtain." The sad fate of Meriwether Lewis's uniform coat well
indicates the straits to which they were reduced. Sergeant Prior
had purchased a much needed canoe from the Caltlamah tribe.
"For this canoe," Lewis wrote on March 17, 1806, "he gave my
uniform laced coat and nearly half a carrot of tobacco. It seems
that nothing except this coat would induce them to dispose of a
canoe which in their mode of traffic is an article of the greatest
value except a wife, with whom it is equal, and is generally given in
exchange to the father for his daughter. I think the United States
are indebted to me another Uniform coat, for that of which I have
disposed on this occasion was but little worn."

When a little later, having decided to travel overland from
where the Columbia River turned away northward, Lewis was in
sore need of horses, he had to sacrifice his sword in exchange for an
"elegant white horse" brought into camp by the Great Chief Yellepet. Yellepet had really wanted a kettle but appeared perfectly
satisfied with the sword. It would seem that the United States was
very near to owing the gallant captain a whole new outfit. He
almost did not need it, for on two occasions on the return journey
he came closer to losing his life than did any other member of the
expedition. The day before Lewis and his section of the party
overtook Clark on the Missouri River below the mouth of the
Yellowstone (down which Clark had traveled), Lewis was accidentally shot by one of his own men. On August 11, 1806, he
recorded the story:

Just opposite to the burnt hills there happened to be a herd of elk on
a thick willow bar, and finding that my observation was lost for the
present I determined to land and kill some of them. Accordingly we
put to and I went out with Cruzatte only. We fired on the elk; I
killed one and he wounded another. We reloaded our guns and took
different routes through the thick willows in pursuit of the elk. I

was in the act of firing on the elk a second time when a ball struck my left thigh about an inch below my hip joint. Missing the bone, it passed through the left thigh and cut the thickness of the bullet across the hinder part of the right thigh. The stroke was very severe. I instantly supposed that Cruzatte had shot me in mistake for an elk, as I was dressed in brown leather and he cannot see very well; under this impression I called out to him "damn you, you have shot me," and looked towards the place from whence the ball had come. Seeing nothing, I called Cruzatte several times as loud as I could, but received no answer. I do not believe that the fellow did it intentionally, but after finding that he had shot me, was anxious to conceal his knowledge of having done so. The ball had lodged in my breeches, which I knew to be the ball of the short rifles such as that he had, and there being no person out with me but him, and no indians that we could discover, I have no doubt in my own mind of his having shot me.

Lewis's encounter with an Indian war party was even more alarming, though it resulted in no casualties. On the upper reaches of the Maria's River (at what is now Cut Bank Creek, not far south of the Canadian border, at the forty-ninth parallel between Alberta and Montana) Lewis and his party of three (the scout Drouillard and the two Fields brothers) ran into eight mounted Blackfoot Indians driving a number of additional saddled horses. After spending an uneasy night in the company of these members of the most dreaded of all the Indian tribes,[7] Lewis and his men awoke to a major crisis:

This morning at daylight the Indians got up and crouched around the fire. J. Fields who was on post had carelessly laid his gun down behind him near where his brother was sleeping. One of the Indians slipped behind him and took his gun and that of his brother unper-

---

7. In 1954 I spent a night at the Rocking Chair Ranch, near Greenough, Montana, as the guest of the late eminent Californian historian Robert Glass Cleland. He showed me the exact spot where Lewis and his three companions had camped overnight at the foot of a small hill, beside the Clearwater tributary of the Big Blackfoot River. Next day they had moved on toward Nine-Mile Prairie on the way to the Continental Divide and unwittingly toward the Blackfoot Indian war party. The scene as it had been in July 1806 came alive for me in July 1954 as Dr. Cleland described it, quoting from memory from the *Journals* of Lewis and Clark. He rolled the phrase "the river that goes to the road that leads to the land of the Buffalo" (which is what the Indians call the Big Blackfoot River) lovingly off his tongue. "What a marvelous name!" he said.

ceived by him. At the same instant two others advanced and seized the guns of Drewyer and myself. J. Fields seeing this turned about to look for his gun and saw the fellow just running off with her and his brother's. He called to his brother, who instantly jumped up and pursued the Indian with whom they overtook at the distance of 50

PRINCIPAL
AMERICAN GOVERNMENT
EXPLORATIONS · 1803-1820
compared with
The ASTORIANS, 1811-12 & 1812-13
and JEDEDIAH SMITH, 1826-28
Lewis & Clark · 1804-05 ——— 1806 ++++++
Pike · 1805-06 —→—→—
Astorians · 1811-12 & 1812-13 ===ᵈ===
Long {1817-18 —→—→ {1819-20 ------ Smith {1826-27 —·—·— {1827-28 ------

or 60 paces from the camp, seized their guns and wrested them from him, and R. Fields as he seized his gun stabbed the Indian to the heart with his knife. The fellow ran about 15 steps and fell dead. Of this I did not know until afterwards, having recovered their guns, they ran back instantly to the camp. Drewyer, who was awake, saw the Indian take hold of his gun and instantly jumped up and seized her and wrested her from him, but the Indian still retained his pouch.

His jumping up and crying "damn you, let go my gun" awakened me. I jumped up and asked what was the matter, which I quickly learned when I saw Drewyer in a scuffle with the Indian for his gun. I reached to seize my gun but found her gone. I then drew a pistol from my holster, and turning myself about, saw the Indian making off with my gun. I ran at him with my pistol and bid him lay down my gun, which he was in the act of doing when the Fieldses returned and drew up their guns to shoot him, which I forbad as he did not appear to be about to make any resistance or commit any offensive act. He dropped the gun and walked slowly off. I picked her up instantly. Drewyer having about this time recovered his gun and pouch asked me if he might not kill the fellow, which I also forbad as the Indian did not appear to wish to kill us. As soon as they found us all in possession of our arms they ran and endeavoured to drive off all the horses. I now hollowed to the men and told them to fire on them if they attempted to drive off our horses. They accordingly pursued the main party who were driving the horses up the river and I pursued the man who had taken my gun, who with another, was driving off a part of the horses which were to the left of the camp. At the distance of three hundred paces, they entered one of those steep nitches in the bluff with the horses before them. Being nearly out of breath I could pursue no further. I called to them as I had done several times before that I would shoot them if they did not give me my horse and raised my gun. One of them jumped behind a rock and spoke to the other who turned around and stopped at the distance of 30 steps from me, and I shot him through the belly. He fell to his knees and on his right elbow, from which position he partly raised himself up and fired at me, and turning himself about crawled in behind a rock which was a few feet from him. He overshot me. Being bareheaded I felt the wind of his bullet very distinctly.

The Indians had decamped with some of the party's horses but left their own behind. Catching four of the best of these, Lewis and his men burned the Indians' baggage as a sign of their displeasure at the unprovoked attack and departed in haste on a forced ride back to the Missouri and their companions. They traveled over ninety miles with only brief halts for rest and food. Lewis now told his men "that it was my determination that if we were attacked in the plains on our way to the point, that the bridles of the horses should be tied together and we would stand and defend them, or sell our lives as dear we could." Fortunately, this was not necessary: "We had proceeded about 12 miles on an East course when we found ourselves near the Missouri: we heard a report which we took to be that of a gun but we were not certain. Still continuing down the north east bank of the Missouri about 8 miles further, being then within five miles of the grog spring we heard the report of several rifles very distinctly on the river to our right. We quickly repared to this joyful sound and on arriving at the bank of the river had the unspeakable satisfaction to see our canoes coming down."

The remainder of the expedition's journey down the Missouri River and back to St. Louis seemed tame by comparison. Old friends and old enemies were met and familiar scenes redescribed. On August 17, 1806, Charbonneau was paid $500 and 33 1/3 ¢ for his services, and departed with Sacagawea for the Upper Missouri again, promising to send the boy Baptiste down to St. Louis to be educated under William Clark's supervision as soon as he was old enough. On September 3, 1806, news from home was passed on to the party by "a Mr. James Airs [Aird] from the Mackinaw by way of Prarie Dechien [Prairie Du Chien] and St. Louis." Wrote Clark:

This Gentleman informed us of many changes and misfortunes which had taken place in the Illinois. He also informed us that General Wilkinson was the governor of the Louisiana, and at St. Louis 300 of the American troops had been cantoned on the Missouri a few miles about its mouth. Some disturbance with the Spaniards in the Nackatosh country is the cause of their being called down to that country. The Spaniards had taken one of the United States frigates in the Mediterranean. Two British ships of the line had fired on an American ship in the port of New York, and killed the Captain's brother. Two Indians had been hung in St. Louis for murder and several others in jail, and that Mr. Burr and General Hamilton fought a duel, the latter was killed.

Thus did the news of the untimely death of Alexander Hamilton two years before first reach the ears of Lewis and Clark, both of whom must have known him and Aaron Burr well.

The expedition was nearly over. The men were paid off and

went their several ways, Sergeant Gass to publish his diary[8] of the expedition (which was conceivably rewritten by an enterprising schoolmaster) in 1807 and to live to a great age. And when the official account of the expedition was finally issued (edited by Nicholas Biddle) in 1814, it constituted, as Bernard De Voto has remarked, "the first report on the West, on the United States over the hill and beyond the sunset, on the province of the American future."[9]

Lewis and Clark performed a great service to the people as well as to the President of the United States. They may not have pioneered either the California or the Oregon trail, but their journey gave heart and inspiration to the whole generation of fur traders and trappers whose journeys and discoveries really opened up these two trails. One of their own men, John Colter, was one of the earliest fur trappers of the Rocky Mountain West. Drouillard was another. Within a year or two of Lewis and Clark's return to civilization the fur trade was in full swing on the upper Missouri and the Yellowstone, Manuel Lisa established his first fort (where Bighorn, Montana, now stands), and the Astorians were following them in their footsteps all the way to the Pacific.

John Jacob Astor, an immigrant from Waldorf, Germany, was directly stimulated by Lewis and Clark's journey to organize the American Fur Company and the Pacific Fur Company in 1808. In July 1810 his overland party, bound for the Far West, left Montreal, and soon afterward he sent the *Tonquin* to sail from New York round Cape Horn to the mouth of the Columbia River. A few months later a rendezvous was effected and the trading post of Astoria, a little inland from Fort Clatsop, established. Subsequently (as Washington Irving[1] and a host of subsequent writers have chronicled) both the *Tonquin* and Astoria were lost by the American and Pacific Fur Companies and the Columbia River trade abandoned to the British. But in the history of the Northwest the fact that Astoria *had* been established in 1811 and that the overland

8. Patrick Gass: *A Journal of the Voyages and Travels of a Corps of Discovery under the Command of Captain Lewis and Captain Clarke . . . 1804, 1805 & 1806 . . . by Patrick Gass . . . one of the Expedition . . . with Geographical and Explanatory Notes by the Publisher* (Pittsburg, 1807; London, 1808; Fr. tr. Paris, 1809). Many later editions; the third was illustrated by six crude engravings, which are usually reproduced in subsequent editions.

9. *Journals of Lewis and Clark*, introduction, lii.

1. *Astoria* (New York, 1846). Many later edns.

Astorians had diverged from the Lewis and Clark route sufficiently to begin the blazing of the great westward wagon trails was to play a significant part in the destiny of the Oregon Country.

Like the achievements of the Lewis and Clark expedition, those of the privately organized Astorians provided an immediate stimulus to the exploitation and settlement of the Far West. The same cannot be said of the work of two other United States government explorers, Zebulon Pike and Stephen Long, of the same generation as Lewis and Clark. Though both traversed many unknown trails and discovered much, they also helped to generate and propagate the myth of the "Great American Desert" lying athwart the advance of the American people westward to the boundaries of the Louisiana Territory and beyond. Two generations of map makers and settlers suffered from the effects of this myth.

In his inimitable way, Walter Prescott Webb has traced[2] the process of "creating the tradition of the 'Great American Desert'" from Coronado and De Soto to Pike and Long and those who echoed them. Pike once said: "These vast plains of the western hemisphere may become in time as celebrated as the sandy deserts of Africa."[3] And James, who accompanied Long, stated categorically that "I do not hesitate in giving the opinion that it is almost wholly unfit for cultivation and of course uninhabitable by a people depending on agriculture for their subsistence."[4] As late as the year 1859, Horace Greeley was telling the readers of the New York *Tribune*, not only that the Great American Desert existed but that "every day's sun is extending it."[5]

Not until the late 1860s did travelers, scientists, and railroad promoters succeed in dissipating this "dust curtain" that Pike and Long had lowered just to the east of the hundredth meridian, to bog down the frontier of settlement short of the High Plains, which they considered uninhabitable. Those hurrying across these plains in the direction of the promised lands of Oregon and Califor-

2. *The Great Plains*, pp. 152–60.

3. Quoted by Webb from *The Expeditions of Zebulon Montgomery Pike*, ed. E. Coues, 3 vols. (New York, 1895), II, 523.

4. Quoted by Webb from *Edwin James's account of an Expedition from Pittsburgh to the Rocky Mountains, performed in the years 1819–1820 under the Command of Major S. H. Long*, ed. R. G. Thwaites, "Early Western Travels," Vol. XVII (Cleveland 1904–7), p. 147.

5. W. P. Webb, p. 159, n. 1.

nia passed them by with averted eyes, but by the end of the nineteenth century they had been converted into one of the most fertile and populous regions of the whole trans-Mississippi West.

Pike and Long were no more fortunate as explorers than they were as geographical diagnosticians. Pike, sent out at the head of a small Army party by Jefferson in 1805 to explore the upper Mississippi, missed its true source. On his second expedition, dispatched by the triple-dealing General James Wilkinson in 1806 to "ascertain the direction, extent and navigation of the Arkansaw and Red

Major Long holds a council with the Pawnees, by S. Seymour, artist to the expedition. From *An Account of an Expedition from Pittsburgh to the Rocky Mountains in the Year 1820* (London, 1823).

rivers," he blundered either by accident or by design into the upper Rio Grande valley in Spanish New Mexico, was detained by the Spanish authorities in Santa Fe, and then sent back under escort via Chihuahua to Nacogdoches, on the Spanish-American border at the Sabine River, the next year. His actual discoveries were unimportant—he sighted and named Pike's Peak but pronounced it unclimbable—but his careful observations[6] of wide areas of the northern Spanish borderlands that he traversed under open arrest,

6. Set down in his Journal first published as *An Account of Expeditions to the Sources of the Mississippi . . . and in the Interior Parts of New Spain . . .* (Philadelphia, 1810). The first London edn. (1811) is called *Exploratory Travels through the Western Territories of North America. . . .*

and the maps he drew, provided much useful information to the Santa Fe traders and the Texas immigrants from the United States of the following generation. Pike himself was killed in the War of 1812.

Long's expedition of 1819–20 was, up to that time, the most ambitious ever to have been sent out by the Americans into the trans-Mississippi West. John C. Calhoun, Secretary of War, said: "It has for its objects the protection of our northwestern frontier and the greater extension of our fur trade." As such, however, it was a great fiasco, owing not so much to Long's leadership as to cheating contractors and the withholding of congressional appropriations. The Yellowstone Expedition, designed to be bigger and better than that of Lewis and Clark on the upper Missouri, had to be abandoned, and Long then led a much reduced party (which nevertheless included professional scientists, topographers, and artists)[7] up the Platte to the Rocky Mountains in 1821. Pike's Peak was climbed and Long's Peak named. On the return journey the upper Arkansas and Canadian rivers were re-explored. Though most of the scientific records of the expedition were lost, enough remained to provide Dr. James with material for his multivolume account of the expedition—and for his disquisition on the Great American Desert. With all its deficiencies Long's was the most important United States government expedition into the Far West that was not strictly military in object until John Charles Frémont set out in 1842. Though it played little or no part in establishing the Oregon Trail or in making the Santa Fe Trail safer for Americans, it did at least help to persuade people to hurry on to a far west that was now beckoning "beyond the sunset, in the province of the American future," and beyond those mountains and deserts which, before the mining and ranching frontiers had been opened up, appeared to offer them nothing at all. Nothing, that is, except hunting and trapping.

7. Samuel Seymour's drawings made on the Long expedition were engraved and printed in London as early as 1823 for the first edn. of James's *Account*; see p. 91 for his "Major Long holds a council with the Pawnees."

CHAPTER IV

Fur Traders and Trappers of the Far West

NORTH AMERICA WAS RICH IN FUR-BEARING ANIMALS, and the fur trade had been important since the seventeenth century, but its importance was to reach a peak in the third and fourth decades of the nineteenth century. During that time it played a leading part, perhaps the leading part, in the exploration of the American Far West.

The fur trappers had to work beyond the farthest fringe of civilization and settlement. To sell their pelts they had to return to the frontier outposts, or the fur traders had to meet them halfway and set up temporary rendezvous in the wilderness. The fur trade required capital and organization; at first its profits had been prodigious, but by the 1840's they had shrunk almost to nothing. Within the active life span of one generation, therefore—after Lewis and Clark's return in 1806 and before Frémont's first expedition set out in 1842—the fur trade experienced its heyday and was beginning to fade away as a major phenomenon of the American frontier. Some who participated in it—Kit Carson, Tom Fitzpatrick, Jim Bridger—lived right through it into new and equally colorful careers after it was over. Others—Jedediah Smith, Harrison Rogers, Sylvester Pattie, William and Milton Sublette—died on the trail, as prisoners of the Mexicans or the Indians or (very rarely) in their beds or blankets. Only the hardy went in for such a life. Only the hardiest and the most fortunate survived.

The fur trade had started in Canada[1] long ago, first with the French and then with the British. The "Company of Adventurers of England Trading into Hudson's Bay" had been founded in the year 1670 to pursue it, and its members and servants had followed and trapped the fur-bearing animal ever since. In its pursuit Alexander Mackenzie had in 1793 reached the Pacific overland in the service of the rival Northwest Company. In 1811 the Northwest Company successfully resisted the challenge of Astor's American Fur Company and reached an agreement with it which confined the Americans to the Rocky Mountain area, and liquidated by purchase their station, Astoria (henceforth known as Fort George), on the Columbia River, in 1813. But the Crown forced the Northwest Company to merge with the Hudson's Bay Company in 1821, better to withstand the Americans. This was timely, for another threat to their monopoly was created in St. Louis in 1822, when William Henry Ashley and Andrew Henry organized the Rocky Mountain Fur Company, bound by no agreement with the Canadians and willing to follow the beaver to the ends of the earth if need be. The Rocky Mountain Company stood up to both its great rivals, Canadian and American, until 1835, when, with the fur trade already beginning to decline and many of its finest leaders either dead (like Jedediah Smith) or in retirement (like General Ashley), it gave up the uneven struggle. That canny German immigrant Astor managed to get out of the trade in 1834 while the going was good, but Dr. John McLoughlin and Sir George Simpson clung desperately to the Hudson's Bay posts at Fort Vancouver and Fort Hall until dispossessed by the Oregon treaty of 1846 with England, which gave the United States everything up the forty-ninth parallel. By that time the fur trade had ceased to be an important factor in the history of the American West.

His time was short, "but in his few allotted years the trapper set his impress forever upon the map of North America and the fate of the United States. He affected the destiny of nations; he changed the future of a continent; he bequeathed to later generations of Americans a tradition of heroic exploration comparable to that of the seamen of Elizabeth or the conquistadores of Spain."[2]

1. See H. A. Innis: *The Fur Trade in Canada* (Cambridge, Mass., 1934), passim.

2. R. G. Cleland: *This Reckless Breed of Men: The Trappers and Fur Traders of the Southwest* (New York, 1950), p. 7.

Cleland's eloquent tribute may be compared with those uttered by Chittenden[3] a half-century and Ruxton[4] a full century earlier. At all levels of achievement—the governors, directors, and factors like Simpson, Ashley, and McLoughlin; the "partisans" and captains like Ogden and Smith; or the rank and file like Jim Baker, Jim Bridger, Jim Beckwith, and "Uncle" Tom Wootton—these fur traders loom somewhat larger than life as it is usually lived. They called Milton Sublette "Thunderbolt of the Rockies," and there was something of an overdisplay of Nature's exuberance about many of his fellows also. Imaginative writers do not need to "write up" the mountain man; rather they have to tone him down to make him sound credible or (in some cases) to get him past the censors. A winter spent with Jim Bridger[5] set up "Ned Buntline" for the rest of a long career as a dime novelist, and many of the stories he wrote about Jim were even true. When a British naval officer met Kit Carson—still in his thirties—at Monterey in 1846, he paid this paladin among mountain men and scouts the ultimate tribute: "Why, he is as famous here as is the Duke in Europe!"[6]

The victim of all this history-making was a harmless, compact, and engaging mammal of from twenty-five to forty pounds full-grown. He could be made into a pet if caught young, but few mountain men were interested in him alive. The intelligence of the beaver has been exaggerated by enthusiastic animal tale-tellers; he was not able to gnaw down a tree so that it fell neatly into place at his dam site in a predetermined direction; nevertheless, the beaver dam and lodge are impressive pieces of animal engineering and architecture. The beaver successfully protected himself against most of his enemies, but man proved too much for him. Using the sex-gland secretions (*castoreum*) of the dead beaver as bait to attract the live one, his human enemy caught him in a steel trap and let him drown himself trying to escape. The beaver's only defense, if not drowned immediately, was to gnaw off an entrapped limb. One mountain man reported: "Between feet and toes we took no

3. Hiram M. Chittenden: *The American Fur Trade of the Far West*, 3 vols. (New York, 1902), I, xiii–ix ff.

4. G. F. Ruxton: *Adventures in Mexico and the Rocky Mountains* (New York, 1848) and *Life in the Far West* (repr. Norman, Okla., 1951). See quotation on pp. 99–101.

5. See below, pp. 106–10.

6. The Honorable Frederick Walpole, R. N.: *Four Years in the Pacific*, 2 vols. (London, 1849), II, 216.

less than 42! We put 150 traps in the water and got 15 beaver."[7] The beaver, if it survived so long, reached full growth at about two years of age, and, says Cecil Alter: "the grandparent whose aging is often related to incisor trouble, finally drops away to Elysium at twelve to fifteen years of age."[8]

The cured "plew" of the adult beaver weighed about a pound and a half and at best would fetch from four to six dollars a pound at the mountain rendezvous or trading fort. This was poor return for all the trouble and risk taken, for the prices of trade goods were very high at these places. Said John Hatcher, a typical mountain man, using the picturesque mountain language: "A little 'bacca, ef it's a plew a plug, an' Dupont an' Galena, a Green River or so, an' he leaves for the Bayou Salade."[9] When, however, beaver plew was down to a dollar a pound, as happened in the early forties, the beaver was hardly worth while trapping any more, and Alexander Barclay, who was later to build Barclay's Fort at the western junction of the two branches of the Santa Fe Trail at Watrous, near Las Vegas, New Mexico, noted in his "Waste Book" (kept while in the employ of the Bents at Fort William, on the Arkansas), under the date August 31, 1846: "Beaver trade stopt at 90¢ plt [pelt]."[1] The trade had in fact been dying for several years,

7. Alexander Ross: *The Fur Hunters of the Far West*, ed. K. A. Spaulding (repr. Norman, Okla., 1956), p. 236.

8. See J. Cecil Alter: *James Bridger: A Historical Narrative* (Salt Lake City, 1925; rev. edn. Columbus, Ohio, 1950). The edn. cited here is *Jim Bridger* (rev. edn. Norman, Okla., 1962), ch. x, pp. 44–9. Like many other writers on the fur-trade era, Alter made use of the classic work of Lewis H. Morgan: *The American Beaver and His Works* (Philadelphia, 1868). A famous drawing of beaver in their natural habitat is that of Karl Bodmer, first publ. in Maximilian of Wied: *Travels in the Interior of North America* (London, 1944), and reproduced in Cleland's *Reckless Breed,* facing p. 14, from Ackermann's engraving of the original watercolor. That attractive plate may also be found below, p. 97.

9. Quoted in W. H. Goetzmann: *Army Exploration in the American West, 1803–1863* (New Haven, Conn., 1959), p. 29. In plain English: "A little tobacco, even if it costs a whole beaver skin for a plug, and some gunpowder and lead, and a hunting knife or so, and he leaves for the trapping country." Bayou Salade is a famous mountain meadow in the Colorado Rockies, near the headwaters of the Arkansas. Salida, Colorado, commemorates the name, at approximately 106° W and 39° N on the map. Bayou Salade was also known as Bayou Salada and South Park.

1. The Barclay Papers (from microfilm copy in the Colorado State Archives, Denver, courtesy of the State Archivist Mrs. D. Renze). The originals are now in the Bancroft Library at Berkeley, Calif., and are quoted from with the permission of the Director Dr. G. P. Hammond.

though incredulous Mountain Men every season expected the price to rise again. Says Ruxton's trapper hero Killbuck: "Howsever, beaver's 'bound to rise'; human natur can't go on selling beaver a dollar a pound; no, no, that ain't a going to shine much longer, I know. There was the times when this child first went to the mountains: six dollars the plew—old 'un or kitten. Wagh! but it's bound to rise, I says agin . . ."[2]

A beaver "lodge" on the Missouri, by Karl Bodmer.

But it didn't. The last rendezvous for the exchange of trade goods for skins were attended by the Rocky Mountain Fur Company in 1838, and the American Fur Company in 1839. A fairly successful rendezvous was held on the Green River in 1840 without the participation of either of these erstwhile giants of the fur

2. G. F. Ruxton: *Life in the Far West, 1846* (repr. Norman, Okla., 1951), p. 18; first pub. serially in *Blackwood's Edinburgh Magazine* (June–November 1848). See App. B (1951 edn.), pp. 235–44, for LeRoy Hafen's learned discussion of the true identity of Killbuck, a fictional name. Hafen favors as the most likely candidate John S. Smith (1810–71), who, as "Uncle John Smith," also attracted the loving attention of Lewis H. Garrard: *Wa-To-Ya and the Taos Trail* (Cincinnati, 1850; Glendale, Calif., 1938), and Henry Inman: *The Old Santa Fé Trail* (New York, 1898).

trade; but the annual series lapsed in 1841, the year of the first overland emigrant party to California, guided by Tom Fitzpatrick, who thus had little time for trapping. That August, Henry Fraeb had his hair lifted by an Indian war party, while his partner, Jim Bridger, was busy building Fort Bridger—on the Black Fork of the Green River—as a permanent trading post. The year 1842 saw the very last *al fresco* rendezvous of the type that had been participated in with such abandon by the mountain men and their (or other people's) squaws.

These remarkable gatherings have been compared not too inaccurately with the great fairs of medieval times in Europe. Borrowing the idea from the fur traders of Canada, General Ashley had initiated the rendezvous system in 1823, after his first organized trapping season as head of the Rocky Mountain Fur Company. The success and convenience of the system, quite apart from providing the lonely fur trappers opportunity for an annual debauch, made the rendezvous the high spot of each year's hunting for almost two decades. A last half-hearted effort was made in 1843 to bring the rendezvous system to life again. On August 12 that irrepressible Scottish sportsman Sir William Drummond Stewart, Baronet, wrote to Jim Bridger: "The compliments of Sir Wm. Stewart to Capt. James Bridger. Come and see us. We have been expecting you for several days, and shall wait for you a few days more come to camp. We have commenced an extensive game of ball, and we want you to come and 'keep the ball in motion,' come . . . and a steed is at your service. Come—hurrah!" This letter was intended to be left on a pole for Bridger at The Old Rendezvous[3] but never reached him. In any case, Jim had trapped few beaver that year. Indians were much more plentiful and even attacked his new fort. He had no time for fun and games with the genial baronet. In 1844 the situation was even worse. James Clyman found Fort Bridger all but deserted on August 31, which should have been the height of the trading season. He didn't see much future for Jim's pride and joy, describing it as "a temporary concern, calculated for trade with the Shoshones and Utahs, which

---

3. Matthew C. Field: *Prairie and Mountain Sketches*, ed. K. L. Gregg and J. F. McDermott (Norman, Okla., 1957), p. 126; quoted in Alter: *Jim Bridger* (1962 edn.), pp. 206–7. A place near present-day Riverton, Wyoming, actually appeared on some maps at that time as "Rendezvous."

is not very valuable. This place is likewise the general rendezvous for Rocky Mountain hunters and trappers. That once numerous class of adventurers are now reduced to less than thirty men. . . ."[4] The mountain men had once numbered over 600! Guiding and supplying the increasing numbers of overland emigrants had now become much more profitable than trapping the beaver. But Jim Bridger at least went on trying, and in 1845 it appears that he attempted to make the best of both worlds, by going to California *and* trapping beaver. On September 17, 1843, A. R. Bouis wrote to Pierre Choteau, Jr.: "Mr. James Bridger arrived at Fort John [Laramie] on the 2d. instant, and delivered Mrs. [Messrs.] Jos. Picotte 840 beaver skins and castorem; 675 dressed deerskins; 25 mules; 24 horses; 1400 California sea shells."[5] Whether Jim Bridger, mountain man, had become Jim Bridger, beachcomber, in an effort to diversify his business is not certain, for he may have obtained the fourteen hundred abalone shells (much prized by the Rocky Mountain and Plains Indians, and used by the latter as ear and nose ornaments) in trade for beaver skins, just about to become a drug on the market at "90¢ plt."

Though George Frederick Ruxton was born in July 1821 at Eynsham Hall, near Oxford, England (the summer before Ashley's first fur-trapping company set out from St. Louis), and died just twenty-seven years later in August 1848 (in that very same St. Louis, just as the era of the fur trade had ended), and though he visited the scenes of the Rocky Mountain rendezvous only after their great days were over, he is recognized as having produced the most vivid contemporary word-pictures of those remarkable scenes. In *Adventures in Mexico and the Rocky Mountains* he writes:

At a certain time, when the hunt is over, or they have loaded their pack animals, the trappers proceed to the "rendezvous," the locality of which has been previously agreed upon; and here the traders and agents of the fur companies await them, with such assortment of goods as their hardy customers may require, including

---

4. *James Clyman, American Frontiersman, His Diaries and Reminiscences* (San Francisco, 1928; repr. Portland, Ore., 1960), p. 99.

5. W. G. Robinson: *S. Dakota Historical Society Collections* (1918), pp. 209–10; quoted in Alter: *Jim Bridger* (1962 edn.), p. 217.

generally a fair supply of alcohol. The trappers drop in singly and in small bands, bringing their packs of beaver to this mountain market, not unfrequently to the value of a thousand dollars each, the produce of one hunt. The dissipation of the "rendezvous," however, soon turns the trapper's pocket inside out. The goods brought by the traders, although of the most inferior quality, are sold at enormous prices—coffee, twenty and thirty shillings a pint cup, which is the usual measure; tobacco fetches ten and fifteen shillings a plug; alcohol, from twenty to fifty shillings a pint; gunpowder, sixteen shillings a pint cup; and all other articles at proportionately exorbitant prices. . . .

A Rocky Mountain rendezvous—Indian encampment on the Green River, by Alfred Jacob Miller.

The rendezvous is one continued scene of drunkenness, gambling, and brawling and fighting, as long as the money and credit of the trappers last. Seated, Indian fashion, round the fires, with a blanket spread before them, groups are seen with their "decks" of cards, playing at euker, poker, and seven-up, the regular mountain games. The stakes are "beaver," which here is current coin; and when the fur is gone, their horses, mules, rifles, and shirts, hunting packs, and *breeches*, are staked. Daring gamblers make the rounds of the camp, challenging each other to play for the trapper's highest stake—his horse, his squaw (if he have one), and, as once happened, his scalp. "There goes hos and beaver!" is the mountain expression when any great loss is sustained; and, sooner or later, "hos and beaver" invariably find their way into the insatiable pockets of the traders. A trapper often squanders the produce of his hunt, amounting to hundreds of dollars, in a couple of hours; and, supplied on credit with another equipment, leaves the rendezvous for another expedition, which has the same result time after time, although one tolerably successful hunt would enable him to return to the settlements and civilised life, with an ample sum to purchase and stock a farm, and enjoy himself in ease and comfort the remainder of his days. . . .

These annual gatherings are often the scene of bloody duels, for over their cups and cards no men are more quarrelsome than your mountaineers. Rifles, at twenty paces, settle all differences, and, as may be imagined, the fall of one or other of the combatants is certain, or, as sometimes happens, both fall to the word "fire."

This has never been bettered, but Ray Allen Billington, in his *American Frontiersman*,[6] has equaled it. His picture supplements and complements that of Ruxton, and draws also upon the whole rich century of publications concerning the fur trade that have followed in Ruxton's wake.

Gradually the trading forts on the upper Missouri, the Yellowstone, the Platte, the Arkansas, and other strategically situated locations, began to take the place of the mountain-valley rendezvous. Smaller forts there had always been, built for both defense (which the rendezvous could not provide) and trade, ever since Manuel Lisa had established himself at the mouth of the Big Horn in the footsteps of Lewis and Clark. Now, in the thirties the large forts began to go up on American territory (and sometimes on Mexican) after the style of the Hudson's Bay Company's Fort Vancouver, which had been established by the Canadians on the Columbia as early as 1824. Forts Union and McKenzie on the upper Missouri, Fort Laramie on the North Platte, and Bent's Fort (or Fort William) on the Arkansas were the most important of these for the fur trade. Bent's Fort, built in 1833-4 by the brothers Charles and William Bent and their partner Céran St. Vrain, near

6. An inaugural lecture, delivered as Vivian Harmsworth Professor of American History at Oxford University, on February 2, 1954 (Oxford and London, 1954), pp. 6–7. See also his *Far Western Frontier, 1830–1860*, New American Nation Series (New York, 1956), Ch. iii.

present-day La Junta, Colorado, was visited by many travelers—
Francis Parkman was there in 1846—but let Ruxton speak again:

Bent's Fort is situated on the left or northern bank of the river
Arkansa, about one hundred miles from the foot of the Rocky
Mountains—on a low and level bluff of the prairie which here slopes
gradually to the water's-edge. The walls are built entirely of adobes
—or sun-burned bricks—in the form of a hollow square, at two
corners of which are circular flanking towers of the same material.
The entrance is by a large gateway into the square, round which are
the rooms occupied by the traders and employés of the host. These
are small in size, with walls coloured by a white-wash made of clay
found in the prairie. Their flat roofs are defended along the exterior
by parapets of adobe, to serve as a cover to marksmen firing from
the top; and along the coping grow plants of cactus of all the
varieties common in the plains. In the centre of the square is the
press for packing the furs; and there are three large rooms, one used
as a store and magazine, another as a council-room, where the
Indians assemble for their "talks," whilst the third is the common
dining-hall, where the traders, trappers, and hunters, and all employés, feast upon the best provender the game-covered country
affords. Over the culinary department presided of late years a fair
lady of colour, Charlotte by name, who was, as she loved to say, "de
onlee lady in de dam Injun country," and who moreover was
celebrated from Long's Peak to the Cumbres Espanolás for slap-jacks
and pumpkin pies. . . .
In the corral, groups of leather-clad mountaineers, with "decks"
of "euker" and "seven-up," gamble away their hard-earned peltries.
The employés—mostly St. Louis Frenchmen and Canadian voya-
geurs—are pressing packs of buffalo skins, beating robes, or engaged
in other duties of a trading fort. Indian squaws, the wives of mountaineers, strut about in all the pride of beads and fanfaron, jingling
with bells and bugles, and happy as paint can make them. Hunters
drop in with animals packed with deer or buffalo meat to supply the
fort; Indian dogs look anxiously in at the gateway, fearing to enter
and encounter the enmity of their natural enemies, the whites: and
outside the fort, at any hour of the day or night, one may safely
wager to see a dozen coyotes or prairie wolves loping round, or
seated on their haunches, and looking gravely on, waiting patiently
for some chance offal to be cast outside. Against the walls, groups of

Indians, too proud to enter without an invitation, lean, wrapped in their buffalo robes, sulky and evidently ill at ease to be so near the whites without a chance of fingering their scalp-locks; their white lodges shining in the sun, at a little distance from the river-banks; their horses feeding in the plain beyond.

The appearance of the fort is very striking, standing as it does hundreds of miles from any settlement, on the vast and lifeless prairie, surrounded by hordes of hostile Indians, and far out of reach of intercourse with civilised man; its mud-built walls inclosing a little garrison of a dozen hardy men, sufficient to hold in check the numerous tribes of savages ever thirsting for their blood. Yet the solitary stranger passing this lone fort, feels proudly secure when he comes within sight of the "stars and stripes" which float above the walls.[7]

Bent's Fort queened it for fifteen years over the whole area of the southern plains. With the possible exceptions of Forts Pierre and Union it was the largest in the trans-Mississippi West. It was certainly "the largest establishment in that vast terrain between St. Louis and the Pacific."[8] Fortunately we know exactly what it looked like, though nothing of its structure has survived above ground. Where Ruxton, Parkman, Thomas Jefferson Farnham, Susan Shelby Magoffin, John Charles Frémont, Alexander Barclay, and many other visitors and residents described it in words, W. M. Boggs (in 1844), Lt. J. W. Abert (in 1845), and Edward Kern (in 1846) captured it in drawings, which have survived, though no photograph is known to have been taken of it before William Bent, then its sole owner, partially destroyed and abandoned it in 1852.[9] The leading artists of the West did not leave paintings of Bent's Fort comparable to those made by Bodmer of Fort Union, Miller of Fort Laramie, and Bierstadt of the rendezvous country of the Wind River Valley and elsewhere, but W. M. Boggs's annotated if crudely drawn bird's-eye view, showing even the Bents billiard

7. *Adventurers in Mexico*, pp. 230–31.

8. *Bent's Fort: National Historic Site*, folder of the National Park Service of the U. S. Department of the Interior (1963). See also David Lavender: *Bent's Fort* (New York, 1954).

9. The site was partially excavated by the Colorado Historical Society in 1954, and the excavation is to be completed by the National Park Service. A reconstruction of the fort adjacent to its original site may also be made, but meanwhile private enterprise has erected a full-scale replica near Morrison, Colorado. See Preface, above, and illustration, p. 104.

room on the roof, allows us to imagine ourselves back in that place where Kit Carson brought in his trophies of the hunt, where Alexander Barclay wielded his telescope (specially imported from England to spy out "hostiles" on the Plains), where Milton Sub-

Bird's-eye view of Bent's Fort as it appeared in 1844; by W. M. Boggs. Note billiard room on roof.

lette died of a gangrenous leg, where Susan Magoffin had her miscarriage, and where Lt. Emory on August 2, 1846, watched the entry of General Kearny's Army of the West.[1]

Bent's Fort was on the mountain branch of the famous Santa Fe Trail just where it left United States for Mexican territory, and was therefore not built for the convenience of the mountain men alone. But they were its most picturesque denizens, even more than the Indians who pitched their lodges around its walls—for it stood

1. W. H. Emory: *Notes of a Military Reconnaissance from Fort Leavenworth to San Diego . . . Made in 1846–47*, U. S. Senate Doc., 30th Cong., 1st Sess., Exec. No. 7 (Washington, D. C., 1848). "I looked in the direction of Bent's Fort, and saw a huge United States Flag flowing in the breeze and straining every fibre of an ash-pole planted over the centre of a gate. The mystery was soon revealed by a column of dust in the east, advancing with about the velocity of a fast walking horse. It was 'The Army of the West.'"

at the meeting place of the hunting grounds of the Cheyenne, Prairie Apache, Arapaho, Commanche, Ute, and Kiowa, and was also visited by bands of Shoshones, Crows, and Gros Ventres. No Indian, not even the lordly Yellow Wolf,[2] or White Thunder, Cheyenne chief and father of Owl Woman, William Bent's first wife, created such a stir as did Old Bill Williams when he rode in from one of his lone and phenomenally successful hunting trips and ordered liquor for all—but mostly for himself. Ruxton knew him well—insofar as any man could know "the old coon"—and has described him unforgettably:

Williams always rode ahead, his body bent over his saddle-horn, across which rested a long heavy rifle, his keen gray eyes peering from under the slouched brim of a flexible felt-hat, black and shining with grease. His buckskin hunting-shirt, bedaubed until it had the appearance of polished leather, hung in folds over his bony carcass; his nether extremities being clothed in pantaloons of the same material (with scattered fringes down the outside of the leg— which ornaments, however, had been pretty well thinned to supply "whangs" for mending moccasins or pack-saddles), which, shrunk with wet, clung tightly to his long, spare, sinewy legs. His feet were thrust into a pair of Mexican stirrups, made of wood, and as big as coal-scuttles; and iron spurs of incredible proportions, with tinkling drops attached to the rowels, were fastened to his heel—a bead-worked strap, four inches broad, securing them over the instep. In the shoulder-belt which sustained his powder-horn and bullet-pouch, were fastened the various instruments essential to one pursuing his mode of life. An awl, with deer-horn handle, and the point defended by a case of cherry-wood carved by his own hand, hung at the back of the belt, side by side with a worm for cleaning the rifle; and under this was a squat and quaint-looking bullet mould, the handles guarded by strips of buckskin to save his fingers from burning when running balls, having for its companion a little bottle made from the point of an antelope's horn, scraped transparent, which contained the "medicine" used in baiting the traps. The old coon's face was sharp and thin, a long nose and chin hob-nobbing

2. "A man of considerable influence, of enlarged views and gifted with more foresight than any man of his tribe . . ." J. W. Abert: *Examination of New Mexico in the Year 1846–47,* U. S. Senate Doc., 30th Cong., 1st Sess., Exec. No. 23 (Washington, D. C., 1848), p. 10. Abert also sketched O-Cum-Who-Wust ("Yellow Wolf") for his report.

each other; and his head was always bent forward, giving him the appearance of being hump-backed. He *appeared* to look neither to the right nor left, but, in fact, his little twinkling eye was everywhere. He looked at no one he was addressing, always seeming to be thinking of something else than the subject of his discourse, speaking in a whining, thin, cracked voice, and in a tone that left the hearer in doubt whether he was laughing or crying.[3]

Old Bill Williams was the most famous of the independent trappers. He sometimes condescended to join a party and occasionally acted as a guide, but never for long. He was essentially a loner. In the end, old (for a mountain man) and ill, with even his iron constitution broken down by dissipation, this one-time preacher who had become more Indian than the Indians was struck down by a war party of his own blood brothers, the Utes, while attempting to salvage some of the equipment left behind by Frémont's ill-fated fourth expedition. His death was as dramatic and as mysterious as that of Jedediah Smith. William Brandon, in his introduction for a new edition of Old Bill's biography,[4] has provided him with a splendid epitaph: "The past-master plainsman, the eccentric old-timer, the weathered rock of experience, scarred by Taos lightning and ancient demigodly deeds, the old scout, who is seldom sober and never wrong." Though he was given a chief's burial by the Utes when they discovered it was he they had killed, Old Bill Williams has no known grave. But, as Mr. Brandon justly observes, he lives on as a type in Western fiction and Western movies without number.

More fortunate in his press agents than Bill Williams—who hardly emerges even from Ruxton's vivid pen as a lovable figure—was Jim Bridger. Everybody liked Jim, from Sir William Drummond Stewart, who had brought out an English Life Guard's dress uniform for him to strut about in at the rendezvous,[5] to General Grenville Dodge, who had his deeds carved in stone. Jim Bridger's

---

3. *Life in the Far West* (1951 edn.), pp. 112–13, 178–9.

4. Alpheus H. Favour: *Old Bill Williams: Mountain Man* (Chapel Hill, N. C., 1936; repr. Norman, Okla., 1962), p. ix.

5. Alfred Jacob Miller drew this remarkable scene. See also M. R. Porter and O. Davenport: *Scotsman in Buckskins* (New York, 1963), passim. Jim Bridger "in armor" faces p. 149.

The Trapper, by Frederic Remington. From Francis Parkman: *The Oregon Trail*, illus. (Boston, 1892).

biographers have served him even better than did Bill Williams's.[6]

Orphaned at thirteen, apprenticed to a St. Louis blacksmith at fourteen, Jim Bridger was all of eighteen years and three days old

6. See Alter: *Jim Bridger* (1962 edn.). The oft-told, sketchily authenticated, and greatly embroidered story of Hugh Glass and the grizzly bear and of Jim's alleged ignominious part in that adventure is carefully analyzed by Alter. But the story goes on being stock-in-trade of the "pulp" merchants.

when on March 20, 1822, he had read to him (for he could not as yet read, and in fact never became adept at the art) Andrew Henry's and William H. Ashley's celebrated advertisement in a St. Louis newspaper "TO ENTERPRISING YOUNG MEN." Another enterprising young man to hear and hearken to that siren song was one Jedediah Strong Smith, who headed west (at the same time Jim did) as a member of Major Henry's fur-hunting party, "a bible in one hand and a rifle in the other."[7] Jim had only a rifle, but it was a trusty snub-nosed Hawken, and with that the poor unlettered orphan was ready for any wilderness.

Forty years later Jim was still on the trail, by this time the most experienced mountain man and guide in all the West and one of the very few survivors of all those enterprising young men. On October 17, 1862, another eighteen-year-old adventurer, Caspar Collins (son of Col. William O. Collins, U. S. Army), wrote home to Mother from Fort Laramie: "We had Major Bridger with us as guide. He knows more of the Rocky Mountains than any living man. He is totally uneducated but speaks English, Spanish and French equally well, besides nearly a dozen Indian tongues. . . . He has been in many Indian battles and has several arrow wounds."[8] One of those arrows, long ago, had been extracted on the Oregon Trail by Dr. Marcus Whitman himself, the Rev. Samuel Parker marveling at Jim's unflinching fortitude during the operation.[9] Young Caspar lovingly describes fifty-eight-year-old Jim Bridger[1] (to whom, as the context makes clear, this apparently generalised description specifically applies): "These old Mountaineers are curious-looking fellows. They nearly all wear big white hats with beaver around it; a loose white coat of Buck or antelope skins, trimmed fantastically with beaver-fur; buffalo breeches with strings hanging for ornaments along the sides; a Mexican saddle, moccasins and spurs, with rowels ten inches long, which jingle as they ride. They have bridles with, sometimes, ten dollars' worth of silver ornaments on; Indian ponies, a heavy rifle, a Navy revolver, a hatchet and a Bowie knife. They have a rawhide lasso tied on one side of the saddle. . . ."[2]

7. Charles Kelly: *Old Greenwood* (Salt Lake City, 1936), p. 9; with Dale Morgan (rev. edn. Georgetown, Calif., 1965), p. 12.
8. Alter, p. 301.
9. Samuel Parker: *Journal*, 3rd edn. (Ithaca, N. Y., 1842), p. 80.
1. Alter, p. 152.   2. Alter, p. 299.

Jim Bridger, photographed as an old man.

Jim stayed on the trail for nearly another twenty years after this, riding his trusty horse Ruff around the fields of his Missouri farm even when almost completely blind, guided only by the horse and by the warning bark of his dog, Old Sultan. He went over the final divide on July 17, 1881, and in 1904—the hundredth anniversary of his birth—his great admirer, Gen. Grenville M. Dodge, had a seven-foot granite column erected to his memory in Kansas City and delivered an oration that, while barely this side of idolatry, was in some ways an even better memorial to the old mountain man. Said Dodge: "Unquestionably Bridger's claim to remembrance rests on the extraordinary part he bore in the explorations of the West. As a guide he was without an equal. He was a complete master of plains and woodcraft. In all my experience I never saw Bridger meet an obstacle he could not overcome." Gen. Dodge's *Biographical Sketch of James Bridger* (1905) expands and documents such praises, and the careful researches of Mr. Alter twenty years later, and in subsequent editions of his definitive biography, have carefully winnowed out the chaff (much of it the product of Jim's own well-developed sense of humor and weakness for leg-pulling) from the Bridger story. Even what remains would seem incredible if only it had not been proved true beyond reasonable doubt by these same careful researches. As Jim himself once remarked: "They said I was the damnedest liar ever lived" when he had described the marvels of what is now Yellowstone National Park.[3]

One cannot have enough of Jim Bridger, but there were other mountain men; none nicer—except, of course, Kit Carson, unless you were an Indian—though many not so nice. Edward Rose, for instance, scalper extraordinary, and a white Crow "chief" in that tribe's wars against the Blackfoot, who "forsook civilization entirely";[4] Jim Beckwith, another Crow convert, who published his own autobiography[5] before being liquidated by poison, probably by one of his own squaws; and, last but not least, Charles Gardner,

3. Who could have expected to believe in a river that ran cold at the top but hot at the bottom (Fire Hole River), petrified tree trunks still standing, and a dark glass cliff (Obsidian Cliff), let alone geysers spouting up seventy feet or more with a terrible hissing noise at regular intervals (Old Faithful), a waterfall three times as high as Niagara (Yellowstone Falls), and springs so hot that meat could be cooked on the top terraces and "delightful baths" taken on the lower ones (Mammoth Hot Springs)! Needless to say, it was an Army officer, John W. Gunnison, and not a mountain man who took the first Mammoth hot bath. See also Alter, pp. 76–8.

4. Billington: *American Frontiersman*, p. 10. For more gory details of Rose's career, see Z. Leonard: *Adventures of Zenas Leonard, Fur Trader and Trapper 1831–1836* (Cleveland, 1904), pp. 262–70.

5. *Life and Adventures of James P. Beckwourth* (his "writing name"), ed. and ghosted by T. D. Bonner (New York, 1856); ed. Charles G. Leland (rev. edn. London, 1892).

or "Cannibal Phil," who hailed from the City of Brotherly Love and who, taking quite literally the old mountain man adage "meat's meat,"[6] when marooned in the mountains by a snow storm, "subsisted comfortably on the flesh of his current squaw."[7]

At his lowest a "case study in the reversion to the primitive"

Dakota (or Sioux) tipis, by Karl Bodmer.

and a curiosity of American history, the fur trapper of the Far West was, at his highest, much more than this, or Cleland's tribute to him[8] would be meaningless. For every Edward Rose there was a Jedediah Smith; for every Jim Beckwith, a Joseph Reddeford Walker; for every Charles Gardner, a Peter Skene Ogden. And

6. "In their willingness to consume anything that walked, swam, wriggled, or crawled, the trappers were strikingly akin to the Indians"—Billington: *Far Western Frontier*, p. 50; cf. Ruxton, *Life in the Far West*, p. 98.

7. LeRoy R. Hafen: "Mountain Men: Big Phil the Cannibal," *Colorado Magazine of History*, XIII (March 1936), 53–8; quoted in Billington: *American Frontiersman*, p. 10. See also *The Mountain Men and the Fur Trade of the West: Biographical Sketches* . . . , ed. Hafen, 3 vols. (Glendale, Calif., 1963–).

8. See above, p. 94.

then of course there was always Kit Carson . . . Kit Carson, who has many other claims to fame, seems, like his most famous employer, John C. Frémont, never to have blazed an entirely new trail across the Far West. True, he has a river, a pass, a city and even a "sink" named after him, but this, like so much of Frémont's geographical nomenclature, was a piece of topographical engineering rather than the recognition of a true discovery. Frémont even gypped Peter Skene Ogden out of the glory of having actually discovered, in 1828, the river which the latter modestly named "the Unknown" but which his men more appropriately christened "the Ogden"—or sometimes "Mary's River," after Ogden's wife. Seventeen years later, points out Cleland's finger of scorn, "John Charles Frémont, the follower of other men's trails, gratuitously dropped the name Ogden and called the river the Humboldt."[9] Baron Alexander von Humboldt had never been within a thousand miles of it, but then Ogden was a partisan of the Hudson's Bay Company and not the agent of manifest destiny and the Benton Enterprises.

Innumerable fur trappers, both famous and obscure, made contributions to the opening up of the ways to the Far West, and both Jim Bridger and Old Bill Williams, each of whom had a remarkable topographical instinct, were among them; but the two men who contributed most were undoubtedly Jedediah Smith and Peter Skene Ogden, while the leader of the most remarkable single journey overland to the Pacific (when its significance for the future development of the area is considered) was Joseph Reddeford Walker. If the lines of travel of the parties led by these three men west of the Continental Divide in the one decade between 1824 and 1834 are superimposed on a map of that area,[1] it is seen that they interlaced it with a network of trails, many of which they were the first, or among the first, white men to follow, and nearly all of which have later proved of inestimable worth to the overland wagon parties of the forties and fifties, to the railroad builders of

9. Cleland: *Reckless Breed*, p. 324. Lt. (later Gen.) Charles C. Frémont, of the U. S. Corps of Topographical Engineers and son-in-law of the influential and aggressive "Western" Senator Benton of Missouri, will reappear often in these pages (especially in Chs. v and vi). He is one of the most controversial figures in American Western history.

1. See maps, pp. 113, 123.

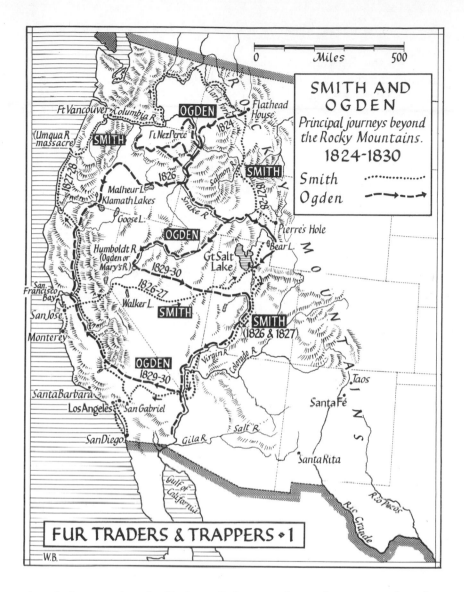

SMITH AND OGDEN

Principal journeys beyond the Rocky Mountains.

1824-1830

Smith ············
Ogden --------→

0   *Miles*   500

Ft Vancouver   Columbia R.   OGDEN   Flathead House

(Umqua R. massacre)   SMITH   Ft Nez Perce   1824

1827-28   1826   Salmon R.   SMITH

Malheur L.   Klamath Lakes   Snake R.   1827-28

Goose L.   Pierre's Hole

OGDEN   Gt Salt Lake   Bear L.

Humboldt R. (Ogden or Mary's R.)   1829-30

1826-27

San Francisco Bay   Walker L.   SMITH

San Jose   SMITH (1826 & 1827)

Monterey   Virgin R.   Colorado R.

OGDEN   1829-30   Taos

Santa Barbara   Santa Fé

Los Angeles   San Gabriel

San Diego   Salt R.   Santa Rita

Gila R.

Gulf of California

R. Grande   R. to Pecos

ROCKY MOUNTAINS

FUR TRADERS & TRAPPERS • 1

W.B.

the sixties, to the tin lizzies of the 1920's, and even to the air-conditioned Cadillacs of the 1960's.[2]

Beginning his career in the fur trade, as has been seen, in 1822, Jedediah Smith was over the Continental Divide in 1824 (at the South Pass, now beginning to come into regular use) and again in

2. J. Alexander Carroll, Western author and editor, told a historical conference in 1961: "I resolved to re-explore every nook and cranny of the West that could be reached by air-conditioned Cadillac." But in an emergency he could not, of course, eat his horsepower or drink his brake fluid.

1825, when he trapped with Ashley on the Green River and around the shores of the Great Salt Lake—which Jim Bridger had first seen, tasted, and spat out in 1824. But Smith's first great expedition into the farthest West was in 1826, when Gen. Ashley, his fortune made, had sold out his interests in the fur trade to his three young associates—Smith, Jackson,[3] and Sublette.[4] Ashley had planned this expedition before he retired, but Smith led it on behalf of the new partnership. Leaving the rendezvous on Bear River, east of Salt Lake, in August 1826 with about fourteen companions, Smith was back there again on July 3, 1827, with three of his men. "My arrival," he wrote, "caused a considerable bustle in camp . . . a small cannon, brought up from St. Louis, was loaded and fired for a salute." Next day being Independence Day, the rejoices were redoubled, "for myself and party had been given up for lost." He told Gen. William Clark in a report dated July 17, 1827: "When we arrived at the Salt Lake we had but one horse and one mule remaining, which were so feeble and poor that they could scarcely carry the little camp equipage which I had along; the balance of my horses I was compelled to eat as they gave out. The company are now starting, and therefore must close my communication. Yours respectfully Jedediah S. Smith."[5] Despite all the hardships he had encountered in eleven months on the trail, this tough young man (he was only twenty-nine years old) was off again on July 13, after less than a fortnight's rest,[6] to rescue and relieve the men he had left behind on the Stanislaus River, in California. Of the eighteen men who accompanied him, he returned with only one member, Arthur Black, of the combined parties of 1826 and 1827. Most of the others were dead. Jedediah Smith did not get back for the summer rendezvous of 1828; indeed, he and his partners were not reunited until the summer of 1829, at

3. David E. Jackson, after whom Jackson (Wyoming), Jackson's Hole, and Jackson Lake were named. As yet he has found no biographer, but *si monumentum requiris*, what's better than the Grand Teton National Park!

4. William L. Sublette, the most famous of five brothers, all of whom were engaged in the fur trade. See further John E. Sunder: *Bill Sublette: Mountain Man* (Norman, Okla., 1959), passim.

5. Quoted in Maurice Sullivan: *The Travels of Jedediah Smith* (Santa Ana, Calif., 1934); see also Dale Morgan's definitive critical biography, *Jedediah Smith and the Opening of the West* (Indianapolis, 1953).

6. The report to Clark, cited above, seems either to have been misdated or else not finished until four days after he set out. See Cleland, p. 87.

Henry's Fork of the Snake River, in Idaho, whence they repaired to the rendezvous at Pierre's Hole, west of the Tetons. There, on August 20, 1829, about 175 trappers gathered.[7] And what a tale Jedediah Smith and Arthur Black had to tell around the camp fires at that rendezvous! Smith, who knew Latin as well as his Bible, may conceivably have had a more than nodding acquaintance with Homer as well. If so, he might well have compared himself to Odysseus, so remarkable and so harrowing had his adventures been in the three years since he had first set out for California, and especially on his second, more tragic, expedition to the Pacific Coast.

On the 1826–7 expedition Smith had not lost a man, though he had left all but two of them behind in California when he decided to scale the high Sierras on his return journey in May 1827. On the 1827–9 expedition, however, which followed virtually the same route from Salt Lake to Southern California—via the Sevier, the Virgin, and the Colorado rivers, across the Mojave Desert to the San Bernardino Mountains and the mission farms of San Gabriel, a route later to become famous as "the Mormon outlet"—Smith lost ten of his men in an Indian ambush while crossing the Colorado at the Mojave villages. Among these was Silas Gobel, one of the two men he had taken back with him across the Great Salt Desert to the 1827 rendezvous, an epic feat of endurance that has been called "one of the greatest single exploits in the whole history of western exploration."[8]

Smith left three of his nine surviving men, one of them badly wounded, in Southern California, but he did not tarry there himself for another visit to the mission of San Gabriel or to San Diego, being unsure of the welcome he would receive;[9] he hurried instead

7. Robert Newell: *Memoranda of Travel in Missouri* (Portland, Ore., 1959), p. 31. Newell was a member of Sublette's supply party, which left St. Louis on March 17, 1829. He wrote a most illuminating diary, survived more than another decade of fur trapping and rendezvous-ing, and finally settled down on a farm in Oregon.

8. Charles Kelly in *Utah Historical Quarterly*, III:1, 27; quoted in Cleland, p. 84.

9. While the Franciscan fathers had been friendly, Governor Echeandía had been distinctly cool toward the Americans in 1826. Smith himself left only a fragmentary account of this first winter of a party of American fur trappers in Alta California, but his clerk and second in command, Harrison Rogers, kept a full diary. The account by this doughty Protestant of his friendly theological disputes with the jolly friars at what he sometimes called "the Mansion" is in H. C. Dale:

to the camp on the Stanislaus, where his 1826 party awaited him, reaching them on July 18. Accompanied by only two of his men—for he realized that the intrusion of the whole party into the Mexican coastal settlements once again would not be tolerated by the authorities there—he then visited the missions of San Jose and Santa Clara for supplies and to attempt to establish friendly relations. Placed under open arrest by a suspicious Father Dúran,[1] he once again found himself back in Monterey, explaining his actions to an even more irascible Governor Echeandía. Before he could get away and back to his men, he had to post a bond for $30,000 (guaranteed by four prominent Yankee residents of Monterey) with the Mexican authorities, and had lost nearly six months. His men had relieved their enforced idleness in the San Joaquin Valley by desultory hunting and trapping, though it was poor beaver country and they had but few traps with them, and by making, under Harrison Rogers, a sight-seeing and shopping[2] visit to San Francisco Bay. It was the new year 1828 before they set out on their return journey. As it was far too late to get across the Sierras, on which snow was already falling, they sloshed their way up the flooded Sacramento Valley to the Feather River. Here beaver were

---

The Ashley-Smith Exploration and the Discovery of a Central Route to the Pacific, 1822–1829 (Cleveland, 1918; Glendale, Calif., 1941). Rogers commanded the party until Smith returned in 1827. He unfortunately perished in the massacre on the Umpqua River on July 14, 1828.

1. Dúran was to tangle some two years later with James Ohio Pattie, another American interloper, over a small matter of payment for smallpox inoculations. See James Ohio Pattie: *The Personal Narrative of James Ohio Pattie of Kentucky* . . . (Cincinnati, 1831; repr. *Early Western Travels, 1748–1846*, ed. R. G. Thwaites, Cleveland, 1905; paperback edn. New York, 1962). Pattie's *Narrative* (publ. by Timothy Flint) is more exciting than it is reliable, but amid exaggerations and much padding—like his (or Flint's) description of Mission San Luis Rey, lifted bodily out of La Pérouse's description of the Carmel mission (see above, Ch. ii, pp. 54–9), printed thirty-three years earlier—it is in essentials authentic. His was the first American book to get into print describing in detail the missions and the life of Mexican Alta California, preceding Dana's *Two Years before the Mast*, for which this claim is often made, by nine years. It is equally good reading.

2. The only "shops" there at that time were occasional merchant ships, come to barter their very mixed cargoes for hides and tallow. The first permanent building in what is now San Francisco was not put up until nearly a decade later. But they could have visited the Spanish presidio (fallen into decay) above the (as yet unnamed) Golden Gate, and the mission of Saint Francis of Assisi, along a cowpath about four miles away. They did find a kindly German merchant, Henry Virmond, who was willing to trade with them out of his ship.

Woman of the Snake tribe, Fort MacKenzie, September 1833,
by Karl Bodmer.

plentiful—one night twenty were caught[3]—and bear were almost
one too many for Rogers, who was nearly killed by one. Elk, deer,
antelope, coyotes, wolves, coons, swan, geese, brant, and wild
ducks also abounded. The Indians, too, were numerous but, fortu-

3. "Great trapping," said Smith, for "I had but 28 traps"—Sullivan, p. 68.

nately, harmless and, in Smith's opinion, "the lowest intermediate link between man and the Brute creation." Apart from the bears, this was truly a hunter's and trapper's paradise. For most of the

Dakota (Sioux) woman and Assiniboin girl, by Karl Bodmer.

men of this party it was to be their last paradise on earth, for when they turned toward the coast in an effort to force themselves up into Oregon, the trail grew worse and worse and the Indians more hostile. They reached the sea on June 8, 1828, and the mouth of the

Umpqua River on July 9. Five days later an Indian attack deci-
mated the party. Only Smith (who had been absent from camp
reconnoitering in a canoe) and three of his men (one of whom
made a lone journey all the way to Fort Vancouver on the Colum-

A Blackfoot Indian on horseback, by Karl Bodmer.

bia) escaped. All their companions, all their gear, and all their furs
were gone. It was utter disaster. They were succored and re-
equipped by the ever hospitable Dr. McLoughlin, who sent a most
dramatic account of their misadventures back to the Hudson's Bay
Company in London[4] and immediately diverted a trapping party
and some of his best hunters to salvage Smith's furs and punish the
Umpqua Indians. For the jolly Harrison Rogers and his once
merry men, they could do nothing except bury eleven skeletons

4. *The Letters of John McLoughlin from Fort Vancouver to the Governor
and Committee, First Series, 1825–38*, ed. E. E. Rich (Toronto, 1941), pp. 68–70.
Letter dated August 10, 1828.

they found "whitening in the sun."[5] Four bodies remained unaccounted for.

But, for Jedediah Smith, this was not yet the end of the trail. Over 700 beaver skins and 39 horses were recovered from the Indians, and though McLoughlin had spent over a thousand dollars on the relief expedition, he and Sir George Simpson, governor-general of the Hudson's Bay Company, refused compensation and paid Smith $3,200 for his furs and horses. After wintering at Fort Vancouver, Smith and Black (the other two men stayed on there) set off on their own—"Sporting with Life or courting danger to madness," in the opinion of Sir George Simpson, who never sent out his own men in parties of less than forty or fifty—up the Columbia Valley to the Grand Coulee, across what is now eastern Washington and northern Idaho, past Lewis and Clark's Traveler's Rest (Missoula, Montana)—where they did not rest—to effect their rendezvous with David Jackson and later with William Sublette. Jedediah Smith had come almost full circle[6] of the American Far West. The cost had been high. Yet Smith's expeditions to California and the Columbia had far-reaching effects. They aroused the interest of mountain men and the United States government in the Far Western territories, particularly California and the Oregon wilderness, which Smith had traversed. They also led the Hudson's Bay Company to send out reconnaissance expeditions as far south as the Gulf of California, and ushered in more than a decade of profitable trapping on the watersheds of California for Dr. McLoughlin and his associates."[7]

The man who led the most important of these Hudson's Bay Company expeditions was Peter Skene Ogden, a man who, in the opinion of Dale Morgan, "stands second only to Smith among the field captains of the fur trade in the decade."[8] Ogden led a party to the Great Salt Lake in May 1825, very soon after Bridger had reached it; in 1826 he went up the Des Chutes and the John Day rivers into hitherto unknown country; in 1827 he visited the Klamath River and explored as far as Mount Shasta; in 1828-9 he made his celebrated discovery of the Unknown River—also known

5. Cleland, p. 113.   6. See map, p. 113.   7. Cleland, p. 116.

8. *Jedediah Smith*, p. 131. Morgan refers scornfully to "a folk belief which has persisted since the days of the Presidential election of 1856 that nothing of importance happened in the west before Frémont's time."

as Mary's and as Ogden's River—which Frémont was to decide should be called the Humboldt. But his name survives at Ogden's Hole, Ogden's Creek, and the city of Ogden,[9] all in Utah. His journeys took him down as far as the Gulf of California on one occasion (1829–30) and he traversed the San Joaquin and Sacramento valleys almost from end to end on his way back north. Taking a brigade out of Fort Vancouver every year from 1824 onward, Ogden had encountered as many difficulties and tribulations as did Smith. He worked his men hard and the casualties among them were many.[1] This may partially explain why he lost so many by desertion to the Americans, notably in his celebrated encounter with John Gardner's party of Ashley's men at Bear Lake in 1825, as a result of which twenty-three of them went over to the enemy. The Hudson's Bay Company never forgot or forgave this rebuff.[2]

The itinerary of Ogden's most far-ranging expedition—that of 1829–30[3]—was from the mouth of the Snake River to the Humboldt Sink across a country "as barren as ever Christian traversed" to the Sevier River, the Virgin, and the Colorado, where twenty-six Mohave Indians were slaughtered, presumably in a move to anticipate any such attack as had been made on Smith's men in 1827. Following the Colorado to its mouth, Ogden then returned through the Yuma country to the San Joaquin, where he encountered an American party under Ewing Young and traveled with it up to the Sacramento for a while. Finally Ogden returned to the Columbia with a thousand beaver skins, only to lose most of them, nine of his men, and the records of his expedition in a boat accident

9. I was disappointed not to find a statue of Peter Skene Ogden in the fine square in the center of the very pleasant city of Ogden, Utah, when I stopped there in 1963. I suspect that if Ogden had been an obscure nineteenth-century Latter-Day Saint and not a Hudson's Bay captain of trappers, he would have been there on his plinth, all right, bearded and frock-coated like the other elect. But of course Ogden did not found the city, and the Mormon elders did. It is much to their credit that they have retained the name.

1. He said: "This life makes a man sixty in a few years. A convict at Botany Bay is a gentleman at ease compared to my trappers." F. C. Elliott: "The Earliest Travelers on the Oregon Trail," *Oregon Historical Society Quarterly*, XVIII, 80.

2. See Frederick Merk: *Fur Trade and Empire* (Cambridge and London, 1931), pp. 274 ff., and *The Letters of John McLoughlin, First Series* (ed. Rich), App. A, for this incident and its effect on Hudson's Bay policy.

3. See map, p. 113.

near the Dalles on the very last lap of his return to Fort Vancouver.[4]

Other Hudson's Bay trapping parties, notably those led by
Laframboise and Work,[5] went down into California in Ogden's
wake all through the thirties, and, as late as 1841, established a
trading post at the little village of Yerba Buena, on San Francisco
Bay, much to the alarm of its Yankee residents. But it was Peter
Skene Ogden, using to a large extent information gleaned from
Jedediah Smith, who had blazed the way for them.

Both Smith and Ogden provided material for the map-makers
of the thirties. Ogden's reports, sent back to London, were used by
Aaron Arrowsmith for his map, published in 1834, and the "J. E.
Smith Route" (though inaccurately and incompletely indicated)
actually appears on Albert Gallatin's famous map, published in
Washington in 1836, which is so much more satisfactory than
Captain Bonneville's map of 1837, made without benefit of Smith's
data and drawing heavily on the gallant Captain's imagination.[6]

Yet it was Bonneville who, in 1833, was responsible for sending out Joseph Reddeford Walker's remarkable expedition—the
only one to rival Smith's and Ogden's in interest and significance
during the mountain-man era. Bonneville accompanied it only as
far as the Great Salt Lake, and Washington Irving called it "a
disgraceful expedition," presumably because it had not followed
Bonneville's limited and somewhat obscure instructions and had
not brought back a wealth of furs; nevertheless, it achieved a
remarkable series of "firsts" in opening up the Far West. The
expedition to California "established his [Walker's] fame as an
explorer and made him one of the historical pathfinders of the
Great West. His trail ran from Salt Lake down the Humboldt
River, across the Sierra Nevada Mountains to the coast, from the

4. See further Alice B. Maloney: "Peter Skene Ogden's Trapping Expedition to California, 1829–30," *California Historical Society Quarterly* [hereafter
cited as *CHQ*], XIX, 308–16.

5. Cleland, pp. 328–42, gives a detailed account of one of these expeditions
and briefly refers to others.

6. For Bonneville, see Goetzmann: *Army Exploration;* Carl I. Wheat:
"Mapping the American West, 1540–1857," *Proceedings of the American Anti-
quarian Society*, LXIV (1954), 19–194; and E. W. Gilbert: *The Exploration of
Western America, 1800–1850: An Historical Geography* (Cambridge, 1933) for
general appreciations of the cartographical significance of Smith and Ogden.
Dale L. Morgan and Carl I. Wheat: *Jedediah Smith and His Maps of the American
West* (San Francisco, 1954) is a specialist study. See especially below, p. 124.

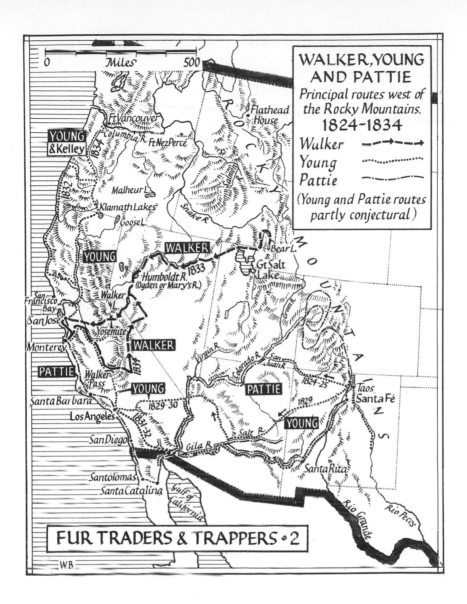

WALKER, YOUNG
AND PATTIE
Principal routes west of
the Rocky Mountains.
1824-1834
Wulker --->--->--->
Young ············
Pattie — · — · — ·
(Young and Pattie routes
partly conjectural)

FUR TRADERS & TRAPPERS ∘ 2

San Joaquin Valley by way of Walker Pass to the Mojave-Colo-
rado basin, up the unknown Owens Valley almost to its source and
back again to the Humboldt"[7] and Salt Lake. His party were the
first white men to see and describe the Yosemite Valley and the
giant redwoods of the Tuolumne Grove, the first to find an easy
route around the south end of the high Sierras (Walker's Pass,
5,250 feet above sea level). It was not his intention to pioneer a
practicable wagon road to California; yet the first two overland

7. Cleland, pp. 307–8.

(1 2 3)

parties of settlers to get through in the 1840's—those of Bidwell-Bartleson and Chiles—followed much of his route of 1833–34, and the second of these had the advantage of Walker himself as guide. He managed to get its wagons as far as Owens Lake and the party itself all the way to Peachtree Valley and the Promised Land. His experiences of 1833–34 were of inestimable value to him and to many others in the years to follow.

A detailed and vivid narrative of the Walker expedition to California, written by Zenas Leonard, one of its members, makes for one of the great stories of the American West.[8] Leonard, a well-trained clerk fresh out of St. Louis, probably produced a better account than Walker himself would have done, for Walker, though not illiterate, was a rough-hewn mountain man, readier with the spoken than the written word. It is true that Leonard may have bowdlerized their adventures a little for the Pennsylvania carriage trade; there is no mention of horse-stealing on the side, and little reference is made to a roistering winter spent in Monterey, in and out of Tom the Trapper's grog shop. But Washington Irving[9] and Joe Meek,[1] who refer to such goings on, both had an ax to grind, and Meek a long bow to draw. Leonard expressed great admiration for Walker as a leader of men. He had to be, for his brigade of "forty thieves" is said to have included such indestructible characters as Bill Williams ("himself"), Joe Gale, Mark Hind, Bill Mitchell, the Meek brothers, Alexis Godey, Antoine Janise, Bill Craig, George Nidever, and John Price.[2] Walker was, says Leonard, "a man well-hardened to the hardships of the wilderness—understood the character of the Indians very well—was kind and affable to his men, but at the same time at liberty to

8. *Narrative of the Adventures of Zenas Leonard,* "written by himself" (Clearfield, Pa., 1839; repr. Cleveland, 1904).

9. *The Rocky Mountains; or, Scenes, Incidents, and Adventures in the Far West; Digested from the Journal of Capt. B. L. E. Bonneville, of the Army of the United States . . . ,* 2 vols. (Philadelphia, 1837). Many subsequent editions, the latest and best being that edited by Edgeley W. Todd (Norman, Okla., 1961).

1. Mentioned in Frances F. Victor: *The River of the West* (Hartford, 1870), though Mrs. Victor may have added some embroidery of her own to Joe's notorious fancywork.

2. Favour: *Old Bill Williams,* pp. 107–8, gives potted biographies of most of these men. Nidever stayed on in California and made quite a name for himself there. See further W. H. Ellison: *The Life and Adventures of George Nidever* (Berkeley, Calif., 1937).

command without giving offense—and to explore unknown regions was his chief delight."[3]

Walker, a fine figure of a man (over six feet tall) and a former county sheriff in Missouri,[4] was, at thirty-five, already "a great name among the Mountain Men."[5] The squaws found him irresist-

Indians hunting the bison, by Karl Bodmer.

ible, and he on his side considered them desirable though not edible. Two of Alfred Jacob Miller's most famous pictures are the head-and-shoulders portrait of *Joseph Walker—The Bourgeois* and the drawing *Bourgeois W —— and Squaw*[6] while yet another, *The Trapper's Bride*, may represent Walker and his latest conquest.

3. Leonard: *Narrative*, p. 33; cf. Jedediah Smith's statement about himself: "I of course expected to find Beaver, which with us hunters is a primary object, but I was also led on by the love of novelty common to all . . ." (Sullivan: *Travels of Smith*, p. 26).

4. As well as policing it, he *named* the County. He called it "Jackson," which was more respectful than Davy Crockett calling his dog "Jackson."

5. George R. Stewart: *The California Trail* (New York, 1962; London, 1964), p. 5.

6. Miller noted: "The sketch exhibits a certain etiquette, the squaw's station in traveling is at a considerable distance in the rear of her liege lord, and never at the side of him." Reproductions of all three of these pictures appear in H. McCracken: *The West of Alfred Jacob Miller* (Norman, Okla., 1951). See also below, p. 126.

But, of all his many adventures, the greatest moment in Walker's life was when he discovered the Yosemite Valley. He asked that this alone be commemorated on his tombstone.

"This Reckless Breed" were men of action but of few words. When Dan Tobin was asked for his recollections of Kit Carson, he just said, "I et many a beaver tail with him." The mountain men

A bourgeois, Joseph Reddeford Walker, and his squaw,
by Alfred Jacob Miller.

lived rough and most of them, like Jedediah Smith, died young. Those who lived into old age, growing garrulous at last in their retirement, as did Jim Bridger,[7] have left behind them a folklore that passes belief but that is probably only a little wider than the truth. Not every mountain man was a John Colter,[8] but most of

7. Jim Bridger was known in his early days as "Old Gabe," not because he had the gift of gab but because the Bible-toting Jedediah Smith likened him to the Archangel Gabriel.

8. John· Colter's escape from his Blackfoot captors alone, unclothed, and unarmed in 1808 is one of the great stories of the West, and it is even quite probably true. See Burton Harris: *John Colter* (New York, 1952).

them had adventures hardly less hazardous than his. The whole
map of the Great West bears the names they gave to streams and
peaks, passes and canyons, lakes and mountain meadows. "Not a
hole or corner but has been ransacked by these hardy men," wrote
Frederick Ruxton. "From the Mississippi to the mouth of the Colorado of the West, from the frozen regions of the North to the Gila

Cavalcade of trappers and Indians with Sir William Stewart on a white
horse, by Alfred Jacob Miller.

in Mexico, the beaver hunter has set his traps in every creek and
stream. All this vast country, but for the daring and enterprise of
these men, would be even now [1847] a *Terra Incognita* to geog-
raphers."[9]

Beside the mountain man the cowboy, riding the range, repair-
ing fences, and, on rare occasions, "painting the town red," seems
almost tame, the train and stage-robbing desperado petty, and the
hijacking gangster of the Prohibition era a sissy. Yet the era of the

9. Porter and Hafen: *Ruxton of the Rockies*, p. 228. In the less dignified
language of the typical mountain man (Black Harris): "I've trapped beaver on
Platte and Arkansa, and away up on Missoura and Yallar Stone; I've trapped on
Columbia, on Lewis Fork, and Green River; I've trapped, marm, on Grand River
and the Heeley [Gila] . . . I've trapped in heav'n, in airth, and hell . . ." (Ruxton: *Life in the Far West*, p. 8).

mountain men, the heyday of the trade in the pelt of the beaver, lasted barely twenty years. By the middle forties the silk hat was in fashion to give it the *coup de grâce*. Those mountain men who survived settled down, grumbling, on farms, went into the cattle industry, became guides and scouts to the overland parties and the armies of the West, or just faded away, as silently as they habitually moved.

CHAPTER V

Breaking the Wagon Trails West

THE THREE GREAT TRAILS ACROSS THE TRANS-MISSISSIPPI West before the building of the transcontinental railroads were the Santa Fe Trail, the Oregon Trail and the California Trail. The Santa Fe Trail continued across from the Rio Grande valley to the Pacific as the Old Spanish Trail to Los Angeles, the Gila River being a less used alternative to San Diego. An even more southerly trail was developed from Memphis across Arkansas, the Indian Country, and Texas to El Paso, Yuma, and San Diego, to be used as the route of the overland stagecoaches. The outbreak of the Civil War soon put an end to its usefulness. It was too roundabout ever to have been an emigrant trail. It carried mail, important small-bulk freight, and affluent or expense-account passengers at considerable speed and in great discomfort. Even less important for the overland migration was the short-lived (1860–1) but spectacular Pony Express, from St. Joseph to Sacramento and San Francisco, carrying, of course, no passengers, but mail, at first at $5 per half ounce—and always at a loss, both in money and in men. The opening of the transcontinental telegraph ended this experiment in 1861, but for another half century, at least, grizzled old bums cadged drinks in bars from Anchorage to the Bowery and back to the Embarcadero with the claim "I rode the Pony Express." A few beery reminiscences culled at fifth-hand from Mark Twain, and a knife scar collected in some tavern brawl but remembered as an Indian arrow wound, were the usual "props," but they often worked. Why, the old timers even walked bow-legged! A few of these "daring young men, preferably orphans" who actually rode the ponies, including (so he always said) "Buffalo Bill" Cody, did manage to wine and dine their way into the twentieth century.

The Pony Express route, which was no new way but just a streamlined version of the (by that time) very much cluttered-up California Trail, closed an era which may be said to have begun, on that particular trail, the memorable evening when Nancy Kelsey, the eighteen-year-old wife of Benjamin Kelsey, put her one-year-old-daughter Ann to bed on "Dr." John Marsh's ranch on the slopes of Mount Diabolo—less than twenty miles short of San Francisco Bay—one November day in 1841. They were the only woman and the only child to stay all the way with the Bidwell-Bartleson party, "the first company of American emigrants to enter California overland."[1]

The Santa Fe Trail may be said to have opened in 1821, fully twenty years before the California and Oregon trails. It could have opened earlier but for the Spanish prohibition on trade between New Mexico and the British and French settlements in the Mississippi Valley. Independent Mexico relaxed this ban, and William Becknell, the involuntary "father of the Santa Fe trade," Thomas James, and the Glenn-Fowler parties, then trading warily in the American-Spanish border country on the upper Arkansas, were all invited to visit Santa Fe and reached it before the end of the year.

1. Stewart: *California Trail*, p. 28. Nancy and Ann Kelsey thus occupy a niche in the Wilderness hall of fame very close to that of Sacagawea and Baptiste Charbonneau. Unlike Baptiste, though, Ann, "having established herself as the first American child to cross the Sierra Nevada and enter California by the central route . . . disappears from history" (Stewart, p. 29), but Nancy lived on until 1895. "Enough incidents happened to me to make a book," she told the press in 1893. "I have seen U. S. Grant when he was little known. I have baked bread for General Frémont and talked to Kit Carson. I have run from bear and killed most all other [sic] kinds of small game" (p. 29). There is no book about Nancy Kelsey, but Stewart offers much interesting biographical information, not only about Nancy and her child but also about the thirty-one men who made up the rest of the party (Ch. i). Several of them became famous, among them James Bidwell, a young schoolmaster from Ohio and the real spark plug of the party, who went on to serve as John Augustus Sutter's right-hand man at New Helvetia, to become a California millionaire, to found the city of Chico, to help nominate Lincoln in the Republican convention of 1860, to serve in Congress, and to run for President (as the Prohibition party candidate) in 1892. See further Stewart: *U. S. Highway 40* (New York, 1953) and *Ordeal by Hunger* (Berkeley, Calif., 1936; rev. edn., 1960; London, 1962).

In 1822, on a second expedition, Becknell pioneered the Cimarron Cutoff, shorter but more hazardous than the better watered "Mountain route" on which Bent's Fort was to be established a decade later. His were the first American wagons to reach Santa Fe. The longer Raton Pass route, used by the pack trains hitherto, was too steep for the wheeled vehicles of the day. By 1831 one caravan of a

Arrival of a caravan at Santa Fe. From Josiah Gregg: *Commerce of the Prairies* (1844).

hundred wagons carried over $200,000 worth of goods to the New Mexican capital: it was ceasing to be a mere outpost of civilization. The trade had its ups and downs, but it continued every year until 1843, after which, in an atmosphere of ever-worsening relations between Mexico and the United States, General Santa Anna reimposed the ban. It was to be finally and triumphantly swept aside by the Army of the West in 1846.

The Santa Fe Trail has had many chroniclers, but pre-eminent among those of a literary turn of mind who actually participated in the trade was Dr. Josiah Gregg. His *Commerce of the Prairies*[2] is a

2. *Commerce of the Prairies, or the Journal of a Santa Fe Trader during Eight Expeditions across the Great Western Prairies and a Residence of Nearly*

vivid and erudite work, on which many later writers have leaned heavily. Gregg himself took part in the trade only between 1831 and 1841, but in his book he surveys its whole development from the first organized caravan of 1822 on which seventy men took about $15,000 worth of merchandise on pack animals to Santa Fe, until 1843, when 350 men and 230 wagons took $430,000 worth there, of which no less than two thirds was later shipped on to Chihuahua, in Old Mexico. Gregg's account of the arrival of a caravan at Santa Fe deservedly gets into all the Western anthologies:

A few miles before reaching the city, the road again emerges into an open plain. Ascending a table ridge, we spied in an extended valley to the northwest, occasional groups of trees, skirted with verdant corn and wheat fields, with here and there a square block-like protuberance reared in the midst. A little further, and just ahead of us to the north, irregular clusters of the same opened to our view. "Oh, we are approaching the suburbs!" thought I, on perceiving the cornfields, and what I supposed to be brick-kilns scattered in every direction. These and other observations of the same nature becoming audible, a friend at my elbow said, "It is true these are heaps of unburnt bricks, nevertheless they are *houses*—this is the city of SANTA FÉ."

Five or six days after our arrival, the caravan at last hove in sight, and wagon after wagon was seen pouring down the last declivity at about a mile's distance from the city. To judge from the clamorous rejoicings of the men, and the state of agreeable excitement which the muleteers seemed to be laboring under, the spectacle must have been as new to them as it had been to me. It was truly a scene for the artist's pencil to revel in. Even the animals seemed to participate in the humor of their riders, who grew more and more merry and obstreperous as they descended towards the city. I doubt, in short, whether the first sight of the walls of Jerusalem were beheld by the crusaders with much more tumultuous and soul-enrapturing joy.

The arrival produced a great deal of bustle and excitement among the natives. *"Los Americanos!"—"Los carros!"—"La entrada*

Nine Years in Northern Mexico, 2 vols. (New York, 1844). Of the many reprints of this book, including a paperback edn., that cited here is the Southwest Press edn. (Dallas, Tex., 1933). See also *Diary and Letters of Josiah Gregg*, ed. Maurice G. Fulton, with an intro. by Paul Horgan, 2 vols. (Norman, Okla., 1941).

de la caravana!" were to be heard in every direction; and crowds of women and boys flocked around to see the newcomers; while crowds of *leperos* hung about as usual to see what they could pilfer. The wagoners were by no means free from excitement on this occasion. Informed of the "ordeal" they had to pass, they had spent the previous morning in "rubbing up;" and now they were prepared, with clean faces, sleek combed hair, and their choicest Sunday suit, to meet the "fair eyes" of glistening black that were sure to stare at them as they passed. There was yet another preparation to be made in order to "show off" to advantage. Each wagoner must tie a bran new "cracker" to the lash of his whip; for, on driving through the streets and the *plaza pública*, every one strives to outvie his comrades in the dexterity with which he flourishes this favorite badge of his authority.

Our wagons were soon discharged in the ware-rooms of the Custom-house; and a few days' leisure being now at our disposal, we had time to take that recreation which a fatiguing journey of ten weeks had rendered so necessary. The wagoners, and many of the traders, particularly the novices, flocked to the numerous fandangoes, which are regularly kept up after the arrival of a caravan. But the merchants generally were anxiously and actively engaged in their affairs—striving who should first get his goods out of the Custom-house, and obtain a chance at the "hard chink" of the numerous country dealers, who annually resort to the capital on these occasions. . . .

The arrival of a caravan at Santa Fe changes the aspect of the place at once. Instead of the idleness and stagnation which its streets exhibited before, one now sees everywhere the bustle, noise and activity of a lively market town. As the Mexicans very rarely speak English, the negotiations are mostly conducted in Spanish.[3]

In its early days, when the caravans were still small, the Santa Fe trade was little hampered by Indians, but before the end of the twenties they had become a major threat to it. Gregg gives several quite literally hair-raising accounts of Indian attacks and white parties' reprisals, and mentions the notorious *Proyecto de Guerra*, adopted in 1837 by the people of Chihuahua, which paid "a hundred dollars . . . for the scalp of a full-grown man, fifty for that

3. Gregg, pp. 66–8.

of a squaw, and twenty-five for that of every papoose!"[4] to deal with constant Apache depredations. An interesting instance of the overlapping of the mountain-man era and that of the wagon trails West was the bringing in of Old Bill Williams and the utilizing of his knowledge of Indian languages and skill in negotiating with the Indians to make safer the passage along the Santa Fe Trail. The famous treaty of Sibley and his fellow U. S. government commissioners with the Osage Indians—Bill Williams's blood brothers and the tribe of his first squaw—at Council Grove (from which

A Comanche village, 1834, by George Catlin.

this famous spot derived its name) on August 10, 1825, was largely Bill's achievement, as was the treaty with the Kansas Indians later that year. The Comanches were another matter, and nobody at this time managed to come to terms with these "Spartans of the Plains" either on the Santa Fe Trail or anywhere else. In 1829, despite military escort under Major Bennett Riley as far as the Mexican border, a large caravan consisting of sixty men and thirty-six wagons, led by Charles Bent and the fiery Colonel Marmaduke, was

4. Gregg, p. 199. He called the Indians "the *Unconquered Sabaeans* of the Great American Desert."

attacked by Comanches during its first unescorted day inside New Mexican territory. Ninety-five hunters under Ewing Young "who might be considered equal to five hundred inexperienced men" turned up to convoy the battered caravan into Taos, to which it had to be deflected instead of going straight to Santa Fe. On the way back, this caravan was protected by a Mexican cavalry force under General Vizcarra; but, though the caravan itself got through, the military escort was badly carved up on the Cimarron

Emigrant train attacked by Comanches, *c.* 1849; by Seth Eastman.

Cutoff while returning to its base. It was near the Cimarron that, two years later, the Comanches caught up with Jedediah Smith, separated from his party and searching for water, and put an end to his short but spectacular career. That year, 1831, Gregg's caravan (it was his first crossing of the Plains) was about a month behind that of Smith and Sublette, and in his account he is somewhat critical of the risks taken by these apparently fearless mountain men: "Capt. Smith and his companions were new beginners in the Santa Fé trade, but being veteran pioneers of the Rocky Mountains, they concluded they could go anywhere; and imprudently set out without a single person in their company at all competent to guide them on the route. They had some twenty odd wagons, and about eighty men . . . every kind of fatality seems to have attended this little caravan."[5] William Sublette finally struggled into Santa Fe after parlaying his way through an "immense horde of Blackfeet and Gros Ventres,"[6] a sadder and wiser man.

These were the teething troubles of the Santa Fe trade; as Gregg points out, "since the year 1831, few or none of the difficulties or dangers which once environed the Santa Fé adventures have been encountered. No traders have been killed by the savages on the regular route, and but few animals stolen from the caravan. On the whole, the rates of insurance upon adventures in this trade should hardly be as high as upon marine adventures between New York and Liverpool."[7] However, political difficulties increased as the Indian menace faded, and it was these that ground the trade to a halt in 1843, the very year that the Oregon migration began on a large scale. The trouble came mainly from the direction of the Republic of Texas, which claimed New Mexico up to the Rio Grande at least, and, given support and encouragement by the United States, would have been prepared to expand westward to the Pacific Ocean. The disastrous Texas-Santa Fe expedition of 1841 had greatly increased tension in the borderlands, and when a party of freebooters, some of whom were Texans, robbed and murdered a prominent Mexican merchant named Chavez in February 1843 near the Little Arkansas (and at least a hundred miles inside U. S. territory), Mexican indignation was intensified, despite the fact that the murderers were later brought to trial and condemned in St. Louis. The last straw was the ignominious Sniveley expedition of 175 men out of North Texas, which, after defeating General Armijo's vanguard inside Mexican territory in the summer of 1843, caused that worthy to retreat with his main force to Santa Fe, but was soon afterward disarmed, when it returned to U. S. territory, by Captain Philip St. George Cooke, U. S. Army, under orders to keep peace along the Trail. As a result of this "second Santa Fe expedition," the Mexican government protested, and demanded damages, to Waddy Thompson, U. S. Minister to Mexico, whose efforts toward maintaining good relations were as much hampered by such incidents as these as by Commodore Thomas ap

5. Gregg, pp. 54–5.

6. Gregg, p. 56. If his identification is correct, these "treacherous savages" were rather far from their usual hunting grounds.

7. Gregg, p. 326.

Catesby Jones's recent seizure (October 1842) of Monterey "by mistake." Santa Anna's decree of August 7, 1843, closed the custom houses at Taos, El Paso, and Chihuahua.

Though these ports of entry were reopened on March 31, 1844, and a certain amount of trade went over the Santa Fe Trail in 1844, the whole enterprise was about to be swallowed up by the onward march of Manifest Destiny. In 1845 Colonel Stephen Watts Kearny led his dragoons on a military reconnaissance showing the flag and the might of the United States as far as the border, and only a year later, as commander of the Army of the West, he was to occupy New Mexico and make it American. After the Mexican War, though Bent's Fort faded out of the picture, the Army established an important new supply depot at Fort Union, near the western juncture of the Mountain and Cimarron routes of the Santa Fe Trail at Watrous, and trade there was heavy once again. "Murphy" wagons, heavier than those used previously, followed both branches, now greatly improved, and by 1860 freighting over the Trail employed nearly 10,000 men and regularly used 3,000 wagons. Large fortunes continued to be made (and lost), and the Indians remained intermittently troublesome, but the era of Becknell and Gregg had passed. Charles Bent was dead, and William Bent abandoned the old fort in disgust when the government refused to buy it from him; but the prosaic army of sutlers and quartermasters at Fort Union, which was just another army camp, indicated that the pioneering days of the famous Trail were over. "In the early and middle forties" Bent's Fort had "assumed the combined proportions of a great Oriental caravanserai and an Occidental mercantile house. Here it stood on the plains, the central point of interest, the isolated refuge of wanderers on a widespread danger-abounding region. Here dwelt the scout, guide and protector of travelers in a strange land. Here at intervals for several years, Kit Carson was a resident hunter supplying the Fort with buffalo meat."[8]

The physical hazards of the Santa Fe Trail were never very great for well-organized and well-armed parties: only the crossing of the Cimarron Desert by the one route and the long, rough pull over the Raton Pass by the other were memorable impediments on

8. A. J. Flynn: "Furs and Forts of the Rocky Mountain West," *The Colorado Magazine*, IX:2 (March 1932), 35.

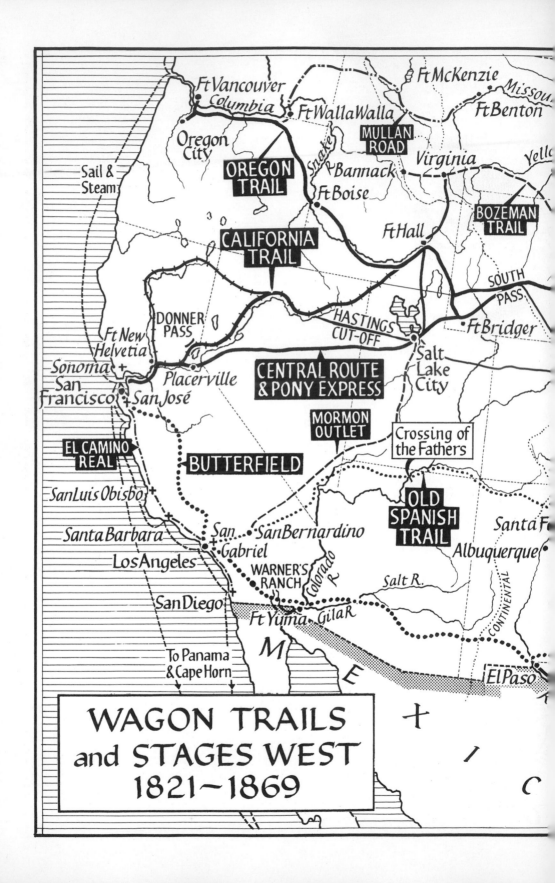

WAGON TRAILS
and STAGES WEST
1821~1869

Ft Union

Lake Superior

Ft Mandan • Bismarck

Medora

Powder R.

tone R.

DEADWOOD
STAGE

Chicago

Lake Michigan

Phil
Kearny

Deadwood

North Platte

Ft
aramie

CALIFORNIA,
OREGON AND
MORMON TRAIL

Missouri R.

South Platte

Platte R.

Council Bluffs
MORMONS

Nauvoo

Ft Kearny

St Joseph

Denver

Ft Leavenworth

Franklin
St Louis

Kansas
City

Bent's Fort

Arkansas R.

SMOKY
HILL ROAD

Springfield

ATON
ASS

CIMARRON
CUT-OFF

SANTA FÉ
TRAIL

Canadian R.

Arkansas R.

Ft Smith

Memphis

Pecos R.

Brazos R.

TEXAS TRAILS

Mississippi R.

BUTTERFIELD
OVERLAND MAIL
1858-1861

Red R.

t Davis

Ft Stockton

Colorado R.

Brazos R.

New Orleans

San Antonio

Galveston

O

SOUTHERN
TRAIL

Nueces R.

Sail &
Steam

Corpus Christi

W.B.

0   Miles   500

the way. But for the danger from Indians the Mountain route could have been one long picnic for younger and more carefree travelers, journeying at the right season and with proper equipment.

The way from the Mississippi Valley to Texas was so easy it could hardly be called a "trail" at all. From 1820 on, in the wake of the first party of settlers taken in under the *empresario* contracts of Moses and Stephen Austin, the Americans poured across the Sabine River by a variety of routes, and many others went by sea to Texas ports and roadsteads from New Orleans. This was a mass migration that neither Spanish nor Mexican government regulation or prohibition could stem or control.

Apart from the ordinary American citizens who went to Texas just to get land, and with no ulterior motives, there were a few active political agitators whose unavowed intention it was to end Mexican rule there and to bring the province into the United States. These were not necessarily agents of the American government, though there is reason to believe that Sam Houston, the most famous of these "activists," was carefully briefed by President Andrew Jackson before he emigrated to Texas in 1832.[9] Some of these men were just free-wheeling souls who believed that the rule of the United States ought to extend all over the American continent, and who enjoyed a fight anywhere. The dedicated agitators, the born trouble-makers and the genuinely disgruntled American settlers who had suffered from the vacillations of Mexican policy and the harshness of Santa Anna's recent measures in Texas, together provided more than enough tinder to produce the revolution of 1835. The heroic resistance by small groups of Americans cut off at the Alamo, in San Antonio, and in Goliad, and their massacre by superior Mexican forces, hardened the resistance of the insurgent Americans and helped to lead them to their eventual victory on the field of San Jacinto (near Houston City), where Sam Houston's amateur soldiers defeated Santa Anna's professionals, captured the proud peg-legged Mexican dictator, and sent him as a gift to Andrew Jackson. Houston survived to become twice President of the Texas Republic and eventually Senator in Wash-

9. The somewhat unsatisfactory evidence for and against this assumption is discussed in the biographies of Jackson (Indianapolis, 1938) and Houston (*The Raven*, Indianapolis, 1929) by Marquis James. See also Eugene C. Barker: *Mexico and Texas, 1821–1835* (Dallas, 1928).

ington for the State of Texas, but the toll of the "patriots" had been heavy. Jim Bowie ("The Knife") and Davy Crockett had both died in the siege of the Alamo, which Texans have never permitted the world to forget.

After Texas became a republic in 1836 (by which year fully 30,000 immigrants from the United States had arrived there), and even more so after the economic depression of 1837 had added an even more compelling incentive, "Gone to Texas,"[1] scrawled on the barns and outhouses of abandoned farms and on the doors of shanties, was a common sight throughout the American South. An oft-told tale of the period is of—

Nightfall and a drizzling rain drove an elderly horseman travel- ing a road to Vicksburg to seek shelter near a roadside fire. As he approached, he saw around it the encampment of a family "a-mov- ing" to Texas—a very common sight in Mississippi in the year 1841. Two bodies wrapped in blankets lay close to the blaze. Near them a tow-headed boy, crying loudly, leaned against a front wheel of a wagon.

The old horseman rode up and addressed him in a mollifying voice, "What's the matter, son?"

"Matter!" roared the piney-woods lad. "Fire and damnation, stranger. Don't you see mammy there shaking with ager! Daddy's gone a-fishing! Jim's got every cent of money there is, playing poker at a bit ante! Bob Stokes is gone on ahead with Nance! Sal's so corned she don't know that stick of wood from seven dollars and a half! Every one of the horses is loose! There's no meal in the waggon! The skillet's broke! The baby's in a bad fix, and it's half a mile to the creek. I don't care a damn if I never see Texas!!!"[2]

The cost of moving family, stock, and worldly goods to Texas was slight. Asa Hoxey, who went to the Austin colony at San Felipe in 1833, estimated it at not more than $10 a head. Would-be emigrants were even urged to make reconnaissances into Texas to select suitable locations and then go back for their families,[3] but it is

1. Often abbreviated into "G.T.T."

2. Recounted in William Hogan: *The Texas Republic* (Norman, Okla., 1946), p. 3.

3. *Texas in 1840, or the Emigrant's Guide to the New Republic* (n.p., n.d.), quoted in Hogan, p. 4.

unlikely that any *empresario* or land agent offered them the cost of the journey or free chicken dinners in the style of later real-estate operators. The classy way of emigrating to Texas seems to have been as a cabin passenger on the steam packet *Columbia* from New Orleans to Galveston, where "the Captain's a gentleman—always at the head of his table—set out in the best style—silver forks, or what looks like silver—large and small, with ivory knives. White waiters, neat and orderly—French Cook . . . and Bedding the finest and whitest linen—water-closets—and lady-like chamber-maid, every thing nice."[4]

The same enraptured passenger found the *New York* of the same line even more sybaritic. As she lay on her "luxurious couch" in her stateroom, surrounded by "blue satin damask and dimity" and by walls of mahogany "polished like the finest pianos," she could "think of nothing but Cleopatra."[5] "Gone to Texas" indeed!

No wonder the Texas immigrants caused the population of the Lone Star Republic to quadruple in ten years. By 1850 the State of Texas had over 212,000 inhabitants, 58,000 of whom were slaves brought in by the United States, for slavery had been abolished in Mexico. The foreign-born population in 1850 was only 12,000, most of whom were Germans imported by the *Adelsverein*, and other German settlement societies,[6] directly from Europe.

The way to Texas, then, was wide open, but the way to California and Oregon was beset with difficulties, especially for wheeled vehicles. Quite apart from badlands and deserts, well-nigh impenetrable forests and deep canyons, none of which had to be crossed on the way to Texas, two high mountain systems and many minor ranges had to be surmounted or circumvented by those who were bound for the Sacramento or the Willamette. An even more arduous task confronted those hardy souls who sought to extend the Santa Fe Trail to Southern California. Indeed, the last way was so difficult that it never was established as a route for wagons, and at one point—preparatory to crossing the Colorado River—pack

4. Mrs. Mary Austin Holley to Mrs. William M. Brand, December 19, 1837 (Holley Papers, Univ. of Texas Lib.); quoted in Hogan, p. 8.

5. Quoted in Hogan, p. 9.

6. For the organized German immigration into the Texas Republic and its importance, see J. A. Hawgood: *The Tragedy of German-America* (New York, 1940), Ch. v.

horses and mules had to be unloaded before they could be led up and down the man-made stone steps.[7]

Although it had previously been brought back into use in places by fur trappers, including the parties of Pattie and Jedediah Smith, this "Old Spanish Trail" was pioneered as a trade route by an enterprising New Mexico merchant, Antonio Armijo, who was later to lead a successful revolution in that province and to be its last governor under Mexican sovereignty. Other pack trains may have reached California by the route earlier, but Armijo's, in 1829, is the first that can be authenticated.[8] According to Armijo's diary of the expedition, published in Mexico City in 1830: "On the 6th of November of the past year, there left from the village of Abiquiu 31 men . . . wishing to discover a route to Upper California and to sell therein some manufactures of their country."[9] It was a roundabout route, first striking northwest from Abiquiu to the four-corners region near Mesa Verde, and then via the Goose Neck Gorge of the San Juan River to the Crossing of the Fathers, which was made with great difficulty on December 8. The Virgin River was reached on January 1, 1830, and San Gabriel mission, via the Mojave River and the Cajon Pass, on January 31. The journey from the New Mexico to the Californian settlement was thus achieved in less than three months. After some profitable trading in California, the expedition did even better on its return journey, the

7. "The Crossing of the Fathers," first blazed by Dominquez and Escalante in 1777, is still a remote and romantic spot. Robert Glass Cleland, a visitor in 1946, offers this description in his *Reckless Breed* (p. 268): "I left the small rowboat in which two companions and I . . . were floating down the Colorado, and made an overland reconnaissance. Without trail or landmarks, we wandered over a high, barren mesa, climbed in and out of a deep canyon, crossed rough naked ridges, and came at last to the crude steps that Father Escalante fashioned a hundred and seventy years before and Citizen Antonio Armijo successfully used a long generation later. They were not steps in the ordinary sense of the word, but shallow grooves, makeshift devices that weary men had cut out of grudgingly yielding rock to check the momentum of their mules and let the slipping, sliding animals regain their balance. Off in the lonely distance we saw a valley, silent, old and vast, that brooded for ever over the ruins and remnants of a broken world . . . a world where Time had never wakened and the centuries and ages lay sleeping in the sun." But man-made dams have now somewhat changed this idyllic picture, and projected ones threaten to destroy it utterly.

8. Cleland, pp. 264–5.

9. Tr. LeRoy R. Hafen, in *Huntington Library Quarterly*, XI:1, 87–101; quoted in Cleland, p. 263.

advance party getting back to Santa Fe in forty days, and Armijo himself in two months.

This became an important route over the next twenty years, taking silver, woollen goods, and blankets to California and bringing back horses and mules and even "small quantities of goods of Chinese and New England manufacture."[1] Unfortunately, many of the horses and mules had not been paid or bartered for but just rounded up and driven off from the extensive Californian *ranchos*. This tended to give the caravans from New Mexico a bad name in California in the course of time, especially as "it is known that the greater part of these *Chaquanosos* . . . are American and English."[2] Certainly "Peg-leg" Jack Smith, and possibly Jim Baker and Old Bill Williams, engaged in this activity; but one who is sometimes accused—Joseph Reddeford Walker—was possibly confused with "Chief Joseph Walkara, the Ute—perhaps the greatest horse-thief the West ever knew."[3]

The California-New Mexico trade over Armijo's Old Spanish Trail languished under this blight. The sleepy Alta California administration tried to control the trade by means of licences and by an official inspection of the horse herds before they left for New Mexico. The government of New Mexico also attempted to give the trade a better character, vesting in caravan captains special authority and punitive powers to enable them to "lead the caravan with as much order as if it were in national service."[4] But the fatal flaw of the Old Spanish Trail was that, unlike the Santa Fe, California, and Oregon trails, it could not be transformed into a wagon route. No covered wagons followed in "the steps of the Fathers," no railroad was to be built along Armijo's route, and although U. S. Highways 30 and 40 now stretch their broad concrete along much of the Oregon and California trails, and U. S. 50 and 350, U. S. 56

1. Quoted in Cleland, p. 270.

2. Eleanor Lawrence: "Horse Thieves on the Spanish Trail," in *Touring Topics* (later *Westways*, publ. monthly by Automobile Club of Southern California, and a mine of popularly presented but often valuable information based on original research about early California history), XXIII: 1, 22–5; quoted in Cleland, himself a frequent contributor to this magazine, p. 271.

3. Cleland (p. 310) thus exonerates his hero Joe Walker, that "figure of heroic proportions in the history of the West, a man of integrity, courage, and simplicity," from the charge of being a despised *chaquanoso*.

4. Ritch MSS (a valuable collection of documents on New Mexican history), Huntington Lib., San Marino, Calif.; quoted in Cleland, p. 275.

and 85, ribbon most of the old wagon roads from the broad Missouri to Santa Fe, Armijo's trail to Mesa Verde and the San Juan Valley is still covered by state roads at the best, while the long haul from Medicine Hat and the Great Goose Necks of the San Juan to Lee's Ferry and Marble Canyon, on the Colorado—more than a hundred miles as the eagle flies, but much further as those two writhing rivers wind—is still traversed by no road at all. You still have to "pack-in" to the Crossing of the Fathers. Escalante's (and Cleland's) wilderness remains undefiled by that importation from a bad Old World, the wheel.

Even as late as 1846 no practicable wagon route existed from Santa Fe to California, for General Kearny and his Army of the West to follow. Kearny himself and his hundred dragoons arrived in California without a wagon train, but he sent Captain Philip St. George Cooke back to command the Mormon Battalion and to make a road. This was achieved (though at one point the wagons had to be dismantled to get them through a narrow mountain defile) when Cooke pushed and creaked his way into San Diego on January 29, 1847, after an epic march.[5] Needless to say, both Kearny and Cooke kept well to the south of the Crossing of the Fathers, and used two variants of the much longer Gila River route, crossing the Colorado near Yuma.

It had not been until 1843 that wheeled vehicles had reached the Dalles of the Columbia River in the Oregon Country, and not until 1844 that the first wagon train managed to cross the Sierras (at Truckee Pass) into the great valley of California. All previous attempts, and there had been many, had failed. Not until the wagons came through was a mass emigration of settlers to these two areas practicable, though a number of pioneering parties had previously struggled through on horse- or mule-back or on foot—like the Bidwell-Bartleson company of 1841, with Nancy and Ann Kelsey. Naturally the 1843 and 1844 parties that first took the wagons through have a high and honorable place in the annals of the westward migration. Elijah Stevens, a typical mountain man, led the one into California, and Dr. Marcus Whitman, a Presbyte-

5. See Ralph P. Bieber and A. B. Bender, eds.: *Exploring Southwestern Trails, 1846–1854,* Southwestern Trails Series, No. 7 (Glendale, Calif., 1938). Henry W. Bigler, one of Cooke's Mormon volunteers, who was later to assist in Marshall's first discovery of gold at Sutter's Mill, wrote an illuminating (and oddly spelled) diary of the march, which is partially printed in "Extracts from the Journal of Henry W. Bigler," *Utah Historical Quarterly,* V (1932).

rian medical missionary, led the other into Oregon. It takes all sorts to make a New World. The old pattern of Conquistador and Friar was repeating itself in a slightly different design on other frontiers and in another century.

The Oregon Trail began with Columbus, says David Lavender,[6] and Captain Robert Gray, who discovered the mouth of the Columbia River, was engaged in the China trade. Because they used water routes wherever possible, neither Mackenzie nor Lewis and Clark may be said to have contributed much, other than in inspiration, to the pioneering of a wagon trail to the Oregon Country. Hunt's Astorians in 1811 and Stuart's returning Astorians in 1812 were the first overland parties to traverse substantial portions of the Oregon Trail proper, though it is uncertain whether either of them actually used the South Pass over the Continental Divide. Ogden's parties explored its western portions between 1824 and 1829, and Ashley's and Henry's men made more familiar its eastern sections (especially the passage of the South Pass) from 1823 onward. But, though the *Missouri Gazette* of St. Louis had, as early as May 15, 1813, said: ". . . it appears that a journey across the continent of N. America, might be performed with a wagon, there being no obstruction in the whole route that any person would dare to call a mountain,"[7] more than two decades were to pass before the first wagon passed over the Oregon Trail all the way from the Mississippi Valley to the Columbia River, and thirty years before the first wagon traveled all the way to the great central valley of California.

"From Independence," founded in 1832, "to the mouth of the Walla Walla was the original Oregon Trail, parent of all the central routes to the Pacific . . . This great highway ran through a wilderness . . . there was nowhere along its line, at the beginning of 1832, even a cabin."[8] The fur-trapping parties of the twenties and early thirties, and even the fur-trading caravans that pursued them to the rendezvous, needed to travel too rapidly to want to experiment with wheeled vehicles. It was the missionaries who first tried to use this cumbersome and much slower means of transportation, and even they suffered many heartbreaking failures be-

6. *Westward Vision*, p. 3.

7. Quoted in W. J. Ghent: *The Road to Oregon* (London and New York, 1929), p. 18.

8. Quoted in Ghent, p. 24.

fore getting a wagon into the Oregon Country. Marcus Whitman
and Henry Spalding first took their missionary wives all the way
from western New York to Fort Vancouver in 1836, riding side-
saddle, and the Reverend and Mrs. Elkanah Walker, the Reverend
and Mrs. Cushing Eels, the Reverend and Mrs. Asa Smith, and the
Reverend and Mrs. William Grey followed, equally uncomfort-
ably, in 1838. These hardy women (several of whom were preg-
nant for part of the journey) rode distances of up to forty-five
miles a day, and four of the six still had enough energy left to write
diaries and journals on the way. From these we learn what "an
unheard-of journey"[9] it was for a woman in those days. The first
wagon train did not follow until 1843, seven years after Narcissa
Whitman and Eliza Spalding. Never underestimate the power of a
woman!

The first wagons were taken through by Dr. Marcus Whitman, by now a veteran of the trail, having first traversed it with
Samuel Parker—who prudently returned by sea—in 1835, but turning back near the Three Forks of the Missouri to recruit more
assistants and to finish his wooing of Narcissa Prentiss, who had
wished to join the 1835 expedition in her own right. Their mar
riage solved an awkward problem of etiquette, though it created
another: Spalding, chosen as Whitman's fellow missionary by the
Presbyterian Board in 1836, had been an unsuccessful suitor of
Narcissa's, and though he was now married to Eliza Hart, he still
harbored some resentment. It speaks well for the good sense of the
two women that this potentially explosive situation was kept under
control throughout the long trek of 1836, and eventually subli-
mated in the course of converting the heathen. Even in 1836 Whitman, a man of great determination, attempted to take a wagon over
the trail. At Fort Hall it had to be cut down to a two-wheeled
vehicle. Narcissa had noted in her diary a week earlier: "Husband
has had a tedious time with the wagon today . . ." and by July 28
she was only too willing to see the last of it: "One of the axle-trees
of the wagon broke today; was a little rejoiced, for we were in
hopes that they would leave it, and have no more trouble with it.
Our rejoicings are in vain for they are making a cart of the back

9. C. M. Drury: *First White Women over the Rockies: Diaries, Letters and
Biographical Sketches of the Six Women who Made the Overland Journey in 1836
and 1838*, 2 vols. (Glendale, Calif., 1963), I, p. 20. A third vol. was pub. in 1966.

wheels this afternoon and lashing the forewheels to it—intending to take it through in some shape or other."[1] Finally, at Fort Boise, even the stubborn Marcus Whitman gave up and the cart was abandoned. It had not been used to any extent, as he had intended, for the ladies to ride in when they grew weary of the side-saddle. When they finally reached Fort Vancouver, Whitman left Narcissa there while he retraced his steps to Walla Walla to establish his Waiilaptu mission.

When the fur trappers Caleb Wilkins, Robert Newell, and Joseph Meek brought the bare chassis (or running gear without wagon beds) of three carts that had been abandoned at Fort Hall by other parties as far as the Columbia River in 1840, Whitman praised their achievement in characteristic language: "Oh, you will never regret it! You have broken the ice, and when others see that wagons have passed, they, too, will pass, and in a few years the valley will be full of our people."[2] There were in 1840 about a hundred Americans in the Oregon Country. "The great migration" was yet to come, but Whitman was right. When it did come it came on wheels, and he came with it.

The Elijah White-Lansford Warren Hastings parties of 1842 abandoned some of their wagons at Fort Laramie (Frémont says that they sold them "at the prices they had paid for them in the States," which is doubtful) and the remainder at Fort Hall, but the wheel-obsessed Whitman was not with them. When the Hudson's Bay Company official at Fort Hall tried to persuade the much larger party of 1843 to do likewise, Whitman, who had joined these emigrants when returning from his famous "ride" eastward through the winter of 1842–43, was foremost among those who refused, and the wagons went through. According to Whitman, this migration consisted of "no less than 200 families, consisting of 1,000 persons of both sexes," with over 200 wagons, 694 oxen, and 773 loose cattle. No sheep were taken, which omission Whitman considered to be a mistake. The famous mountain man Captain John Gannt was their guide as far as Fort Hall (from there Joseph Reddeford Walker led some of them down into California); Peter H. Burnett (who was to become the first Governor of California under the Constitution of 1849) was their first captain, and James W. Nesmith (later Senator for Oregon) his orderly sergeant. But it

1. Drury, I, 75.   2. Quoted in Ghent, p. 46.

was Marcus Whitman who got the wagons through to the Columbia, as testified to by Jesse Applegate,[3] captain of the slower "Cow Column" after the emigration of 1843 split up into two sections: ". . . it is no disparagement to others to say that to no other individual are the emigrants of 1843 so much indebted for the

Interior of the first Fort Laramie in the 1830's, by Alfred Jacob Miller.

successful conclusion of their journey, as to Dr. Marcus Whitman." Applegate also calls Whitman "that good angel" of the emigrants.

The Protestant missionary impulse in the Oregon country had by this time almost exhausted its momentum. The Methodist pioneers in the Willamette Valley, Jason and Daniel Lee, had turned to farming; Jason as "promoter, developer, business adviser and

3. This classic account of the migration was published as "A Day with the Cow Column," *Transactions* of the Oregon Pioneer Association (1876); repr. *Oregon Historical Society Quarterly* (December 1900), by the Caxton Club, ed. Joseph Schafer (Chicago, 1934), and by Champoeg Press, ed. Dorothy Johansen (Portland, Ore., 1952).

constant advocate of the Americanization of the country"[4] played a leading part in the Champoeg constitutional convention, which provided a ready-made "American" form of government for the emigrants of 1843. In 1842 the American Board had sought to liquidate the Presbyterian missions and only the persuasiveness of Whitman had given these a reprieve. The Indians, never very co-operative after their first inquisitiveness about the white man's religion had been satisfied, were now growing positively un-friendly. This unfriendliness and suspicion were to culminate in the tragedy of the Whitman massacre of 1847. Only Father de Smet and his fellow Roman Catholics continued to work with success among the Northwestern Indians after this, but it was the Protes-tant missionaries who had spearheaded the settlement of the Ore-gon Territory from the United States.

The Oregon treaty of 1846 belongs rather to diplomatic his-tory than to the history of the Westward Movement, but it was the Oregon migration of 1834–46 which made that treaty so favorable to the United States. Although the Americans had put hardly a settler *north* of the Columbia River by the treaty year, they had by then so many in the Willamette Valley, and had been so active in the Walla Walla region, that Simpson and McLoughlin decided that the Hudson's Bay Company—"H.B.C." ("Here Before Christ"), as the trappers said—should evacuate not only Fort Boise and Fort Hall but also Fort Vancouver, their headquarters on the north bank of the Columbia, and retire to Fort Victoria, on Van-couver Island. This cut the ground from under the feet of a vacil-lating British government. Lord Aberdeen had never said "The Columbia River line or fight," and he now persuaded his colleagues and the British people to accept the 49th parallel as the mainland border all the way to the Straits of Juan de Fuca. McLoughlin, broken and disappointed, took up residence in Oregon City, in "enemy territory," and even applied for United States citizenship. But a crude and insensitive generation of American frontiersmen cold-shouldered the man who had done so much, more even than Whitman, for them. Jedediah Smith, the Lees, the Whitmans, Wyeth, even Hall Jackson Kelley and William Slacum (who, he rightly suspected, were up to no good), Lansford Warren Has-tings and Elijah White (who, whether he suspected it or not, were

4. W. J. Ghent: "Jason Lee," in *Dictionary of American Biography* (New York, 1933), X, 112.

also active and conscious agents of Manifest Destiny)—all these men and women, and others, were succored, supplied, or protected by Dr. McLoughlin. Many of them testified to his kindness and generosity. But he could also be fierce! When the Reverend Herbert Beaver, an Englishman who came as Anglican chaplain to the Fort, made insulting remarks about Mrs. McLoughlin—who was of mixed Scottish and Indian blood—McLoughlin booted him around the compound and probably regretted that he could not do the same to Mrs. Beaver, who was as bigoted and obnoxious as her spouse. Narcissa Whitman formed an unfavorable impression of Beaver, and in a letter dated October 25, 1836, she wrote: "He seldom draws the line of distinction between the righteous and the wicked, and when he does it is so faintly that it is scarcely perceptible."[5] She also disliked the way he conducted his services. He on his side objected to Narcissa's conducting the singing of hymns out of church. And so it went on. The good Presbyterian ladies obviously preferred the Papist McLoughlin to their fellow Protestant. These squabbles must have enlivened a long, wet winter.

The Great Migration of 1843, piloted on wheels to the promised land by Marcus Whitman and his Cayuse Indian assistant Stickus, was followed in 1844 by three parties—about 1,500 persons all together—despite the admonition of the *Missouri Republican*, June 11, 1844: "No man of information or in his right mind, would think of leaving such a country as this, to wander over a thousand miles of desert and five hundred of mountains to reach such as that. . . ."[6] The old mountain man James Clyman (tired of farming and shopkeeping in the Midwest) helped to guide one of the parties, along with his companion of many a trail, "Black" Harris, and has left a vivid diary of the journey.[7] The 1845 party was guided by Stephen Meek, who recklessly led a portion of it by a mythical short cut through the Cascades, and fifty to seventy persons lost their lives before the party could be extricated from this "worst disaster of the Oregon road,"[8] and Meek himself was

5. Drury, I, 106, n. 49, See also ed.: *Reports and Letters of Herbert Beaver 1836-38*, ed. T. E. Jesset (Portland, Ore., 1959), in which James Douglas's report on the "Beaver Affair" (Oct. 5, 1838) is also included.

6. Quoted in Lavender, p. 388, where he also discusses the estimates of the size of the 1844 migration to the Oregon Country. Ghent's estimate (p. 83) is much smaller.

7. *James Clyman, Frontiersman*, ed. C. L. Camp (Portland, Ore., 1960).

8. Lavender, p. 395.

nearly lynched by irate survivors. But upwards of three thousand emigrants had taken the trail that year, and the great majority came through, bringing their hundreds of wagons with them. The Oregon Trail, though still difficult, was now becoming a beaten track.

Only about 1,350 persons went to Oregon in 1846: the Mexican War had broken out, and news of the Oregon treaty came through too late to exert much influence; even so, it was many more than went to California, despite Caleb Greenwood's propagandist efforts at Fort Hall, and Lansford Warren Hastings's printed exhortations that California must be Americanized, as Oregon had been, by sheer weight of numbers. Hastings even cast himself in the role of "President of California" when the Texas game should have been played there, but he was on the wrong side of the Sierras, as it happened, when the Bear Flag movement,[9] which might have given him his chance briefly to achieve this ambition, broke out in June. It was in 1846 that he changed from an Oregon to a California booster[1] and started trying to persuade California-bound emigrants to take the fateful Hastings Cutoff across the deserts of Utah and Nevada, but his book had already compared Oregon unfavorably with California, even though in it he was still seeking to attract emigrants to both. By the time Hastings wrote, wagons had won their way through to the Columbia and the Sacramento valleys without benefit of his advice (which, incidentally, tended to be recklessly inaccurate). Elisha Stevens led the first wagon train safely across the Sierras into California in 1844 but did not write a book about it. In consequence, perhaps, less than two hundred emigrants reached California overland in 1845, but they had an easier time than Stephen Meek's "cutoff" section of the Oregon emigrants. In 1846 the numbers reaching California rose to around five hundred,[2] excluding the survivors of the Donner party.

The story of the Donner party is one of the best known and

9. See below, p. 167.

1. So much did the Oregon settlers fear the effects of Hastings' efforts that they called a public meeting on June 15, 1846 (*Oregon Spectator*, Oregon City, June 25, 1846), "for the purpose of sending an express to meet the emigration from the United States to this country, in order to prevent their being deceived and led astray by the misrepresentation of L. W. Hastings, who is now on his way from California for that object. . . ." Quoted in C. H. Carey's intro. to L. W. Hastings: *The Emigrant's Guide to Oregon and California*, (facs. of orig. 1845 edn. Princeton, 1932), p. xviii.

2. Ghent, p. 87; cf. Stewart, pp. 143-84.

most spine-chilling in the history of the West.[3] Losing time by bad organization and judgment, as well as suffering the effects of overly heavy but inadequate equipment, the party was also weakened by dissensions. James Reed, a natural leader in times of difficulty, was "banished" for having killed another member in a brawl, and forced to go on ahead to California alone. After struggling over the dreadful Hastings Cutoff across the grim Nevada Desert, the party was caught by unusually early snowfalls in the California Sierras near the present Truckee Pass (not far from Squaw Valley, famous today as a winter-sports area) and forced to camp there until rescue parties could arrive from the Sacramento Valley in the spring of 1847. Food ran out and some members of the party managed to subsist on the hides of their dead cattle, which at first they had used to roof their tents and dug-outs. Others resorted to cannibalism, to some extent at least, though it has never been proved that any member of the party was actually killed in order to be eaten. Enough, anyway, died of starvation and exhaustion. The diaries and accounts of survivors and rescuers (including two obviously honest and very vivid letters written by a girl of twelve, Virginia Reed, along with the diary of the Irishman Patrick Breen) authenticate the *fact* of cannibalism, though they do not establish all its circumstances. Without its practice, some of the children who survived might not have lived through the ordeal.

That "Year of Decision," 1846, in which the Donner party set out for California, also saw the outbreak of the Mexican War. The aggressive diplomacy of Andrew Jackson was followed up by actions on the part of both the Tyler and Polk administrations which thoroughly, and understandably, alarmed Mexico, already put on her guard by the Texas revolution of 1835, the two Texan "invasions" of New Mexico, and the premature and mistaken seizure of Monterey by an American naval squadron under Commodore Thomas Ap Catesby Jones in 1842. Countermeasures were taken on the Texas border, in New Mexico, and in California, but these did not stop further "Yankee" infiltration into these regions. Mexico sought the assistance of European powers against the United States, but the price she would have had to pay would have been too high, even had effective help been available against a now powerful nation, very conscious of its manifest destiny to dominate

3. See George Stewart: *Ordeal by Hunger* (Berkeley, Calif., 1936; 1960); repr. in "The Frontier Library" (London, 1962), intro. Marcus Cunliffe.

the whole North American continent. The presidential election of
1844 had brought this sentiment into the open in the United States
in its crudest and most extreme forms, as the calls for "All Mexico"
in the South and "Fifty-four-forty or Fight" in the North demon-

Donner Lake, *c.* 1870. From *Harper's Magazine.*

strated. The term "Manifest Destiny" was not coined until 1845,[4]
but the ideal that it crystallized had long existed—even back to the
days of John Adams and Thomas Jefferson—and between 1844
and 1846 this was translated into action, leading to the outbreak of
the Mexican War in May 1846. Though an armed clash with

4. "Manifest Destiny" was a phrase first used by the Irish-American newspaper editor John L. O'Sullivan in July 1845 with regard to the crisis caused by
the proposed annexation of Texas. It immediately gained wide currency. The use,
meaning, and origins of the term are discussed exhaustively in S. K. Weinberg:
Manifest Destiny (New York, 1925), and re-examined more recently and somewhat less mordantly in Frederick Merk: *Manifest Destiny and Mission* (Cambridge, Mass., 1962). See also John A. Hawgood: articles on "Manifest Destiny" in
British Essays in American History, ed. H. C. Allen and Peter Hill (London and
New York, 1957), and in *Collier's Encyclopedia* (New York, 1963–).

Britain was avoided (and British Columbia and Alberta saved for the Crown) by the Oregon settlement, Mexico declared that she would regard the American annexation of Texas as a *casus belli*. She had already withdrawn her minister from Washington and refused to receive a special envoy from President Polk, when a minor clash between Mexican and American soldiers on the Rio Grande—toward which river General Taylor had moved his forces forward from the Nueces, which the Mexicans claimed to be the true border of Mexico, and the Texas Republic gave Polk his opportunity to declare war in self-righteous terms. Even without a formal declaration a state of war already virtually existed, and fresh "incidents" were continuing to occur at frequent intervals in New Mexico and in California as well. Kearny had "shown the American flag" to Governor Armijo in the former in 1845, and Frémont to General Castro in the latter in the spring of 1846. The Army of the West and the California Volunteers were soon to come into existence. American naval squadrons were equally active; the Navy was, in fact, to beat the Army in the race to occupy Upper California and rule it as conquered territory.[5]

By the Treaty of Guadalupe Hidalgo, in January 1848, Mexico was formally to cede the conquered provinces of New Mexico (then much larger than the present state) and Upper California, and to recognize the annexation of Texas, but she did not lose Lower California, Sonora, Chihuahua, or Coahuila, and, apart from the small and peaceable Gadsden Purchase (1853), the integrity of her northern borders, as established in 1848, have been respected by the government of the United States ever since. "Punitive" or policing expeditions sent into Mexico against the Apaches or against Mexican "border ruffians" such as Pancho Villa were withdrawn when the trouble ended.

The Mexican War, and the extension of U. S. territory in which it resulted, ranks in importance with the Louisiana Purchase in the history of the American West. It brought not only California and New Mexico into the Union, but also most of Arizona and

5. The complicated campaigns of the Mexican War can be followed in summary form in O. A. Singletary: *The Mexican War* (Chicago, 1960), and in much greater detail in the older J. H. Smith: *The War in Mexico*, 2 vols. (New York, 1919). John A. Hawgood's article in *Collier's Encyclopedia* (1963–) attempts to relate the planning and execution of the campaign of the Mexican War to the ideas of American expansionists and to assess its importance in the history of the West.

major portions of Colorado, Nevada, and Utah. It also gave to the United States her empire on the Pacific, for which she had so long striven.

In 1847 only ninety wagons headed for California, half the number of 1846, though twice the 1845 figure. The War with Mexico was the cause of this slump. "We can only wonder that anyone at all started" in 1847, says Stewart. The news of what had happened to the Donner party would also have had its dampening effect. Many more wagons and people went to Oregon that year, and most of the emigrants who made their way there now took the Applegate Road through southern Oregon into the upper Willamette Valley, but some of those who took the earlier route over the Blue Mountains gave the measles to the Cayuse Indians, and thus indirectly caused the Whitman massacre of November 29, 1847. The traditional fate of the medicine man who could not cure his patient was death, and Whitman, Narcissa, and the others who died at the mission that day were victims of this stern aboriginal law. The news of the massacre all but stopped further emigration to Oregon by the more northerly route for a time. Joe Meek's ride to St. Louis and Washington, D. C., as "Envoy Extraordinary and Minister Plenipotentiary of the Republic of Oregon to the Court of the United States" (as the press described him[6]), resulted in the organization of the Oregon Territory and the arrival there—via Santa Fe and then from Los Angeles and by sea—of Governor Lane in March 1849. For very obvious reasons 1847 was to be the last year in which the emigration to Oregon was larger than that to California, though "no one setting out for California in the spring of 1848 knew about the finding of gold."[7] Neither did the news that the Mexican War was over and California officially ceded to the United States reach the emigrant parties that set out from the Missouri assembly points in the spring of 1848. The avalanche did not begin, therefore, until 1849. Then "in a single year the numbers so increased that for *one* person who traveled the trail to California in '48, *fifty* traveled it in '49," Stewart points out.

In the gold-rush years every possible variant on the California and Oregon Trails that had not been used before was explored and adopted, or found wanting and abandoned. The Lassen route, the

6. Lavender, p. 399.
7. Stewart: *California Trail*, p. 193.

Carson route, and the Salt Lake Cutoff had, like the Hastings
Cutoff, been used before the gold rush. The Mormon Trail of 1847
followed the way blazed by the Donner party through the Wa-
satch Mountains to Salt Lake, improving upon the route of Brig-

ham Young and his advance party of 1846. This was the greatest
contribution made to the opening up of the West by that ill-fated
band, apart from the imperishable and gruesome saga of their
crossing the Sierras. It was, indeed, the earlier wagon parties which
made things easier and quicker for the later parties, just as the pack-
mule parties and the parties on foot, guided by the know-how of
mountain men, pointed the way for the first wagon parties. It is a
complete myth that John Charles Frémont, whose first expedition

of 1842 did not even reach the Sierras, and whose second in 1843 met but did not lead the first wagon parties on their way West,[8] was either the "Pathfinder" or the "Pathmarker" of the West, though he and his wife (who never went West until 1849, and then by sea) may well be claimed as the West's greatest popularizers. Brigham Young had read Frémont's *Report* of the Expedition of 1843-4 and was influenced by it to settle his people around the Great Salt Lake,[9] but the Mormon Trail was just another variant— using the north bank of the Platte River instead of the south bank —of the trail followed by Oregon and California pioneers for the past twenty years, and by hundreds of wagons for the past ten years, for Fort Hall, where wagons tended to be abandoned in the early days, was beyond the Salt Lake. Frémont "located no new pass or any new route to Oregon"[1]—or indeed to California. Frémont's Peak was not the highest in the Rockies, as he claimed, and had in all probability been previously climbed by Bonneville's men. The Sierras had previously been crossed in winter by Jedediah Smith. In fact it is difficult to discover any real "first" in the discovery and opening up of trails to and through the West for Frémont. He only caught up the Great Migration of 1843 as Jesse Applegate's Cow Column floated down the Columbia River on flatboats on the last weary lap of its long journey. But he wrote it all up incomparably, and his *Reports* became bestsellers. "For a

8. But this myth is an old soldier that never dies. On April 11, 1945, Senator Capper, of Kansas, had printed in the *Congressional Record* (79th Cong., 1st Sess.) the claim by the popular novelist Paul Wellman concerning Frémont's second expedition: "It was this expedition, with the consequent publicity attending it, which more than any other single factor led to the great rush of immigrants to the West." Yet Wellman goes on to disclose that "nearly 1,200 immigrants" were already assembled at Kansas City in 1843 when Frémont arrived there at the beginning of his expedition! Who came first, the pioneer or the publicist?

9. Frémont's first *Report* was published as a Senate Document in 1843, and his second in 1845. They were many times reprinted, as by Henry Polkinhorn, in one volume of 278 pages (Washington, D. C., 1845). The *National Intelligencer* had somewhat uncritically claimed: "The Great Salt Lake, the Bear River Valley, and the rivers, the valleys and the mountains of Upper California, may be said to be now first brought to the knowledge of civilized man by these expeditions"; and Brigham Young, in an interview with *The New York Times* (which Frémont quotes in his *Memoirs of My Life*, Vol. I—no other was published—pp. 415-16), acknowledged his debt to Frémont, though saying Frémont had "made a mistake" in describing the Great Salt Lake as "partially fresh" (a statement Frémont denied).

1. Goetzmann: *Army Exploration*, p. 93.

whole generation of people his report and map were to serve as guides for their trek to the promised empire of the Pacific."[2] Boys of all ages had their imaginations fired by the Frémont *Reports*. The poet Joaquin Miller tells how his family read them on their Ohio farm by candlelight: "I never was so fascinated. I never grew so fast in my life. . . . I fancied I could see Frémont's men, hauling the cannon up the savage battlements of the Rocky Mountains, flags in the air, Frémont at the head, waving his sword, his horse neighing wildly in the mountain wind, with unknown and un-named empires on every hand. . . . I began to be inflamed with a love for action, adventure, glory and great deeds, away out yonder under the path of the setting sun."[3]

The wagon trails West were thus all firmly established before the era of the gold rush put an almost impossible strain on their much traveled ways, despite the fact that a majority of the Argo-nauts were to arrive in California by sea. Down to 1857 more than 165,000 people crossed the continent to California overland. The number of animals they took with them must have approached a million.

It was in 1857 that a new phenomenon appeared upon the Plains, providing a singular contribution to the history of Western transportation. This was the handcart, the little brother, as it were, of the covered wagon; and it was Mormon ingenuity and dogged-ness that produced the remarkable handcart experiment of 1857–60. During these years approximately three thousand people walked the whole distance from Iowa City, the assembly point, to Salt Lake City, pushing or pulling handcarts until they reached the promised land. During the same period only 5,200 migrated to Utah by wagon team.[4] It was a time of tribulation and near bank-ruptcy for the Church of Jesus Christ of Latter Day Saints, and during these years their whole desert kingdom was in jeopardy. First came the crop failures and famines of the "grasshopper years"

2. Ibid.

3. *Overland in a Covered Wagon*, ed. S. G. Firman (New York, 1930), pp. 42–3; quoted in Goetzmann, p. 84. The family went West to the Willamette Valley in 1852, and "Joaquin," as he now began to call himself (after another of his heroes, Joaquin Murieta, the Mexican-Californian bandit), went to California in 1856. See further *Dictionary of American Biography*, XII, 621–2.

4. G. E. Larson: *Prelude to the Kingdom: Mormon Desert Conquest—A Chapter in American Co-operative Experience* (Francetown, N. H., 1947), pp. 235–6.

1855–6, and then the "declaration of war" on the Mormons by President Buchanan's government and the occupation of the territory by U. S. troops. The handcart experiment did not save the day, but it contributed a great deal toward maintaining morale and preventing the inward migration from falling to an insignificant trickle, which might have resulted in disaster for the missions abroad and spelled ruin to the Church at home. Brigham Young, the head of the Mormon church, initiated the handcart experiment

Mormons crossing the plains with a handcart.

with brave words that he himself could hardly have entirely believed, saying: "If it is once tried, you will find that it will become the favorite method of crossing the plain." And it was, of course, by far the cheapest. Three of the five handcart companies organized in 1856 reached their destination in good order, welcomed on their last day's tramp "home to Zion" by enthusiastic Saints, weeping and "speechless with joy." Two other companies, starting later, ran into bad weather, and 67 of the 500 in the Willie company and no fewer than 135 of the 567 in the Martin contingent died on the way. "With more than 200 dead it was a far greater disaster than that of the oft-publicized Donner Party."[5]

It was partially to prevent the recurrence of such disasters that the Brigham Young Carrying and Express Company (popularly known as the X.Y. Company) was formed in 1857 to carry the mails "by swift pony express" and to prepare a wagon line to haul freight. A successful bid was made to carry a monthly U. S. mail from Independence to Salt Lake City, and the first mail went through in twenty-six days. Staging points were set up and a number of regular settlements established along the route, mostly by using labor and materials supplied free by the Saints, at the behest of Brigham Young. A new class of "express missionaries" was created, and these young men were strung out along the trail, outfitted and supplied by wealthier and older members of the church.[6] Unfortunately, this enterprising development, anticipating in many ways the great express and staging enterprises of the sixties,[7] was brought to an end by the U. S. government's cancellation of the four-year mail contract on June 10, 1857—barely six months after it had been signed—and by the "Utah War" of 1858, which resulted in the evacuation of all the outposts of Zion outside the Salt Lake Basin and, indeed, a brief "exodus" from the capital itself by its entire Mormon population as the U. S. Army marched in.

For a short time it appeared that the tragic history of the Mormon church during the 1830's and 1840's might now be continued, after a decade of promise and achievement in Utah. But the steady hand of Brigham Young (contrasting with the somewhat unsteady policy of President Buchanan in Washington) was at the helm, and the Saints returned to resume their remarkable colonization work.[8]

The tragedies of earlier days had shown that religious fervor was not enough to found and consolidate a new settlement and to put into operation revolutionary social and economic ideas there, unless accompanied by organizing ability of a very high order. Joseph Smith, the Prophet and founder of the church, lacked this

5. Arrington: *Great Basin Kingdom,* p. 158.

6. Arrington, pp. 167–8.   7. Arrington, passim.

8. Arrington, Ch. xii, passim. Some historians are kinder to Buchanan and more critical of Young in the matter of the Mormon War than is Arrington. See, e.g., Norman Furniss: *The Mormon Conflict* (New Haven, Conn., 1960).

ability, and he was constantly at loggerheads, right up to his assassination in 1844, with his associates in the Church as well as with the hostile "gentiles" outside it. Brigham Young was an organizing genius, who not only had vision but could also compel the loyalty of his people and even secure the grudging admiration and aid of the world outside. Founded in New York State in 1830, the Mormon sect, gaining adherents and enemies as it went, moved its headquarters first to the Western Reserve of Ohio (1831) and then to Jackson County, on the Missouri frontier. In 1833 they were banished to Clay County, across the river, and many returned to Kirtland, Ohio. The next Zion was to be Far West, Missouri (1837), and Kirtland was then evacuated. Again the building of "a Kingdom of God in the Wilderness" by the new sect encountered implacable local opposition despite the economic progress made. In 1839 the whole community was moved back across the Mississippi to Quincy, Illinois, and Joseph Smith established his new—and last —capital at nearby Nauvoo ("beautiful place" in Hebrew), as he rechristened a swampy village hitherto known as "Commerce." By 1844 there were over twenty-five thousand Mormons living in Nauvoo and the adjacent area. Nauvoo was to be a model city; it was planned on a grand scale, and several imposing buildings (for a frontier community) were completed. Then disaster struck again. The almost open practice of polygamy (despite numerous "official denials" that it existed) by Joseph Smith and other members of the Mormon hierarchy undoubtedly served to intensify the opposition of the "gentiles" in neighboring communities, and this led to the rioting and demonstrations in which Joseph Smith and his brother Hyrum lost their lives in 1844—and also to the final exodus to an even "further west" in 1846–7, led by Brigham Young, the new head of the Church.

The move into the Salt Lake Valley was to get away from the United States and from interference by its intolerant citizens and officials, whereas most other Americans who migrated to the Far West in those days fervently hoped that the Stars and Stripes would soon follow them—into Oregon, New Mexico, Texas, California, and even beyond. Indeed, many of these other Americans were motivated, in part at least, by such patriotic sentiments in deciding to make the difficult journey across the plains or around the Horn. How different it was with the Mormons! Their religious fervor and iron discipline took them into the "Great Basin King-

dom" when it was still an uninhabited (and believed to be uninhabitable) region nominally owned by Mexico. Here within a year
manifest destiny had caught up with them, and within two years
"that damn flag," as a Mormon elder called it, was flying over their
latest Zion, for, by the Treaty of Guadalupe Hidalgo, all of the
Utah Territory, all of the Mormons' proposed "State of Deseret,"
became part of the United States.[9]

But this time the Mormons were not to be dislodged. Utah had
to wait a half century for statehood,[1] but long before that time the
Mormon economic and social experiment had succeeded, and
though the religious beliefs and practices of the Saints (even after
the complete banning of polygamy by the church) continued to
arouse opposition—though also to secure converts throughout the
world—the United States had learned how to live with them and
they with the United States.

It cannot be said that, but for the Mormon example, the
inhospitable Great Basin area between the Rockies and the Sierras
and Cascades could *never* have been settled, and that Americans
and immigrants alike would have continued to leap-frog over it to
Oregon and California. But Mormons were the first to *prove* that it
could be settled and could support a large, self-sufficient, and
growing population. This was their greatest contribution to the
history of the American Far West, and it was a very impressive
one. They were there before the railroads, before the overland
stages, even before the gold rush. Never in the history of human
migration have a dedicated people more decisively made the desert
blossom like a rose.

9. See Ch. xi, pp. 369–81.
1. Arrington, Ch. xiii, passim.

CHAPTER VI

By Land and Sea
to El Dorado

I
N 1838 AN ELDERLY SCOTSMAN, WHO HAD NEVER BEEN
there, published the first *History* in the English language
of little-known California.[1] His book was widely read
on both sides of the Atlantic and received favorable notice
in the London *Times*.[2] In 1840 a young Harvard student, who had
shipped for two years before the mast in the trade between Boston
and Pacific coast ports, printed his experiences, and his book became a best-seller.[3] He described the uninhabited mist-shrouded
shores of San Francisco Bay, the high cliffs of Capistrano, the
desolate wasteland of the San Pedro anchorage, the pleasant social
life of the rustic provincial capital, Monterey. In 1841–42 a young
French attaché, from his country's legation in Mexico City, visited
the two Californias (describing the Franciscan missions one by
one), spent time at the Russian establishments at Fort Ross and
Bodega Bay, and penetrated as far as the outpost of civilization
recently established on the upper Sacramento by an enterprising
Swiss emigrant. His book, too, attracted considerable attention.[4]

1. Alexander Forbes (of Tepic): *A History of Upper and Lower California, from their first discovery to the present time, comprising an account of the
climate, soil, natural productions, agriculture, commerce, etc. A full view of the
Missionary Establishments and condition of the free and domesticated Indians.
With an appendix relating to Steam Navigation in the Pacific* . . . (London,
1839).

2. September 6, 1839.

3. R. H. Dana, Jr.: *Two Years before the Mast* (Boston, 1840); critical ed.
John H. Kemble (San Francisco, 1964).

4. M. Duflot de Mofras: *Exploration du Territoire de L'Orégon, des
Californies, et de la Mer Vermeille, executée pendant les Années 1840, 1841, et
1842* . . . , 4 vols. (Paris, 1844); tr. M. Wilbur, 2 vols. (San Francisco, 1937).

On November 12, 1842, a Prussian diplomat in New York wrote to a colleague in London: "Upper California is one of the finest countries in the world . . . It is only necessary that it should be in the possession of an active, industrious and energetic people."[5]

Such a people (though the Prussian diplomat thought the Germans would qualify) were the citizens of the United States, a certain number of whom had already found their way, by sea or overland, to California by the year 1840. "The Yankee Exodus" of the generation after the War of 1812 brought a number of men from Massachusetts and other parts of New England into this remote pastoral utopia, some to trade and go away, others to stay. John Cooper came to Santa Barbara and Monterey in 1823 and married into the powerful Vallejo family; Abel Stearns came to the pueblo of Los Angeles in 1829 and married Arcadia, beautiful daughter of Juan Bandini; Thomas Oliver Larkin, Cooper's half-brother, came to Yerba Buena and then to Monterey in 1832, and, after a shipboard romance on the long voyage from Boston to California via the Sandwich Islands, married an American widow, Rachel Holmes. Theirs were the first all-American children to be born in Mexican Alta California. Meanwhile, trappers were seeping over the mountains and deserts, seeing California and finding that it was good. Some of these, like William Wolfskill and Isaac Graham, decided to stay. Not until 1841 was the first organized immigrant party (that of Bidwell and Bartleson)[6] to find its way into the California valleys overland, but individuals, like John Marsh, Harvard graduate and amateur physician and surgeon, who went by way of Santa Fe in 1836, had arrived earlier. A few other foreigners also arrived before 1840, but the Americans predominated. There were, in that year, still fewer than 300 alien residents in Upper California.[7]

5. Friedrich von Roenne (Prussian Minister in Washington) to a fellow Prussian diplomat in London (Minister Christian von Bunsen). MS letter in German in Prussian Secret State Archives, Merseburg, D.D.R. Photostat copy in Library of Congress, Washington, D. C. Roenne mentions Forbes's book as the latest authority on Upper California. See John A. Hawgood: "A Projected Prussian Purchase of California," *Southern California Quarterly* (December 1966).

6. See above, Ch. v, p. 130.

7. Thomas Oliver Larkin, in 1856, compiled a list of "Names of British Subjects and Citizens of the United States who resided in Alta California—prior to 1840." He calculated that "during this period, there were living in California, a few French, Germans, Portuguese, and Italians (not forty), and thirty to forty

Upward of a hundred of these foreigners were summarily arrested in April 1840 at the orders of Governor Alvarado (who had seized power in a revolution in 1836, assisted by some of these very same foreigners) and deported in irons to Tepic, in western Mexico, in order to be sent for trial in Mexico City.[8] Although his motives are still somewhat obscure, Alvarado was certainly influenced by his fear that these foreigners, and particularly the Americans among them, were gaining too much influence in Upper California and might eventually take it over, as had so recently happened in Texas. The U. S. government had for some time been casting longing eyes on San Francisco Bay, which most Americans considered to be the only part of the province worth having, and two of the United States' envoys in Mexico, Anthony Butler (1835) and Waddy Thompson (1842), unsuccessfully opened negotiations for the purchase of all or part of California, to include the coveted bay. Between these two attempts Lieutenant Charles Wilkes, of the U. S. Navy, visited the bay in the course of his exploring expedition, and added his praises of it to those of others, and a year later, on October 20, 1842, Commodore Thomas ap Catesby Jones actually took possession of Monterey, the Californian capital, on behalf of his country, under the mistaken impression that war had broken out between the United States and Mexico and that a British naval squadron was on its way to put California under the protection of Her Majesty Queen Victoria. Though he evacuated the port within three days, apologized to the newly arrived Mexican governor, Micheltorena, and sailed away after participating in a fiesta held in his honor at Los Angeles by the fun-loving Californians, who never let either business or politics interfere with pleasure, the incident distinctly worsened Mexican-American relations, already strained by the arrest of Isaac Graham and his fellow foreigners in 1840, and everybody now knew that the first action of the U. S. Navy in the actual event of war would be to seize California and keep it. In this trigger-happy atmosphere, men of good will, like Thomas Oliver Larkin, who had been

---

natives of the Sandwich Islands and Foreigners of Color." This list—containing the names of 162 persons identified as Americans, 60 as English, 21 as Irish, and 15 as Scotch—appears as an appendix in John A. Hawgood, ed.: *First and Last Consul* (San Marino, Calif., 1962), pp. 109–18.

8. They were released in Tepic, however, owing to the intervention of Eustace Barron, the British consul there, and were afterward repatriated.

appointed U. S. consul in the Californias in 1843 by Tyler's administration, and General Mariano Guadalupe Vallejo, the leading landowner in the north of the province, worked against time to settle California's future in a peaceful way. Both of them realized that it lay with that of the United States, and Larkin worked openly to this end, supported by an additional appointment in 1845 as confidential agent by the Polk administration. He was to be overtaken by the events of the spring and summer of 1846, when first of all J. C. Frémont, in California (without explicit orders) on his third "exploring" expedition, defied the Californian authorities for a time after General Castro had ordered him to withdraw his force of very warlike looking Topographical Engineers, and then lent covert encouragement to an insurrection among the American settlers known as the Bear Flag Revolution. The American-dominated "California Republic" set up in Sonoma (where Vallejo, although the Americans' best friend, had been captured and imprisoned by the insurgents) lasted only three weeks, but it justified all the worst fears of the Spanish Californians and alienated many of them who had hitherto been friendly toward the United States.[9]

On July 7, 1846, the U. S. Navy did reoccupy Monterey and take possession of Upper California, this time for keeps, for the war with Mexico had finally broken out on the Rio Grande and Commodore J. D. Sloat now felt justified in obeying his secret orders without risking a repetition of the Ap Catesby Jones fiasco of 1842. Within days the Stars and Stripes were also flying over Yerba Buena, New Helvetia, and (replacing the short-lived Bear Flag) Sonoma. Frémont and the "messenger of destiny" who had chased after him into the Oregon—Lieutenant Archibald Gillespie, of the U. S. Marines[1]—organized the California Volunteers, who

9. For the background of the American infiltration and conquest of California, see R. G. Cleland: *The Early Sentiment for the Annexation of California . . . 1835–1846* (Austin, Tex., 1915); John A. Hawgood: "Patterns of Yankee Infiltration in Mexican California," *Pacific Historical Review*, XXVII (February 1958), 27–37, and "J. C. Frémont and the Bear Flag Revolution: A Reappraisal," *Univ. of Birmingham Hist. Journal*, VII (1959), 80–100; repr. in rev. form in *Southern California Quarterly*, XLIV:2 (June 1962), 67–96. More general works on the subject are R. G. Cleland: *From Wilderness the Empire* (New York, 1944), Ch. xii, pp. 193–205, and Ch. xiii, pp. 206–21; and Norman Graebner: *Empire on the Pacific* (New York, 1953), passim.

1. See Werner Marti: *Messenger of Destiny* (San Francisco, 1960), for a full treatment of the thrilling and mystifying mission of this dashing and choleric leatherneck secret agent and courier, "licensed"—and only too happy—"to kill."

marched to Monterey and were then shipped down south to complete the American conquest of California. This was not accomplished quite so easily as the almost bloodless occupation of the north, and General Kearny's hundred dragoons suffered a technical reverse, at least, at San Pasqual (when they arrived there after a long march from Santa Fe) at the hands of the Californians, who had previously rallied and thrown the high-handed Gillespie out of the pueblo of Los Angeles. Resistance ended at the Capitulation of Cahuenga Pass early in 1847, although the American commanders, Commodore R. F. Stockton, J. C. Frémont (whom Stockton had appointed military governor of California), and Stephen Kearny, who had come over the mountains and deserts to "pull rank" on them both, continued their private war against each other for some months longer. The consequence of this dispute was the famous Frémont Court Martial of 1847–48.[2] With the departure of Stockton, Frémont (under open arrest), and Kearny, the military government settled down to its proper business of completing the absorption of Upper California as part of the United States, under Colonel R. B. Mason and his adjutant, Lieutenant William Tecumseh Sherman, who had arrived by sea in 1847. The Treaty of Guadalupe Hidalgo, negotiated by Nicholas Trist in Mexico City in February 1848 (though news of its terms took several months to reach Monterey), handed over California officially to the United States. Two weeks earlier, gold had been discovered by James Marshall in the tailrace of John Augustus Sutter's sawmill at Coloma, on the south branch of the American River, a tributary of the Sacramento.

After that, California was never the same again. 1848 was also the Year of Revolutions in Europe. Marshall made his great discovery on January 24: the Treaty of Guadalupe Hidalgo was signed on February 2; King Louis Philippe lost his throne on February 24; Prince Metternich fell from power in Vienna on March 13; on March 15 the daily *Californian*, San Francisco's first newspaper, had an item at the bottom of the third column of the second page which read:

2. The published report of this *cause célèbre* reads like a novel, and it is remarkable that it has never been dramatized or filmed. Extensive extracts from the proceedings appeared in the press, but the full report took the form of a *Message* from President Polk. (Exec. Doc. No. 33, 30th Cong., 1st Session [Senate]. Washington, D. C., 1848, 447 pages.)

GOLD MINE FOUND

In the newlymade raceway of the Saw Mill recently erected by
Captain Sutter on the American Fork, gold has been found in
considerable quantities. One person brought thirty dollars worth to
New Helvetia, gathered there in a short time. California, no doubt,
is rich in mineral wealth; great chances here for scientific capitalists.
Gold has been found in almost every part of the country.

Nobody paid much attention, even in San Francisco, to this obscure item, but an era had ended on the shores of the Pacific and a
new age had begun, just as assuredly as at the Hofburg and at
Versailles, in Frankfurt and in Prague. Not until early in May,
when Sam Brannan, a recusant Mormon elder who had led a ship-
load of Saints round Cape Horn to California the previous year, ran
through the streets of San Francisco (still, despite its grand new
name, a tiny village of several hundred inhabitants on Yerba Buena
Cove) flourishing in his hand a bottle of dust that glinted in the sun
and shouting "Gold! Gold! Gold from the American River!" did
even a local gold rush begin. It was to take another half-year for
the East and the outside world to realize the extent and importance
of the gold discoveries initiated by James Marshall.

A half-hearted attempt on the part of its first discoverers and
their immediate associates to keep the gold mining secret was ended
by Brannan.[3] Within a month of his action San Francisco was
emptied of its able-bodied men and boys; its two newspapers (one
recently transferred from Monterey) ceased publication, and the
furniture of its only hotel (the owner of which, former U. S. Vice-
Consul William Leidesdorff, had recently died) was put up for
auction; the complete crews of most merchant vessels in the harbor
deserted, and naval vessels had to put out to sea to avoid a similar
fate. The American army of occupation soon consisted only of
officers. The military governor had to cook his own dinner. (His
adjutant had gone out on horseback to head off enlisted men escap-
ing inland toward the mines.) James Marshall and Sam Brannan
had really started something.

It had not been until 1842 that the U. S. government first
openly showed its intention to secure California by force if necessary. Less than four years later California was American-occupied

---

3. He had taken the gold dust in trade from a thirsty and garrulous miner
at his general store at Sutter's Fort, on the Sacramento.

territory, and seven years later it was the most desirable place on earth for millions of people, hundreds of thousands of whom faced every imaginable hardship to reach the El Dorado it had become. A sleepy Mexican province, with a population of less than 15,000 in 1845, was to become by 1850 a state of the American Union, humming with every kind of human activity and enterprise—but with the pick and shovel, the pan and sluice, the "Long-Tom" and

Sutter's Fort—New Helvetia. From F. Soulé: *Annals of San Francisco* (1856).

the flume[4] dominating the scene—and boasting a population of close on a hundred thousand. Another quarter-million at least were converging on California from all parts of the world—from China, Chile, the Antipodes and the Cape of Good Hope, and, possibly from Samarkand, Timbucktu and Kamchatka, from Madagascar and Sarawak. The great gold rush was on.

4. See illus., pp. 175–7. They are also described in detail by "Dame Shirley" (op. cit.).

The 1848 gold rush was a local one. This is how (in the words of Walter Colton) it happened in Monterey:

June 20, 1848 . . . My messenger has returned with specimens of gold, he dismounted in a sea of upturned faces. As he drew forth the yellow lumps from his pockets, and passed them around among the eager crowd, the doubts, which had lingered till now, fled. . . . The excitement produced was intense; and many were soon busy in their hasty preparations for a departure to the mines. The family

Beach of Yerba Buena Cove, winter 1849–50. From F. Soulé: *Annals of San Francisco* (1856).

who had kept house for me caught the moving infection. Husband and wife were both packing up; the blacksmith dropped his hammer, the carpenter his plane, the mason his trowel, the farmer his sickle, the baker his loaf, and the tapster his bottle. All were off for the mines, some on carts, some on horses, and some on crutches, and one went in a litter. . . .[5]

From San Francisco, Thomas Larkin, the American consul, wrote to the Secretary of State in Washington, on June 28, 1848:

5. Walter Colton: *Three Years in California* (New York, 1850), pp. 240–7.

Three fourths of the houses in the town on the Bay of San Francisco are deserted . . . every blacksmith, carpenter and lawyer is leaving; brick-yards, saw-mills and ranches are left perfectly alone. A large part of the volunteers at San Francisco and Sonoma have deserted . . . vessels are losing their crews . . . both our newspapers are discontinued . . . San Francisco has not a justice of the peace left. . . . Every bowl, tray, warming pan and pigin has gone to the mines. Everything in short that has a scoop in it that will hold sand and water. All the iron has been worked up into crow-bars, pick axes and spades. . . .[6]

The story was the same in Sonoma, San Jose, and Santa Cruz. The fever was somewhat slower to reach San Luis Obispo, Santa Barbara, Los Angeles, and San Diego, but well before the end of the year these little towns had emptied of their folk too, and migrant miners had begun to come up out of Mexico. John Charles Frémont, leading the remnants of his disastrous fourth expedition by the southern route from Santa Fe to begin a new life on the property he had purchased, through the agency of Thomas Larkin, in California, met on the Gila River, in February 1849: "A large party of Mexicans from Sonora, several hundred in number . . . From them was received the news of the discovery of gold in California, and this large party were on their way to California to hunt for Gold."[7] Frémont persuaded the Sonorans to go with him to his Mariposa grant, for which he had paid Larkin $3,000. According to Jessie Frémont (with, in this case, pardonable exaggeration) it proved to be "the richest gold-bearing estate in the country. Soon the bags of gold, in lumps, in dust, in rich bits of rock, began to accumulate in inconvenient quantities,"[8] filling up all the drawers and cupboards (when taken to Monterey) of the house the Frémonts shared with Señora Alvarado.

6. G. P. Hammond, ed.: *The Larkin Papers* (Berkeley, Calif., 1951–64), VI, 301–4.

7. "Great Events during the Life of J. C. Frémont and Jessie Benton Frémont," written by Lieutenant Francis and Jessie Frémont (typescript with MS revisions in Bancroft Library, Berkeley, Calif.: Doc. CB.397, Pt. I, Vol. 1, p. 97). Although not itself published, this narrative was extensively used by Mrs. Frémont in her various publications and by Allan Nevins in his biography of Frémont. The original narrative is quoted here with the permission of the Director of the Bancroft Library, Dr. G. P. Hammond. It is to be printed in full by the Univ. of Illinois Press in the forthcoming "Frémont Papers."

8. Ibid, p. 101.

It will be noted that the news of the gold discoveries had not yet reached Santa Fe when Frémont left that city in January 1849 after the failure of the fourth expedition. It had reached the East Coast a little earlier, but the extent of the discoveries was not fully realized until President Polk, in his annual *Message* on December 5, 1848, published a glowing account of them, based upon the special report of Colonel Mason, the military governor of California, and on other information received through official channels:

It was known that mines of the precious metals existed to a considerable extent in California at the time of its acquisition. Recent discoveries render it probable that these mines are more extensive and valuable than was anticipated. The accounts of the abundance of gold in that territory are of such an extraordinary character as would scarcely command belief, were they not corroborated by the authentic reports of officers in the public service, who have visited the mineral district, and derived the facts which they detail from personal observation. Reluctant to credit the reports in general circulation as to the quantity of gold, the officer commanding our forces in California visited the mineral district in July last, for the purpose of obtaining accurate information on the subject. His report to the War Department of the result of his examination, and the facts obtained on the spot, is herewith laid before Congress. When he visited the country, there were about four thousand persons engaged in collecting gold. There is every reason to believe that the number of persons so employed has since been augmented. The explorations already made warrant the belief that the supply is very large, and that gold is found in various places in extensive districts of country.

Information received from officers of the navy, and other sources, though not so full and minute, confirm the accounts of the commander of our military force in California. It appears also, from these reports, that mines of quicksilver are found in the vicinity of the gold region. One of them is now being worked, and is believed to be among the most productive in the world.

The effects produced by the discovery of these rich mineral deposits, and the success which has attended the labours of those who have resorted to them, have produced a surprising change in the state of affairs in California. Labour commands a most exorbitant price, and all other pursuits but that of searching for the precious metals are abandoned. Nearly the whole of the male population of the country have gone to the gold district. Ships arriving on the coast are deserted by their crews, and their voyages suspended for want of sailors. Our commanding officer there entertains apprehensions that soldiers cannot be kept in the public service without a large increase of pay. Desertions in his command have become frequent, and he recommends that those who shall withstand the strong temptations, and remain faithful, should be rewarded.

This abundance of gold, and the all-engrossing pursuit of it, have already caused in California an unprecedented rise in the price of the necessaries of life.[9]

Colonel Mason's own account, dated August 17, 1848, told of his visit in June "twenty five miles up the American Fork, to a point now known as the Lower Mines or Mormon Diggins [*sic*]":

The hill sides were thickly strewn with canvas tents and bush arbours; a store was erected, and several boarding shanties in operation. The day was intensely hot, yet about two hundred men were at work in the full glare of the sun, washing for gold—some with tin pans, some with close woven Indian baskets, but the greater part had a rude machine, known as the cradle.

This is on rockers, six or eight feet long, open at the foot, and at its head has a coarse grate or sieve; the bottom is rounded, with small cleets nailed across. Four men are required to work this machine; one digs the ground in the bank close by the stream; another carries it to the cradle and empties it on the grate; a third gives a violent rocking motion to the machine; whilst a fourth dashes on water from the stream itself. The sieve keeps the coarse stones from entering the cradle, the current of water washes off the earthy matter, and the gravel is gradually carried out at the foot of the machine, leaving the gold mixed with a heavy fine black sand above the first cleets.

The sand and gold mixed together are then drawn off through augur holes into a pan below, are dried in the sun, and afterwards separated by blowing off the sand. A party of four men thus

9. This famous *Message* has been reprinted many times. It is to be found, of course, in Richardson: *Messages of the Presidents;* but in more convenient form it was included, together with a number of other valuable documents, as an appendix to J. C. Frémont: *Geographical Memoir*, p. 68. Repr., ed. Allan Nevins, was published (San Francisco) in 1965.

employed, at the lower mines, averaged $100 a day. The Indians, and those who have nothing but pans, or willow baskets, gradually wash out the earth, and separate the gravel by hand, leaving nothing but the gold mixed with sand, which is separated in the manner before described. The gold in the lower mines is in fine bright scales, of which I send several specimens.[1]

Frémont also printed a letter written by a naval officer on the U. S. *Dale* and published in the New York *Courier and Enquirer*.

How the California mines are worked, by C. Nahl.

Dated San Jose, Lower California, November 17, 1848, the letter mentioned some of the results of several more months of the local California gold rush:

> The *rancheros* have left their farms, and unless supplies are sent into the country there must be a famine. I *saw* a man who paid six hundred dollars for a barrel of flour.
>
> Every thing in the shape of goods and provisions commands the highest prices at the mines, payable in gold—which has been sold at the mines for five dollars per ounce, *Troy* weight, and in some cases for even less. At San Francisco and Monterey it sells for from ten to twelve dollars in trade. A vessel sailed a short time before our arrival at Monterey, for Mazatlan, with twelve hundred pounds of this gold, which I found upon our arrival sold for over sixteen dollars

1. Frémont: *Geographical Memoir* (1849), p. 69.

per ounce, *avoirdupois* weight. The gentleman who owns this gold came out to this country in January, 1847, in one of the store-ships chartered in Boston, to bring out provisions for the squadron; he brought out with him between four and five thousand dollars worth of goods, which he bought at auction for a venture. He located in San Francisco, and in August of the same year, he told me that with the goods he brought out, and his purchase of two lots, he was

Hydraulic mining at French Corral, California.

worth thirty thousand dollars. Lots bought originally for fifteen dollars are now worth five or six thousand dollars; all of this took place before the discovery of the mines. This gold has been assayed and found to be twenty-three and a half carats fine—pure virgin gold. The largest piece found weighs twenty-five pounds, in one solid block; the next weighs seven pounds, and so on, down to fine black sand.[2]

2. *Geographical Memoir*, p. 78.

A ship sailed from Boston for San Francisco the day after Polk's *Message* was published, and thus had the technical honor of carrying the first of the "Argonauts" around the Horn. Three weeks later 335 people were on their way to the mines of California by the "short" sea route via Panama, and in 1849 over 6,000 (including members of John Augustus Sutter's own family) used this difficult and fever-ridden route. One of these trans-Isthmian forty-niners, a man named Collis P. Huntington, paused at Panama City to open a store and earn the first installment of what was to become one of the greatest fortunes to be earned by a California

River mining, by C. Nahl.

resident during the next half-century. He was later to move on to Sacramento and become the biggest of the fabulous Big Four. Meanwhile, people were pouring around the Horn and overland, by every established trail, and a few novel ones, to the mines. The *California*, the first steamship to open William H. Aspinwall's Pacific Steamship Navigation Company's "regular" service, left New York on October 6, 1848, before the gold fever had really started, and reached San Francisco on February 28, 1849, to find it in full swing. This ship carried Jessie Frémont to a dramatic reunion with her "lost" husband (at Chagres, to which she had traveled overland from Panama, she had been told that he had probably not survived his fourth expedition) and hers is one of the most vivid descriptions of the sea and Isthmian route in '49.[3] The *California* had a royal reception at the Golden Gate and at Yerba Buena Cove, where "A few low houses, and many tents, such as they were, covered the base of some of the wind-swept treeless hills, over which the June fog rolled its chilling mist. Deserted ships of all sorts were swinging with the tide."[4] The *California* itself was almost immediately to lose nearly its entire crew.

By early 1849 from 4,000 to 5,000 persons (nearly all of them men) had reached the mines from outside California. By the end of 1849 the figures had reached between 40,000 and 50,000 including many foreigners. By the middle of 1850 there were at least 20,000 foreigners in California out of a population of around 100,000. Of these 100,000, only about eight in a hundred were women. Not all of these women were housewives. "The miners came in '49, the whores in '51," runs the ribald old song, but even by 1851 resolute, literate (as will be seen), and respectable women were coming around the Horn, across the Isthmus, and along the overland trails to upstage and outnumber the "soiled doves" of the cribs and honky-tonks. Mrs. Megquier, Mrs. Clappe ("Dame Shirley"), and Mrs. Sarah Royce were notable among this later group.[5]

California's population explosion by immigration was phenomenal; indeed, considering the short time in which it occurred, it can hardly be said to have been matched in recorded statistical history. Before the end of 1852—the peak year of the California gold boom—the state had a quarter of a million inhabitants (or over fifteen times as many as at the beginning of 1848), and by the

3. Jessie B. Frémont: *A Year of American Travel* (New York, 1878; repr. San Francisco, 1960), passim. Another eloquent traveler, the Swiss Carl Meyer (who was probably a mining engineer, so accurate and detailed are his technical descriptions of the diggings), left New Orleans in February 1849, reached Monterey in July, and spent the autumn and winter at the mines. He met the Frémonts at Mariposa, and stayed in California until 1852. See Carl Meyer: *Bound for Sacramento* (*Nach dem Sacramento*, Aarau, Switzerland, 1856); ed. Henry R. Wagner, tr. Ruth F. Axe (Claremont, Calif., 1938); see also his *Prospectus to Form a Society for Emigration to California* (Aarau, Switzerland, 1852); tr. Ruth F. Axe (Claremont, Calif., 1938).

4. Frémont: *A Year of American Travel* (1878 edn.), p. 97. This was the *California*'s second voyage to San Francisco, returning undercrewed and overpassengered from Panama, where she had returned after the first outward voyage, to start the projected service. See also Carl Meyer: *Bound for Sacramento*.

5. All three wrote valuable diaries or letters, which have been published. See Bibliographic Note, p. 430.

MODERN
CALIFORNIA

U.S. Highways
National Parks & Monuments
Franciscan Missions Santa Inez · 1804
(some names shortened)

0   Miles   200

census of 1860 **the figures had risen** to 380,000 (or half as many again). By 1860 the population of Oregon had crept up to only 52,000 (from a population approximating that of California in 1848), and that of Utah, despite the Mormon Church's tremendous efforts to colonize and settle its chosen land, to just over 40,000.[6] The increase in each of these rich and attractive territories was thus only fourfold in the twelve years, whereas California's was nearly thirtyfold.

Not all of the California immigrants became miners, and of those who went to the mines, many ceased to remain there. By the end of 1848 there were approximately only 5,000 men at the mines, by the end of 1849 about 40,000, by the end of 1850 about 50,000, by the end of 1852 certainly 100,000. Even in 1860, when the bonanza days were long over, fully 82,573 men stated "miner" as their occupation in the U. S. Census returns. Of the 35,000 Chinese in California in 1860, perhaps three-quarters were still living in the mining counties and "reworking placer ground sold to them or abandoned to them by discouraged white men . . . It is entirely possible that by the close of the decade of the fifties one quarter of the working miners may have been Chinese."[7]

The mining population of California did not fall spectacularly after the early gold rushes—unlike those in so many other states and territories—because the mines remained rich, even though the gold was becoming harder and more expensive to get year by year. At the height of the boom, in 1852, over $81 million in gold came out of California mines; in 1853–54 the "take" was down to just under $70 million each year; between 1865 and 1885 the yearly figures fluctuated between $15 million and $20 million, and the lowest figure of any year up to 1900 was just over $11 million. California thus entered the twentieth century still very much the Golden State, with a half-century's production of that precious metal totaling over $1,300,000,000, or an average of $26 million a year. These are heady figures, and that thirteen hundred million dollars have played no inconsiderable part in swaying the destinies of both America and the world ever since. Parlayed into much greater sums by astute financial manipulators like Collis and Henry Huntington, Leland Stanford and George Hearst, this capital has created "empires" for them or their families matching those of the

6. Rodman W. Paul: *Mining Frontiers of the Far West* (New York, 1963), p. 15, gives the 1848 figures for California as "about 14,000 other than Indians," and for Oregon (including Washington) as "perhaps 10–12,000 whites and half-breeds." Utah's census figures for 1850 and 1880 were 11,380 and 40,273. For further details, see R. W. Paul: *California Gold* (Cambridge, Mass., 1947), pp. 23–5.

7. Paul: *Mining Frontiers*, pp. 35–6.

Caesars of old; their hard-bitten faces have launched a thousand ships and woven—and unwoven—a hundred thousand miles of railroad. They have founded universities, created great research libraries, assembled fabulous collections of Old Masters, piled newspaper upon newspaper, bought presidents, sold senators, purchased crown jewels for their wives and crown princes for their daughters, and built themselves palaces to live in and mausoleums to lie dead in, which rival (or at least mimic) Knossos, Tivoli, Helicarnassus, and the Taj Mahal.[8]

Hardly any of the great California millionaires of the half-century after 1848 had actually *worked in* the mines: four of the greatest fortunes were made by men who supplied the miners with goods and who, with unnecessary denigration, have been labeled the "four grocers of Sacramento." Everything began with Sutter's roving enterprise, Marshall's discovery in the tailrace, Sam Brannan's town cry, Colonel Mason's report, and President Polk's *Message*. "Gold! Gold! Gold from the American River" (and from all the other places where men, encouraged and emboldened by this discovery, sought for and found precious metals and other riches throughout the American Far West) built Nob Hill, bought *The Blue Boy*, and reassembled a Spanish monastery stone by stone—but with all modern conveniences added, including a carved and paneled elevator for the tycoon, and gold-plated waste pipes for his mistress' bathroom—on a high hill overlooking the coast of California. But not every California (or Nevada, Colorado, or Arizona) millionaire, or his heir, was like Dorothy Parker's "wealthy son of a bitch." The astronomical vulgarity of San Simeon[9] and the poor (but at least pious) taste of the Stanford Memorial Chapel[1] are canceled out by the restraint with which are displayed the wonders of Henry Huntington's San Marino,[2] the tomes of Adolf Sutro,[3]

8. The striking similarity of the Henry E. Huntington Mausoleum at San Marino to the Jefferson Memorial in Washington, D. C., is of a different order! It is by the same architect, but was executed first. On a much smaller scale, it is therefore rather a prototype than a copy.

9. Now a state historical monument, viewable by the public at $2 a head, but with an extra $2 fee for the private—and most vulgar—parts.

1. Mistakenly rebuilt after an act of God—and who can blame Him—had knocked it about a bit in April 1906.

2. The Henry E. Huntington Library and Art Gallery at San Marino, Calif.

3. What survived the 1906 earthquake and fire of the magnificent library of this German-Jewish immigrant engineering genius is now housed in a special

the treasure houses of the De Youngs,[4] and the gifts and foundations of many other equally public-spirited and even more publicity-shy California plutocrats. Not all their gold came out of the South Fork of the American River, but there a page of history was turned to disclose many leaves of gold that would follow after.

Not every gold-rush merchant became rich. One moderately successful member of that profession, Stephen Chapin Davis,[5] on his second venture in California (the first, in 1850–51, was a total failure, but he fell in love with the country and returned there in 1852), amassed 190 ounces of gold dust and a check for $350 as "the result of my two years labor" before he finally returned home to Nashua, New Hampshire, in 1854. The gold dust he guarded with his Colt revolver and a fierce dog while in California, and "slept with my money under me" when crossing the steamy Isthmus of Panama (on board ship the pursers took charge of it, at a commission of one per cent of its value on each voyage). Once in New York: "We went down to Wall St. to sell our dust. . . . I had 170 oz's which I sold at 17.60. . . . I took a check on Gilbert & Sons, of Boston, for $2,900, Ward [his more cautious companion] taking all his in cash." Davis' earnings thus amounted to less than $1,500 a year, and the cost of his outward passage had to be deducted from that. His return trip was paid for in gold dust out of the 190 ounces he had started back with. Davis died in 1856 at the age of twenty-four after another mercantile adventure, in which he sold 865 barrels of New Hampshire apples in Liverpool, England, at a profit of nearly 900 per cent (far better than he had ever done with California's gold, and netting him and his partner nearly $5,000 each) was certainly a more typical gold rush merchant, in his ups and downs of fortune, than Collis P. Huntington, who died in 1900 a multi-millionaire.

Possession or lack of business ability was a big factor in the success or failure of a gold-rush merchant, but whether a miner struck it rich or not seems to have been sheer luck. Even the most skilled tin or lead miner from the Middle West or from Europe, or

---

building on the campus of the Roman Catholic University of San Francisco, to the credit of all concerned.

4. The De Young Museum and Art Gallery in Golden Gate Park, San Francisco, is one of the World's finest. The De Young money was greatly augmented by newspaper publishing, as was—at first—the Hearst fortune.

5. B. B. Reynolds, ed.: *California Gold Rush Merchant: The Journal of Stephen Chapin Davis* (San Marino, Calif., 1956), passim.

the most experienced and hard-working silver miner from Mexico, tended to do no better than the merest greenhorn straight from college, plow, or office. Charles Pancoast, the Quaker forty-niner[6] who stuck to mining (with a little ranching and shopkeeping on the side) for five years until in 1854 he returned to Philadelphia and the drug business for which he had been trained, not only records his own lack of success:

My loss of $1,600 in the turning of the Stanislaus; the high cost of living without production on the Merced; and now the loss of my

Monte in the mines, by J. D. Borthwick. From his *Three Years in California* (1857).

Mules, with other expenses, had so reduced my capital that after paying my passage from San Francisco [to try his luck afresh at Trinity River, in northern California] I had now about ten dollars. My continued Misfortunes and the prospect before me were enough to crush the spirits of almost any man; but Youth, Health, Spunk, Energy and Perseverance are not readily subdued.[7]

6. A. P. Hannum, ed.: *A Quaker Forty-Niner: The Adventures of Charles Edward Pancoast on the American Frontier* ("written by himself"), foreword by J. B. McMaster (Philadelphia and London, 1930), passim.

7. Hannum, p. 306. "Uncle Charlie" Pancoast was then thirty-three years old. He died in 1906, at the age of eighty-eight.

but also recounts the remarkable good fortune of another:

> We then went out prospecting to Mt. Ophir, and reached a point where we could see the Yosemite Valley; but as it was reputed to have no Gold in it we did not regard it as worthy of our attention. We had no luck the first day; but as we were returning I found an abandoned Claim with a good show of Gold, and the next day we carried our clumsy heavy rocker up a high mountain to these Diggings. We left our Tent where it was and climbed this Mountain, averaging $12.00 to $16.00 each per day. In front of our Tent was a small Boulder, that we were in the habit of using as a seat. One Sunday a young Miner who was making us a friendly visit remarked "This stone has Gold in it; I see a speck." He washed off the dirt and we could see another speck or two. He asked if he might have the stone and we answered in the affirmative. He then went up to a speculative Store Keeper on the Flat [Big Oak Flat] and brought him down to look at it. The Store Keeper gave him $200 for it, broke it up, and obtained $3,000 worth of Gold—a prize we lost from our ignorance.[8]

Tales like these, both true and false—and Charles Pancoast was a particularly reliable narrator, though, when he set down his reminiscences many years later, his memory often played him false on place names and dates—have been preserved by innumerable forty-niners and by those who followed them in search of "the elephant"[9] in later years. One example of such late-comers was the Englishman J. D. Borthwick, who was not only a skilled observer but also a gifted artist. His book *Three Years in California*, illustrated by himself, appeared as early as 1857.[1] Almost casually he states: "In May 1851 I happened to be residing in New York, and was seized with the California fever. My preparations were very soon made and a day or two afterwards I found myself on a small barque about to sail for Chagres with a load of California emi-

---

8. Hannum, p. 291. This, at one fell swoop, was as much as Stephen Davis made in two years of storekeeping. Once again, though, it was not the miner who struck it rich.

9. "I have seen the elephant," or, according to the *Oxford English Dictionary*, "I have seen the elephant from trunk to tail," was the picturesque forty-niner way of saying that one had seen everything.

1. The edn. cited here is that publ. by William Blackwood (Edinburgh and London, 1857), "with eight illustrations by the Author," one of which is repr. above, p. 183.

grants."[2] By the time he had arrived at the mines, after sundry adventures, many of the diggings had been "worked out" by the crude methods then still employed, but "every place in the mines had its tradition of Wonderful events which had occurred in the olden times; that is to say, as far back as '49—for three years in such a fast country were equal to a century."[3]

Without exaggeration, Borthwick remarked: "Certainly no country ever so rapidly advanced to so high a position as California; but it is equally true that no country ever commenced its career with such effective population, or with the same elements of

San Francisco, 1854. From F. Soulé: *Annals of San Francisco* (1856).

wealth to work upon . . . the attractions offered by California were such as to draw to it a complete ready-made population of active and capable men, of every trade and profession."[4] When Sir Richard Burton reached California overland via Salt Lake City in 1860, he found "At Sacramento—the newer name for New Helvetia—a capital mass of shops and stores, groggeries and hotels," but

2. Borthwick, p. 3.

3. Borthwick, p. 322. Two longer extracts from this book are included in M. M. Quaife, ed.: *Pictures of Gold Rush California*, Lakeside Classics Series (Chicago, 1949). Other contemporary works quoted from *in extenso* in this anthology include H. R. Helper: *The Land of Gold;* D. B. Woods: *Sixteen Months in the Gold Diggings;* Bayard Taylor: *Eldorado;* and Alonzo Delano: *Life on the Plains and among the Diggings.* Also included are two articles: "California in 1848," New York *Herald* (September 1, 1848); and "How the Gold Was Mined," *Harper's Monthly Magazine* (April 1860), as well as selections from the works of Walter Colton (*Three Years in California*) and Louise Clappe (*The Shirley Letters*), already cited in this chapter. A comprehensive gold-rush bibliography is Carl Wheat: *Books on the Gold Rush* (San Francisco, 1949).

4. Borthwick, pp. 381–2.

it was San Francisco, the El Dorado of the West, where "a tolerable opera, a superior supper, and the society of friends made the arrival exceptionally comfortable," and where "Mr. Consul Booker placed my name on the lists of the Union Club, which was a superior institution to that of Leamington,"[5] that most aroused his admiration. A generation later, James Bryce found San Francisco equally impressive and very much larger. But the most dramatic account of the mushroom growth of that metropolis under the stimulus of the gold rush was recorded by that "pioneer of pioneers," Richard Henry Dana. To the 1869 edition of his classic *Two Years before the Mast*, first published in 1840, he added an appendix entitled "Twenty-four Years After." Here are its opening paragraphs:

It was in the winter of 1835–6 that the ship *Alert*, in the prosecution of her voyage for hides on the remote and almost unknown coast of California, floated into the vast solitude of the Bay of San Francisco. All around was the stillness of nature. One vessel, a Russian, lay at anchor there, but during our whole stay not a sail came or went. Our trade was with remote missions, which sent hides to us in launches manned by their Indians. Our anchorage was between a small island, called Yerba Buena, and a gravel beach in a little bight or cove of the same name, formed by two small projecting points. Beyond, to the westward of the landing-place, were dreary sand-hills, with little grass to be seen, and few trees, and beyond them higher hills, steep and barren, their sides gullied by the rains. Some five or six miles beyond the landing-place, to the right, was a ruinous presidio, and some three or four miles to the left was the Mission of Dolores, as ruinous as the presidio, almost deserted, with but few Indians attached to it, and but little property in cattle. Over a region far beyond our sight there were no other human habitations, except that an enterprising Yankee, years in advance of his time, had put up, on the rising ground above the landing, a shanty of rough boards, where he carried on a very small retail trade between the hide ships and the Indians. Vast banks of fog, invading us from the North Pacific, drove in through the entrance, and covered the whole bay; and when they disappeared we saw a few well-wooded

5. Richard F. Burton: *The City of the Saints and across the Rocky Mountains to California* (London, 1861); rev. edn., intro. and notes by Fawn M. Brodie (New York, 1963; London, 1964), pp. 557–8, cited here.

islands, the sand-hills on the west, the grassy and wooded slopes on the east, and the vast stretch of the bay to the southward, where we were told lay the Missions of Santa Clara and San José, and still longer stretches to the northward and north-eastward, where we understood smaller bays spread out, and large rivers poured in their tributes of waters. There were no settlements on these bays or rivers, and the few ranchos and missions were remote and widely separated. Not only the neighbourhood of our anchorage, but the entire region of the great bay was a solitude. On the whole coast of California there was not a lighthouse, a beacon, or a buoy; and the charts were made up from old and disconnected surveys by British, Russian, and Mexican voyagers. Birds of prey and passage swooped and dived about us, wild beasts ranged through the oak groves, and as we slowly floated out of the harbour with the tide, herds of deer came to the water's edge, on the northerly side of the entrance, to gaze at the strange spectacle.

On the evening of Saturday, the 13th of August 1859, the superb steamship *Golden Gate*, gay with crowds of passengers, and lighting the sea for miles around with the glare of her signal lights of red, green, and white, and brilliant with lighted saloons and state-rooms, bound up from the Isthmus of Panama, neared the entrance to San Francisco, the great centre of a world-wide commerce. Miles out at sea, on the desolate rocks of the Farallones, gleamed the powerful rays of one of the most costly and effective lighthouses in the world. As we drew in through the Golden Gate, another light-house met our eyes, and in the clear moonlight of the unbroken Californian summer we saw, on the right, a large fortification, protecting the narrow entrance, and just before us the little island of Alcatraz confronted us—one entire fortress. We bore round the point towards the old anchoring-ground of the hide ships, and there, covering the sand-hills and the valleys, stretching from the water's edge to the base of the great hills, and from the old presidio to the mission, flickering all over with the lamps of its streets and houses, lay a city of one hundred thousand inhabitants. Clocks tolled the hour of midnight from its steeples, but the city was alive from the salute of our guns, spreading the news that the fortnightly steamer had come, bringing mails and passengers from the Atlantic world. Clipper ships of the largest size lay at anchor in the stream, or were girt to the wharves; and capacious high-pressure steamers, as large and showy as those of the Hudson or Mississippi, bodies of dazzling light, awaited the delivery of our mails, to take their cruises up the bay, stopping at Benicia and the United States Naval Station, and then up the great tributaries—the Sacramento, San Joaquin, and Feather rivers—to the far inland cities of Sacramento, Stockton, and Marysville.

The dock into which we drew, and the streets about it, were densely crowded with express-wagons and hand-carts to take luggage, coaches and cabs to take passengers; and with men—some looking out for friends among our hundreds of passengers—agents of the press, and a greater multitude eager for newspapers and verbal intelligence from the great Atlantic and European world. Through this crowd I made my way, along the well-built and well-lighted streets, as alive as by day, where boys in high-keyed voices were already crying the latest New York papers; and between one and two o'clock in the morning found myself comfortably abed in a commodious room in the Oriental Hotel, which stood, as well as I could learn, on the filled-up cove, and not far from the spot where we used to beach our boats from the *Alert*.

Sunday, August 14th. When I awoke in the morning, and looked from my windows over the city of San Francisco, with its storehouses, towers, and steeples; its court-houses, theatres, and hospitals; its daily journals; its well-filled professions; its fortresses and lighthouses; its wharves and harbour, with their thousand-ton clipper ships, more in number than London or Liverpool sheltered that day; itself one of the capitals of the American Republic, and the sole emporium of a new world, the awakened Pacific; when I looked across the bay to the eastward, and beheld a beautiful town on the fertile, wooded shores of the Contra Costa; and steamers, large and small, the ferry boats to the Contra Costa, and capacious freighters and passenger-carriers to all parts of the great bay and its tributaries, with lines of their smoke in the horizon—when I saw all these things, and reflected on what I once was and saw here, and what now surrounded me, I could scarcely keep my hold on reality at all, or the genuineness of anything, and seemed to myself like one who had moved in "worlds not realised."[6]

6. Signet Classics (New York, 1964), pp. 341–71; and Penguin Travel and Adventure Series (London, 1948), pp. 356–87, cited here. John H. Kemble's splendid critical and illust. edn. (San Francisco, 1964) is the best hard-cover one as yet.

HUTCHINGS'

CALIFORNIA MAGAZINE.

VOL. II.   NOVEMBER, 1857.   No 5.

THE DISCOVERY OF GOLD IN CALIFORNIA.

GEN. JOHN A. SUTTER.

[*From an Ambrotype by R. H. Vance.*]

THE DISCOVERY OF GOLD IN CALIFORNIA.

> Ours is the age of gold,
> And ours the hallowed time.—*Mellen.*

To the lovers of history, nothing can be more welcome and valuable than the un-varnished narrative of events, from the actors themselves: therefore, we feel the greater pleasure in presenting our readers with the following statements, with which we are favored: one from the good old pioneer, Gen. John August Sutter; and the other from Mr. James W. Marshall, the favored discoverer of the gold—and who, unitedly, are the fathers of *The Age of Gold.*

It was in the first part of January, 1848, when the gold was discovered at Coloma,* where I was then building a saw-mill. The contractor and builder of this mill was James W. Marshall, from New Jersey. In the fall of 1847, after the mill seat had been located, I sent up to this place Mr. P. L. Wimmer with his family, and a number of laborers, from the disbanded Mormon Battalion; and a little later I engaged Mr. Bennet from Oregon to assist Mr. Marshall in the mechanical labors of the mill. Mr. Wimmer had the team in charge, assisted by his young sons, to do the necessary teaming, and Mrs. Wimmer did the cooking for all hands.

I was very much in need of a saw-mill, to get lumber to finish my large flouring mill, of four run of stones, at Brighton, which was commenced at the same time, and was rapidly progressing; likewise for other buildings, fences, etc., for the small village of Yerba Buena, (now San Francisco.) In the City Hotel, (the only one) at the dinner table this enterprise was un-kindly called "another folly of Sutter's," as my first settlement at the old fort near Sacramento City was called by a good many, "a folly of his," and they were about right in that, because I had the best chances to get some of the finest locations, near

* The Indian name and pronunciation is Cul-lu-mah, (beautiful vale,) now Americanized Coloma.

the settlements; and even well stocked rancho's had been offered to me on the most reasonable conditions; but I refused all these good offers, and preferred to explore the wilderness, and select a territory on the banks of the Sacramento. It was a rainy afternoon when Mr. Marshall arrived at my office in the Fort, very wet. I was somewhat surprised to see him, as he was down a few days previous; and when, I sent up to Coloma a number of teams with provisions, mill irons, etc., etc. He told me then that he had some important and interesting news which he wished to communicate secretly to me, and wished me to go with him to a place where we should not be disturbed, and where no listeners could come and hear what we had to say. I went with him to my private rooms; he requested me to lock the door; I complied, but I told him at the same time that nobody was in the house except the clerk, who was in his office in a different part of the house; after requesting of me something which he wanted, which my servants brought and then left the room, I forgot to lock the doors, and it happened that the door was opened by the clerk just at the moment when Marshall took a rag from his pocket, showing me the yellow metal: he had about two ounces of it; but how quick Mr. M. put the yellow metal in his pocket again can hardly be described. The clerk came to see me on business, and excused himself for interrupting me, and as soon as he had left I was told, "now lock the doors; didn't I tell you that we might have listeners?" I told him that he need fear nothing about that, as it was not the habit of this gentleman; but I could hardly convince him that he need not to be suspicious. Then Mr. M. began to show me this metal, which consisted of small pieces and specimens, some of them worth a few dollars; he told me that he had expressed his opinion to the laborers at the mill, that this might be gold; but some of them were laughing at him and called him a crazy man, and could not believe such a thing.

SUTTER'S FORT IN 1848..

After having proved the metal with aqua fortis, which I found in my apothecary shop, likewise with other experiments, and read the long article "gold" in the Encyclopedia Americana, I declared this to be gold of the finest quality, of at least 23 carats. After this Mr. M. had no more rest nor patience, and wanted me to start with him immediately for Coloma; but I told him I could not leave, as it was late in the evening and nearly supper time, and that it would be better for him to remain with me till the next morning, and I would travel with him, but this would not do: he asked me only "will you come to-morrow morning?" I told him yes, and off he started for Coloma in the heaviest rain, although already very wet, taking nothing to eat. I took this news very easy, like all other occurrences good or bad, but thought a great deal during the night about the consequences which might follow such a discovery. I gave all my necessary orders to my numerous laborers, and left the next morning at 7 o'clock, accompanied by an Indian soldier, and vaquero, in a heavy rain, for Coloma. About half way on the road I saw at a distance a human being crawling out from the brushwood. I asked the Indian who it was: he told me "the same man who was with you last evening." When I came nearer I found it was Marshall, very wet; I told him that he would have done better to remain with me at the fort than to pass such an ugly night here; but he told me that he went up to Coloma, (54 miles) took his other horse and came half way to meet me; then we rode up to the new Eldorado. In the afternoon the weather was clearing up, and we made a prospecting promenade. The next morning we went to the tail-race of the mill, through which the water was running during the night, to clean out the gravel which had been made loose, for the purpose of widening the race; and after the water was out of the race we went in to search for gold. This was done every morning: small pieces of gold could be seen remaining on the bottom of the clean washed bed rock. I went in the race and picked up several pieces of this gold, several of the laborers gave me some which they had picked up, and from Marshall I received a part. I told them that I would get a ring made of this gold as soon as it could be done in California; and I have had a heavy ring made, with my family's coat of arms engraved on the outside, and on the inside of the ring is engraved, "The first gold, discovered in January, 1848." Now if Mrs. Wimmer possesses a piece which has been found earlier than mine Mr. Marshall can tell,* as it was probably received from him. I think Mr. Marshall could have hardly known himself which was exactly the first little piece, among the whole.

The next day I went with Mr. M. on a prospecting tour in the vicinity of Coloma, and the following morning I left for Sacramento. Before my departure I had a conversation with all hands: I told them that I would consider it as a great favor if they would keep this discovery secret only for six weeks, so that I could finish my large flour mill at Brighton, (with four run of stones,) which had cost me already about from 24 to 25,000 dollars—the people up there promised to keep it secret so long. On my way home, instead of feeling happy and contented, I was very unhappy, and could not see that it would benefit me much, and I was perfectly right in thinking so; as it came just precisely as I expected. I thought at the same time that it could hardly be kept secret for six weeks; and in this I was not mistaken, for about two weeks later, after my return, I sent up several teams in charge of a white man, as the teamsters were Indian boys. This man was acquainted with all hands up there, and Mrs. Wimmer told him the whole se-

cret; likewise the young sons of Mr. Wimmer told him that they had gold, and that they would let him have some too; and so he obtained a few dollars' worth of it as a present. As soon as this man arrived at the fort he went to a small store in one of my outside buildings, kept by Mr. Smith, a partner of Samuel Brannan, and asked for a bottle of brandy, for which he would pay the cash; after having the bottle he paid with these small pieces of gold. Smith was astonished and asked him if he intended to insult him; the teamster told him to go and ask me about it; Smith came in, in great haste, to see me, and I told him at once the truth—what could I do? I had to tell him all about it. He reported it to Mr. S. Brannan, who came up immediately to get all possible information, when he returned and sent up large supplies of goods, leased a larger house from me, and commenced a very large and profitable business; soon he opened a branch house of business at Mormon Island.

Mr. Brannan made a kind of claim on Mormon Island, and put a tolerably heavy tax on "The Latter Day Saints." I believe it was 30 per cent, which they paid for some time, until they got tired of it, (some of them told me that it was for the purpose of building a temple for the honor and glory of the Lord.)

So soon as the secret was out my laborers began to leave me, in small parties first, but then all left, from the clerk to the cook, and I was in great distress; only a few mechanics remained to finish some very necessary work which they had commenced, and about eight invalids, who continued slowly to work a few teams, to scrape out the mill race at Brighton. The Mormons did not like to leave my mill unfinished, but they got the gold fever like everybody else. After they had made their piles they left for the Great Salt Lake. So long as these people have been employed by me they have behaved very well, and were industrious and faithful laborers, and when settling their accounts there was not

* Mrs. Wimmer's piece weighs about five dollars and twelve cents. The *first piece*, Mr. Marshall says, weighed about fifty cents.

SUTTER'S FORT, IN 1857.

one of them who was not contented and satisfied.

Then the people commenced rushing up from San Francisco and other parts of California, in May, 1848: in the former village only five men were left to take care of the women and children. The single men locked their doors and left for "Sutter's Fort," and from there to the Eldorado. For some time the people in Monterey and farther south would not believe the news of the gold discovery, and said that it was only a '*Ruse de Guerre*' of Sutter's, because he wanted to have neighbors in his wilderness. From this time on I got only too many neighbors, and some very bad ones among them.

What a great misfortune was this sudden gold discovery for me! It has just broken up and ruined my hard, restless, and industrious labors, connected with many dangers of life, as I had many narrow escapes before I became properly established.

From my mill buildings I reaped no benefit whatever, the mill stones even have been stolen and sold.

My tannery, which was then in a flourishing condition, and was carried on very profitably, was deserted, a large quantity of leather was left unfinished in the vats; and a great quantity of raw hides became valueless as they could not be sold; nobody wanted to be bothered with such trash, as it was called. So it was in all the other mechanical trades which I had carried on; all was abandoned, and work commenced or nearly finished was all left, to an immense loss for me. Even the Indians had no more patience to work alone, in harvesting and threshing my large wheat crop out; as the whites had all left, and other Indians had been engaged by some white men to work for them, and they commenced to have some gold for which they were buying all kinds of articles at enormous prices in the stores; which, when my Indians saw this, they wished very much to go to the mountains and dig gold. At last I consented, got a number of wagons ready, loaded them with provisions and goods of all kinds, employed a clerk, and left with about one hundred Indians, and about fifty Sandwich Islanders (Kanakas) which had joined those which I brought with me from the Islands. The first camp was about ten miles above Mormon Island, on the south fork of the American river. In a few weeks we became crowded, and it would no more pay, as my people made too many acquaintances. I broke up the camp and started on the march further south, and located my next camp on Sutter creek (now in Amador county), and thought that I should there be alone. The work was going on well for a while, until three or four traveling grog-shops surrounded me, at from one and a half to two miles distance from the camp; then, of course, the gold was taken to these places, for drinking, gambling, etc., and then the following day they were sick and unable to work, and became deeper and more indebted to me, and particularly the Kanakas. I found that it was high time to quit this kind of business, and lose no more time and money. I therefore broke up the camp and returned to the Fort, where I disbanded nearly all the people who had worked for me in the mountains digging gold. This whole expedition proved to be a heavy loss to me.

At the same time I was engaged in a mercantile firm in Coloma, which I left in January, 1849 — likewise with many sacrifices. After this I would have nothing more to do with the gold affairs. At this time, the Fort was the great trading place where nearly all the business was transacted. I had no pleasure to remain there, and moved up to Hock Farm, with all my Indians, and who had been with me from the time they were children. The place was then in charge of a Major Domo.

It is very singular that the Indians never found a piece of gold and brought it to me, as they very often did other specimens found in the ravines. I requested them continually to bring me some curiosities from the mountains, for which I always recompensed them. I have received animals, birds, plants, young trees, wild fruits, pipe clay, stones, red ochre, etc., etc., but never a piece of gold. Mr. Dana, of the scientific corps of the expedition under Com. Wilkes' Exploring Squadron, told me that he had the strongest proof and signs of gold in the vicinity of Shasta Mountain, and further south. A short time afterwards, Doctor Sandels, a very scientific traveler, visited me, and explored a part of the country in a great hurry, as time would not permit him to make a longer stay.

He told me likewise that he found sure signs of gold, and was very sorry that he could not explore the Sierra Nevada. He did not encourage me to attempt to work and open mines, as it was uncertain how it would pay, and would probably be only profitable for a government. So I thought it more prudent to stick to the plow, notwithstanding I did know that the country was rich in gold, and other minerals. An old attached Mexican servant who followed me here from the United States, as soon as he knew that I was here, and who understood a great deal about working in placers, told me he found sure signs of gold in the mountains on Bear Creek, and that we would go right to work after returning from our campaign in 1845, but he became a victim to his patriotism and fell into the hands of the enemy near my encampment, with dispatches for me from Gen. Micheltorena, and he was hung as a spy, for which I was very sorry.

By this sudden discovery of the gold, all my great plans were destroyed. Had I succeeded with my mills and manufactories for a few years before the gold was discovered, I should have been the richest citizen on the Pacific shore; but it had to be different. Instead of being rich, I am ruined, and the cause of it is the long delay of the United States Land Commission, of the United States Courts, through the great influence of the squatter lawyers. Before my case will be decided in Washington, another year may elapse, but I hope that justice will be done me by the last tribunal — the Supreme Court of the United States. By the Land Commission and the District Court it has been decided in my favor. The Common Council of the city of Sacramento, composed partly of squatters, paid Alpheus Felch, (one of the late Land Commissioners, who was engaged by the squatters during his office), $5,000, from the fund of the city, against the will of the tax-payers, for which amount he has to try to defeat my just and old claim from the Mexican government, before the Supreme Court of the United States in Washington.

SUTTER'S MILL, IN 1848.

Unfortunately for Gen. Sutter, he had one failing—*his heart was too large and confiding.* The men who shared most largely in his princely hospitality and confidence, were the first to take advantage of it, by stealing away his possessions. His generous nature taught him to feel that all *white men* were *honest*—but he did not find them so ;—a mistake to which is attributable his present impoverished circumstances. Now, when he should be enjoying the fruit of his long and enterprising labors in peace, he is annoyed with contentions and lawsuits innumerable—simply *in trying to hold his own!* Even the quiet and pleasant Hock Farm—his homestead —(a spot which is ever sacred to the heart of an American)— was sold, not long since, under the hammer of the sheriff. Recently, however, it has been redeemed, at a great sacrifice. And this is the man to whom we are so much indebted for the gold discovery. May God forgive us Californians, for our shameful indifference to the Old Pioneer.

—

The following is Mr. Marshall's account of his discovery of the gold :—

Being a millwright by trade, as there was a ready cash sale for lumber, I con-cluded to seek a location in the mountains and erect a mill, to supply the valley with lumber. Some time in April, 1847, I visited New Helvetia, commonly known as the "Fort," where I made my resolution known to John A. Sutter, sen., and requested of him an Indian boy, to act as an interpreter to the mountain Indians in the vicinity of the American river—or Rio del los Americanos, as it was then called. At first he refused, because, he said that he had previously sent several companies, at various times, and by different routes, for that purpose, all of whom reported that it was impossible to find a route for a wagon road to any locality where pine timber could be procured, and that it was the height of folly to attempt any such thing.

Capt. Sutter at length, however, promised me the desired interpreter, provided I would stock some six or eight plows for him first, of which he was in immediate want, which I readily agreed to do. While I was employed upon this job there was much talk at the Fort concerning my contemplated trip to the mountains ; and Messrs. Gingery, P. L. Wimmer and Mc-Lellan having resolved also to take a trip, with the same object in view, came where

I was working, and asked me where I expected to find a road and timber, and I promptly gave them my views and directions.

They departed, I believe in company, but finally separated, and P. L. Wimmer found pine timber and a road, on what is now known as the Sacramento and Diamond Springs road, and about the 12th of May, Gingery and Wimmer commenced work, about thirteen miles west of the (now called) Shingle Spring House.

On the 16th of May, having completed my work for Capt. Sutter, I started, with an Indian boy, —— Treador, and W. A. Graves, (who is now residing in Butte county, and who had assisted me in my work, and heard the conversation between myself, Gingery, Wimmer and McLellan,) accompanied me for the purpose of seeing the mountains. On the 18th of May we entered the valley of Culluma [Coloma] ; and on the 20th Gingery joined our company. We then traveled up the stream now called Weber creek—the Indian name of which is Pul-Pul-Mull—to the head of the creek ; thence higher in the mountains until we arrived at the South Fork of the American river, where it divides into two branches of about equal size ; from whence we returned by Sly Park and Pleasant Valley to the Fort.

On my arrival I gave Capt. Sutter an account of my trip, and what I had discovered. He thereupon proposed to me a partnership ; but before we were ready to commence operations, some persons who had tried, in vain, to find Culluma, reported to Sutter that I "had made a false representation, for they could find no such place." To settle matters, Capt. Sutter furnished me with a Mission Indian, who was Alcalde of the Cosumnes tribe, as an interpreter and guide—trusting partly to the Indian's report, as to the propriety of the proposed co-partnership.

The report which I had made on my first trip having been fully confirmed by observations on the second, the co-partnership was completed, and about the 27th of August we signed the agreement to build and run a saw-mill at Culluma. On the third day (I think) afterwards, I set out, with two wagons, and was accompanied by the following persons, employed by the firm of Sutter & Marshall, viz.: P. L. Wimmer and family, James Barger, Ira Willis, Sidney Willis, Alex. Stephens, Wm. Cunce, James Brown, and Ezekiah Persons.

On our arrival in the Valley we first built the double log cabin, afterwards known as Hastings & Co.'s store. About the last of September, as Capt. Sutter wanted a couple of capable men to construct a dam across the American river at the grist-mill—near where the Pavilion now stands—I sent the two Willis', as the most capable ; (Wm. Cunce being in feeble health, left about the same time ;) and I received Henry Bigler, Israel Smith, Wm. Johnston and —— Evans in return ; and shortly afterwards I employed Charles Bennet and Wm. Scott, both carpenters. The above named individuals, with some ten Indians, constituted my whole force.

While we were in the habit at night of turning the water through the tail race we had dug for the purpose of widening and deepening the race, I used to go down in the morning to see what had been done by the water through the night ; and about half past seven o'clock on or about the 19th of January—I am not quite certain to a day, but it was between the 18th and 20th of that month—1848, I went down as usual, and after shutting off the water from the race I stepped into it, near the lower end, and there, upon the rock, about six inches beneath the surface of the water, I DISCOVERED THE GOLD. I was entirely alone at the time. I picked up one or two pieces and examined them attentively ; and having some general knowledge of minerals, I could not call to mind more than two which in any way resembled this —sulphuret of iron, very bright and brittle ; and gold, bright, yet malleable ; I then tried it between two rocks, and found that it could be beaten into a different shape, but not broken. I then collected four or five pieces and went up to Mr. Scott (who was working at the carpenter's bench making the mill wheel) with the pieces in my hand, and said, "I have found it."

"What is it?" inquired Scott.

"Gold," I answered.

"Oh! no," returned Scott, "that can't be."

I replied positively,—"I know it to be nothing else."

Mr. Scott was the second person who saw the gold. W. J. Johnston, A. Stephens, H. Bigler, and J. Brown, who were also working in the mill yard, were then called up to see it. Peter L. Wimmer, Mrs. Jane Wimmer, C. Bennet, and J. Smith, were at the house; the latter two of whom were sick; E. Persons and John Wimmer, (a son of P. L. Wimmer), were out hunting oxen at the same time. About 10 o'clock the same morning, P. L. Wimmer came down from the house, and was very much surprised at the discovery, when the metal was shown him; and which he took home to show his wife, who, the next day, made some experiments upon it by boiling it in strong lye, and saleratus; and Mr. Bennet by my directions beat it very thin.

Four days afterwards I went to the Fort for provisions, and carried with me about three ounces of the gold, which Capt. Sutter and I tested with *nitric acid.* I then tried it in Sutter's presence by taking three silver dollars and balancing them by the dust in the air, then immersed both in water, and the superior weight of the gold satisfied us both of its nature and value.

About the 20th of February, 1848, Capt. Sutter came to Coloma, for the first time, to consummate an agreement we had made with this tribe of Indians in the month of September previous, to wit:—that we live with them in peace, on the same land.

About the middle of April the mill commenced operation, and, after cutting a few thousand feet of lumber was abandoned; as all hands were intent upon gold digging. In December, '48, Capt. Sutter came again

to Coloma, and some time in that month sold his interest in the mill to Messrs. Ragley & Winters, of which new firm I became a member. The mill was soon again in operation, and cut most of the lumber of which the town of Coloma was built.

The *first piece of gold* which I found, *weighed about fifty cents.* Mr. Wimmer, having bought a stock of merchandise some time about May or June, 1848; and Mrs. Wimmer being my treasurer, used four hundred and forty dollars of my money to complete the purchase; and among which was the first piece of gold which I had found. Where that went, or where it is now, I believe that nobody knows.

J. W. MARSHALL.

This is the unvarnished statement which the writer received from the lips and pen of Mr. James W. Marshall himself; and being unacquainted with him personally, I went to several gentlemen in Coloma— among whom were several old pioneers still resident there—to ascertain, if possible, whether or not Mr. M.'s statements were true and trustworthy, and the answer invariably was, in substance, "Whatever Mr. Marshall tells you, you may rely upon as correct." I moreover read the affidavits of several of the men who were present when the gold was discovered by Marshall, and which affidavits were affirmatory of the facts which are stated.

There is another fact I wish here to mention, that it may be recorded in the remembrance of the English, as well as the American public. It is this: Mr. Hargraves, the discoverer of gold in Australia, was mining in Coloma in the summer of 1849, and went to Sutter & Marshall's mill for some lumber; and as he and Marshall were leaning against a pile of lumber, conversing, Mr. H. mentioned the fact that he was from Australia. "Then why," replied Marshall, "don't you go and dig gold among your own mountains? for, what I have heard of that country, I have no doubt whatever that you would find plenty of it there."

"Do you think so, indeed?" inquired Hargraves.

"I do," was the answer.

"If I thought so I would go down there this very autumn," was Hargraves' reply. He went; and with what result, the millions of pounds sterling which have since poured into the British treasury can give the history.

Mr. Hargraves, for this discovery, received from the British Government the sum of £5,000, (or twenty-five thousand dollars,) and from the Australian government £10,000, or $50,000, making $75,000.

Mr. Marshall is almost denied the credit of the discovery, by some unprincipled persons, and his reward from the United States Government is, alas! what? At this very moment wronged of every dollar and every foot of land which he possessed, he would not have, but for the daily charity of comparative strangers, even a cabin in which to lay his head to rest at night— and, is this, kind readers, *gratitude?—our* gratitude? to the man by whose instrumentality a new age—THE GOLDEN AGE—has been inaugurated.

In August last, anxious to obtain an excellent portrait of Mr. Marshall, I journeyed to Coloma for that purpose; and, although Mr. M. cheerfully gave every information in a very simple and straightforward manner concerning the history of the country and of the men who figured in it around Coloma, at an early day, he could not be prevailed upon to allow his likeness to be taken. After returning to this city, a letter was penned to him, urgently asking for it, and the following answer was received, which, while it denies the request, will also show the just bitterness of his spirit at the treatment he has received:—

Coloma, Sept. 5th, 1857.

DEAR SIR:—In reply to your note received three days ago, I wish to say that I feel it a duty I owe to myself to retain my likeness, as it is in fact *all I have that I can call my own*, and I feel like any other poor wretch—I want *something* for self. The sale of it may yet keep me from starving; or, if may buy me a dose of medicine in sickness; or pay for the funeral of a—dog—and such is all that I expect, judging from former kindnesses. I owe the country nothing. The enterprising energy of which the orators and editors of California's early golden days boasted so much, as belonging to Yankeedom, was not national, but individual. Of the profits derived from the enterprise, it stands thus—

Yankeedom,...................$600,000,000
Myself Individually,..........$000,000,000

Ask the records of the country for the reason why; they will answer—I need not. Were I an Englishman, and had made my discovery on English soil, the case would have been different. I send you this in place of the other. Excuse my rudeness in answering you thus.

I remain, most respectfully,

J. W. MARSHALL.

Is this, then, the reward befitting the dignity and gratitude of a great nation and people—like our own—for that discovery which has poured hundreds of millions of wealth into the laps of the people and the treasury of our country; and, in addition to giving us the stability consequent upon the establishment of a metallic currency, (which is the desire and envy of all nations) has spread prosperity across the broad acres of every State in the Union? while *the individual* who has been the cause of this, is allowed almost to starve of hunger and exposure in our mountains! Who, then, is there among us that does not feel his cheek glow with shame at such ungrateful neglect? Let him answer, for he needs our pity. If the Executive ear is closed against a fit reward for such an important service, let you and I, gentle reader, put our hand into our own pocket, and if we find it empty, let us deny ourselves some little luxury, if needs be, that we may yet, in some measure, wipe out the disgraceful stain from our history, by seeing that James W. Marshall, the discoverer of gold in California, has at least a fertile farm which he can call his own, and where he may spend his remaining days in comparative ease,—without the humiliation of dependence upon strangers, after the benefit he has conferred upon our country, and the world.

CHAPTER VII

The Mining Boom
Moves Inland

W HAT A CLOVER FIELD IS TO A STEER, THE SKY TO THE lark, a mudhole to a hog, such are newer diggings to a miner," wrote the *Daily Oregonian* on July 12, 1862,[1] and by that date this irresistible urge had taken California's Argonauts—and many others who followed them more directly to fresh fields—all over the trans-Mississippi West and even up into Canada and Alaska. Nevada and Colorado had become mining territories almost as fabulous as the Golden State itself, and were, for a shorter time and on a smaller scale, experiencing a similar hothouse growth and efflorescence. Miners were also finding the precious metals, though in much smaller quantities, in Oregon and the Washington Territory (resulting in a backwash of population from California, which had stolen so many of the Oregon Country's early immigrants in '49), as well as in Idaho, Montana, and Arizona. These territories were still largely in the hands of the Plains Indians, proud tribes who resented, and reacted to, every advance of the white man, and many a lone prospector or small underguarded party bit the dust and lost their hair at the hands of Sioux, Blackfoot, or Apache war parties, instead of hitting pay dirt and striking it rich, before the inland mining empire became firmly established. But established it was, and new discoveries in the Dakotas, in Utah, and in the center and extreme south of Arizona, as well as the discovery of fresh bonanzas in

1. Quoted in W. J. Trimble: *The Mining Advance into the Inland Empire* (Madison, Wis., 1914), p. 158.

Nevada and Colorado—such as the revival of Virginia City's Comstock boom in the 1870's, and the Cripple Creek rush at the very end of the 1880's—kept the mineral empire expanding, and the roving miners on the move, almost to the end of the century.

Even then some of these old-timers (who had often been boys in their teens in '49, could still heft a pick or at least stake a claim and dream) were off to Dawson City, in the frozen North, and the fabulous Klondike. The Manuel brothers, Fred and Moses, offer a case in point.² Starting off from their home in Minnesota, they reached Montana in 1866 and 1867 respectively, when Moses was only nineteen. Not striking it rich there, they next tried Utah, then thought of going to Arizona but changed their minds and tried their luck in Idaho. "Finding more Indians than gold," they trekked down through the Nevada and eastern California deserts (prospecting all the way) into Arizona. Then, in 1874, Moses went by sea up to British Columbia and the Alaska border and found some gold, but even more cold, at Great Slave Lake. Retreating from the inhospitable climate, he thought he'd try South Africa next (where the Rand was beginning to boom) but was deflected at Portland, Oregon, to the Black Hills of South Dakota. He rejoined his brother in Helena, Montana, then beginning to grow up around the notorious Last Chance Gulch. Pursued by hostile Indians and nearly buried by snowstorms, they made it across Wyoming to the new promised land and started working three claims known as the Homestake, Old Abe (Fred was a Union Army veteran!) and Golden Terra. These they made yield enough to be able to sell them in 1876 for $70,000, $45,000, and $35,000, respectively, to interests connected with the ubiquitous George Hearst (who in these days picked up and threw away mines with almost as much abandon as later his son did newspapers). Fred and Moses then "retired" back to Minnesota with their hard-gotten gains. But the itch was still upon Moses, now an "old-timer" of twenty-nine. He went back to Helena, Montana, and was eventually blown up in a mine explosion in 1905, on the move to the last. Fred took a line of lesser resistance and joined the health seekers in Southern California. Like Wyatt Earp, he died peacefully in his bed at Los Angeles. There is no monument anywhere—except the mine itself, which continues to produce to these discoverers of the Homestake Mine, one of the richest in all the West.

The California Argonauts dispersed to the four winds—wherever they smelled metal—in search of daughter lodes. They were tough and they died hard. Mark Twain has idealized them in a magnificently overwritten epitaph as:

erect, bright-eyed, quick-moving, strong-handed young giants—the strangest population, the finest population, the most gallant host that ever trooped down the startled solitudes of an unpeopled land. And

2. See Rodman Paul: *Mining Frontiers*, pp. 183–5.

where are they now [1871]? Scattered to the ends of the earth—or
prematurely aged and decrepit—or shot or stabbed in street affrays—
or dead of disappointed hopes and broken hearts—all gone, or
nearly all. . . .[3]

Mark Twain was to meet some of the Argonauts, not yet so decrepit
as they were later to become, when he arrived in Carson City, the
territorial capital of Nevada, as "Mr. Secretary's secretary," one
eventful summer's day in 1861. He describes in *Roughing It* how

in 1858 silver lodes were discovered in "Carson County" [then part
of Utah] and then the aspect of things changed. Californians began
to flock in . . . Congress passed a bill to organize "Nevada Territory." At this time the population of the territory was about twelve
to fifteen thousand [about the same as California before the Gold
Rush]. . . . By and by I was smitten with the silver fever. "Prospecting parties" were leaving for the mountains every day, and
discovering and taking possession of rich silver-bearing loads and
ledges of quartz. Plainly this was the road to fortune. The great
"Gould and Curry" mine was held at three or four hundred dollars a
foot when we arrived; but in two months it had sprung up to eight
hundred. . . . The Gould and Curry claim comprised twelve
hundred feet and it all belonged originally to the two men whose
name it bears. Mr. Curry owned two-thirds of it—and he said that
he sold it out for twenty-five hundred dollars in cash, and an old
plug horse that ate up his market value in hay and barley in seventeen days by the watch. And he said that Gould sold out for a pair of
second-hand government blankets and a bottle of whiskey that
killed nine men in three hours, and that an unoffending stranger that
smelled the cork was disabled for life. Four years afterwards the
mine thus disposed of was worth in the San Francisco market
$7,600,000 in gold coin.[4]

Even more fabulous than the Gould and Curry mine was the
Comstock. Indeed, Comstock was the name given not only to one
famous mine but also to a whole mining area. It is ironic that the
man after whom this immensely rich lode was named was himself
just a claim-jumper on it, though others were to benefit from his
claim far more than either he or the original discoverers. He was to

3. *Roughing It* (1871; Signet Classics edn., New York, 1962), pp. 309–10.
4. Twain (1962 edn.), pp. 146–7, 242.

die a failure and by suicide years later in Montana, once again in search of the crock of gold that had eluded him in Nevada. Henry Thomas Paige Comstock's story has been superlatively told by "Dan de Quille" (William Wright) in probably the best and certainly best-known contemporary account of the Nevada mining boom, *The Big Bonanza:*[5]

> In the evening of the day on which the grand discovery was made by O'Riley and McLaughlin, H. T. P. Comstock made his appearance upon the scene.
>
> "Old Pancake," who was then looking after his Gold Hill mines, which were beginning to yield largely, had strolled northward up the mountain, toward evening, in search of a mustang pony that he had out prospecting for a living among the hills. He had found his pony, had mounted him, and, with his long legs dragging the tops of the sagebrush, came riding up just as the lucky miners were making the last clean-up of their rockers for the day.
>
> Comstock, who had a keen eye for all that was going on in the way of mining in any place he might visit, saw at a glance the unusual quantity of gold that was in sight.
>
> When the gold caught his eye, he was off the back of his pony in an instant. He was soon down in the thick of it all—"hefting" and running his fingers through the gold, and picking into and probing the mass of strange-looking "stuff" exposed.
>
> Conceiving at once that a wonderful discovery of some kind had been made, "Old Pancake" straightened himself up, as he arose from a critical examination of the black mass in the cut wherein he had observed the glittering spangles of gold, and coolly proceeded to inform the astonished miners that they were working on ground that belonged to him.
>
> He asserted that he had some time before taken up 160 acres of land at this point, for a ranch; also that he owned the water they were using in mining, it being from the Caldwell spring, in what was afterwards known as Spanish Ravine.
>
> Suspecting that they were working in a decomposed quartz vein, McLaughlin and O'Riley had written out and posted up a notice, calling for a claim of 300 feet for each and a third claim for

5. *The Big Bonanza: An Authentic Account of the Discovery, History and Working of the World-Renowned Comstock Lode of Nevada* . . . (Hartford, Conn., 1876); ed. Oscar Lewis (repr. with orig. illus., New York, 1947), pp. 25-7.

the discovery, which extra claim they were entitled to under the mining laws.

Having soon ascertained all this from the men before him, Comstock would have "none of it." He boisterously declared that they should not work there at all unless they would agree to locate himself and his friend Manny (Emmanuel) Penrod in the claim. In case he and Penrod were given an interest, there should be no further trouble about the ground.

Comstock discovering silver, 1859. From Dan De Quille: *The Big Bonanza* (Hartford, Conn., 1876).

After consulting together, the discoverers concluded that, rather than have a great row about the matter, they would put the names of Comstock and Penrod in their notice of location.

This being arranged to his satisfaction, Comstock next demanded that one hundred feet of ground on the lead should be segregated and given to Penrod and himself for the right to the water they were using—he stoutly asserting that he owned not only the land, but also the water, and, as they had recognized his right to the land, they could not consistently ignore his claim to the water flowing upon it. In short, he talked so loudly and so much about his water-right that he at last got the hundred feet, segregated, as he demanded. This hundred feet afterwards became the Spanish or Mexican mine, and yielded millions of dollars.

De Quille's account of Comstock's later misfortunes is in the vintage style of the man who gave Mark Twain his basic training as a reporter:

After Comstock's wife ran away with the strolling miner he thought best to let her continue on her travels unmolested. He opened a store at Carson City with the money received for his mining interests in Virginia City and also had a branch store at Silver City, a town on Gold Canyon, about three miles below Gold Hill, which was laid out in the summer of 1859.

He soon broke up in the mercantile line, losing everything. He trusted everybody—all went to his stores and purchased goods without money and without price, and at last his old friends the Piute Indians came in and carried away the remnants. Comstock made them all happy, male and female, by passing out to them armfuls of red blankets and calico of brilliant hues.

His stock in the Carson store was as good as was seen in most trading establishments of the kind at that day, but his Silver City branch never amounted to much, the stock consisting principally, as the miners said, of blue cotton overalls, pick-handles, rusty bacon, "nigger" shoes, and "dog-leg" tobacco.

After losing all of his property Comstock left Nevada and went to Idaho and Montana, through which countries he wandered and prospected for some years, always hoping that some day he would come upon a second Comstock lode. He was always ready to join every expedition that was fitted out to explore new regions, as the "big thing" seemed to him to be ever just ahead.

In 1870 he joined the Big Horn expedition in Montana, and this was his last undertaking. When near Bozeman City, on September 27, 1870, he committed suicide by shooting himself in the head with his revolver. The Montana papers said it was supposed that he committed the act while laboring under temporary aberration of mind, and this was doubtless the case, as his was by no means a sound or well-balanced brain.[6]

6. *The Big Bonanza*, p. 48. The whole of Ch. ix (pp. 45–8) is hilariously devoted—apart from its unhappy ending—to "Comstock's Matrimonial Venture." Old Pancake literally *bought* his wife from a Mormon, who found her surplus to

In his later years Comstock wrote a long and somewhat lugu-brious autobiographical letter, which was published in part in the St. Louis *Republican*, giving a well-edited version of how he discovered and then lost the Comstock Lode. Here is the middle part of that letter, as reproduced in *The Big Bonanza* (pp. 50–1):

Riley and McLaughlin were working for me at the time of the Ophir discovery. I carved the cut in and went after my party to take up the lead and form my company. Manny Penrod, Peter Riley, Patrick McLaughlin, "Kentuck," or Osborne, and myself formed a company. With my party I opened the lead, and called it Comstock lode; that is the way they came by their interests; I gave it to them.

We started to rocking with my water; had only a small quantity to rock with. We made from five to ten and twelve pounds a day, and the dust was from $9 to $12 an ounce—went that at Brewster's bank, Placerville, California, where I did my business.

I continued owning the claim, locating 1,400 feet out for myself, for the use of my water to the company. I also located the Savage claim; showed the ground to old man Savage. I located the Gould & Curry—went into the valley and got old Daddy Curry to come down, and put him in possession of it.

I also owned the Hale & Norcross, and kept Norcross for a year to work in that ground. I also owned the principal part in Gold Hill and leased it out to Walsh and Woodruff—leased to them 950 for 760—don't now remember which. Now I will tell you how I sold it; it has never been told as it ought to be told throughout the United States for my benefit, and it shall be.

Sandy Bowers, I gave him his claim of 20 feet in Gold Hill. Bill Knight, I gave him his claim; Joe Plato, I gave him his. Joe is dead now, and his widow is awful rich.

I was working this claim, the Ophir, and taking out a good deal of ore; I did not know what the ore was worth, being in the wilderness then, with no road to get out or into from California. It

---

requirements, in return for "a horse, a revolver and sixty dollars," and he demanded and received a regular bill of sale. She soon ran away from him with a "seductive youth of the town," but Comstock offered $100 reward for her apprehension, which was won by a "dead-broke" Placerville miner. "By practising eternal vigilance Comstock managed to keep his wife that winter, but in the spring . . . she ran away with a long-legged miner . . . finally [she] came to anchor in a lager-beer cellar in Sacramento."

was an awful wilderness! I took several tons of the ore and transported it by ox-teams, to best advantage, through the mountains of California, and Judge Walsh was my agent and helped me.

Now during this time I was taking out large gold and silver specimens, and took one specimen, weighing 12 pounds, and boxed it up and ordered it sent to Washington City. I instructed John Musser, a lawyer at Washoe, to send it; I don't know whether it ever reached there or not. I wanted Congress to see it, and the President, for it was the first gold and silver ore mixed ever found in the United States.

I went on working, and Judge Walsh and Woodruff were there for two months, trying every day to buy me out. My health being bad I sold the claim to them on these terms: I was to get $10,000, and did get it at last; and I was to receive one-eleventh of all that ever came out of the claim during my natural life, and at my death was to will it to whoever I pleased; also, to receive $100 per month.

That was the contract; and two men, Elder Bennett and Manny Penrod, witnessed it; but my health was bad, and before I had the contract of sale recorded, Woodruff and Walsh sold it out. Having taken no lien on the property, I never got a dollar, from that day to this, except what was at first received.

I am a regular born mountaineer, and did not know the intrigues of civilized rascality. I am not ashamed to acknowledge that. Well, I had a store in Carson City and was lying in the back room sick and helpless. I told Ed. Belcher to take all my papers, and the contract between Judge Walsh and Woodruff and myself, and put them under my pillow. I could speak, but couldn't help myself a bit. They all said I would die, and said: "Boys, let's pitch in and help ourselves!" And they did pitch in; and I never saw the papers afterwards. And the Gold Hill I leased to Walsh and Woodruff; and then Frink and Kincaid got it, and I never got anything for it; and the 160 acres of ground on which Virginia City is built is my old recorded ranche. I used to raise all my potatoes and vegetables on it, and had the Indians do the work for me.

Virginia City was first called Silver City. I named it at the time I gave the Ophir claim its name. Old Virginia and the other boys got on a drunk one night there, and Old Virginia fell down and broke his bottle, and when he got up he said he baptized that ground Virginia—hence Virginia City.

So much for H. T. P. Comstock and his lode of mischief! "Old Virginia" was an equally colorful character and came to an equally violent end. Says De Quille (pp. 52–3):

James Fennimore, better known as James Finney and familiarly called "Old Virginia" by all the old settlers of Washoe, he being a native of the state of Virginia, came to the mines on Gold Canyon in 1851. He came from the Kern River country, California, where he had a "difficulty" with a man and, believing he had killed him, took a little walk across the Sierra Nevada Mountains, dropping the name of Fennimore and calling himself James Finney.

Although fond of the bottle, Old Virginia was by no means a loafer. He had his sprees, but these were generally followed by seasons of great activity.

He was very fond of hunting, and when not engaged in mining or prospecting he was ranging the mountains and valleys in search of deer, antelope, and mountain sheep. He was interested in nearly all the enterprises of the early Johntown and Gold Hill mines, but missed being in the Ophir at the time of the discovery of silver, having sold his interest in the Six-mile Canyon diggings the previous season.

He was killed in the town of Dayton, in July 1861, by being thrown from a "bucking" mustang that he was trying to ride while a good deal under the influence of liquor. He was pitched head-first upon the ground, suffered a fracture of the skull, and died in a few hours. At the time of his death he was possessed of about $3,000 in coin and had been talking of returning soon to his native state.

An old Piute brave who had known both Comstock and Fennimore pronounced a joint epitaph on them to De Quille (p. 53):

"Hoss kill um Ole Biriginey, Comstock he kill heself. Comstock owe me fifty-five dollar; old Birginey owe me forty-five dollar! Me think . . . maybe both too much whisky."

Though the first discoverers failed to make great fortunes out of them, the western Nevada mines proved to be enormously rich. Between 1859 and 1869 about a hundred million dollars' worth of gold and silver—the latter constituting two thirds of this—was extracted from them, but by the late sixties their productivity was beginning to decrease. The Comstock Lode produced 16½ million dollars' worth of precious metals in 1867 alone, but only 8 million dollars' worth in 1869, while, it was estimated, the Ophir mine "has taken out thirteen millions of dollars, but used it nearly all up in expenditures, and probably not returned to the stockholders so much as they have paid in."[7] But it was George Hearst's one-sixth share in the Ophir mine, acquired in 1859, that brought him his first fortune, and people like Judge Walsh and Almarin B. Paul also did very well out of coming to Washoe in '59 and buying out Comstock and Company. The first ten years of production, however, and the fortunes made therein, constituted only a small bonanza beside the Big Bonanza of 1873 and the following years, when the Comstock Lode, recapitalized, exploited by new and more scientific methods, and benefiting from the completion of the transcontinental and feeder railroads, became "the richest spot in the world,"[8] making men like John Mackay, William Ralston, William Sharon, James Fair, James Flood, Samuel Curtis, William O'Brien, and J. P. Jones as rich, every one of them, as Croesus.[9]

The four Bonanza Kings, comparable to the Big Four of California, were Mackay, Fair, Flood, and O'Brien. They all came via California and were of Irish extraction. Mackay was born in Dublin, and had been a ship's carpenter, while Fair was born in Ulster, but they always worked very closely together. "The pair generally hold a grand council on all matters of moment. When this council is in session at the private office of the works [of the Consolidated Virginia and California mining companies] the miners, in passing back and forth, hold up their fingers to one another as a sign that no noise is to be made . . ."[1] The silences of John Mackay and of James G. Fair were worth about $50,000 a day at the height of the

7. Samuel Bowles: *Our New West* (Hartford, Conn., 1869), p. 289.

8. The title of Ch. lxiv, *The Big Bonanza.*

9. "Although Mr. Mackay is now [1876] worth fifty or sixty million dollars, yet like Mr. Fair [worth $30 or $40 million], he spends much of his time, when at Virginia City, in the lower levels. Almost every morning at six o'clock he descends into one or another of his mines," says De Quille (p. 398), who makes Mackay the hero of his book, even dedicating it to this "Prince of Miners and 'Boss' of the Big Bonanza." Unlike so many of the mineral nabobs, Mackay remained unspoiled and unassuming. It remained for his ambitious wife and extravagant children to discover the primrose path. His granddaughter, Ellen Mackay, married the famous song writer Irving Berlin. Mackay himself lived until 1902, and after his death his business manager told the press: "I don't suppose he knew within twenty millions what he was worth."

1. De Quille, p. 401.

Big Bonanza. A dividend of $10 per share, or over a million dollars, was being paid *every month* after all mining expenses had been met. "Out of the first bonanza, into the top of which O'Riley and McLaughlin luckily struck their picks, was taken about $20,000,000 before the deposit was exhausted; out of the consolidated Virginia Mine alone has already been taken $15,500,000 and as yet [1876] they have hardly begun working in real earnest."[2] Peter and Pat's celebrated water hole of 1859 was only about four feet deep; the Big Bonanza of 1873 had to be worked 1,500 feet below the surface, and Fair estimated the cost of mining and milling as high as $17 per ton of ore. But it was worth between $100 and $200 a ton, so why worry!

Eventually the Comstock Lode was to produce over 300 million dollars' worth of ore (between 1859 and 1880), and the Virginia City and Gold Hill area became "an industrial suburb of California and particularly of San Francisco."[3] The boom city that Dana had beheld with eyes of wonder in 1859 boomed again, after California's own gold rush had petered out, under this shower of Comstock gold and silver. Had he returned again, in 1883, after another twenty-four years, the author of *Two Years before the Mast* would once more not have recognized San Francisco. The mansions of the rich, no longer festooned around George Gordon's elegant South Park,[4] were climbing to the crest of "Nob Hill" (on California Street) in ever-increasing grandeur. There the Fair and Flood mansions were beginning to look even the ornate palaces of "Boss" Crocker and Leland Stanford in the eye. Among lesser men, great wealth was no longer rare in this true "City of Gold." Joseph L. King, chairman of the San Francisco Stock and Exchange Board for many years, once remarked in all seriousness: "Prior to the Civil War, extremely wealthy men in California were not so numerous . . . and one could name our millionaires on his

2. De Quille, p. 380.   3. Paul: *Mining Frontiers*, p. 56.

4. Conceived by George Gordon, an English forty-niner, who brought George H. Goddard, the architect of the Holland Park Estate in London, out to design and develop South Park. South Park's houses no longer exist, but Mount Goddard in the High Sierras, which was named after him, constitutes a more enduring monument to their architect. Dr. Albert Shumate, past president of the California Historical Society, is engaged on a study of Gordon's South Park, the buildings of which strikingly resembled those of the Holland Park Estate. Unlike Holland House itself, the estate survived the bombs of the London blitz almost intact.

finger ends. Men possessing $100,000 were considered well off, while a $50,000 citizen was always addressed with the prefix of 'Mister.' "[5] To be called Mister after the wealth of the Big Bonanza hit town, one presumably had to be worth at least a million!

The whole of Nevada (mushroomed into a State of the Union in 1864) has had a smaller population at all times—in 1859, in 1883, and also in 1959—than the city of San Francisco at the same dates. Every advance of the Western mining frontier increased the fortunes of San Francisco's already rich "Misters," lent prestige to the city's mint and its stock exchange, and expanded its port facilities. San Francisco was not only the principal outlet for all this wealth (though after 1869 some of it was transferred East via the new transcontinental railroad), but also the main source of the capital increasingly needed to keep the mines working productively and to develop new ones.

In the sixties and seventies everybody tried to visit Virginia City and many people wrote books about it, whether they were local chroniclers (Twain, De Quille, John Hittell), Easterners (Horace Greeley, Samuel Bowles, Henry Villard), or Europeans (Sir Richard Burton, Charles Dilke). Dilke, fresh down from Cambridge and on a world tour that was to produce his influential book *Greater Britain* (1869), to help spearhead his country's revived interest in empire, wrote:

> To see Virginia City and Carson since I first heard their fame in New York had been with me a passion. . . . Virginia City has passed through its second period—that of "vigilance committees" and "historic trees"—and is entering the third, the stage of churches and "city officers" or police.
>
> The population is still a shifting one. A by-law of the municipality tells us that the "permanent population" consists of those who reside more than a month within the city. At this moment [autumn 1867] the miners are pouring into Washoe from Montana, from Arizona and from Utah, coming from the gayeties of the largest mining city, to spend their money during the short fierce winter.[6]

"From Montana, from Arizona and from Utah . . ." The mining frontiers of the Far West were already extended far be-

5. *History of the San Francisco Stock and Exchange Board* (San Francisco, 1910), pp. 256-7; quoted in Paul: *Mining Frontiers*, p. 57.

6. Vol. I (London and Philadelphia, 1869), p. 166.

yond the Mother Lode and the Comstock by the middle sixties. Halfway across Nevada, in the middle of nowhere, Samuel Bowles, journeying by stagecoach in the party of Schuyler Carfax, later Vice-President of the United States, in the summer of 1865, found

Virginia City, Nevada. From *Harper's Magazine*.

the most representative mining town we had yet seen. . . . Beginning in 1863, Austin had in a year's time a population of six to eight thousand, fell away in 1865 to four thousand, and now probably has no more than three thousand. Its houses are built anywhere, everywhere, and then the streets get to them as best they can; one side of a house will be four stories, the other one or two,—such is the lay of the land; not a tree, not a flower, not a blade of green grass anywhere in town; but the boot-blacks and baths and barbers are of European standards; it has a first-class French restaurant and a daily newspaper; the handsomest woman, physically, I ever saw presided, with almost comic queenliness, over one of its lager beer saloons; gambling went on openly, amid music, in the area of every "saloon"

—miners risking to this chance at night the proceeds of the scarcely less doubtful chance of the day; while the generally cultivated and classical tone of the town may be inferred from this advertisement in the daily paper:—

"Mammoth Lager Beer Saloon, in the basement, corner Main and Virginia streets, Austin, Nevada. Choice liquors, wines, lager beer and cigars, served by pretty girls, who understand their business and attend to it. Votaries of Bacchus, Gambrinus, Venus or Cupid can spend an evening agreeably at the Mammoth Saloon."[7]

Teaming in Washoe. From Dan De Quille: *The Big Bonanza* (1876).

Reaching Virginia City a little earlier than Dilke, Bowles also discerned signs that this once wild mining camp—"the 'cussedest' town in the States, its citizens expecting 'a dead man for breakfast' every day," as Dilke had put it—was beginning to settle down:

We found in Virginia, the original "Washoe" of mining history, many contrasts to and improvements upon Austin. It is three or four years older; it puts its gambling behind an extra door; it is beginning to recognize the Sabbath, has many churches open, and closes part of its stores on that day; is exceedingly well built, in large proportion with solid brick stores and warehouses; and though the fast and fascinating times of 1862–63 are over, when it held from fifteen to twenty thousand people, and Broadway and Wall street were not more crowded than its streets, and there are tokens that its great mines are nearly dug out, it still has the air of permanence and of profit, and contains a population of seven or eight thousand, besides the adjoining town or extension of Gold Hill, which has about three thousand more.

7. *Our New West*, p. 279.

The situation of Virginia is very picturesque; above the canyon or ravine, it is spread along the mountain side, like the roof of a house, about half way to the top. Directly above rises a noble peak, fifteen hundred feet higher than the town, itself about six thousand feet high; below stretches the foot-hill, bisected by the ravine; around on all sides, sister hills rise in varying hights, rich in roundness and other forms of beauty, but brown in barrenness, as if shorn for prize fight, and fading out into distant plain, with a sweet green spot to mark the rare presence of water and vendure.[8]

For a whole decade, from 1865 to 1874, the Comstock Lode was, as the miners put it, in "borrasca," or clouded over. But the clear sky of the biggest bonanza of all was just around the corner. The shares of the Consolidated Virginia Mine, organized by Washoe's new Big Four out of several earlier workings that were now considered to be worthless by other mining experts, stood at $1 each in 1870 but had skyrocketed to $700 by 1875. That was when the mine was bringing in $50,000 a day. Dividends of nearly $75 million were paid by the company between 1875 and 1881.[9] Then the skies clouded over again for Virginia City, this time for good. The 38-million-dollar production of the Comstock Lode in 1875 fell to less than a million and a half dollars in 1881. As early as 1878, unemployment among the Washoe miners had become a serious problem and they began to drift away like Comstock capital. The Comstock skills and mining know-how were to be exported all over the United States—indeed, all over the world. But in 1880 the population of Virginia City was still over 15,000 (a figure it had first reached as early as 1863), compared with a peak figure of 20,000 in 1875. It never did quite become a ghost town, and by the time of its centennial in 1959 it had been rescued from oblivion by tourism, perhaps for an even more unpleasant fate.[1]

8. *Our New West*, pp. 280–1.

9. G. H. Smith: *The History of the Comstock Lode, 1850–1920* (Reno, Nev., 1943), p. 259; quoted in Paul: *Mining Frontiers*, p. 80. Smith's figures are more reliable, as well as more up to date, than those in E. Lord: *Comstock Mining and Miners* (Washington, D. C., 1883); ed. D. F. Myrick (repr. Berkeley, Calif., 1959).

1. As a not-so-venerable fossil, presided and tinseled over until recently by a pair of bizarre entrepreneurs of by-gone glamour, Lucius Beebe and Charles Clegg, two somewhat incandescent refugees from the bright lights of Broadway, and co-authors of *Virginia and Truckee* (Stanford, Calif., 1950) and *Legends of the Comstock Lode* (Oxford, 1957). These are works to enliven an idle hour

For obvious reasons, the mining rush into western Nevada from 1858 on was from the West. Not so the almost simultaneous rush into the Colorado Rockies. This came mainly across the Plains from the Middle West and the East, and therefore contained a much higher proportion of greenhorns, though most of the early discoveries were made by seasoned miners, and Horace Greeley[2] reckoned that three out of every ten participants in the Pike's Peak gold rush had previously worked in California.

The Colorado Rockies were virtually uninhabited in 1858; the Indians whose hunting grounds they were still lived in the Stone Age and would have had little use for precious metals had they found any; the mountain men who roamed its slopes and found the way through its passes were after beaver, not gold. But a whole new profession, that of prospector, had been created by the California experience since 1848—men who sought to locate new mines rather than exploit them, and who were willing to take quick and moderate payments for their claims, as has been seen in Nevada. A member of the fraternity, one W. G. Russell, a disappointed forty-niner who had returned, still not rich, to his native Georgia, organized a party to prospect the Pike's Peak region in the summer of 1858. On Cherry Creek, near its confluence with the South Platte, considerably to the north of Pike's Peak itself, they found small quantities of placer gold. As this was not enough to satisfy them, they moved on, prospecting the eastern slopes of the Rocky Mountains, all the way to what is now Wyoming. But travelers' tales exaggerated their successes, and the newspapers of the Midwest, which was still stagnant economically as a result of the Panic of 1857, filled their columns and spread their headlines with stories of A NEW ELDORADO IN KANSAS TERRITORY. After a winter of feverish preparation, about a hundred thousand gold seekers, nearly all of them greenhorns, started to rush across the Plains from Kansas City, Independence, Omaha, and many other assembly points as soon as the snow was off the prairie. Meanwhile, Russell's party had returned to winter on Cherry Creek, where they met a party from Lawrence, Kansas, which had also found

---

rather than to pore over seriously, for while there is no harm, neither is there much good in them, or for that matter in the other enterprises of this *Ersatz* Twain. Beebe's very readable last work was *The Big Spenders* (New York, 1966).

2. *An Overland Journey from New York to San Francisco in the Summer of 1859* (New York, 1860), p. 15.

but little gold, and the two groups turned to the frustrated frontiersman's favorite off-season pastime, the laying out of town lots and the creation of metropolises on paper. Denver and Aurora—one might as well have gold in the name even if there was none in the creek—were laid out, as were two other more ephemeral cities near where Cherry Creek and the South Platte converged. When the fifty-niners began to swarm in the following spring, they found plenty of real estate but no gold awaiting them. Of the hundred thousand who started out, it is reckoned that one half never even arrived, having turned back discouraged by those returning from Pike's Peak (or thereabouts) "busted." Of those who did reach the region, half had left again before the end of 1859. If this was the greatest fiasco in American gold-rush history, it was not without its good effects: a hitherto entirely unpopulated area did acquire a population of about 25,000 in one year, and those who failed at mining, real-estate dealing, and politics[3] could turn to the ever-present last resort of agriculture, for, unlike most parts of the California and Nevada mountains, the Eastern Rockies contained many fertile high valleys—like the remarkable series of "parks" the mountain men had used and Ruxton and Frémont had so eloquently described—while the Plains just to the east of them, including the Cherry Creek-South Platte area itself, were level and ready for the plow.

While the empire builders of Cherry Creek wrote prospectuses and banged gavels in their winterized log cabins, an experienced "miner-forty-niner" named George A. Jackson went out and found gold in usable quantities in January 1859 at Chicago

3. Politics was the third largest industry in early Colorado—long before the territory had even acquired that name—and a perfect pastime for the short, cold winter days and colder, longer winter evenings of 1858-9. When the Cherry Creek settlements had no more than a hundred inhabitants, these elected thirty-five delegates to petition Congress for Territorial status. By the spring of 1859 their ambition had grown to the extent of proclaiming themselves "the State of Jefferson." An unsympathetic Congress kept them waiting until 1861 even for territorial status, and until 1876 for statehood, but there was no harm in trying. It was his observation of the situation in Colorado at this time that prompted Albert D. Richardson, in his entertaining *Beyond the Mississippi* (Hartford, Conn., 1867), p. 77, to coin the often quoted aphorism: "Congregate a hundred Americans anywhere beyond the settlements and they immediately lay out a city and apply for admission into the Union, while twenty-five of them become candidates for the United States Senate." This was almost literally true of the settlers along Cherry Creek in 1858. See further W. and W. H. H. Larimer: *Reminiscences of General William Larimer and His Son* . . . (Lancaster, Pa., 1918), passim.

Creek, but kept it dark until April. Meanwhile, John H. Gregory —another far-ranging Georgian—hiked in mid-winter up the nearby north branch of Clear Creek, also west of Denver, and, by early spring (just when the earliest would-be Argonauts of '59 were catching their first glimpse of Pike's Peak), had really struck it rich in a quartz vein, on May 6. He panned out nearly a thousand dollars' worth of gold in a few days. True footloose prospector that he was, Gregory sold out his claim quickly for a mere $21,000 and disappeared from history.[4] But, unknown to the elusive Gregory, "angels" were hovering around his head that still chilly May day in 1859, and as these angels included such well-known Eastern journalists as Horace Greeley, Henry Villard, and Albert D. Richardson, all of whom descended on Gregory Gulch and unleashed their goose quills in June, the resultant publicity was enormous. Though their books took some time to appear—Greeley's and Villard's in 1860, Richardson's[5] not until 1867—their articles were in print within weeks of their visit, and they dropped their rivalry to combine in a remarkable and enthusiastic joint statement[6] that materially helped to turn the ebb tide back from Colorado in '59 into a real California-style gold rush during the latter half of the year.

The Gregory diggings did not turn out to be very rich and were soon exhausted, but their discovery set men, with renewed hope, prospecting all over the eastern slopes of the Colorado Rockies, and, before the year was out, a number of other equally promising strikes had been made. Colorado's mineral "belt" was found to be almost as extensive, though by no means as rich (gold was never found in the profusion of that at Mariposa, for instance), as the Mother Lode of California, and stretched about 200 miles northeast (in Boulder County) to southwest (in San Juan County), as far east as South Park,[7] and as far west as the upper Colorado River.

4. For the little that is known of him, see C. Bancroft: "The Illusive Figure of John H. Gregory, Discoverer of the First Gold Lode in Colorado," *Colorado Magazine*, XX (1943), 121–35.

5. See further Bibliographic Note below, p. 432.

6. Repr. in LeRoy R. Hafen: *Colorado Gold Rush Contemporary Letters and Reports, 1858–59* (Glendale, Calif., 1941), pp. 376–82.

7. Said Samuel Bowles (*Our New West*, p. 187), who prayed that it would not be done, for he loved the place: "An intelligent investigator of the subject tells me that the whole of South Park would pay three to four dollars a day for the

Colorado's gold attracted an inordinate number of people, considering that only 25 million dollars' worth was taken out in the decade of 1858–67. The best years were 1862 and 1863, with nearly 3½ million dollars' worth each, while 1864 to 1868 were slump years, in which people seeped away again from the mines and from the territory as a whole. The population of Colorado, over 34,000 in 1860, was only 39,000 by 1870, a mere net gain of 5,000; it has been estimated that fully sixty per cent of the territory's immigrants of the sixties failed to stay there. Even Denver, the supply metropolis of the local mining areas, had only 4,759 inhabitants by 1870. Samuel Bowles, an acute first-hand observer of Colorado's recession of the middle sixties, wrote of the territory as having been saved by agriculture, though he discerned an upward turn in her mining fortunes by 1868:

When we first visited the country, in 1865, the original era of speculation, of waste, of careless and unintelligent work, and as little of it as possible, of living by wit instead of labor, of reliance upon eastern capital instead of home industry, was, if not at its hight, still reigning, but with signs of decay and threatening despair. In the next two years, 1866 and 1867, affairs became desperate; the population shrunk; mines were abandoned; mills stopped; eastern capital, tired of waiting for promised returns, dried up its fountains; and the secrets of the rich ores seemed unfathomable. Residents, who could not get away, were put to their trumps for a living; and economy and work were enforced upon all. Thus weeded out, thus stimulated, the population fell back on the certainties; such mining as was obviously remunerative was continued; the doubtful and losing abandoned; the old and simple dirt washing for gold was resumed, and followed with more care; and farming rose in respectability and promise. The discovery and opening of specially rich silver mines near Georgetown kept hope and courage alive, and freshened speculation in a new quarter; but the main fact of the new era was that the people went to work, became self-reliant, and, believing that they "had a good thing" out there, undertook to prove it to the world by intelligent and economic industry.

---

labor of washing it over." This may well have been true, for an old-timer, on a wager, panned enough gold to pay for drinks all around out of the dust in the main street of Dutch Flat, Calif., just outside the old gold-rush-period hotel, in 1963, over 110 years after the gold rush there.

These were the kernel years of Colorado; they proved her; they have made her. Her gold product went down, probably, to say a million dollars, in each of 1866 and 1867; but it began at once, under the new order of things, to rise; and agriculture also at once shot up and ahead, and directly assumed, as it has in California, the place of the first interest, the great wealth. No more flour, no more corn, no more potatoes at six cents to twelve cents a pound freight, from the Missouri River; in one year Colorado became self-supporting in food; in the second an exporter, the feeder of Montana, the contractor for the government posts and the Pacific Railroad; and now, in the third year (1868), with food cheaper than in "the States," she forces the Mississippi and Missouri valleys to keep their produce at home or send it East. She feeds the whole line of the Pacific Railroad this side the Continental Divide, and has even been sending some of her vegetables to Omaha. Her gold and silver product ran up to at least two millions in 1868, got out at a profit of from twenty-five to fifty per cent, and is certainly to be at least three millions in 1869. Her agricultural products were near twice as much, certainly three millions for 1868, and perhaps four millions; though it is difficult to make as certain estimates in this particular, and the Indians worked great mischief with the ingathering of the crops the past fall.[8]

The perspicacious and well-informed Bowles (as befitted a vice-presidential adviser and public relations man in the Age of Johnson) had already discerned that silver as well as agriculture might come to the rescue of Colorado. He was proved right, for by 1874 the annual value of her silver production exceeded $3 million and had passed that of her gold. Though her older and most prosperous mining camps, such as Georgetown and Central City, continued to produce silver as well as gold ("indeed, there is silver in all the gold ores and gold in all the silver ores of the State," wrote Bowles), but at increasing cost as more and more expensive ore-crushing and separating machinery was introduced, her most spectacular silver mines were not opened up until 1877, when Leadville, well to the south of most of the other diggings, began to boom as soon as a smelter was established there by a German-trained metallurgist named August Meyer, and jumped in size in eighteen months from a tiny hamlet to a large city. By 1880 it had nearly 15,000 inhabitants, twenty-eight miles of streets, and an

8. *Our New West*, pp. 179–81.

opera house, and had been reached by the railroad (via the Arkansas Valley). Only Denver, with over 35,000 inhabitants (nearly
a tenfold increase during the decade and now the state capital), was
larger. Leadville's phenomenal prosperity was floated on a sea of
silver, and it soon took the title of America's chief silver-producing
center away from Virginia City and Gold Hill. Leadville's silver

Chestnut Street, Leadville. From Frank Fossett: *Colorado: Its gold and
silver mines* (New York, 1879).

production, worth $2 million in 1878, rose to $9½ million in 1879
and $11½ million in 1880. The area also produced lead (worth
nearly $2 million in 1879), copper, and zinc, and its richness in these
baser metals was to carry its prosperity on even into the twentieth
century. The silver princes of Leadville's heyday surpassed in pic-
turesqueness, if not in out-and-out wealth, the big four of the Big
Bonanza. H. A. W. Tabor, a semi-illiterate miner, who bought
himself an actress ("Baby Doll" eventually became his second wife,
and survived in reduced circumstances until 1935), an opera house
for her to perform in, and a seat in the U. S. Senate for his own
performances, was the most fabulous of these, but the Dexters and
the Healys ran the Tabors close. And all this happened over 10,000
feet above sea level!

Leadville put Colorado back on the map as a leading producer of precious metals, but it was Cripple Creek, on the western slopes of Pike's Peak, that kept her there. Not until 1890 was its gold first found, but thenceforward it almost literally poured out, and "Cripple Creek became Eldorado, a miniature California with modern conveniences,"[9] including (by 1894) the telephone, electric light and power, and two railroads. By this time it had a population of 10,000 and was still growing fast. This was a very sophisticated gold rush indeed: even its *demi-monde* arrived (by Pullman) straight from Paris.

After 1894, gold "attained an overwhelming primacy"[1] over silver in Colorado, production during the decade 1895–1904 totalling $229 million. By the year 1897 Colorado was producing more gold annually than California. The production of silver had dropped spectacularly after its virtual demonetization, and the repeal of the Sherman Act[2] in 1893 had both curbed domestic demand and lowered its price. It was down to under $7 million by 1905, compared with over $23 million in Colorado's best silver year. But the state entered the twentieth century as America's top producer of the two precious metals combined, and accounted for one third of the country's total production. It was still possible to say in 1910, over fifty years after the Pike's Peak gold rush and the strike at Gregory's Gulch, that "Colorado is pre-eminently a mining region, and to this fact it owes its colonization."[3]

The biggest bonanzas of California, Nevada, and Colorado were nowhere matched in the other states and territories of the Union, but this was not for want of trying, especially in Montana, Idaho, Utah, Arizona, New Mexico, and, finally, the Dakotas. For brief spells the gold or silver mines in one or the other of these regions topped the production of the Big Three, as when the Boise Basin of Idaho alone did better than all of Colorado between 1863 and 1866.[4] Idaho's mining frontier moved rapidly southward from the first discoveries on the Clearwater River in 1860 to the Salmon

9. Paul: *Mining Frontiers*, pp. 132–3.

1. Article on "Colorado" in *Encyclopaedia Britannica*, 11th edn. (1910), VI, 720.

2. An act forced through Congress by the "silver bloc" in 1890, under which the U. S. government had to purchase 4½ million ounces of silver a month at a fixed ratio of 16 ounces of silver to 1 ounce of gold.

3. *Encyclopaedia Britannica* (11th edn.), VI, 720.

4. *U. S. Geological Survey for 1896–1897*, P. III, p. 655; cited in Paul, p. 139.

River valley in 1861 and then to the Boise Basin in 1862. Mining camps like Oro Fino and Florence lived and died in rapid succession during these years, for "the miners of Idaho were like quicksilver," who "ran after any atom of gold in their vicinity."[5] As the Boise Basin contained the most gold, they stayed there longest, and by the summer of 1864, its population was over 16,000. The relative inaccessibility of these Idaho mining camps, especially from the east, tended to make them the resort of the roughest and toughest elements from the California, Nevada, and Oregon territories' fields. "Before these adventurers, now eastbound and no longer facing west, there arose the vast and formidable mountain ranges which in their time had daunted even the calm minds of Meriwether Lewis and William Clark. But the prospectors and the pack-trains alike penetrated the Salmon River range. . . . Here the indomitable packer from the West, conquering unheard-of difficulties, brought in whiskey, women, pianos, food, mining tools. Naturally all these commanded fabulous prices. The price for each and all lay underfoot . . ." says the inimitable Emerson Hough.[6] Life was short as well as brutish in Oro Fino, Florence, Placerville, Centreville, and Boise City in those days, and by the mix-sixties the survivors had begun to move on to new eldorados, reputedly far richer. By 1870 the bloom was off the Boise Basin. "The decline in the production of Idaho is due to the exhaustion of the creek and gulch claims of the older placer-mining districts of the Boise Basin. The greater portion of these claims have been turned over to Chinamen, who are content with small earnings and who will maintain, no doubt for many years to come, a moderately productive industry in these abandoned fields," wrote the U. S. Commissioner of Mining Statistics in March 1871.[7] The California story was thus repeating itself in the Territory (so designated in 1863) of Idaho, and "the heathen Chinee" took over what the white man disdained. "The fact is," continued Raymond, "that new fields of mining nearer the railroad are draining Idaho of her nomadic mining population." Quartz mining, requiring fewer men and much

5. H. H. Bancroft: *Works*, XXXI, 427; quoted in Paul, p. 139.

6. *The Passing of the Frontier*, "Chronicles of America Series," Vol. XXVI (New Haven, Conn., 1918), pp. 59–60. This picturesque writer is great fun but must be read with some restraint.

7. R. W. Raymond: *Statistics of Mines and Mining . . . West of the Rocky Mountains* (Washington, D. C., 1872), p. 187.

more expensive machinery, was still in its infancy there. The agent of the ubiquitous Wells Fargo Company in Boise City, W. A. Atlee, estimated the territory's total yield of gold and silver for the year 1870 at only $6 million. His estimate for 1869 had been $2 million higher.[8] But there were compensations. Sixty years after Lewis and Clark, this area had at last been opened up to settlement. Depots created for the miners on the supply route from the Columbia River, like Walla Walla and Lewiston, burgeoned as cities, and did not die when the mining boom was over. The area contained much fertile land, even if also the impassable ranges of the Bitterroot Mountains and the unnavigable rapids and falls of "the River of No Return." "As the placer mines decline," said the *Boise Statesman* on July 1, 1870, "persons forsake them for the more permanent pursuits of farming and stock-breeding . . . the grain, hay and vegetable crop of Boise and other agricultural districts is better than ever." Those who had seen enough of the elephant could now settle down and raise cattle, but those who still wanted to raise hell (and strike it rich in the bargain) went "over the hill" again into what is now Montana, the next magnet for the footloose miner.

In Montana the tough miners of Idaho, who had many of them been the dregs of more westerly and earlier mining areas, met, and mingled explosively with, more sedentary and law-abiding elements from the Mississippi Valley or from Utah and Colorado, who were part of the orthodox westward movement and not the backwash of California, Nevada, and British Columbia. Again an earlier mining-frontier pattern repeated itself, and a vigorous and ruthless vigilante movement came into being to rid Montana—on the end of a rope—of men like the notorious Henry Plummer (who, in true "Western" style, first managed to get himself elected sheriff) and the somewhat overpublicized desperado Slade.[9]

Minor gold discoveries had been made in Montana as early as

8. Raymond, p. 187.

9. Two well-known frontier classics have glamourized both the villains and the vigilantes of Montana. Though somewhat overwritten, both were the works of eyewitnesses: T. J. ("Professor") Dimsdale: *The Vigilantes in Montana* (Virginia City, Mont., 1866; rpr. Norman, Okla., 1953); and N. P. Langford: *Vigilante Days and Ways*, 2 vols. (Boston, 1890). For the true but still not too sober facts, see M. G. Burlingame and K. Ross Toole: *A History of Montana*, 3 vols. (New York, 1957). Mark Twain (*Roughing It*) made, from hearsay, a sort of hero-villain of Slade.

1852, and James and Granville Stuart[1] tried their luck at Gold Creek in 1858, but Bannack (1862), Alder Gulch (1863), and Last Chance Gulch (1864) were the really big strikes that gave the Montana gold fields national and international fame. Parties that had set out for Idaho from the east and from Colorado were deflected to this area in 1862, while one company of Oregon-bound settlers from St. Paul left half its members behind prospecting the Grasshopper Diggings (Bannack), the first large-scale Montana mining camp. Meanwhile, the Idaho miners were seeping in over the mountains, the Plummer gang among them. On his first day in Bannack, Plummer killed a man and won the usual speedy acquittal. "Life in Bannack at this time was perfect isolation from the rest of the world," wrote Nathaniel Langford. ". . . all the great battles of the season of 1862—Antietam, Fredericksburg, Second Bull Run—all the exciting debates of Congress, and the more exciting battles at sea, first became known to us on the arrival of the newspapers in the spring of 1863." The news of the organization of the Territory of Idaho (including Montana and Wyoming) on March 3, 1863, must have trickled into Bannack almost as slowly. Alder Gulch, less remote and much richer, had a more rapid growth. Its chief camp, the nostalgically named Virginia City, had a population of ten thousand within two years of the first discovery there in May 1863. The first year's yield of gold out of Alder Gulch was worth over $10 million; eventually the gulch's yield would be worth over $120 million. When young "J. Sidney Osborn"[2] first reached Virginia City, Montana Territory, on June 6, 1865, just turned twenty-one and with only $2 left out of his original $3,500, the place was not yet very prepossessing—but the vigilantes had done their work. The robbers were dead, the crack

1. See Granville Stuart: *Journals and Reminiscences*, ed. P. C. Phillips, 2 vols. (Cleveland, 1925), passim.

2. A pseudonym taken from Thackeray's *Vanity Fair*, which this omnivorous reader greatly admired. His "name in the States" had been James Knox Polk Miller. Born on April 26, 1845, just after the inauguration of the "dark-horse President" from Tennessee, Miller had absconded from New York in 1864, pocketing $3,500 from a business in which he was partner with an uncle; and after trying his luck, with little success, as a merchant—selling cigars to the "gentile" minority—in Salt Lake City, he moved on to booming Virginia just under a year later. His frank and illuminating diary has been published as *The Road to Virginia City*, ed. Andrew F. Rolle (Norman, Okla., 1960), whose researches into Miller's career provided the information used here.

The PACIFIC NORTHWEST and the "BIG SKY" COUNTRY

U.S.Highways ▭
National Parks ▨

(225)

of pistols had ceased, and the people felt safe: they could walk the streets without constant exposure to danger, according to Langford's testimony. Young Miller wrote down in his diary (June 7, 1865) a first impression of Alder Gulch:

> From Nevada's [Nevada City's] west end to the east end of Virginia City is about 3 miles. The houses and stores are mostly on one street and are built of loggs, mud and stones with dirt roofs. The street runs along "Virginia Gulch" where, for a width of 500 to 1000 feet, shovelled, uplifted & piled, it looks as if an enormous Hog had been uprooting the soil. My board and lodging at the Missouri House[3] are to cost me $14 pr. week. Mr Ray is proprietor of the establishment. "Puss" Ray, a very friendly girl, is one of the *attractions* of the house.[4]

Miller's first Sunday in Virginia City (June 11, 1865) was an eye-opener after the austerities of his months in the City of the Saints:

> There was nothing visible to remind a person in any degree that it was Sunday. Every store, saloon and dancing hall was in full-blast. Hack running, auctioneering, mining, and indeed every business, is carried on with much more zeal than on week days. It made me heartsick to see it.[5]

But even Miller was deflected from going to church that day, being asked to take tickets at the door of the Montana Theater for his friends of the road north, "The Keystone Gymnastic Troupe." "I spent the evening at the Montana Theater," he confessed. "Today showed me an entirely new phase of life." Failing next day to get a bookkeeping job he had been promised, Miller almost decided to throw in the sponge after this first discouraging week in Virginia City and move on to San Francisco. Soon afterwards he obtained a good position; yet, by June 8, 1866, he was "$5 worse off than nothing, after a year's work in such a country as this, $3,500 worse off than when I left the states. I much doubt whether the Lord ever intends to let me make another 'Pile.'" However, only ten

---

3. There were also a California Hotel, a Virginia Hotel, a Wisconsin House, an Idaho Hotel, and a Nebraska House. All carried advertisements in the *Montana Post*, according to Rolle (p. 75, n. 4).

4. Rolle, p. 75.

5. Rolle, p. 77.

days later, he netted "a gain of $563.14 since June 8"[6] by a success-
ful speculation in salt, and after this he did not look back. By June
18, 1867, he was in St. Louis, staying at the Southern Hotel, attending a theater production of *The Black Crook*,[7] with a pair of rented
opera glasses and enough money ($2,000) saved up for a year of
carefree travel.[8] Miller had taken French lessons while still in Virginia City, and he was Paris-bound. By June 29, 1867, he was
departing from New York on a French steamer, "a slight thumping
in my heart as even to a matter-of-fact person the ocean is a wide
gulf to separate one from his friends." But "The Elephant" had the
last laugh, for, after visiting not only Paris but also Rome, Alexan-
dria, Cairo, and Jerusalem, he was back in Montana (at Helena)—a
year, to the day, after he had left.[9] He set up a business at Deer
Lodge but moved on to Deadwood, South Dakota, the center of a
new gold rush, in 1876. His switch from storekeeper to builder and
real estate developer was most profitable, one that ultimately saw
him president of the Deadwood Central Railroad Company. It will
be noticed that, in his entire career, James Knox Polk Miller never
once staked a claim, panned for gold, or tunneled for silver. But he
struck it rich and made his "pile" all the same before he died of
tuberculosis in Santa Barbara, California, in 1891, at the age of
forty-six. His was a not untypical life of America's mining frontier
—if one ignores his trips to Paris, Rome, Cairo, and Jerusalem, and
his weakness for Charlotte Brontë.[1]

The last boom year in Montana was 1868, and the gold and
silver production of the Territory worth just over $9 million in

6. Rolle, p. 96.

7. "I found that the play was one which owed its popularity to the scenic
effects, the beautiful dancing, and the scant amount of clothing covering the
dancer"—Rolle (Diary, July 17, 1867), p. 131. *The Black Crook*, by Charles M.
Barras, was described on its title page (Philadelphia, 1866) as "A Most Wonderful
History Now being Performed With Immense Success in All the Principal
Theatres Throughout the United States."

8. He had thought of going to college instead, but after looking over
Princeton's prospectus, he decided that it would cost him at least $3,000 to attend
that seat of learning.

9. Rolle, p. xii.

1. "Business dull, my work heavy as usual. After supper took up 'Jane Eyre'
by Currer Bell. Became very interested in it and read until 2 or 3 o'clock in the
morning. . . . Poor Jane, you have loved as only passionate characters can. . . .
Mr Rochester, how I felt the similarity of many points of his character, as drawn,
and my own"—Rolle (Diary, August 24, 1865), p. 79.

1870, according to Raymond,[2] but by that time Last Chance Gulch had managed to get itself rechristened Helena and called "cosmopolitan" by a newly arrived Episcopal bishop. The bishop's wife was amazed at the opulence of the local ladies, who called on her "arrayed in silk and adorned with gold and jewels"; and she and her husband either did not guess or did not care to inquire how some of these adornments had been earned in this community still over eighty per cent male in 1870.[3] Helena went on to become the territorial, and eventually state capital, while its displaced rival, Virginia City, went into decay. The latter, like its neighbor Nevada City, has been reconstructed for the tourists of the twentieth century. Butte, too, nearly died as a gold-mining center, to be saved by silver mining and then, even more spectacularly, by copper.

In the 1870's the mining frontier moved eastward again—like J. K. P. Miller—into the Black Hills of the Dakota Territory. This was Sioux Indian country, guaranteed to the tribe by a treaty concluded as recently as 1868. As early as 1874, according to a San Francisco editorial of that year, "the glowing reports of Custer's expedition to the Black Hills have had the effect of exciting a lot of prospectors who want some new country to work in."[4] Prospectors were already in the territory, dodging both the Indians and the Army, before the end of 1875, and they were not deterred by the fate of Custer and his men in the summer of 1876. Finally, in the spring of 1877, the Indian title was extinguished and the region officially opened to exploitation. But by that time several thousand eager miners or prospectors had "jumped the gun." Deadwood Gulch and neighboring Lead were the richest mining camps. Here the familiar frontier patterns of '49, '59, and '62 were repeated. This hitherto uninhabited area, over 200 miles from the nearest railroad until the 1890's, saw the return of stagecoach days, and *The Attack on the Deadwood Stage* by road agents became almost as famous a bar-room picture as *Custer's Last Stand*. A

2. *Statistics of Mines and Mining* . . . , p. 204; cf. Bowles: *Our New West*, p. 402: "The present [1869] gold production of the Territory is about eight millions of dollars a year, and the population twenty-five thousand."

3. Daniel S. Tuttle: *Reminiscences of a Missionary Bishop*, quoted in Paul: *Mining Frontiers*, pp. 140–1.

4. San Francisco *Mining and Scientific Press*, September 19, 1874; quoted in Paul: *Mining Frontiers*, p. 177.

theater was opened in Deadwood as early as June 1876;[5] a Methodist (who was soon to be killed by Indians) and a Congregationalist preacher arrived before the end of the year, shortly followed by a Roman Catholic priest. The Salvation Army was also soon on the scene. In June 1877 George Hearst and his fellow California capitalists moved in on the new bonanza and purchased the Home-

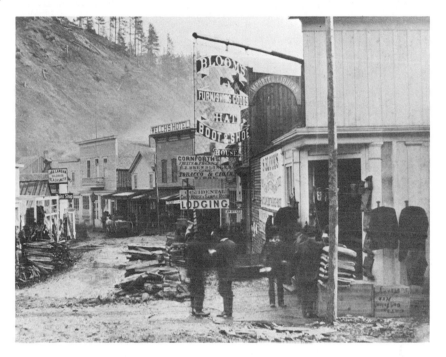

Deadwood, South Dakota, in its heyday, as photographed by F. J. Haynes. From Freeman Tilden: *Following the Frontier* (New York, 1964).

stake and associated mines from the Manuel brothers.[6] "Wild Bill" Hickok arrived, briefly to bestride the narrow gulch like a colossus until he was shot in the back, as every schoolboy knows, in a tavern brawl. "Calamity Jane" reached the height of her "reputation" in Deadwood and lived on, like "Baby Doll," long after she had lost

5. At the Gem Theater *The Mikado* was to run for 130 nights, the Lord High Executioner being especially appreciated, but the theatre was ruined by such competition as street carnivals, dance halls, bar room quartets and the Salvation Army. Riegel: *America Moves West*, p. 508.

6. See above, pp. 200–1.

both her man and her looks. Even as early as July 1878 Deadwood City was said by a leading mining engineer, who had visited many other similar areas in their early days, to be no longer a rough camp, but already a place of some refinement, where "all the conveniences, and even the luxuries of life can be obtained . . . in no other district is justice more ably administered or greater security afforded to life and to property."[7] If Janin's assertion—and it does seem that Wells Fargo conveyed $60 million in bullion out of Deadwood without loss—can be accepted, then it seems that mining frontiers developed with great precocity in the late 1870's, as compared with "the days of Forty-nine." Indeed, both Leadville and Cripple Creek experienced a similar rapid advance to sophistication, sobriety, and sabbatarianism. By 1880 there were 3,570 professional miners in the Dakota Territory, according to the census figures, which indicated that the Black Hills gold rush was not at any time on the scale of those in California, Nevada, and Colorado, or even of the smaller ones in Oregon, Idaho, and Montana. But, once again, population had been rapidly drawn to a remote and hitherto entirely unsettled area, and though Deadwood was to fade to a pale shadow of its former self before the end of the century, the Homestake mine, at Lead, remains famous and productive to this day.[8] And out of this frontier, in addition to Wild Bill (who had also flourished his gun elsewhere), came yet another, somewhat more mythical, "folk-hero"—Deadwood Dick, darling of the dime novelists.

South Dakota and southern Arizona rival each other in the history books, in Hollywood, and in popular literature as the "last and wildest" of the American mining frontiers. This was not strictly true of either, though Tombstone and Deadwood did perhaps run in roughly parallel grooves during the late seventies and early eighties.

Arizona had experienced earlier mining "boomlets," even in Spanish and Mexican days, and the ubiquitous *Norte Americano*

7. Louis Janin: *Report on Some of the Leading Mining Claims . . . in the Black Hills* (n.p., 1879); quoted in Paul: *Mining Frontiers*, p. 181, from a typescript copy of the rare orig. publication in the possession of James A. Noble, of Pasadena, Calif.

8. Nearly $6½ million in gold and silver came out of South Dakota's mines in 1902. Gold production alone was worth nearly $7¾ million in 1908, "the greater part coming from the Homestake Mine," according to the *Encyclopedia Britannica* (11th edn.), XXV, 508.

prospectors were at last on home ground there after 1848 and (in the extreme south) 1853. Men from California "struck it," but somewhat poorly, near Yuma and Ehrenburg in the late fifties, and moved on up to Prescott and Wickenburg (named after a veteran

Schieffelin Hall, Tombstone, by C. M. Palmer.

miner) in the early sixties. Tucson, near the famous mission of San Xavier del Bac, was Arizona's first "wide-open" mining town, but more as a place in which to roister and obtain a grub stake than as the center of a very productive region. Tucson was still, in the sixties, liable to have to stand siege at the hands of raiding Apaches.

Ed Schieffelin, the discoverer of the famous Lucky Cuss silver mine at Tombstone, which started that community on its heady career, was not an itinerant forty-niner or fifty-niner. Indeed, he had only been born (in Pennsylvania) in 1848, months after James Marshall's great find, but had been taken to California as a boy of ten, and by the age of seventeen he was working a claim in Jackson, Oregon.[9] After trying his luck in Nevada, Utah, and Idaho, Schieffelin drifted down to Arizona. Other prospectors, including one Bronkaw, in 1858, had already made some discoveries in the extreme south of Arizona and then lost their hair to the Apaches. The Army was against Ed's going into this dangerous country even in 1878, but he did so anyway, earning himself a fortune, rather

9. See further H. H. Bancroft: *Works*, XVII, 589 n.

than the tombstone predicted by the soldiers. Then, in the best prospecting tradition, he sold out in 1880 and moved to the flesh-pots of Los Angeles.

"The Lucky Cuss" was the first Tombstone silver mine to be worked, but others were soon opened up. The Contention mine

TOMBSTONE
ARIZONA
"The Town Too Tough To Die"

MECCA OF TOURISTS, HEALTH SEEKERS AND LOVERS OF WESTERN LORE

The "Lucky Cuss" Mine, Tombstone, by C. M. Palmer.

alone produced $1,676,000 in 1882 and by May 1883 had yielded over $5 million and paid out nearly half that amount in dividends, an exceedingly high net yield. The early eighties were the heyday of Tombstone, when the population rose to some 13,000 and the Earps and Clantons stalked each other along Frémont Street at the back of (but not inside) the O.K. Corral, while the young Reverend Endicott Peabody gave exhibitions of fisticuffs[1] in the Crystal Palace Saloon in aid of his Episcopal church funds before returning east to become headmaster of Groton and mentor of Franklin Delano Roosevelt. But at about the time the Apache menace was finally removed by the surrender and internment of Geronimo, the flooding of the Tombstone mines and the demonetization of silver administered the *coup de grâce* to the prosperity of the area. Fitful attempts to restart the silver mines were made, but Tombstone's great days were over. Its fifteen city blocks shrank to two or three; its magnificent town hall (built in 1881 and now a national historical monument) and its massive court house echoed with emptiness. Finally, Tombstone ceased to be even a county seat and began to fall apart at the seams. Rescued from oblivion in the 1920's and 1930's by writers like Stewart Lake and Walter Noble Burns,[2] and restored to the public eye by Hollywood and the television networks in more recent years, Tombstone, sadly diminished, may now be said to ride again, but on the silver screen rather than on a silver stallion.

The spotlight had swiveled back to Nevada early in the twentieth century. Tonopah's gold (and silver) in 1900, and Gold-field's (1903), reopened the bonanza mining frontier there; Rhyolite's promise (1905) kept it alive. But by 1908 this new boom was over and Rhyolite (built in the grand manner) had become a ghost metropolis in the desert.

1. A science acquired at Cheltenham College, England, where he had been educated until 1876, although he was a New Englander by birth.

2. See below, Bibliographic Note, p. 433.

CHAPTER VIII

The Revolution in

Western Transportation

J UST AS THE AMERICAN COLONISTS WERE STILL BUILDING
Queen Anne houses in Virginia and New England in the
1750's, so was the American West still extensively using
stagecoaches in the 1880's, nearly half a century after
they were beginning to be supplanted by railroads east of the
Mississippi. By 1865 there were still only 3,272 miles of railroad
in the whole of the trans-Mississippi West, but a network of over
ten times that mileage (35,085) east of the river. It was 1854 before
the first railroad reached the Mississippi, not until 1859 that the
Missouri was finally touched on its middle course (opposite Hannibal); while at the close of the Civil War, Oregon still had only
19 miles of rail. By then California had 214 miles of railroad, but
the California Stage Company alone "operated 28 daily stage lines
covering over 1,970 miles of California road. On these it used 1,000
horses and 134 coaches, and employed 184 agents, drivers, and
hostlers."[1] Between 1858 and 1890 over 600 of the renowned and
elegant Concord coaches "were manufactured by Abbot, Downing,
and Company, of Concord, New Hampshire," and "it may be
presumed that the largest share of these found service on Far West
roads."[2] It was not until well after the Civil War that railroad

1. O. O. Winther: *Via Western Express and Stage Coach* (Stanford, Calif.,
1936), pp. 153–6; and *The Transportation Frontier: Trans-Mississippi West, 1865–
1890* (New York, 1964), p. 46.
2. Winther: *Transportation Frontier*, p. 61.

ARREST. STAGE ROBBER.

About one o'clock P. M. on the 3d of August, 1877, the down stage between Fort Ross and Russian River, was stopped by a man in disguise, who took from Wells, Fargo & Co.'s express box about $300 in coin and a check for $205 32, on Granger's Bank, San Francisco, in favor of Fisk Bros. On one of the way-bills left with the box, the robber wrote as follows :

> I've labored long and hard for bread—
> For honor and for riches—
> But on my corns too long you've trod,
> You fine haired sons of bitches.
> BLACK BART, the Poet.

Driver, give my respects to our friend, the other driver; but I really had a notion to hang my old disguise hat on his weather eye.

Respectfully B. B.

It is believed that he went into the Town of Guernieville about daylight next morning.

———

About three o'clock P. M , July 25th, 1878, the down stage from Quincy, Plumas Co., to Oroville, Butte Co., was stopped by one masked man, and from Wells, Fargo & Co.'s box taken $379 coin, one diamond ring said to be worth $200, and one silver watch valued at $25. In the box, when found next day, was the following :   [Fac simile.]

*here I lay me down to sleep
to wait the coming morrow
perhaps success perhaps defeat
And everlasting sorrow
I've labored long and hard for bread
for honor and for riches
But on my corns too long you've tred
You fine haired sons of bitches
let come what will I'll try it on
My condition can't be worse
And if there's money in that Box
Tis munny in my purse
Black Bart
the P o 8*

About eight o'clock A. M. of July 30th, 1878, the down stage from La Porte to Oroville was robbed by one man, who took from express box a package of gold specimens valued at $50, silver watch No. 716,996, P. S. Bartlett, maker.

It is certain the first two of these crimes were done by the same man, and there are good reasons to believe that he did the three.

There is a liberal reward offered by the State, and Wells, Fargo & Co. for the arrest and conviction of such offenders. For particulars, see Wells, Fargo & Co.'s "Standing Reward" Posters of July 1st, 1876.

It will be seen from the above that this fellow is a character that would be remembered as a scribbler and something of a wit or wag, and would be likely to leave specimens of his handwriting on hotel registers and other public places.

If arrested, telegraph the undersigned at Sacramento. Any information thankfully received.

J. B. HUME, Special Officer Wells, Fargo & Co.

The Black Bart reward poster—with facsimile of his "poem."

transportation began to play a significant part on Far Western frontiers. When it did it tended to follow the lines of older trails.

Frederick Jackson Turner, father of the "frontier hypothesis,"[3] pointed out long ago: "The buffalo trail became the Indian

WILL BE
EXHIBITED
FOR ONE DAY ONLY!

AT THE STOCKTON HOUSE!
THIS DAY, AUG. 12, FROM 9 A. M., UNTIL 6, P. M.

THE HEAD
Of the renowned Bandit!

JOAQUIN!
AND THE
HAND OF THREE FINGERED JACK!
THE NOTORIOUS ROBBER AND MURDERER.

"JOAQUIN" and "THREE-FINGERED JACK" were captured by the *State Rangers*, under the command of Capt. Harry Love, at the Arroya Cantina, July 24th. No reasonable doubt can be entertained in regard to the identification of the head now on exhibition, as being that of the notorious robber, *Joaquin Muriatta*, as it has been recognised by hundreds of persons who have formerly seen him.

Joaquin Murieta exhibition poster, 1853. From Yellow Bird (John Rollin Ridge): *The Life and Adventures of Joaquin Murieta* (San Francisco, 1857).

trail, and this became the trader's 'trace'; the trails widened into roads and the roads into turnpikes and these in turn were transformed into railroads."[4] With the exception of the trans-Missis-

3. See below, Chs. xi and xii.

4. F. J. Turner: *The Frontier in American History* (New York, 1920), p. 14. The famous "title essay," in which this passage occurs, was first published in 1893. It proved to be of seminal importance.

sippi West, where turnpikes, for instance, could hardly be established on the Oregon Trail across the Plains, and were thus supplanted by toll ferries and bridges, this was the usual pattern. The first transcontinental railroad followed almost exactly the routes of the old Oregon-California trails of the 1840's, while Promontory Point in Utah, where the Union Pacific and Central Pacific were finally joined, was right in the middle of Jim Bridger's old fur-hunting and Indian-fighting ground of the twenties, above Bear River Bay of the Great Salt Lake. The Atcheson, Topeka, and Santa Fe Railroad was to follow approximately the line of the old Santa Fe Trail, the Southern Pacific (up from San Diego to San Francisco) that of the Camino Real, past the Franciscan missions of San Juan Capistrano, San Gabriel, San Fernando, San Buenaventura, Santa Barbara, San Luis Obispo, San Miguel, and Santa Clara. The great Union Station at Los Angeles stands on the edge of the old Spanish Plaza; Hollywood film stars, jet-propulsion experts, and atomic scientists detrain from the Chief and Super-Chief at the Pasadena Depot of the Santa Fe line just two or three miles from where Jedediah Smith and his men staggered into the San Gabriel Mission after crossing the American wasteland; the Third Street Rail Terminal at San Francisco is even nearer to Mission Dolores, built in 1776 and named in honor of Saint Francis of Assisi.

But, before all this could happen, pack horses and covered wagons without number would have to stamp and rut these trails, to be followed by the handcarts of the Mormons, the stagecoaches, and the Pony Express; the great railroad surveys, both government and privately sponsored, would have to be made; the Indian menace would have to be met and countered; the bandit gangs and lone road agents dealt with, by the "suspended sentences" of vigilantes, the rough "equalizing" justice of frontier marshals, and the relentless sleuthing of the Pinkertons.[5]

Owing to the nature of the rivers of the West, and of the terrain beyond the Mississippi, canals played a most inconspicuous

5. "Black Bart," the most celebrated and successful stagecoach robber in all the West, was finally traced, by an assiduous Wells Fargo detective, through the laundry mark on his handkerchief. The hilarious and true story of this elderly, engaging, and poetically inclined Raffles is well told in Winther: *Via Western Express*, pp. 86–90 (see also illustrations, p. 94). The anticlimactic nature of Black Bart's capture and consignment to St. Quentin Jail can almost be regretted. The Scarlet Pimpernel betrayed by his blood group! Dick Turpin identified by his palm prints! Achilles fatally scratched by a bobby pin! Siegfried catching his death of cold! A Black Bart reward poster is reproduced on p. 235.

part in the transportation history of this area. In 1840 the United States had in use almost exactly as many miles of canals (3,326) as of railroads (3,328), but west of the Mississippi the mileage of each was nil. By 1850, canal-building even east of the Mississippi had virtually stopped—the Chicago and Illinois Canal, opened in 1848, being the last important one—leaving the total national canal mileage at only 3,698, compared with an increased railroad mileage of 8,879; yet, west of the Mississippi, there were still only four miles of railroad (in Missouri) and no canals at all. There were still no canals in 1860 but trans-Mississippi railroad mileage had risen to 1,814.[6]

If canals can be ignored in the trans-Mississippi West, river traffic cannot. In 1804–05, Lewis and Clark had tried to get by water all the way to the Pacific, when the country between the middle Missouri and the mouth of the Columbia River was still unexplored and its terrors unguessed at. They had found the Missouri fairly easily navigable as far as Great Falls, and the Columbia uneasily and intermittently navigable from its confluence with the Snake down to the ocean. Columbia River navigation, indeed, owing to the many rapids and gorges, never became easy. The first small steamboat on its waters, the Hudson Bay Company's *Beaver*, plied from 1836 onward between Fort Vancouver and the ocean and up and down the Willamette, but could not penetrate beyond the Dalles. Only after 1850 did steamboats become important in the Columbia River and Puget Sound areas, and finally "combination steamer, wagon-freighting, pack train and stage coach services were established that effectively linked the Columbia River watershed with that of the Missouri."[7] This was quite obviously a transitional and somewhat makeshift "transportation chain," awaiting the completion of the Northern Pacific Railroad, which was not until 1883. Meanwhile, the Oregon Steam Navigation Company, organized in 1860, managed to establish a virtual monopoly

6. From a table in G. R. Taylor: *The Transportation Revolution, 1815–1860*, The Economic History of the United States, Vol. IV (New York, 1951), p. 79; based on *Hunt's Merchant's Magazine* and H. V. Poor: *Manual of the Railroads of the United States*. Louisiana is not considered to be a trans-Mississippi state in the figures given here. In 1850 it had 14 miles of canals and 89 of rail, compared with 335 miles of rail in 1860. Minnesota (not a state until 1859) and Oregon are also excluded from the table.

7. Winther: *Transportation Frontier*, p. 83; and more fully in *The Old Oregon Country* (Stanford, 1950), Ch. xii.

of river transportation in the Pacific Northwest, and had to be bought up at the high price of $5 million by Henry Villard, the promoter of the Northern Pacific, in 1879, when he sought to establish a co-ordinated rail and steamboat empire—which he was able to do with considerable success.[8]

Nothing entirely adequate could be done about bridging the bulk transportation gap between the Missouri and the Columbia rivers until the rail came through in 1883, but the Mullan Road,

The steamer *Yellowstone* on April 19, 1833, by Karl Bodmer.

built from Fort Benton, at the head of navigation of the Missouri, to Fort Walla Walla, near the confluence of the Columbia and the Snake, became a major freighting route, as did the Bozeman Trail, from Fort Laramie on the North Platte to Virginia City and Bannack in Montana, carrying many thousands of tons of goods between the Atlantic and the Pacific drainage areas before the

8. See further J. B. Hedges: *Henry Villard and the Railways of the Northwest* (New Haven, Conn., 1930), passim.

Northern Pacific came through. These supplemented the older Oregon and California trails as well as the more recently established Central Overland Road, going more directly westward from Denver through Salt Lake City to the Nevada mines and the Pacific.

Missouri River transportation became big business as soon as steamboats arrived to replace the cumbersome pirogues and keelboats, which were well-nigh impossible to navigate upstream without superhuman efforts. The first steamboat puffed its way laboriously upstream in 1819, but it required another forty years before the tortuous 3,100 midstream mileage from St. Louis to Fort Ben-

Camp of the Gros Ventres on the Upper Missouri, by Karl Bodmer.

ton was completely spanned by steam. After 1860 Fort Benton became for a few years a major river port.[9] From the forties on, regular steamship lines were in operation north of Council Bluffs, but it was as early as 1832 that the American Fur Company's *Yellowstone* had struggled up to Fort Union at the mouth of the river after which she was named. Thence, in 1833, she carried a

9. Paul Sharp: *Whoop-Up Country: The Canadian American West, 1865–1885* (Minneapolis, 1955), passim.

German prince, Maximilian of Wied, his huntsman-valet Dreidop-pel, and the Swiss artist he had under contract, Karl Bodmer, on a sight-seeing and scientific expedition into the Far West. They managed to get by steamboat as far as Fort McKenzie, just east of the Great Falls, but had to complete their journey beyond Fort Union by keelboat. Prince Maximilian's *Travels* and Bodmer's drawings and paintings have preserved a remarkable picture of life on the upper Missouri in those early days. Both the *Yellowstone* and the *Assiniboin,* the steamboats they used, appear in Bodmer's port-folio, and he made a splendid sepia-tone watercolour of an episode during the keelboat journey.[1] George Catlin, a much cruder painter, had preceded Bodmer up the Missouri on the *Yellowstone* in 1832, but though he, too, drew pictures of the little steamer, he was much more interested in Indian portraits for his famous "Gal-lery"[2] than in river scenery. Jacob Miller, while he did not paint the Missouri journey, has left pictures of many other Western rivers, including, notably, the Green and the Platte.

Even before 1860 the lower half of the Missouri had become very busy indeed, rivaling even the Mississippi in density of traffic. An average of nearly a steamboat a day tied up at Fort Leaven-worth in 1859. On the eve of the Civil War, St. Louis had out-stripped even New Orleans as a steamboat-passenger center (over a million passengers used it annually from 1855 on), and "it is signifi-cant to note that more of these vessels operated between St. Louis and the upper Mississippi and Missouri river points than between the

1. *Reise in das Innere Nord-Amerika in den Jahren 1832 bis 1834* (Koblenz, 1839; Eng. tr. London and New York, 1843); repr. as *Travels in the Interior of North America,* ed. R. G. Thwaites, "Early Western Travel Series" (Cleveland, 1905). Bodmer's *Atlas,* or portfolio of drawings, was issued as a separate volume and was reissued in the Thwaites edn. (the most easily accessible) on a reduced scale and in black and white. The original folio *Atlas* was issued in black and white, in three colors, in full color (now very rare), and in part color (the costumes only). Some editions appear to have been pirated, according to Bernard De Voto: *Across the Wide Missouri* (New York, 1947; London, 1957), p. 453. De Voto offers a useful critical essay, "The First Illustrators of the West" (ibid., pp. 391–415), and reproduces ten of Bodmer's plates, six in color. See *American Heritage* (April 1963) for twenty-nine color reproductions of Bodmer's original water colors painted on the expedition (from the collection of the Northern Natural Gas Co., now on permanent loan to the Joslyn Art Museum in Omaha, Neb.).

2. Catlin's Indian Gallery and other Western paintings were exhibited not only in the East but also in Europe, and attracted widespread attention. Copies of most of these are preserved in the Smithsonian Institution, Washington, D. C., where a selection is on permanent exhibition.

city and New Orleans and other lower Mississippi River ports."[3]
After 1860, with the pushing of steam navigation up to Fort Benton and the opening of the gold and silver mines of Idaho, Montana, and the Dakotas, Missouri River traffic boomed as never
before. Young James Knox Polk Miller's embarkation for Cythera
at Fort Benton on the *Waverly* on June 2, 1867, bound for St.
Louis (and Paris), took him to Omaha in ten days and ten hours,[4]
and the *Waverly* passed forty-seven other vessels between Fort
Benton and Yankton alone. The journey was not without other
incidents:

> June 4. . . . This morning a negro, one of the boat hands, fell
> overboard. No effort was made to save him . . ."
>
> June 5. . . . Passed a point and saw the remains of a trading post
> . . . burned by the Indians . . ."
>
> June 6. . . . rushed on deck, found the entire force of the boat
> engaged . . . in shooting buffalo . . . they were hoisted
> aboard and duly skinned and cleaned for the table . . .
> Shortly after dinner we passed a war party of Indians about
> 75 in number . . . a passenger shot at a beaver but missed
> him.
>
> July 7. . . . a sharp trial of speed took place, which was soon
> brought to a close by the collision of our boat with the
> bank of the river, thereby disabling one of the paddle wheels
> and causing a detention of four hours . . .
>
> July 8. Started at daylight. Our first exploit was to run into the
> "G. A. Thompson," smashing their cookhouse and seriously
> disarranging their breakfast . . .
>
> July 9. . . . Passed the bank today where the Indians attacked the
> "Big Horn," and killed one man, while wooding a few weeks
> since.
>
> July 10. . . . It blew so fiercely that the boat was turned round and
> round, frequently driving us against the bank. We were
> finally forced to tie up. A soldier taken with delirium
> tremens is howling hideously below the hurricane deck
> upon which I am watching the sun set. . . .
>
> July 11. . . . reached Choteau Agency where, for the first time
> since leaving Benton, I saw some signs of cultivation.

3. Winther: *Transportation Frontier*, p. 25.
4. Rolle: *Road to Virginia City*, p. 128.

July 12. . . . Passed Sioux City and reached Decatur . . . purchased . . . butter at .25¢. Quite different from the price
at Benton, where we paid $2.50 per lb.[5]

Never a dull moment! And, to end up with, the *Waverly* left
Miller behind in Omaha, as he tarried too long at "Shoat's Billard
Saloon, a beautiful hall with twelve tables and a splendid bar." He
chased after the boat (which had his gold dust on board) in the
Stonewall, but, failing to catch up with her at St. Joseph, took a
train "by Northern Missouri R. R. from St. Joseph to Weston,
thence went by ferry at $1.00 apiece fare to Leavenworth," and
again by train to Jefferson City, where he "found that the *Waverly*

Stagecoach (Wells Fargo).

had passed ten hours ago." Finally he reached St. Louis, by train,
two hours ahead of the *Waverly*. His gold dust recovered, he went
out "on the town."[6] After this his progress was rapid: "Having
breakfasted in Missouri, lunched in Illinois, dinned [*sic*] in Indiana
and supped in Ohio," and having purchased a ticket to New York
for $36 on the Baltimore and Ohio, Miller reached Washington,
D. C., on June 21, just nineteen days out of Fort Benton. "I visited
the Smithsonian Institution and in the evening went to see Ben Zoub

5. Rolle: *Road to Virginia City*, pp. 120–5.
6. See above, Ch. vii, pp. 226–7.

Zoub Arab Jugglers. I was delighted with the Capitol buildings
. . ." He had left Helena, Montana, by Wells Fargo stagecoach
on May 28. Had he not missed the *Waverly* at Omaha, the whole
trip from Fort Benton to New York would have cost him just
$137.

The year of Miller's downstream trip, 1867, was Fort Benton's
peak year for arrivals from the east by river. Forty-three steamers
tied up and disgorged "ten thousand passengers, eight thousand
tons of mining equipment and seven thousand tons of foodstuffs
and other goods . . . twenty-five hundred men, three thousand
teams, twenty thousand oxen and mules and six hundred wagons
were needed to transport all this on from Fort Benton."[7] Fort
Benton retained some importance until 1890, long after the lower
Missouri River traffic had been driven to the wall by the railroad
network. Sioux City, Yankton, and Bismarck all had their days as
river ports as the railroads reached these cities from the east, by-
passing the older, slower water route (even for heavy freight) via
St. Louis, Independence, St. Joe, and Omaha. Bismarck also became an important staging point down to Deadwood and the Black
Hills, and at this metropolis, where river, road, and rail met, the
young British scholar and politician James Bryce found an amazing
mirage of future greatness when he visited the Dakota territorial
capital in 1883:

> I happened to be at the city of Bismark [*sic*] in Dakota when this
> young settlement was laying the corner-stone of its Capitol, in-
> tended to contain the halls of the legislature and other State offices
> of Dakota when that flourishing Territory becomes, as it soon must,
> a State, or perhaps, for they talk of dividing it, two states. The town
> was then only some five years old, and may have had six or seven
> thousand inhabitants. It was gaily decorated for the occasion, and
> had collected many distinguished guests—General U. S. Grant, sev-
> eral governors of neighbouring States and Territories, railroad po-
> tentates, and others. By far the most remarkable figure was that of
> Sitting Bull, the famous Sioux Chief, who had surprised and slain a
> detachment of the American army some years before. Among the
> speeches made, in one of which it proved that as Bismark [sic] was
> the centre of Dakota, Dakota the centre of the United States, and
> the United States the centre of the world, Bismark [*sic*] was des-

7. Winther: *Transportation Frontier*, p. 80.

tined to "be the metropolitan hearth of the world's civilization," there came a short but pithy discourse from this grim old warrior, in which he told us, through an interpreter, that the Great Spirit moved him to shake hands with everybody. However, the feature of the ceremonial which struck us Europeans most was the spot chosen for the Capitol. It was not in the city, nor even on the outskirts of the city; it was nearly a mile off, on the top of a hill in the brown and dusty prairie. "Why here?" we asked. "Is it because you mean to enclose the building in a public park?" "By no means; the Capitol is intended to be in the centre of the city; it is in this direction that the city is to grow." It is the same everywhere from the Mississippi to the Pacific. Men seem to live in the future rather than in the present: not that they fail to work while it is called to-day, but that they see the country not merely as it is, but as it will be, twenty, fifty, a hundred years hence. . . .[8]

But, alas, "eighty years hence" Bismarck had a population of only a little over 20,000 and was still not the center of the world. The capitol, rebuilt as a fine skyscraper, remained on the edge of town. In its grounds there is, appropriately, a statue of Sacagawea and Baptiste Charbonneau.

While the Missouri was the longest navigable and most important river of the trans-Mississippi West, many other rivers saw a busy steamboat traffic until the railroads reached them and took away their freight and passengers. Everywhere they helped to advance the frontier. Both the Arkansas and the Red River of the South were navigable for nearly a thousand miles. The Minnesota River, meandering across the state of that name to St. Paul, on the Mississippi, was linked up to the Red River of the North for freighting purposes by a giant "portage" of cart trails, past Pembina, Minnesota, into Canada, and navigation on the Red River was financed from the Twin Cities, which benefited mightily. By 1874 the Red River Transportation Company was operating five steamers and twenty barges. St. Paul still had nearly 2 million tons of river freight and nearly 1½ million river passengers as late as the year 1884; in fact, some river traffic survived there even into the twentieth century.[9]

8. James Bryce: *The American Commonwealth*, 3 vols. (London and New York, 1888), III, 643–5.

9. Winther: *Transportation Frontier*, pp. 77–8.

In the Far West even the Colorado was found to be navigable for steamers as far inland as the desert outpost of Fort Yuma. The first steamer in San Francisco Bay was a little tub belonging to the American Vice-Consul William Leidesdorff, a former sailing-boat captain who died early in 1848. She did not survive her owner, but she made one trip up the Sacramento before being wrecked, and steamboats began to ply regularly on both that river and the San Joaquin after the gold rush started. Sacramento and Stockton soon became important river ports. By the early 1850's luxurious steamboats such as could have graced the Mississippi itself kept regular

Fargo, Dakota. Head of steamboat navigation on the Red River of the North, drawn by W. A. Rogers.

schedules between San Francisco and Sacramento City and ports higher up the Sacramento and Feather rivers. John Augustus Sutter, the founder of New Helvetia and the squire of Hock Farm, wrote to an old school friend in Germany, who in 1852 had asked how he and his family could emigrate to California:

> Each day steamers go from San Francisco to Marysville, and they all halt here at Hock Farm . . . every day four large steamboats pass by the house, and stop on request. I myself use them a lot as it is so convenient to get here in this way. Just two miles above us is the flourishing town of Marysville, sixty miles below is Sacramento City

where my Fort still stands, and we are about 150 miles from San Francisco, the great metropolis [*Weltstadt*]. If I leave here about midday, and stop a while at Sacramento, I can still be in San Francisco early the next morning. When I first arrived there, it had only four houses.[1]

It had also taken eleven days for Sutter to reach the site of Sacramento, where he built his fort, from San Francisco Bay, when he had arrived as the first white pioneer in the upper Sacramento Valley in August 1839. He must also have had in mind his odyssey of five years (1834–9) spent in reaching California from Switzerland when he advised his friend, in the same letter:

The journey via the Isthmus of Panama or via San Juan de Nicaragua by steamer would not only cost a lot for a large family, but the long stay in Panama is very expensive, and one also risks catching Panama fever, as was the case with my wife and my younger son. It would therefore be best to make the journey from Boston or New York in a clipper ship round Cape Horn. This sort of sailing ship is very big, sails remarkably fast and makes the journey in 90 to 100 days from New York or Boston to San Francisco.[2] You are much more comfortable on these ships and much less exposed to danger than on the steamships, and the cost of living is barely one third as much. These fine ships have not long been in service and not very long ago the journey round Cape Horn lasted from 5 to 6 months. There is a House in Boston which each month sends one of these ships here with passengers, and it comes to another House in San Francisco which has business connections with the first. It can therefore be arranged that one can pay in advance and make sure of a passage or reservation for one's friends. If it is all right by you I will, directly after receiving your letter, pay the fares in San Francisco and immediately send the documents that will secure a passage for seven persons. You will then have simply to pay for the journey as far as Boston or New York. . . . An Emigration will be coming

1. The letter from which this passage (tr. orig. in German) is taken, was written on May 1, 1852, at "Hock Farm, Sutter County, California," and addressed to Jakob Friedrich Hess, of Kandern, Baden, Germany. It is quoted from here with the kind permission of Jacob Frederick Hess, Jr., of Canton, Ohio, great-great-grandson of the addressee, and a tr. is printed in *University of Birmingham Historical Journal* (Birmingham, Eng., 1965), X, no. 1, pp. 90–94.

2. The fastest run of the famous clipper ship *Flying Cloud* from Boston to San Francisco (in 1854) was 89 days, 8 hours. See R. A. Rydell: "The Clipper Ship Era," *Pacific Historical Review*, XVIII: 1 (1949), 70–83.

here overland this summer and autumn which it is reckoned will be at least 75,000 strong. This journey would be too troublesome for you, as it needs wagons and cattle and the necessary supplies of food have to be transported, while it requires at least 5 to 6 months for the journey from Missouri here.

Sutter's letters gives a very good idea of the improvement in communications between the East and the Sacramento Valley of California in the four years since the first gold discovery—when Leidesdorff's little launch had been the only steamship in Californian waters. The clipper ships remained the most comfortable, if not the fastest, means of making this journey until the trans-Isthmian railroad was completed in 1855, by which time luxurious steamships were running regularly down from East Coast and Gulf ports to the Isthumus of Panama and up from there to California. The overland stagecoaches were to carry passengers and mail from St. Louis to San Francisco between 1858 and 1861 even faster, though at considerably more discomfort for the former, than the steamer and Isthmian railroad route.[3]

The story of Western stagecoaching would be a romantic one even if a stage had never been robbed by a road agent. The drivers were colorful characters, written about by Western travelers with almost Dickensian zest. Billy Carll, Billy Hamilton, Clark Foss, Charlie Parkhurst, Hank Monk, and men who were known simply as "Sage Brush Bill," "Cherokee Bill," and, even more simply, as 'Alfred'—just plain 'Alfred,'[4] were among the best known of them. Hank Monk keeps getting into literature—including Mark Twain's *Roughing It*—as the driver who gave the great and pompous Horace Greeley his comeuppance on one celebrated occasion. This oft-told tale has various versions, but always ends with these memorable words: "Keep your seat, Horace, and I'll get you there on time." If Hank Monk was the most famous Jehu in all the West,

3. The first Butterfield Overland Mail, which left St. Louis on September 16, 1858, reached San Francisco at 7:30 a.m. on October 10. The steamer *John L. Stephens,* carrying mail that had also left St. Louis on September 16 and gone East by train, arrived in San Francisco from Panama at 5:00 p.m. on October 16. See L. H. Wright and J. M. Bynum, eds.: *The Butterfield Overland Mail* (San Marino, Calif., 1942; repr. 1955), p. 133, n. 154, and passim. This is an annotated repr. of dispatches sent to the New York *Herald* by Waterman L. Ormsby, its special correspondent and the only through passenger on the first westbound stage. Ormsby and the overland mail went through in 23 days, 23 hours.

4. Winther: *Via Western Express*, p. 69.

the polite, profane, laconic, 'baccy-chewing, cigar-smoking "One-eyed Charlie" Parkhurst was the most singular. It was discovered only at his death in 1879 that "he" had been a woman!

The "stagecoach kings," the men who organized the Western Express routes and turned them into big business during the fifties and sixties, were almost as colorful as their drivers. Men of great ability and much ruthlessness, most of them came from the East with the gold rushes and had been in the business there. The first "regular" stagecoach service in California, started in the autumn of 1849, was anything but an express. One John Whistmann drove an old French omnibus the fifty miles from San Francisco to San Jose in nine hours when the weather was fair, charging "thirty-two dollars or 'two ounces' " for the trip. At about the same time, James Birch took passengers from Sutter's Fort to Mormon Island and Coloma (where gold had first been discovered) on the American River for the same fare. He was his own driver and promised to be "Through by Daylight!" The newly founded Sacramento *Placer Times* wrote up Birch's Stage on March 9, 1850, as "*the* line to get to the Mines in a hurry"[5]—which was what every forty-niner wanted. Birch, who was to be one of the earliest magnates of the road, soon discovered the publicity value of a long and impressive-sounding title for his stage operations. In 1851 he founded The Telegraph Line of the United States Mail Stages to run from Sacramento to the diggings at Rough and Ready, Grass Valley, and Nevada City. Continuously expanding his activities, Birch merged with his competitors in northern California to become president of the California Stage Company on January 1, 1854. By January 5, 1855, Governor John Bigler was able to announce proudly to the state legislature that "inland travel between all the principal parts of the State by means of stages has . . . been rendered expeditious and comfortable."[6] It had also become much cheaper. The fare from Sacramento to Coloma was now down to $5. By 1860 the California Stage Company had extended its services to Portland, Oregon, 710 miles from Sacramento, on a daily schedule. In 1857 Birch had also won a post office contract to convey mails and passengers twice a month between San Diego and San Antonio, Texas. The 1,500-mile pull, across inhospitable deserts most of the way, and through even more actively inhospitable Apache country

5. Winther: *Via Western Express*, p. 7.
6. Winther: *Via Western Express*, p. 12.

(where a military escort had to be provided), took thirty days. James Birch himself would have been wiser to stick to his own slow "Jackass Mail" and brave the Apache arrows, but instead he took the steamship *Central America* out of San Diego, bound for New York, and was drowned when she sank on September 11, 1857.[7] The first mail had left San Antonio on August 9 and reached San Diego on the 31st.

By 1857 many other hands were already grasping at the torch that James Birch let fall. As early as 1851 a mail and passenger route was established to run each month from Salt Lake City to Sacramento. From Independence via Salt Lake City to Sacramento, mail could now be conveyed in an elapsed time of two months, and from the East Coast to the West Coast in about ten weeks. A monthly mail service had been started along the Santa Fe Trail from Independence and on from Santa Fe to San Antonio, Texas, in 1850, via El Paso. Birch's San Antonio to San Diego line, also via El Paso, was a logical completion of this network, but it was much too slow to satisfy those who wanted rapid transit from the Mississippi Valley to the Pacific slopes, and for this reason the famous Butterfield Overland Mail was born in 1858. After a tremendous struggle between the proponents of rival routes, and a good deal of lobbying in Washington, President Buchanan's Postmaster-General Brown awarded a contract on September 16, 1857 (just a week after Birch's unhappy demise), to John Butterfield,[8] of New York, a founder of the American Express Company. According to the terms of this contract, Butterfield would take the U. S. mails from St. Louis and Memphis to San Francisco by a roundabout southern route which, after reaching El Paso, roughly coincided with Birch's route as far as San Diego, but then continued up through California, by Los Angeles and the San Joaquin Valley, to San Francisco Bay. The distance was more than 2,750 miles and the contract was a rich one—a mail subsidy of $600,000 for six years. But Butterfield was a friend of President Buchanan; Postmaster-General Brown's home town was Memphis; and Jefferson Davis, from Mississippi, the Secretary of War, threw all his powerful weight in favor of the Overland Mail passing through southern, and not central, states and territories. Butterfield's associates in the venture were the western stagecoach pioneers W. B. Fargo and

7. Wright and Bynum: *Butterfield Overland Mail*, p. 145 *n.*
8. See *Dictionary of American Biography*, III, 174–5.

W. D. Dinsmore. Eastern capitalists put up most of the money. Beginning on September 16, 1858, as specified in the contract, the Butterfield Overland Mail was a resounding success from the start. By 1860 it was carrying more mail than the inter-ocean steamers. It never did get mail or passengers through from St. Louis to San Francisco in under twenty-one days ("inside twenty-five days" was required by the mail contract), as Butterfield prophesied it would, but it came pretty close to it. Waterman Ormsby's twenty-three days, twenty-three hours on the first westward run[9] stood as a record for a long time. The trip seems to have shaken up that intrepid young journalist somewhat. Despite his statement on arrival at San Francisco that he felt fine and was willing to return East in the same way, he seems, in fact, to have gone back to New York by steamer.[1]

Even had the Overland Stage reduced its time to twenty days, it would not have satisfied a generation craving for even greater speed of communication. To meet that craving, the Pony Express was born on April 3, 1860. It took only mail (and not much of that) from St. Joseph, Missouri, to Sacramento, California, in under ten days, at the exceedingly high rate of from $2 to $10 an ounce. The Pony Express carried 34,753 items of mail before it was discontinued in October 26, 1861, just two days after the even faster transcontinental telegraph line was completed. The Pony Express carried far too little mail, and was much too expensive to its promoters, the staging firm of Russell, Majors, and Waddell, to make a lasting contribution to the transportation revolution of the West; but, as "promotion," it was in every way a fabulous achievement. It went to the heads of contemporaries[2] and has been keeping old men from the chimney corner and young men from the office desk ever since.

The Pony Express was only one of the many enterprises of Russell, Majors, and Waddell. William H. Russell and William B. Waddell began their western activities as government freight con-

9. See Ch. v.

1. Wright and Bynum, p. ix.

2. For one of many ecstatic contemporary accounts of the Pony Express and its riders, see the illus. article in *Hutchings' California Magazine*, repr. in its orig. form below, pp. 266 ff. Even Mark Twain (in *Roughing It*) was sufficiently overawed by the Pony Express to write an unusually dead-pan and entirely worshipful account of it. It is one of his best pieces of reporting—and probably his straightest.

tractors on the Santa Fe Trail in the early fifties. They provisioned the U. S. Army's Utah expeditionary force and "for about five years . . . dominated the freighting business on the plains."[3] Then they branched out—disastrously, as it was to prove—into stage-coaching and mail carrying. Their Leavenworth and Pike's Peak Express ran to the new mining frontier in Colorado from February 1859, about which time they also began carrying the mails (and some passengers) from St. Joseph to Salt Lake City. The Leavenworth and Pike's Peak Company went into liquidation before the year was out and was absorbed in the new and grandly titled Central Overland California and Pike's Peak Express Company, another Russell enterprise. Their aim was to dominate all stage, freight, and mail-carrying services between the Missouri and the Pacific Coast, and the froth on this heady idea was the spectacular Pony Express. On March 6, 1861, two days after President Lincoln's inauguration, the Butterfield Overland Mail (which ran through no fewer than four of the eleven southern states that were to secede from the Union and only one state—California—that was not) ground to a halt. Congress and the Post Office Department had already taken steps to transfer the Overland Mail to the central route, entirely through northern-dominated territory. Jefferson Davis was no longer in Washington to say them nay, as he was off in Richmond organizing a rival government. The new Overland Mail contract provided for a daily service between St. Joseph and Sacramento, to take thirty-five days or less (ideally, twenty-three, matching Butterfield's achievement further south). The Central Overland Company was to operate the section between the Missouri River and Salt Lake City, but the Butterfield Company (now presided over by Dinsmore) was to retain the lucrative route from Salt Lake to Virginia City, Nevada (this was the period of the earlier Comstock boom). The western end of the route from Virginia City to Sacramento was sublet to the Pioneer Stage Company. From there to San Francisco the river-steamer service was by this time so good that even the Pony Express used it. (On the first run, the ship carried both rider *and* horse from Sacramento in order that they could gallop up from the Embarcadero to the post office in Portsmouth Square and be subjected to a civic reception. The pony, it was reported by onlookers, by this time appeared some-

3. Winther: *Transportation Frontier*, p. 26. Their story is told in detail in R. W. and M. L. Settle: *Empire on Wheels* (Stanford, Calif., 1949).

what dazed.) Soon, of course, a railroad was to be completed up the Sacramento Valley. Had it been running by 1861, the unfortunate quadruped would probably have been put on board the train! Indeed, when the new Central Overland Stagecoach service began on July 18, 1861, it started at Hannibal, Missouri, and ended at Folsom, California, because by this time these two places had become railheads. Mails and passengers completed their westward safari by train on the newly opened Folsom to Sacramento railroad, the first in California. The Central Overland California and Pike's Peak Express sank under the weight of its Pony Express deficit and its none too profitable management of the Missouri to Salt Lake stage, and the gibe leveled at the company by its restive employees and a heartless press—that C.O.C. & P.P. stood for "Clean Out of Cash and Poor Pay"—was soon no exaggeration. Early in 1862 the company was declared bankrupt, and the chief creditor, one Benjamin Holladay, moved in for the kill. Holladay was to become the biggest stage and express tycoon of them all in the years that followed. The discredited C.O.C. & P.P. had its name shortened to the more manageable Overland Stage Company, and in case anybody should doubt who was now really boss, it soon became The Holladay Overland Mail and Stage Company. Nobody dared to make a play on words with those initials!

Benjamin Holladay's tentacles were now all over the West. He had a line up from Salt Lake City to Virginia City (Montana) on a new mining frontier, and others to Boise City (Idaho), Walla Walla (Washington), and the Columbia River valley. Hardy travelers could now go by stage all the way from Hannibal (reached by rail from eastern points) to The Dalles of the Columbia, courtesy of Ben Holladay (who constantly traveled his own stages to keep up standards and improve the service[4]). His competitors were impressed but not overawed. The Butterfield interests counterattacked in 1865 by founding the Butterfield Overland Dispatch, to play between Atchison, Kansas (by then an important railroad town), and Denver by the Indian-infested Smoky Hill Road, a variant on the old Leavenworth and Pike's Peak route. Holladay, scenting danger from the competition, made the B.O.D. an offer and bought it out in March 1866, when it was in temporary financial difficulties and growing tired of pulling arrows out of the

---

4. See further J. V. Frederick: *Ben Holladay: The Stagecoach King* (Glendale, Calif., 1940), passim.

coachwork and upholstery. But he continued to operate the Smoky Hill Road, and his empire had grown so big that people were beginning to call him "the Napoleon of the West." He didn't seem to mind! But what he did mind was the progress of the first transcontinental railroad, started by virtue of the Pacific Railroad Act of 1864 and now laying its inexorable ribbons of steel westward from Omaha and eastward from Sacramento.

The Holladay Overland Mail and Stage Company did not operate directly west of Salt Lake City, and the California Stage business had been dominated by Wells Fargo after the failure of

Indian attack on the Overland Express. From *Harper's Magazine*.

Adams and Company (a bank as well as an express company) in 1855. Wells Fargo bought out the Pioneer Company and was operating in Nevada as well as California, and soon it controlled the stage and express routes all the way to Salt Lake City itself. By 1866 the two giants stood face to face across the Bonneville salt flats, and it was only a question of which would swallow up the other. Holladay, when he took over the Butterfield Overland Dispatch Company, appeared to be the more likely winner, but, in an abrupt about-face almost as dramatic as the other Napoleon's action in the matter of the Louisiana Purchase, he sold out to Wells Fargo in November 1866 for a million and a half in cash, $300,000 in Wells Fargo stock, and a directorship in their company. This *douceur* no doubt made it easier for him to contemplate another change of corporate image, and see his name dropped from the title of the routes he had established or taken over. Henceforth "Wells, Fargo, and Company" operated all the way from the Missouri to the Pacific, and it was this great enterprise, not the astute Ben Holladay, which had to make the agonizing reappraisal of its operations that the driving of the golden spike at Promontory Point on May 10, 1869, rendered necessary. Wells Fargo survived, but not, probably, in a form of which Ben Holladay would have approved.

Ceremony at Promontory Point, Utah, May 10, 1869.

The driving of the gold and silver spikes by Leland Stanford and Thomas C. Durant amid the puffs and snorts of the C.P.'s *Jupiter* No. 60 and the U.P.'s No. 119, standing face to face on that memorable day, was the culmination of a long struggle, stretching right back into the 1840's, to achieve a transcontinental railroad. What was a dream to Asa Whitney, an unrealized ambition of Thomas Hart Benton, and a will o' the wisp for John C. Frémont (on his disastrous fourth expedition of 1848) became a reality only when the first train went through from Omaha to Sacramento. A journey which had never been completed by stagecoach passengers in less than twenty-one days, and which the Pony Express riders had brought down by superhuman efforts to just under nine days (carrying only a small *mochila* of gold-plated mail), could now be completed in a week by anybody who had the fare—and the stamina to go through without a break. In American transportation history, May 10, 1869, was the most important date since the opening of the Erie Canal in 1825, not to be matched until Wilbur Wright wobbled across the sands of Kitty Hawk and made the first

Laying the track of the Pacific Railroad. From Samuel Bowles: *Our New West* (Hartford, 1859).

sustained powered flight in a heavier-than-air machine in 1903, and Henry Ford, with more immediate practical effects, produced the first Model T automobile in 1907. General Grenville Dodge, chief engineer of the Union Pacific, describes the memorable occasion:

The Central Pacific had made wonderful progress coming east, and we abandoned the work from Promontory to Humboldt Wells, bending all our efforts to meet them at Promonotory. Between Ogden and Promontory each company graded a line, running side by side, and in some places one line was right above the other. The laborers upon the Central Pacific were Chinamen, while ours were Irishmen, and there was much ill-feeling between them. Our

Irishmen were in the habit of firing their blasts in the cuts without giving warning to the Chinamen on the Central Pacific working right above them. From this cause several Chinamen were severly hurt. Complaint was made to me by the Central Pacific people, and I endeavored to have the contractors bring all hostilities to a close, but, for some reason or other, they failed to do so. One day the Chinamen, appreciating the situation, put in what is called a "grave" on their work, and when the Irishmen right under them were all at work let go their blast and buried several of our men. This brought about a truce at once. From that time the Irish laborers showed due respect for the Chinamen, and there was no further trouble.

When the two roads approached in May, 1869, we agreed to connect at the summit of Promontory Point, and the day was fixed so that trains could reach us from New York and California. We laid the rails to the junction point a day or two before the final closing. Coming from the East, representing the Union Pacific, were Thomas C. Durant, Vice President, Sidney Dillon, who had taken a prominent part in the construction of the road from the beginning, and John R. Duff, directors, together with the consulting engineer and a carload of friends. From the West the representatives of the Central Pacific were its President, Leland Stanford, Mr. Collis P. Huntington, Mr. Crocker, Mr. Hopkins[5] Mr. Colton, and other members of that company, and Mr. Montague, chief engineer, and a detachment of troops from Camp Douglass, Salt Lake City. The two trains pulled up facing each other, each crowded with workmen who sought advantageous positions to witness the ceremonies, and literally covered the cars.[6]

"It was a bright but cold day," he added. "After a few speeches we all took refuge in the Central Pacific cars, where wine flowed freely, and many speeches were made." Samuel Bowles, writing in 1869, described the whole journey on the new railroad from Omaha to San Francisco Bay and compared it with his stagecoach ride over the same route in 1865.[7] He spared no superlatives:

There will speedily be other railroads across our Continent. The rivalries of sections, the temptations of commerce, the necessi-

5. The "Big Four" grocers of Sacramento; see above, p. 181.
6. Grenville M. Dodge: *How We Built the Union Pacific Railway and other Railway Papers and Addresses* (n.p., n.d.), pp. 15–16.
7. *Our New West*, Ch. iii, pp. 45–74.

ties of our political system, will add at least two more through lines within a generation's time. But this, the first, will forever remain the one of history; the one of romance. Its construction in so short a time was the greatest triumph of modern civilization, of all civilization, indeed. The work was seriously begun on the California side in 1864; on the eastern end in 1866; and the early part of the year 1869 witnessed its entire completion.[8]

The second transcontinental railroad link to be completed was across the great American Southwest and was owing to the enterprise and initiative of the promoters and builders of the Atcheson, Topeka, and Santa Fe Railroad, which also followed a historic trail. Said to "start nowhere and go nowhere," it is true that it had to veer southward down the Rio Grande valley past Albuquerque rather than continue west from the transportation "dead end" of New Mexico's capital. It is also true that it could get running rights to the Pacific Coast only by making costly and often disadvantageous agreements with the monopolistic Southern Pacific (successor to the Central Pacific) and its president, the inflexible Collis P. Huntington. But Santa Fe trains did run through. They were over the Raton Pass (after an epic struggle for track-laying priorities with the Denver and Rio Grande Railroad) in 1878 and into "La Cuidad de la Santa Fé de San Francisco" itself by 1878; by 1883 the Atlantic and Pacific Railroad (now a subsidiary of the Santa Fe Company) had been pushed as far as Needles, on the Colorado River, at the California-Arizona border; joint-tracking rights were secured with Huntington's Southern Pacific from Mojave to San Francisco, and a line from Barstow down to San Diego was completed by the California Southern, another Santa Fe subsidiary. Thus by blood, sweat, and not a few tears (shed in chagrin at Mr. Huntington's hard terms and his even more exacting interpretation of agreements), the Atcheson, Topeka, and Santa Fe Railroad system reached the Pacific Coast a decade and a half after the U.P.-C.P. joint enterprise.[9] The Santa Fe Railroad eventually was extended at both ends to run from Chicago to the Pacific Coast

8. *Our New West*, p. 68.

9. No railroad ever used the pass discovered by Joseph Reddeford Walker in 1834, despite his strong advocacy of this route in a verbal statement made before a committee of the California state legislature in 1853. For this statement, see Pat Adler and Walt Wheelock: *Walker's R.R. Routes—1853* (Glendale, Calif., 1965), which contains useful maps.

over its own lines. It also reached the Gulf of Mexico at Galveston and even right across Old Mexico from Nogales to the port of Guaymas, on the inner side of the Gulf of California. Its attempt to control and complete a more ambitious route across Mexico via Chihuahua to Topolobampo failed.[1]

Old-time locomotive crossing the Plains. From *Harper's Magazine.*

1. These two Mexican subsidiaries of the Santa Fe were both in Kino country (see above, Ch. ii, pp. 42 ff.). If he could have lived to 1882 and traveled up from the gulf to his missions at Magdalena and to Tubac by the Sonora Railway, this unflappable Jesuit would probably only have remarked "I told you so," and he would have shown Christian sympathy for another promoter and dreamer, one A. E. Stilwell, who in 1912 wrote: "The Kansas City, Mexico and Orient Railroad [surely the grandest of all those grand railroad names, but to be absorbed by the Santa Fe in 1928] is one of the greatest enterprises of today; it opens one of the treasure houses of the world in the mines of Mexico; it will build a port that will rival any on the Pacific coast . . . the port of Topolobampo . . . will have its line of steamers to the Orient, Central and South America, New Zealand and Australia . . . and the one hundred miles of the Fertile River Valley [Rio de la Fuerte], as rich as the Nile, will contribute great earnings to the road"—quoted in L. L. Waters: *Steel Trails to Santa Fe* (Lawrence, Kan., 1950) pp. 367–8. Alas, the line was never completed across the Sierra Madre, and Topolobampo remains a sleepy little Mexican fishing village. A rusty nationalized single-track runs up the Rio de la Fuerte as far as San Pedro, to the dead end of Stilwell's ambitions.

The way to finance transcontinental railroads through government aid had been pointed to by Senator Thomas H. Benton in
his unsuccessful bill of 1849, which advocated the sale of public
land to assist the building of a line from St. Louis to San Francisco,
and in 1850 the first federal grant of land to a railroad—though
not a transcontinental one—was made. By 1853 the clamor for
railroads to the Pacific from different parts of the Union caused
Congress to pass the Pacific Railroads Survey Act. This act called

for four possible routes—between the 49th and 47th parallels, between the 38th and 39th, along the 35th, and along the 32nd, to be explored and reported on by the Topographical Engineers of the Army. Enormous amounts of data were collected by these four surveys, and published in eleven huge and sumptuously illustrated volumes between 1855 and 1860. These surveys[2] were much more detailed and scientific than Frémont's better written but far more impressionistic reports of the 1840's. Each one worked out a practicable route from the Mississippi Valley to the Pacific, but not one of them was to be followed very closely by any of the five transcontinental railroads that were actually completed between 1869 and 1893, because the promoters of these made their own surveys and often, for political, financial, or other reasons, diverged considerably from the shortest, the easiest, or the most logical routes. But some were better than those that had been officially surveyed, for "the routes selected for survey were those with the most political support."[3]

The Central and the Union Pacific benefited from the two Pacific Railroad acts passed by Congress in 1862 and 1864, and signed by President Lincoln, to the extent of many millions of acres of land[4] and also received substantial cash subsidies, in the form of government bonds,[5] for every mile of line. The generous terms made millionaires of both the constructors and the operators of the first transcontinental railroad, and notably of Sacramento's Big Four, who acted in both capacities.

The next transcontinental railroad project to receive a federal

2. See G. L. Albright: *Official Explorations for Pacific Railroads* (Berkeley, Calif., 1921), and W. H. Goetzmann: *Army Exploration in the American West, 1803–1863* (New Haven, Conn., 1959), ch. vii. The 47th–49th parallel survey is typical of all four. It was led by Isaac Stevens, the first territorial governor of Washington, and its principal artist was John Mix Stanley, who in some eighty engravings publ. in the volumes has left a striking and imperishable picture of the American West along its northern borders, from Lake Superior to Puget Sound and the Columbia River Valley as it appeared in the 1850's.

3. Goetzmann: *Army Exploration*, p. 277.

4. For each mile built, ten alternate (odd-numbered) sections of government land on either side of a two-hundred-foot right of way were granted to the railroad.

5. These bonds were interest-bearing and redeemable in thirty years, but they were also instantly negotiable, so could be used to finance the laying of the tracks. The subsidy per mile varied from $16,000 across the Nebraska prairies to $48,000 in the stretches over the Rocky Mountains and the Sierras.

subsidy was not quite so generously treated. An act passed on July 4, 1864, authorized the construction of a line from Lake Superior to Puget Sound, to be called the Northern Pacific. This line received twice as much land per mile as the C.P.-U.P., but no cash subsidy. It was short of money from the start, and although authorized by Congress in 1869 to mortgage its assets, it fell into the hands of Jay Cooke, the Philadelphia financier to whom a railroad was strictly a speculation and not a public service, and was involved in his bankruptcy in 1873, when the line had reached only as far west as Bismarck. Henry Villard, another Eastern promoter, whose interest in the West dated from his visit to the gold mines at Gregory Gulch in 1859 as a journalist,[6] took over the ailing N.P. and pushed it through to Portland by 1883 and to Seattle by 1887. It was owing to this line that the real "Lewis and Clark country" was at last opened up to large-scale settlement, for the N.P. not only passed the site of the Mandan villages near Bismarck, but also ran up the Yellowstone River, over the Bozeman Pass, past the Three Forks of the Missouri to Missoula (Traveler's Rest), while one branch extended from Spokane to the Dalles and Portland. At the other end of the line, Minneapolis and St. Paul (Duluth was the second eastern terminal) went mad in 1873 in a huge celebration graced by the presence of President Chester A. Arthur, General Grant, General "Phil." Sheridan, and Carl Schurz. It was Henry Villard's finest hour, and "within four years St. Paul's population had doubled."[7]

Yet another transcontinental line, the Great Northern, was to be built without any federal subsidy at all, either in land or in cash. This was nearer to the Canadian border than the N.P. and approximated more closely the route surveyed in the fifties by Isaac Stevens. This was achieved by the financial genius of James J. Hill—the "Jim Hill" of the famous "Railroad Bum Song"[8]—and it was completed from Duluth to Seattle in 1893. It became one of the most successful of all the great trunk lines, despite the competition of the privately owned Canadian Pacific and the government-sponsored Canadian Trunk, both spanning the continent not far north of the border. The Great Northern, ninety years after, pursued the

6. See above, Ch. vii, p. 217.
7. Winther: *Transportation Frontier*, p. 116.
8. Oh I like Jim Hill; he's a good friend of mine
   And that's why I'm hiking down Jim Hill's main line. . . .

ghosts of Lewis and Clark, and the fur traders who followed them, even further, for it ran along the upper Missouri Valley where Forts Union and McKenzie had once stood and past Cut Bank on Maria's River, near where Lewis and three of his men had once stood off a Blackfoot war party. Browning, the Blackfoot tribal capital, is now a station on the Great Northern just before it climbs over the Continental Divide through the Lewis Range and descends Pacificward to Columbia Falls, above Flathead Lake, in the land of the "Big Sky."[9]

The 32nd parallel route, near the Mexican border and through Texas, was a gigantic battle ground of the Western and Eastern railroad tycoons Collis. P. Huntington, of the Southern Pacific, and Thomas Scott, of the Pennsylvania Railroad; the apple of Scott's eye was the Texas and Pacific project, which was chartered in 1871 and started from Marshall, Texas. He linked his eastern railroad empire up with this line at Dallas in 1873 and started pushing it across the northern Texas plains. Meanwhile, the Southern Pacific had bridged the Colorado and reached Yuma, Arizona. Without federal aid or sanction, it then struck across the Arizona and New Mexico territories to El Paso. The Texas and Pacific, which had meanwhile come under the control of another Wall Street wizard, Jay Gould, joined up with the Southern Pacific in an uneasy, and somewhat unholy, alliance in 1882. Once again Collis Huntington was to welsh on his agreements and to establish control over a more direct route across Texas to New Orleans before the end of the same year. Thus was established the famous Sunset Route. Now the fifth of the great transcontinental railroads had two prongs across Texas, one pointing through Fort Worth and Dallas at what was to become oil-rich North and East Texas, and the other, through San Antonio, at the cattle and staple-crop empires of the sub-tropical Gulf Coast area.

The Texas and Pacific thus never went beyond Texas; the Atlantic and Pacific (starting from Springfield, Missouri) had also been squeezed between the upper grindstone of the Acheson, Topeka, and Santa Fe and the nether grindstone of the Southern

9. A. B. Guthrie, Jr., gave the name *Big Sky* to his best-selling novel of the fur-trading era (New York, 1947); repr. in The Frontier Library (London, 1965). He comes from Choteau, Montana, has lived at Great Falls, and now (when not in Hollywood) makes his home at Twin Lake. Just over the mountains, in the Big Blackfoot Valley, is the Rocking Chair Ranch of the late R. G. Cleland. See map, p. 225.

Pacific, and it, too, never reached the promised land. The mills of Collis P. Huntington, also, ground exceeding small, and at one time he controlled all the transcontinental roads except the Great Northern. Another ambitious project, the Kansas Pacific, promoted by John Charles Frémont, reached Denver, connected with the U.P. at Cheyenne in 1871, and then gave up.

It was not until the twentieth century that a sixth transcontinental railroad joined the original five across the United States from the Mississippi to the Pacific, when the Chicago, Milwaukee, St. Paul, and Pacific railroad reached Seattle in 1909. New routes, but not through routes, led from Chicago as far as Montana (the Chicago, Burlington, and Quincy, and the Chicago and Northwestern), from Salt Lake City to the Columbia River (the Oregon Short Line, continuing the U.P.), from Pueblo to Salt Lake City (a branch of the Denver and Rio Grande[1]), from San Francisco to Portland (the California and Oregon, a subsidiary of the S.P.), down the San Joaquin Valley from Mojave to San Francisco (an extension of the Atlantic and Pacific–Santa Fe system), from Los Angeles to Salt Lake City (the San Pedro, Los Angeles, and Salt Lake Line), and finally (in 1911) from San Francisco to the Salt Lake (the Western Pacific more or less paralleling the half-century-old Central Pacific). The opening of the Panama Canal in 1915 may be said to have effectively ended all dreams of new transcontinental railroads, though, as has been seen, A. E. Stilwell still had one more magnificent dream in his pipe as late as 1912.

By 1915, too, it was already possible to cross the continent (hopefully, and sometimes even to arrive) by automobile. The Lincoln Highway Association had been founded in 1914 to promote what is now U. S. 40 into a hard surfaced route all the way. This, along with the other transcontinental highways of the next quarter-century, brought to an end the great age of the railroads, just as they in their time had ended the era of the stagecoach and the covered wagon. One man, Ezra Meeker, managed to straddle the whole transportation revolution:

> Out in the State of Washington a seventy-six-year-old man with long white hair and beard started east with an ox team along the road he had traveled westward in 1852. He intended to stop at all the small

1. For the trials, tribulations and triumphs of this remarkable intramontane narrow-guage line, see R. Athearn: *Rebel of the Rockies* (New Haven, Conn., 1962), passim.

towns, organize civic-minded citizens and enlist their help to mark the once famous trail. His trip elicited immediate response. In the East great crowds lined the roads to see him. He drove into New York City and stopped his ox team to be photographed in Wall Street. He went to Washington and shook hands with the great Rough Rider. Ezra Meeker had achieved his mission, but he had only begun to be famous as an overland pioneer. In 1916—aged eighty-six—he made the trip again in an automobile with a covered wagon top and camp outfit. The daring experiment of crossing the continent in a motor car, he said, was one of his ambitions in life. And it was an achievement, surely enough. The Lincoln Highway Association had not been organized until 1914, and people still wrote books about motoring from coast to coast. The dusty, rutted roads bore no resemblance to the modern highways tourists travel today on U. S. 40 to the Northwest [sic] or U. S. 30 through the Donner Pass [sic] to San Francisco. . . .

The Covered Wagon, with accompanying strains of "Oh, Susanna," proved one of the most popular pictures of the silent screen, and with its success the Overland Trail became an American epic. The year following the picture's opening on Broadway, an aviation meet was held in Dayton, Ohio. An old biplane appeared in the western sky. It sailed down to the field, circled, came to the ground and taxied along the track before the grandstands. Two goggled figures sat in the tandem cockpit. They pulled off their helmets, and the crowd beheld white-haired Ezra Meeker, aged ninety-four. He had made his last trip, high in the air, above the Oregon Trail.[2]

That was 1926. A year later a young man, almost as young as Ezra Meeker had been when he drove an ox team west in 1852, started out from St. Louis eastward. Like James Knox Polk Miller in 1867, he was Paris-bound. On the wings of *The Spirit of St. Louis*, Charles Augustus Lindbergh was to make the first solo flight across the Atlantic. Ezra Meeker, at ninety-five, lived into yet another transportation era, in which the wheels of Marcus Whitman had come full circle.

2. Jay Monaghan: *The Overland Trail* (New York, 1947), Epilogue, pp. 412–13. In fact, it is U. S. 30 that goes to the Pacific Northwest and U. S. 40 through the Donner Pass to San Francisco; see Stewart: *U. S. 40*, passim.

HUTCHINGS'

CALIFORNIA MAGAZINE.

Vol. V.   JULY, 1860.   No. 1.

THE PONY EXPRESS.

SWIMMING THE STORM-SWOLLEN STREAM.

WE are not about to insist that the Pony Express is the greatest of all the great enterprises of modern times, nor are we contemplating the running down of others, by way of proving that this individual one is particularly and pre-eminently *the* enterprise of the present day; but we shall show that in speed of transmitting news and letters, nothing has ever equaled it on this continent.

We remember with what enthusiastic

welcoming the first Overland Mail was received here, on the 10th of October, 1858, which had made the trip from St. Louis to San Francisco, via Los Angeles, in the unprecedented short time of twenty-three days and twenty-one hours. This was a great achievement, and should not be overlooked, especially as a better average of speed has been made from that time to this, almost in every instance anticipating the mail steamer's news.

Nor should we overlook the demonstration of joy everywhere manifest, when the pioneer mail steamship, the *California*, plowed the waters of the bay, on the 28th day of February, 1850; and the actual benefits that have arisen from passenger and mail transportation by the steamships of this and other companies from that time to this, with all their high prices and abuses—and heaven knows they have been high enough and bad enough. Yet, to suppose them out of the way, before the Pacific Railroad is built, would be to suppose one of the most deplorable extremities to which California could be reduced, especially as it would be utterly impossible to convey, overland, the thirty or more dray loads of mail matter sent by every steamer; to say nothing of the four hundred or more passengers that depart semi-monthly for the Atlantic ports. We wish to offer no plea in justification of the exhorbitant rates of passage charged, nor the over-crowding and other abuses to which travelers have to submit, simply because they cannot help themselves; but to ask a question arising from the circumstances of the case. "After all, what could we do without them—at least, until the railroad is built?" and which at present appears very doubtful. Therefore, while we remember the one with just exultation and pride, let us not forget the other in ingratitude—however great the humiliation we may feel, that through the selfish conniving of interested politicians, who cannot be accredited

with being statesmen—a greater good, the Pacific Railroad, is indefinitely postponed. With this brief allusion to these valuable public enterprises, we can with a better conscience proceed to speak of a private one of equal importance, in a new and commercial point of view—THE PONY.

This Express was established by Majors, Russell & Co., whose principal office is at Leavenworth, Missouri, and who have had the mail contract from St. Joseph, Mo., to Salt Lake City, for several years. When gold had been discovered, and mining settlements began to flourish at Pike's Peak, this enterprising company organized a branch Express to that point also.

Early in the present year the plans for the establishing of the Pony Express from St. Joseph to San Francisco, were perfected, and Major Solomon, U. S. Marshal for California, was authorized to select and procure as fine a collection of fleet-footed and muscular horses, as could be found in the State.

This accomplished, Mr. W. W. Finney was dispatched as general road agent, and who arrived here in March last, with the intention of starting the Pony on the first day of April, ensuing. But owing to the difficulty of arranging the stations beyond Placerville, on account of several severe snow storms having rendered the trails almost impassable, it was found next to impossible to get feed for the animals, and provisions for the men packed out at any price; and but for the kindness of Mr. Halliday, who promptly cashed the drafts of the company, a still further delay would have been inevitable; yet owing to this well-timed assistance, Mr. Finney was enabled to purchase trains of pack mules, and thus prosecute the work of stocking the stations, which he did with untiring energy.

All things being in readiness, early on the morning of the third of April, the "Pony" was placed at the door of the

PASSING AN EMIGRANT TRAIN ON THE PLAINS.

Alta Telegraph Company, on Montgomery street, San Francisco, decked with a small U. S. flag on each side of his head, and a neat pair of leather bags *in the mochila** of the saddle, on which was painted "Pony Express." At a few minutes before 4 o'clock, P. M., of the same day, in order to be in time for the Sacramento boat, the first messenger left the office, on his arduous undertaking.

At 5 P. M. of the same day, the first Pony Express was dispatched from St. Joseph, with St. Louis dates up to the time of starting.

As many of our readers have probably never crossed this portion of the continent, perhaps they would like to accompany the Pony—at least in imagination—for the purpose of seeing the country; which, if it be not as instructive, or as life-like as an actual trip, can be taken in less time, at a smaller expense, and with

* As the reader is probably aware, the "mochila" is the common, though Spanish name, for the leather covering of a California saddle.

considerable less fatigue, danger, inconvenience and exposure than is traveled by every expressman on the route.

The moment the St. Joseph's ferry-boat touches the western side of the Missouri river, the "rider" mounts his steed and dashes up the steep bank and across the heavily-timbered alluvium on the margin of the stream. The beautiful undulating country, carpeted with green, or covered with flowers; the songs of the birds, the wild bees prospecting for honey, even the declicious flavor of the strawberries that grow in bounteous profusion on every hand, are alike unheeded—for onward he hastens.

The loud peals of thunder, and the fierce flashes of lightning, or even the falling of the drenching rain, detains him not. What though the storm-swollen banks of the streams are full to overflowing, so that even the landmarks for crossing are altogether invisible, it deters him not, for in it he plunges and speeds along on his rapid course, undismayed.

Whether sun-dried or soaked, snow-covered or frozen, by day or by night, in starlight or darkness, be he lonely or merry, forward he hastens, until the thrice welcome station is just there, in sight, when he leaps from his saddle, and with full heart rejoices that his task for the present is fully accomplished, Here another, whose horse, like himself, has been waiting, perhaps without shelter, quickly takes the *mochila*, which contains all the letters. On his saddle he throws it, then jumps to his seat, shouts a hearty " Good-night, boys," and is lost in the distance, He rides on alone, over prairies and mountains, whether up hill or down, on rough ground or smooth, among true friends or foes, he hies swiftly on, until in the shadowy distance the relay is seen, and his duty's performed.

Again and again, from station to station, this is often repeated, until from the Carson, across the Sierras, a message announces the " Pony's arrival," with news from St. Louis in eight days or less.

The following table, kindly furnished us by Mr.——————— of the Alta Telegraph office, will not only indicate the general route traveled, but the number, name and distance of the principal stations :

From St. Joseph to 1st Station	25
Kinnekuk	25
3d Station	23
Marysville on Big Blue	45
5th Station	30
Little Blue	65
Up Little Blue	35
Fort Kearney	50
Plum Creek	40
Cottonwood	40
Crossing South Platte	85
Ash Hollow	18
Rush Creek	36
Larence Fork	21
Chimney Rock	18
Scott's Bluff	25
Horse Creek	15
Fort Laramie	35
Horse-shoe Creek	42
Deer Creek	58

Platte Bridge	25
1st Crossing Sweetwater	54
3d do do	40
Last do do	50
South Pass	10
Dry Sandy	12
Little Sandy	18
Big Sandy	6
Green River	20
Ham's Fork	20
Miller's Fork	20
Fort Bridger	12
Bear River	40
Weber River, mouth Echo Canon	30
Salt Lake City	42
Hot Springs	20
Camp Floyd	27
Rush Valley	24
Simpson's Springs)	27
Dug Way (Well) } Desert	20
Fish Springs)	30
Pleasant Valley	46
Shell Creek	45
Thousand Spring Valley	34
Ruby Valley	21
Two Springs	18
Next Station	12
Willow Creek	25
Antelope Creek	18
Mouth of Cañon	28
Cold Springs	20
Reese's River	20
Willow Creek	13
Sink of Carson River	50
Walker's River	22
Up Walker's River	14
Carson River	14
Miller's Station	12
Carson City	18
Placerville	100
Sacramento City	50
San Francisco	118
Total	1996

Up to the time of interruption by the breaking out of the Washoe Indian war, eight trips had been successfully made, in which the average number of letters carried from this side to the east was ninety-two, and those from the east, fifteen. From each way a steady increase was observable.

On the breaking out of the Indian disturbances, the volunteers, we are informed, without any regard whatever to the wants of the Express, pressed the

DISTANCING THE OVERLAND MAIL STAGE.

stock from several stations into their service, and omitted to restore it; stores were appropriated in a similar manner; thus materially crippling the efficiency of the company before the Indians had molested it in any way.

No sooner had actual hostilities commenced than Indian aggression began to be manifest upon the route of the Pony, as the following dispatch from C. H. Ruffin, an employee of the company, located at Miller's Station, to W. W. Finney, road agent:

"Miller's Station, May 31.

"I have just returned from Cold Springs —was driven away by the Indians, who attacked us night before last. The men at Dry Creek Station have been killed, and it is thought the Robert's Creek Station has been destroyed. The Express turned back after hearing the news from Dry Creek. Eight animals were stolen from Cold Springs on Monday. Hamilton is at the Sink of the Carson, on his way in with all the men and horses. He will get to Buckland to-morrow."

We cannot do better here than re-publish the following well-written letter, to the S. F. *Bulletin*, as it tells of the intrepidity and daring, and we regret to say, the melancholy end of a courageous man:—

IN MEMORIAM.
PLACERVILLE, May 31, 1860.
Editor Bulletin: You will oblige many by publishing the following tribute to the memory of a brave man:

Bartholomew Riley died last night, at Carson City, of a rifle-shot wound received at Cold Springs Station, on the Pony Express route, on the 16th of May. He had received an honorable discharge from Company E of the 10th Regiment of U. S. Infantry, at Camp Floyd, and was *en route* to California, where he has brothers and sisters residing, when intelligence of the Indian outrage at Williams' ranch was first brought to Carson. As might be expected from a gallant soldier, he did not hesitate what course to pursue, but at once threw himself into the ranks of the ill-fated volunteers, under Major Ormsby. During the trying scenes of that bloody day, at Pyramid Lake, he was conspicuous among them all for the intrepidity and gallantry of his conduct. Like the white plume of Henry of Navarre, his course was where the battle raged fiercest and the bullets flew thickest, but he heeded them not. More than one of the dusky enemy were made painfully aware of the unerring accuracy of his aim, whilst his were the friendly hands that performed the last kind service for the lamented Ormsby.

Among the last to leave the field, Riley did not reach Buckland's until near daylight, just as the Express going East arrived, on the 15th May. The rider upon whom devolved the duty of going forward with the Express shrinking from its performance, and when there seemed no alter-

CROSSING THE SIERRAS IN A SNOW-STORM.

native but a failure, Riley, fresh from the battle-field and tired as he was, stepped forth and volunteered to ride to the next change, a distance of 85 miles. He did so in excellent time.

On the following day, by the accidental discharge of a weapon in the hands of a friend, he received wounds from which he died last night. "He sleeps his last sleep —he has fought his last battle." May the last trump "awake him to glory again."

Thomas Flynn, the rider of the Pony Express from Genoa to Sink of Carson, who came in on Thursday night, informs us, says the *Territorial Enterprise* of June 2d, that the last Pony Express going East was turned back at Dry Creek, 250 miles east of here. No word there had been heard of the Express coming from the East. Six Pike's Peakers found the body of the station keeper horribly mutilated, and all the animals missing at Simpson's Park, as reported last week. Mr. Hamilton and Ruffin, with others of the Pony Express, took the stock from Smith's Creek, and camped at night at Cold Springs; Ruffin and Hamilton, while on guard, were fired

on by the Indians. The whole party on hearing the shots saddled up and moved off. They, in the moving, overtook some emigrants with 3,000 sheep; some forty men were with the sheep train. That party is now safe at Miller's Station. Josephus, a friendly Pah-Ute, who has been in the employ of the Pony Express Company, advised Flynn to leave with his stock from the Sink of Carson immediately. He heeded the warning, and attributes his safety to that fact.

It is ascertained beyond doubt, that most of the stations from Carson Valley to Camp Floyd, have been destroyed by the Indians, and it is thought that several of the employees have been murdered, and the stock driven off. Mr. Finney, with the intention of ascertaining the situation of the men and the condition of the stations, and with the view of re-establishing the Express, appealed to the public for men, well armed and provisioned, and $1,000 for their pay. This met with a prompt response, at 2 P.M., of June 9th, from twenty picked men, who were to start under Mr. F., but as he was indisposed, they left Carson City the same morning without him, well armed and mounted.

Where the country was favorable, the stations were distant from each other between 25 and 75 miles, according to the necessities of the route. The last Express that came through, made the trip from St. Joseph to Carson City, in less than six days' actual traveling time; but owing to the stock being run off, was delayed at the stations. The storms this spring, at the time the Pony was running, were very severe on the riders, and the roads were never in a worse condition. Besides, owing to the great depth of snow on the Sierras, but one trail (and that very narrow), was beaten; and as this was blocked up in many places with pack trains and travelers on their way to the Washoe silver mines, much detention was caused.

The company feel confident of being able to make the time regularly from St. Joseph to Carson Valley, in from five to six days. With all the drawbacks of the first few trips from St. Joseph to Carson City, the following excellent time was made:

First express from St. Joseph through to San Francisco, in 10 days; 2d, 14 days; 3d, 9 days; 4th, 10 days; 5th, 9 days; 6th, in 9 days. Those going eastward, were taken from San Francisco through to St. Joseph. By putting on a daily express and two riders, instead of one, that company affirm that it will carry the entire letter mail from San Francisco to St. Joseph, within six days. Of course this would be of immense advantage to the public. If this could be carried into effect, without injury to the overland mail, via Los Angeles, we should like to see it done.

On the evening of the 23d ult, another express arrived safely at Carson City, with St. Louis dates to the 9th, under guard of fifty mounted U. S. troops, as an escort to protect them from massacre by Indians, and to assist in re-establishing the stations destroyed. They met the twenty armed volunteers who took the last out-going express from Carson City.

THE CALIFORNIA WILD PLUM.

It is very probable that many of our readers who dwell in the principal mercantile cities are unaware that in the mountains of this State there are not less than two varieties of a very excellent wild plum. One is almost the size—although we have seen some much larger—and shape of that given in our engraving, the other is a little smaller, oblong, and almost the shape and color of a damson when ripe. This latter variety has not yet been examined and classified by botanists; but if some of our friends who are coming to the city will bring a good specimen with them and leave it with us, we will see that this is done.

Both varieties of this plum grow on low bushes, and not on trees like other wild plums at the east, and are about the height and conformation of the illustration given on page 10.

They generally grow in patches or groups, at the heads of ravines, at an altitude seldom less than two thousand feet above the sea, and mostly in open localities adjacent to pine forests, but not directly in it. The bushes are found near to each other, and the two varieties frequently grow in the same group, though not from the same root.

Both are excellent edibles, although those that are round are the first ripe and better, eaten as fruit or stewed as sauce, and preferred by some palates; but when the oblong plum is thoroughly ripe, its rich acetous flavor, in our estimation, far excels the other, and which makes a delicious preserve.

Just before the fruit is fit for use, a large proportion of its leaves drop off,

CHAPTER IX

The Indian Problem
and Its Solution

HE WOODLAND INDIANS OF THE EAST HAD SOMETIMES fought the colonists and sometimes allied themselves with them against other foes. In the struggles between the French and the Spaniards, the French and the British, the Royal forces and the revolted colonists, the Indians had been used by both sides. From time to time Indian leaders, like King Philip and Pontiac, had put up a broader resistance to the white man than the usual sporadic defense or attack employed by the chiefs of individual tribes. Of the various attempts made to end Indian warfare by treaty or by insulating the Indian hunting grounds from the settlements of the white men, the most ambitious was the famous Proclamation Line drawn by the government of King George III along the crest of the Appalachians in 1763. All beyond this line was to remain Indian hunting grounds in perpetuity. Almost immediately Edmund Burke perceived that the Proclamation Line would be useless to stop the westward surge of the white settlers, who, already restive under British rule, would only find it a new grievance. His eloquent prophecy was very soon to come true:

Many of the people in the back settlements are already little attached to particular situations. Already they have topped the Appalachian mountains. From thence they behold before them an immense plain. . . . Over this they would wander without possibility of restraint; they would change their manners with the habits of their life; would soon forget a government by which they were disowned; would become hordes of English Tartars; and pouring down upon your unfortified frontiers a fierce and irresistible cavalry, become masters of your governors and your counsellors, your collectors and comptrollers, and of all the slaves that adhered to them. . . . Such would be the unhappy result of an endeavour to keep as a lair of wild beasts, that earth, which God, by an express Charter, has given to the children of men. . . .[1]

Burke's philosophy, put more crudely, was also that of the colonial and American settler who equated the Indians with the wild beasts, headed for extermination as the wilderness was tamed. Unlike the Middle American Indians, those of the North did not provide the white man with a labor force for the fields or the mines, nor were they suitable, except to a very limited extent, as house servants. Even when converted to Christianity, they tended to cling to their tribal ways and continued to live in their tribal long houses, tepees, pueblos, or hogans. There were just enough of them—perhaps half a million at the time of the Mexican War of 1846, when their systematic extermination may be said to have commenced—to be a nuisance to the white man, but not enough to be his tool in the creation of a new and powerful nation. Thus, slavery was introduced, and the willing, cheerful, malleable, and prolific Negro became the hewer of wood and the drawer of water for the American South—remaining so even after emancipation. The North, with a different climate and economy, was able to draw upon ever-increasing immigration from Europe for its basic labor force. In neither section was any serious attempt made to integrate the Indian with the economy or the social institutions of the white communities. This applied to even such adaptable peoples as the Five Civilized Tribes of the East and the Pueblo Indians of the Rio Grande valley, who were far from being the wild Stone Age savages many white men imagined all Indians to be. Oddly enough, a "tame" Indian was no more highly regarded than a wild Indian in white circles; indeed, he was denied the respect sometimes accorded to such untameable figures as Sitting Bull, Chief Joseph, or Geronimo. The Indian who "came over" into a white community all too often remained a second-class citizen (and in the

1. *The Works of Edmund Burke*, 12 vols. (London and Boston, 1866-7), II, 131-2.

civic sense he rarely, if ever, was able to exercise a citizen's rights);
in white communities intermarriage with Indians was rare—between white women and red men, virtually nonexistent. Most of
the "squaw men" of the furthest frontier concluded strictly temporary alliances with Indian brides, making full use of the looseness of
the marriage tie among the tribes, and often lived part of each year
as Indians, in the villages of their squaws, adopted as members of
the tribe. Stable communities of squaw men, like the Hudson's Bay
headquarters at Fort Vancouver on the Columbia River, were rare,
and greatly resented by bigoted white visitors like the Reverend
Mr. Beaver.[2] When the mountain men visited Bent's Fort and
similar establishments to trade and carouse, they tended to leave
their Indian wives outside the walls. "A wife in the tepee" was a
well-understood term. Sometimes the mountain men in question
would have another more favored squaw, or a Mexican wife, waiting for him inside—an additional reason for parking the other one
extra-murally, as if she were one of his ponies or mules. An Indian
man living in a white community tended to be looked upon with
the sort of suspicion that Negroes did not attract. (Compare the
villainous "Injun Joe" of *Tom Sawyer* with the delightful "Jim" of
Huckleberry Finn.) However, the half-breed—to the same extent
as the half-Negro—though the victim of much unreasonable
prejudice, could "pass over" much more easily than the full-blood,
and some, like Baptiste Charbonneau, were even made pets of by
the white man, accepted as their equals (for most purposes), and
shown the great world.[3]

The Declaration of Independence rightly accused the British
monarch and his agents of using the Indians against the colonists:
"He has endeavored to bring on the inhabitants of our frontiers the
merciless Indian savages whose known rule of warfare is an undis-
tinguished destruction of all ages, sexes and conditions." Great
Britain continued to use Indian allies against her colonists and ex-
colonists right up to the end of the War of 1812. Tecumseh, the

2. See Ch. v, p. 151.
3. Prince Paul of Württemberg took Baptiste back to Germany with him in
1823, where this natural gentleman moved as easily amid the stiff etiquette of the
Schloss as he had in the free and easy life of lodge and rendezvous. He had, of
course, as a youth received an education in the ways of the white man in St. Louis,
as William Clark's ward, and he had the high prestige of being the son of
Sacagawea.

Indian "nationalist" leader, and his brother, "The Prophet," sided with the British.[4] This undoubtedly further hardened the hearts of the American frontiersman against the Indian. By 1815 the policy of "Indian removal" into remote and supposedly barren regions well beyond the Mississippi had already been put into operation. The Great American Desert of Pike and Long seemed to have been expressly created by an all-foreseeing Providence to receive these outcasts, far from "the Garden of the World" that was the white man's heritage. The traveler and trader H. M. Breckenridge asserted in 1817 that the Indian nations "will continue to wander over those plains, and the wild animals, the elk, the buffalo, will long be found there; for until our country becomes supercharged with population, there is scarcely any probability of settlers venturing far into these regions."[5] Removal of the eastern tribes, therefore, into what men were beginning to call the Indian Country seemed at the time a permanent solution to the Indian problem.

As early as 1790 the half-Scottish, quarter-French, Creek Indian chief Alexander McGillivray had signed away some of his tribe's lands to the U. S. government in return for a perpetual guarantee of the remainder. This was only the beginning of a long process that ended with all that were left of the Five Civilized Tribes of the Carolinas, Georgia, and Florida being pitchforked across the Mississippi. The infamous Indian Removal Act of 1830 had the effect of expelling the Creeks and Cherokees from Georgia and Alabama (which had become a state in 1819), and the Chocktaws and Chickasaws from Mississippi (a state since 1817); the removal was expedited by state laws that were much more radically anti-Indian than existing federal legislation, and President Jackson, to his lasting shame (he was, after all, an old Indian fighter and too old a dog to change his habits and prejudices), did nothing to protect the members of the unfortunate civilized tribes. The removal caused much misery and suffering, and nearly a quarter of

4. See Alvin M. Josephy, Jr.: *The Patriot Chiefs* (New York, 1961; repr. The Frontier Library, London, 1963), passim, for details of the career of Tecumseh and those of eight other Indian "patriot" leaders.

5. *Views of Louisiana: Containing Geographical, Statistical and Historical Notices of that Vast and Important Portion of America* (Baltimore, 1817); repr. in Early Western Travels Series, ed. R. G. Thwaites (Cleveland, 1904–7), p. 72; quoted in Henry Nash Smith: "The Garden and the Desert," Ch. xvi of *Virgin Land* (Cambridge, Mass., 1950; paperback edn., New York, 1957, p. 203, cited here).

the whole Cherokee nation died on the way before the survivors were finally resettled west of the Mississippi in 1839. The Seminoles were brought out from Florida and resettled in the Indian Territory by 1842, but they had fiercely resisted their removal and it cost the United States a seven years' long war of great cruelty on both sides.

The tribes of the old Northwest, crushed at Fallen Timbers by Anthony Wayne in 1794, signed away their lands to the Americans in a series of treaties, some extorted under duress, beginning with that at Greenville in 1795. Tecumseh's efforts to prevent the handing over of any more land north or west of the Ohio River by any tribe ended with his death in 1813, and in 1816 the Sauk Indians signed away part of eastern Missouri as well as additional lands in Wisconsin and Illinois. This was the beginning of the erosion of the Indian trans-Mississippi West. Second thoughts on the part of the Sauk chieftain Black Hawk, when a minor leader of his tribe, Keokuk, sought to hand over even more land, led to the Black Hawk War of 1832 and the opening up of Iowa, as well as the rest of Wisconsin, to white settlement. A treaty concluded at Prairie du Chien on the Mississippi in 1825 had guaranteed certain of their ancestral lands both east and west of that river to the Chippewa, Sauk, and Foxes, Menominee, Iowa, Sioux, Winnebago, Ottowa, and Potawatomi, but within a few years the remainder of the Old Northwest—the great area between the Ohio and the upper Mississippi rivers—was utterly lost to the Indians. By 1846 only about 150 Potawatomi were left in Indiana; the rest had departed west of the Mississippi.

What were left of the Woodland Indians were, for the most part, "jumbled west of the Mississippi,"[6] having to share the traditional hunting grounds of the Plains Indians, who did not always take kindly to these intruders. In 1834 the High Plains had been set aside as Indian Country, to be administered by a Bureau of Indian

6. William Brandon: *The American Heritage Book of Indians* (New York, 1961), p. 252. The narrative portions of this book, for which Mr. Brandon was responsible, have been repr. in a paperback edn. (New York, 1963) and though the orig. edn. was magnificently illus., it is the narrative that is the most valuable part of the book. This constitutes a comprehensive and sensitive treatment of the fate of the Indians of North America, to which this present ch. is greatly indebted. An attempted "popularization" of Mr. Brandon's fine prose, by the eds. of *American Heritage*, in the art-paper pages on which the illus. are printed in the hardcover edition, is much less satisfactory.

Chief Joseph's Retreat→→

1784

CHINOOK

CAYUSE

Columbia R.

BLACKFEET   ASSINIBOINE

FLATHEAD

ARIKARA

1742   MANDAN

WALLA WALLA

WASCO

Yellowstone R.

4
5

⊗
Umpqua Massacre

KLAMATH

PAIUTE

NEZ PERCE

Wallowa L.

7

CROW

CHEYENNE

MODOC

LAVA BEDS

WASHOE

Snake R.

Pierre's Hole

Humboldt R.

SHOSHONE

BUFFALO

Great Salt Lake

N. Platte R.

ARAPAHO

Republican

MIWOK

[Numerous small tribal groups]

PAIUTE

UTE

S. Platte R.

1700

PAWNEE

ANCIENT INDIAN SITES

Colorado R.

NAVAJO
HOPI

☐ Mesa Verde

Cimarron R.

1682

Canadian

MOJAVE

MARICOPA   PIMA

YUMA

Gila R.   PAPAGO

ZUÑI

P
U
E
B
L
O
S

☐ Casa Grande

1714

KIOWA

A P A C H E

COMANCHE

BUFFALO

Pecos R.

Rio Grande

DISTRIBUTION OF PRINCIPAL INDIAN TRIBES & GROUPS c.1800

"Five Civilised ⎫ original   **CREEK**   *after 19TH cent.*   CREEK
Tribes"   ⎭ location   *removal*

PRINCIPAL RESERVATIONS
as finally established c.1890

CULTURE of the PLAINS INDIANS
·········· *c.1800*

Spread of ⟩⟩⟩⟩⟩ 1700   Distribution of
the Horse   Buffalo c.1800 ⟞⟞

Spanish horses acquired by Indians c.1650

SIOUX MIGRATIONS

Original hunting grounds
Ⓗ Hunkpapa Ⓣ Teton Ⓢ Santee
Ⓞ Oglala Ⓑ Brulé Ⓨ Yankton

BATTLES

❶ Bloody Run ❷ Fallen Timbers
❸ Tippecanoe ❹ Little Big Horn
❺ Rosebud ❻ Horseshoe Bend
❼ Fetterman Massacre

BUFFALO

CHIPPEWA

Lake Superior

OJIBWA

SAUK & FOX

L. Huron

Lake Michigan

L. Ontario

IROQUOIS CONFEDERACY (FIVE NATIONS)

PONCA

1738

OMAHA

Platte R.

IOWA

OTOE

Mississippi R.

Lake Erie

❶

❷

INDIAN BOUNDARY 1812

Ohio R.

SHAWNEE

Cumberland R.

❸

y Hill R.

Arkansas R.

OSAGE

MISSOURI

Missouri R.

PROCLAMATION LINE OF 1763

CHEROKEE

CREEK

SEMINOLE

CHICKASAW

CHOCTAW

CHEROKEE

CHICKASAW

CHOCTAW

❻

CREEK

Savannah R.

Brazos R.

Colorado R.

Red R.

BUFFALO

INDIAN WESTWARD REMOVALS

SEMINOLE

SEMINOLE (remnants)

Gulf of Mexico

0 Miles 500

W.B.

Affairs, established in Washington in 1832. But the policy of a "permanent Indian frontier"[7] was soon in ruins under the inexorable pressure of more and more white settlers. Many inroads were made by these on the Indian Country, and the overland parties which began to take wagons across it in the direction of the Pacific Coast in the early forties were forced to traverse it, even if they did not stop and settle in it. The treaties that had guaranteed their trans-Mississippi lands to the Indians "as long as the stars shall shine and rivers flow" began to be systematically abrogated in 1853, the year of Jefferson Davis's railroad surveys, and in 1854 the Kansas-Nebraska Act, for the purpose of which Stephen A. Douglas, of Illinois, secured the cancellation of the 1834 act, reduced the Indian Country to the much more restricted confines of what is now the state of Oklahoma, which was speedily to be reduced to the position of an island in the ever-advancing white man's West. Kansas and Nebraska became territories in the fifties; and the Dakotas, Montana, Wyoming, Idaho, Colorado, New Mexico, and Arizona in the sixties—the first step in the direction of their massive settlement by white men. The Mormons had already broken the "Indian barrier" before the 1840's were over, to establish Zion in the Great Basin kingdom beyond the hunting grounds of the Plains Indians or the haunts of the buffalo herds. The unfortunate red man was beset on all sides. He continued to give up land by treaty, but, more often than not, his land was simply taken from him, while the U. S. government made treaties only to break them.

No wonder was it that in 1862 the Plains Indians abandoned their mood of fatalistic acquiescence in the depredations of the white man and, while the sons of the Great White Father were engaged in slaughtering each other in the Civil War, chose to return to a more active defense of their treaty rights and their heritage. After twenty years of only intermittent and small-scale trouble on the Indian frontier—during which some tribes, like the Winnebago, had been peaceably moved on no fewer than five times—the Sioux decided to resist, and were followed by the Cheyennes and other tribes. In 1862 the Secretary of the Interior

7. During the 1830's this "frontier" ran approximately from the south shore of Lake Superior down to Green Bay; then across northern Wisconsin to the Mississippi River; down that river nearly to Fort Crawford; through east-central Iowa to the Missouri line; and along the northern and western boundaries of Missouri and the western boundary of Arkansas to the Red River.

himself had sought to justify further Indian dispossessions as simply "yielding to necessity."[8]

If the Secretary of the Interior, sitting on the right hand of the Great White Father himself, could say in 1862 that "the government has always demanded the removal of the Indians when their lands were required for agricultural purposes by advancing settlements," whatever their treaty rights, it was only to be expected that local and state officials in frontier regions would express themselves even more crudely on the subject. Thus, in 1864, the white agent of the Osage Indians in Kansas said of the lands he was supposed to be protecting from them: "The Indian lands are the best in the State, and justice would demand, as well as every consideration of policy and humanity, that these fertile lands should be thrown open to settlement and the abode of civilized and industrious men."[9] The Governor of the Colorado Territory went even further in 1870: "God gave us the earth, and the fullness thereof . . . I do not believe in donating to these indolent savages the best portion of my territory, and I do not believe in placing the Indians on an equality with the white man as landholder."[1]

Between 1862 and 1877 the more the Indians resisted, the more the white man hardened his heart. "Whereas in the early sixties, no one thought of limiting the extent of Indian reservations in the Plains and Rocky Mountains, except as concerned mineral lands, yet by 1871 the Secretary of the Interior had come to the conclusion that the solution of the Indian problem was simply to remove all Indians to the Indian Territory [Oklahoma].[2] Virtually no new reservations had been created in the frontier or unsettled areas of the West since 1862, and in 1871 Congress forbade the making of any more Indian treaties. President Grant's annual *Message* for 1872[3] accepted this policy, depicting Oklahoma as a land flowing with milk and honey, where the government could "protect the Indians from inroads of white men for a term of years, until they become sufficiently advanced in the arts of civilization to

8. *Report of the Secretary of the Interior* (1862), p. 11; quoted in R. M. Robbins: *Our Landed Heritage* (Princeton, 1942; paperback edn., Lincoln, Neb., 1961, p. 233 cited here).

9. *Report* (1864), p. 536; Robbins, p. 231.

1. *Report* (1870), p. 627; Robbins, p. 231.

2. Robbins, p. 233.

3. Richardson: *Messages and Papers of the Presidents*, VII, 200.

guard their own rights." The ominous words "for a term of years" did not escape the notice of either redskins or palefaces, and by 1890 even this last asylum in the Indian Territory was to be extinguished, apart from one small Osage reservation, and the description "Cherokee Strip" became subject to a startlingly modern interpretation.

By the end of 1876 the western tribes' resistance was broken, the Custer massacre of June of that year only having bestirred the U. S. government and Army to greater efforts to bring "the Indian menace" to an end. The Sioux (who had been guaranteed this area by treaty as recently as 1868) had the Black Hills—now known to be rich in gold—taken away from them after the Custer affair, and gave little more trouble. Meanwhile, the Shoshones and Bannocks in Idaho (1872), the Crows in Montana, and the Utes in Colorado (1873) had been pushed and cajoled off the major part of their lands—the Utes losing 4 million acres—and the unfortunate Modocs of Oregon ejected forcibly from theirs (1873) after the incident of "Captain Jack" and General Canby in the larva beds.[4] The Kansas Indians were to be squeezed off their remaining lands—toward which the Santa Fe Railroad was already huffing and puffing —in 1877.

But, enough is enough, and as some of the bitterness of the Custer defeat began to die down (though not in 7th U. S. Cavalry circles), the glimmerings of a more humane attitude toward the Indian on the part of the government appeared. President Hayes, a civilian, and his Secretary of the Interior, the liberal-minded German immigrant Carl Schurz (a veteran of the revolutions of 1848 in Europe and the liberator of Professor Kinkel from the king of Prussia's jail), attempted some reforms. In his 1877 *Message*[5] Hayes even spoke of "broken promises and acts of injustice on our part," and, in his 1880 *Message*,[6] urged the passing of legislation that would remedy some of these injustices. Hayes and Schurz were before their time, but humanitarian sentiment was to be aroused

4. See J. P. Dunn: *Massacres of the Mountains* (Indianapolis, 1887); repr. from orig. plates with illus. as in the 1st edn. in The Frontier Library (London, 1963), Ch. xviii, pp. 461–97. This old classic contains some of the best accounts ever written of "The Indian Wars of the Far West," which is its subtitle, and is free from much of the blind prejudice against the red man of most of Dunn's contemporaries.

5. Richardson: *Messages*, VII, 401.

6. Richardson: *Messages*, VII, 576.

more strongly in the following year, 1881, by the publication of what has been called "The Indians' *Uncle Tom's Cabin*," by Helen Hunt Jackson (best known for *Ramona*, her novel of early California). *A Century of Dishonor*[7] was a flaming full-scale indictment of the white man's treatment of the Indians, containing long unsparing descriptions of such unsavory episodes as the Chivington massacre at Sand Creek in 1864. This book had a wide circulation, and was extensively reviewed and discussed in the press, and even quoted in Congress. Liberal journals like *The Nation*[8] were heartened in their crusade for better treatment of the red man, but it was not until the Cleveland administration that the Democratic party's first incumbent of the White House since before the Civil War sponsored the Dawes Act of 1887, which allowed Indians (who had hitherto been disbarred from it) to enter on the public domain of the United States, and to hold lands in severalty (instead of only collectively as members of tribes). This permitted them to benefit for the first time from the Homestead laws and to look forward to full U. S. citizenship, but it also meant that the remaining reservation land could now be subdivided, and, while Indians were guaranteed homesteads on it, a great deal was to fall into the hands of white settlers in the ensuing years. By 1892 over 26 million additional acres of Indian reservation land had been returned to the public domain to be a "free-for-all" to which the white settler helped himself much more freely than the Indian. On April 22, 1889, the Indian Territory itself had been effectively broken up, and the Five Civilized Tribes removed from the land guaranteed them in perpetuity after earlier removals. The "boomers" swarmed over this land, by train, stagecoach, on horseback, by bullock wagon, on bicycles, and on foot; the "sooners" who had jumped the starting gun of this land rush were already there.[9]

The Indians must have wondered exactly what, and whom, the Dawes Act had been designed to protect. While Senator Dawes and President Cleveland undoubtedly meant well by the red man, the Secretary of the Interior was able to report that "the reserva-

7. New York and London, 1881; repr. with intro. by Andrew F. Rolle (New York, 1965).

8. *The Nation*, on July 13, 1876, less than a month after the Custer massacre, had very courageously called the deliberate pauperization of the Indians in the process of getting hold of their lands "shocking," with "nothing in our religion, or manners, or laws, or tradition or polity, to give it any countenance or support."

9. See below, Ch. xi, p. 365.

tion system and the continuance of tribal relations have been broken . . . a constant effort has been made to suppress the influence of the Indian chiefs."[1] By 1906, Robbins points out, "through the breaking up of the reservation system, some 75,000,000 acres, or about three-fifths of the Indian land released by the Dawes Act of 1887, had been appropriated by whites."[2] The Indian's lands were vanishing even more rapidly than the original American himself.[3] But the Burke Act of 1906 threw a sop in his direction by granting him full title to the lands he had managed to keep (in less than the twenty-five years prescribed by the Dawes Act) if he behaved himself.

Eventually, Brandon estimates: "Of the approximately 150 million acres owned by the Indians in 1880, most of it guaranteed by treaties made less than 30 or 40 years before, over 90 million acres—an area more than twice the size of Oklahoma—was abstracted from the Indian's pocket."[4] By the 1920's, when the Indian population, instead of obligingly vanishing altogether, had actually begun to increase again in the United States—and a quarter-Indian from Oklahoma, Charles Curtis, actually became Vice-President in 1929—there was not enough land left in their possession for them to live on. The remaining reservations tended to become overcrowded rural slums. It was not until 1934, when a new and extremely liberal head of the Bureau of Indian Affairs put through as part of Franklin D. Roosevelt's New Deal legislation the Indian Reorganization Act, that the "allotment" of Indian lands under the Act of 1887 was stopped, and regeneration through the once despised tribal organization sought. Some of the more cohesive tribes

1. *Report* (1892), p. 8; Robbins, p. 284. A fierce protagonist of the view that Indian culture was negligible, and that the tribal organization must therefore be broken up everywhere and Indians as individuals integrated with white communities, was Gen. Richard Henry Pratt. He "admitted biological equality for the red man" and put his beliefs into practice in his Carlisle Indian School. See Elaine G. Eastman: *Pratt: The Red Man's Moses* (Normon, Okla., 1935), passim; and *Dictionary of American Biography*, XV, 175–6 (by John Bakeless). Pratt, however, was as fiercely against the integration of the Negro into his school. What a shock it must have been to him when one of Carlisle's renowned graduates, Sylvester Long (or "Buffalo Child Long Lance"), who entered the institution as an eastern Cherokee and later claimed to be a Blackfoot, turned out to be in fact "the son of a Negro school janitor and a half-blood Croatian woman"—Eastman, p. 201.

2. *Our Landed Heritage*, p. 284.

3. By 1900 the number of Indians in the U. S. was down to 250,000.

4. *Book of Indians*, p. 408.

had kept their tribal systems going through the lean years, but a great many were broken beyond recall. The eloquent and energetic John Collier[5] did his best, but his act of 1934 had really been bolting the stable door after the horses were stolen. The Indians regained only about three of the 90 million acres of land lost by them since 1880, and in 1950 the liberal policy of 1934 was abandoned. A new policy aimed at the forced "integration" of the Indian (against whom there was by now little active or militant prejudice in most parts of the country)[6] with American society was tried but soon found both wanting and extremely objectionable by all but the most bigoted of right-wing extremists. With the passing of McCarthyism and the gathering to his fathers of Senator "Pat" McCarran, of Nevada—who disliked "the first Americans" (the Indians) and the latest Americans (the immigrants) with equal vehemence—the so-called termination program (an unfortunate description used by an inept administration, and so redolent of the jargon of the concentration camp or, at best, of the hospital for incurables) was discontinued. Among the tribes to be "terminated" under this program while it lasted was that of the Menominee, whose small reservation near Green Bay, Wisconsin, was eliminated. They had shown the bad judgment of locating themselves on valuable timberland, now becoming scarce in the cut-over North Woods.[7]

The causes of the Indian wars of the Great Plains during the 1860's and 1870's were many and complex; it would be far too simple to explain them as the inevitable clash of the irresistible white man with the irremovable redskin. In contrast to the Indians of the plains, those of the East, the Old Northwest, the Pacific

5. Head of the Bureau of Indian Affairs from 1933 and author of *Indians of the Americas* (New York, 1948), a warm-hearted, if not overscholarly, survey and tract.

6. Even before this time intermarriage with "the first Americans"—provided they had integrated themselves with the white American way of life—was beginning to be widely tolerated. See, e.g., Conrad Bercovici: *Round the World in New York* (New York, 1924), passim.

7. I spent some days camping on the Menominee reservation in the summer of 1929 with my friends the late Professor Felix Keesing and his wife, Marie, anthropologists from New Zealand, who found in the life and problems of the Menominee some similarities to those of the Maori. The Menominee appeared to my lay eye to be a simple, friendly people, living just above the margin of subsistence and entirely incapable of facing the rough and tumble of American competitive society.

Northwest, California, and the Great Basin frontier showed their resistance in a more sporadic, more episodic, and more despairing way—apart from the Apaches, who belonged to the Great Plains as well as to the Southwest. In a way, the whole problem had been created by the white man letting the horse be taken over by the Plains Indians as a primary feature of their culture and as one of their chief weapons of war, along with the rifle, which they also obtained from him. The Plains Indians were hardly formidable when Coronado encountered them in 1540, nor indeed for another century and a half. Had the Great Plains been resolutely colonized by Europeans then, Indian opposition could have been but slight.

Dakota (or Sioux) weapons, by Karl Bodmer.

The Plains Indians were relatively few, compared with the Pueblo Indians of the Rio Grande valley, who let themselves be dominated by a handful of Spanish soldiers and settlers in the seventeenth century, with only one revolt of major proportions. But the horse came up the Rio Grande valley with the Spaniards, spreading rapidly over New Mexico into what are now Colorado, Montana, Alberta, and Saskatchewan, into Texas, Oklahoma, Kansas, Nebraska, the Dakotas, and Manitoba, and into Iowa and Minnesota. Such Indian tribes as the Comanches, the Cheyennes, the Shoshones, the various branches of the Sioux, the Pawnees, the Crows, and finally the Blackfoot, had their whole way of life transformed before the end of the eighteenth century by the coming of the horse. Says Brandon: "The trudging foot people of the plains were thrown into panic by enemies transformed into centaurs 9 feet tall who could dash upon their victims with the speed of the screaming wind. Mounted Shoshonis were attacking the

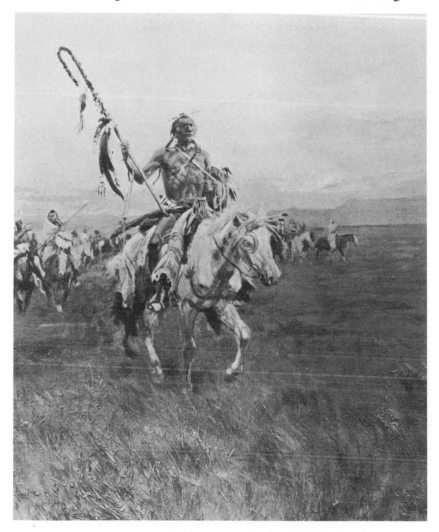

The Medicine Man, by Charlie Russell.

Blackfoot by 1730 . . . the horse-frontier, moving in from the south and west, and the gun frontier, advancing from the east, met on the Great Plains in a spectacular clash and created the figure that has obsessed the world ever since as the archetype of the

American Indian: the feather-streaming, buffalo-chasing, wild-running, recklessly fighting Indian of the Plains."[8]

During the first half of the nineteenth century the Plains Indians were mainly content to fight each other, leaving the white man alone, especially when he traveled in large parties or settled *en masse*. Tribal prestige came less from scalping odd white men and driving off their horses and cattle than from "counting coups" in the elaborately formalized internecine warfare of the Plains, the rules of which, in a barbaric way, resembled a code of chivalry. Tribes had their hereditary enemies, but, more often, their battles were for some temporary advantage, like the possession of a disputed hunting ground, or of a proportion of another tribe's horses or women. The obtaining of prisoners for torture or sacrifice does not appear to have been practiced on a large scale, certainly not on that of the Aztecs; even the taking of scalps was by no means widely practiced until the white man began to demand them as evidence from friendly Indians engaged in mercenary warfare on his behalf with "hostiles," before the payment of head money or trade goods would be made. Above all, Indian warfare in the Plains and the Rockies was on a very small scale; many tribal units ran into hundreds rather than thousands, and a war party of as many as a hundred braves was unusual. A large Indian village on the move was virtually impossible of concealment, as Dull Knife learned when Colonel Ronald S. Mackenzie, 4th U. S. Cavalry, surprised his Cheyenne village of about 1,500 Indians—only 400 to 500 of them warriors—on the Red Fork of the Powder River in Wyoming on November 25, 1876, and utterly destroyed it.[9] Up to the end

8. *Book of Indians*, pp. 333-4. Immediately after his final resistance had been broken, this centaur, this "fighting Indian of the Plains," could safely be depicted in all his glory and glamour by artists such as Charles Russell and Frederic Remington. Since the days of Bodmer, Catlin, and Miller, half a century earlier, the Plains Indian had grown larger than life, a figure of epic proportions. Out of the watercolors and the oils of Charles Russell this noblest savage of them all stares down his long nose at lesser men and less heroic days. See, for example, the illustration, p. 287.

9. This was a Pyrrhic victory, for the Cheyennes left only thirty bodies behind when they retreated (though they later admitted to having had forty warriors killed); Mackenzie withdrew his force and "elected to let General Winter administer the *coup de grâce*," and on the night after the battle, with the thermometer at 30° below, "eleven Cheyenne babies froze to death in the arms of their mothers" on the bare slopes of the Big Horn Mountains—Lessing G. North, Jr.: "Mackenzie against Dull Knife: Breaking the Northern Cheyennes in 1876," in *Probing the American West*, ed. Ross Toole (Santa Fe, 1963), pp. 90–1.

of the Civil War, even the U. S. forces engaged in convoy and garrison duty in the West and in occasional punitive or "flag-showing" expeditions were very small.

The whole U. S. Army consisted of only 6,000 men in 1830, over a quarter of whom became deserters before the year was out. By 1841 the army was only 11,000 strong. Nearly all the "one-year volunteers" of the Mexican War interpreted their terms of enlistment very strictly, some of them downing rifles even in the midst of battles, others having to be disbanded before their time for mutinous conduct, and many more simply deserting. General Kearny's force of dragoons which rode through the West to impress the Indians in 1845 was only 600 strong, and his Army of the West of the following year,[1] the largest force to be mustered there up to that time, contained only 1,800 men. Of these he took a mere 300 with him beyond Santa Fe and was content to have just a hundred accompany him all the way to California. Colonel Doniphan worked wonders in his expedition down the Rio Grande valley to Chihuahua with not more than a thousand men. During the fifties and the Civil War the Army continued to be very thin on the ground in the West. The railroad survey parties of 1853–55 were small and lightly armed, preferring to parley with, rather than fight, the Indians and, on the whole, managing to do so quite successfully.[2] About 2,000 men was all the Army could spare to garrison the western forts before 1865. A command in the West was regarded as miserable exile and one that most well-connected West Pointers managed to avoid. Only when generals and brevet-colonels became two-a-penny, at the end of the War between the States, did men of both integrity and ability come into positions of authority in the regular western Army, and then it was often too

1. See above, Ch. vi, p. 168.

2. Gov. Stevens, when at Fort Union, on the upper Missouri, with his Pacific Railroad Survey party in 1853, recruited the services of Medicine-Snake-Woman, the Blood Indian squaw of Alexander Culbertson, the *Bourgeois* at the Fort, to smooth the way for him through the Blackfoot and Gros Ventres country. So successful were she and her equally cooperative cousin, Little Dog, that the United States was able to conclude a treaty with the Blackfoot for the first time in 1855. The general and his party went through the Blackfoot country unmolested, which is more than can be said for the Union Pacific Railroad (the route of which he pioneered) a decade later, by which time the whole northern Indian frontier was aflame. There were limits to what even "Mothers of the Mixed Bloods" could do! See John C. Ewers: "Mothers of the Mixed Bloods: The Marginal Woman in the History of the Upper Missouri," *Probing the American West*, pp. 62–70.

late to coerce the Indians peaceably. Meanwhile, the Indian Bureau of the Department of the Interior, and the War Department, continued to fight each other when not preying on the unfortunate red man it was their duty to protect and civilize. The Indian grew to distrust them both and this led to the first large-scale revolt of the Sioux in Minnesota in 1862. Little Crow, with 1,300 warriors, went on the rampage and killed over 700 white settlers. The state militia was able to deal with this outbreak, and 400 Indian prisoners (thirty-eight of whom were subsequently executed) were put on trial for murder and other crimes at St. Paul. All the remaining Sioux lands in Minnesota were confiscated.

It was the militia, too, that "dealt with" the Cheyennes in southern Colorado Territory in 1864, this time with far less provocation and far more savagely. The Fort Wise[3] treaty of 1861 took away the land guaranteed to the Arapahos and Cheyennes by Tom Fitzpatrick's famous treaty of 1851 and since overrun by the miners of the "Pike's Peak or Bust" gold rush, who knew no law and recognized no property rights, red or white. The Indians who stood in the way of the exploitation of the Territory's mineral and agricultural resources were ordered to a new reservation in the Sand Creek Valley of southeastern Colorado. In June 1864, after three uneasy years of non-compliance, Black Kettle and his band of some 500 Cheyennes moved down to Sand Creek and encamped peaceably under a flag of truce. They had decided to resist the proclamation of the territorial governor no longer. Here they were attacked by the paranoic "Colonel" J. M. Chivington (by profession a minister of religion!) and his blood-lusting Colorado militiamen—who had been urged by their superior officers to spare neither man, woman, nor child—and over half of them—about two hundred women and children and seventy men—massacred in cold blood. Casualties among Chivington's "boys" were negligible, but the consequences for future Indian-white relations and the reputation of the white man in the West were to be momentous. More than a hundred years later "the Chivington massacre" continues to be spoken and written about in tones of horror and incredulity. It is America's St. Bartholomew.[4]

3. Fort Wise was a new military post near the site of Bent's Old Fort, on the Arkansas.

4. The details of the massacre at Sand Creek and the number of Indians killed are still hotly disputed, but Chivington's responsibility for his men's excesses

Upon the Northern Plains the Sioux took sweet revenge for the thirty-eight hangings[5] in St. Paul after Col. H. B. Carrington led a detachment along the Bozeman Trail to keep it open for the wagons and stages. He built three forts—Reno, Phil Kearney, and C. F. Smith—on the trail, and it was near Fort Kearney in December 1866 that Lt. Col. Fetterman and his entire force of eighty-one men were exterminated by a much larger band of Sioux, led by Crazy Horse. More effective action against the hostiles was demanded, both by the Press and by Congress, especially as the Cheyennes and Arapahos had redoubled their depredations further south since the Sand Creek massacre. A peace commission meeting at Fort Laramie decided to evacuate the Powder River area and thus abandon the Army's policing of the Bozeman Trail, but General William Tecumseh Sherman, a member of the commission, put in a minority report to the effect that "all [Indians] who cling to their old hunting grounds are hostile and will remain so until killed off . . . we must take chances and clean out Indians as we encounter them." His former comrade in arms in the G.A.R., General Philip Sheridan, new commander of the Department of Missouri, had at his disposal only 2,600 men, of whom 1,200 were cavalry, to look after the entire Central Plains, and General Hancock, in the Northern Plains, was even worse off, despite having such formidable Indian fighters as "Buffalo Bill" Cody (who now became Sheridan's chief scout) and George Custer, another "boy general"—like Mackenzie—of the Civil War, but now back to his substantive rank of lieutenant colonel. Not much could be done with an army of this size to cover all the West. Custer's book *My Life on the Plains*, published in the year of his death, speaks of

---

is not and was even admitted by himself. The congressional investigation into the affair disclosed much damning evidence (*U.S. Senate Reports of Committees*, 39th Cong., 2nd Ser., Doc. 156); quoted at length in Jackson: *A Century of Dishonor*. J. P. Dunn: *Massacres of the Mountains* (Indian, 1886), ch. xiii, pp. 342–82, attempts a defense of Chivington and concludes: "as a matter of retaliation and a matter of policy, whether these people were justified in killing women and children at Sand Creek is a question to which the answer does not come so glibly. . . . Sand Creek is far from being the climax of American outrages on the Indian" (p. 382).

5. Hanging was the greatest humiliation an Indian could suffer. One brave, condemned and in irons, cut off his own feet in order to be able to escape the hangman.

frustration after frustration. Custer was no friend of the Indian but at least he wanted to be allowed to fight him properly.[6]

The ten years of Indian warfare which spanned the period between the Fetterman massacre and the tragedy of the Little Big Horn witnessed no other reverses comparable to these for the U. S. Army in the West. The transcontinental railroads split the buffalo herds of the Plains, and first the southern, then the northern, herds were exterminated. The Plains Indians, deprived of the main basis of their economy, gradually let themselves be hounded into reservations, as "wards" of the government, there to attempt to settle down to farming or cattle ranching, if they turned their hands to anything at all. Those who continued to put up even a token resistance were only the most resolute, the most untamable, and the ones possessing outstanding leaders. This was the age of the last generation of great Indian heroes.

Two of these heroes were Crazy Horse and Sitting Bull. Both were Teton Sioux (or "Lacotas," as they called themselves), but Crazy Horse belonged to the Oglala branch of the tribe and Sitting Bull to the Hunkpapa. Both these men came to overshadow Red Cloud, the great war chief of the Sioux, who had driven the Americans from the Bozeman Trail in 1868. After he made his peace with the white man and agreed to settle at the agency that was given his name, Red Cloud, the hero of eighty coups, was pushed aside by these younger men, to whom continued resistance, against whatever odds, was a holy duty inspired by their dreams. Crazy Horse was the son of a medicine man of the same name, and Sitting Bull a medicine man in his own right. The former was primarily a man of action, the latter a planner and schemer. In his own day Sitting Bull achieved the greater fame, which was not exactly dimmed by his participation in Buffalo Bill's great Wild West Show during the eighties, but Crazy Horse (who was killed while a prisoner in 1877) has latterly been claimed his equal, if not his superior, as the last effective war leader of the Sioux.[7] It is clear

6. See George Custer: *My Life on the Plains* (St. Louis, 1876). This book was reissued in a greatly expanded form—from 330 to 590 pages—as *Wild Life on the Plains* "by a Corps of Competent Authors and Artists" in 1891. Custer's name did not appear on the title page of that new edn., though his part of the text was repr. from the orig. plates.

7. Mari Sandoz: *Crazy Horse* (New York, 1942), and Alvin Josephy: *The Patriot Chiefs* take this view; but William Brandon: *American Heritage Book of*

that the Indians they led and inspired did not seek to place the one above the other, for they performed different functions in peace and in war, and were at the heads of different groups in a loose federation of tribes and sub-tribes. When the old warrior Kicking Bear painted his celebrated pictograph[8] of the Battle of Little Big Horn, in 1898, he put Crazy Horse and Sitting Bull side by side, and the same size, in the middle of the battlefield, along with Rain-in-the-Face and himself. When Sitting Bull was interviewed by a journalist during his Canadian exile, however, he stated that he himself was never in the thick of the fight and never once saw

An Indian version of "Custer's Last Stand." Pictograph by Kicking Bear.

Custer alive, as his was the task of guarding the village and directing the packing up of the lodges by the squaws[9] in case they had to move away.

Crazy Horse first achieved prominence during the Fetterman massacre of December 1866, when he led a decoy party, although

Indians, p. 347, thinks that revisionism has gone too far, saying: "There was a fashion for some years among Western historians of belittling Sitting Bull's importance: recent scholarship seems to have restored him to the place of eminence he held in his own day."

8. Now in the Southwest Museum at Los Angeles.

9. *Wild Life on the Plains*, pp. 407–16. Sitting Bull was very positive about his inactive role in the battle: "You did not personally witness the rest of the big fight? You were not engaged in it?" asked the anonymous journalist, to whom he replied: "No, I have heard it from the warriors" (p. 412).

he was already a "shirt wearer" at the age of twenty-four—the age at which Custer had become a brevet brigadier-general, a comparable rank. From that time on he was in nearly every important engagement of the Sioux and their allies with the U. S. Army until the end.[1] Black Kettle had been killed on the Washita River in Oklahoma, in an engagement with Custer, which earned this dashing officer the not unmerited title of "Long Hair the Squaw Killer" among the Indians, because thirty-eight women and children were slaughtered along with about a hundred warriors. The heart had already gone out of Black Kettle even before Sand Creek, and those Cheyennes who continued to resist now tended to throw in their lot with Crazy Horse and the Sioux. Crazy Horse never lost a battle with the Americans and never signed a treaty with them. Red Cloud, on the other hand, was a "used-up man" as a resistance leader after his famous visit to Washington in 1870, where he was wined and dined by President Grant. His speech on Indian grievances at the Cooper Union Institute in New York, though, indicated that he still had great potentialities as a lobbyist, and he might have served the Indian cause better by remaining among eastern fleshpots than by returning to play a Quisling role on the North Platte. During this return visit to Washington he made no progress in his efforts to keep for the Sioux their hunting grounds south of the Platte, and in 1873 he acquiesced in their removal of the Red Cloud Agency northward to the White River. This was a threat to the Indian "holy land" in the Black Hills, by which Sitting Bull set such store, and drew the dissident Sioux and Cheyenne groups closer together in their "retreat" on the Rosebud River in Montana. The Northern Pacific Railroad survey parties were probing through the Yellowstone country at that time, protected by "Long Hair the Squaw Killer" himself and his 7th U. S. Cavalry (now transferred from Oklahoma). They had several skirmishes with Crazy Horse's Indians that year, but in 1874 Custer was back with a much larger force, with which he decided to reconnoiter the Black Hills and test rumors that they were full of gold. This was probably the most provocative and questionable episode in the whole career of the "Glory Hunter," as one of his

1. See further Robert Utley: *The Last Days of the Sioux Nation* (New Haven, Conn., 1963), and *The Custer Legend* (New York, 1962). Mr. Utley, chief historian of the National Park Service, was once a ranger at the Custer Battlefield National Monument. See also D. Jackson: *Custer's Gold* (New Haven, 1966).

biographers has called him, for he certainly exceeded both the letter and the spirit of General Sheridan's orders. Prospectors and other gold-hungry civilians followed him into the Black Hills, and even if the Army had tried to remove them (which it did not), it probably would have failed, for Custer's force numbered only 1,200, including newspaper correspondents, government scientists, and the usual Custer family hangers-on. Crazy Horse declared open season on the prospectors (for this was Indian country, still guaranteed to the red man by the treaty of 1868 and subsequent solemn promises in Washington). The prospectors on their side howled for protection, and in 1875 Red Cloud was again taken to Washington for a new round of dissipation and arm-twisting. More and more of the agency Sioux and Cheyennes went off to join the hostiles under Crazy Horse, sensing that a sell-out of the Black Hills was imminent. Twenty thousand Indians flocked to the Red Cloud Agency to meet the U. S. commissioners, but the Oglala and the Hunkpapa Sioux were conspicuous by their absence. The day was saved, for the moment, by Red Cloud's demanding the astronomical sum of 600 million dollars for the Black Hills, to which the commissioners, perhaps mindful of the recent "bargain-basement" Alaska purchase,[2] countered with a niggardly offer of $6 million, and the council dispersed. The Sioux were all ordered into the agencies, and when large numbers of them disobeyed the Department of the Interior in the early spring of 1876, their "pacification" was turned over to the Army. By March 1 General Crook had opened his campaign against the hostiles. It began badly when, some days later, Colonel J. J. Reynolds attacked the camp of Two Moons and his Cheyennes (who were actually on their way to the Agency with peaceful intent) and, though destroying it, was forced to retreat. Reynolds was court-martialed and Crook deprived of a useful base for further operations on the Powder River. Crook returned to the Platte, and Two Moons, his mind changed by this unprovoked attack, joined forces with Crazy Horse. Crazy Horse was now named head of all the Oglalas, in peace and in war, and at the Sun Dance ceremonies of the Hunkpapa early in June, he heard Sitting Bull's prophecy of imminence of a fierce battle—a fairly safe prediction, for Crook was already advancing again up the

2. The United States paid Russia a mere $7,200,000 for this acquisition in 1867. New Mexico and California had cost only $15,000,000 in 1848, and the Louisiana Territory a similar sum in 1803.

Rosebud. On June 17 a skirmish since dignified as "the Battle of the Rosebud" occurred, in which Crook lost nine soldiers and a number of auxiliaries, and Crazy Horse, who was himself in the thick of

Indian necklace made from sixteen trigger-finger bones of Custer's men.

the fight, eleven braves. Both sides withdrew, Crook deciding that he needed reinforcements before advancing again, a decision that left General Terry, with Custer's force under his direct command, to advance alone. Custer's precipitate rush up the Rosebud ahead of the other two forces under Terry's command led him to the exposed position on the Little Big Horn on June 25 which cost him and all the men of five companies of the 7th Cavalry their lives. Two hundred and fifty men died in the "last stand," and about forty survivors of the three companies under Major Reno and the three under Captain Benteen, who were able to beat a retreat, were wounded. The Indians, who numbered several thousand, also retreated, without waiting for Gibbon and Terry. They had won a battle, but it soon became obvious that they had lost the war. The whole American nation, aroused and humiliated by the news of what has been called "this moment of truth" just before the centennial celebrations of Independence were due to be held, both expected and insisted upon a massive retaliation. By September 1876 Crook, greatly reinforced, was "mopping up." Sitting Bull led a handful of his tribe across the border into Alberta in February 1877 rather than surrender; Crazy Horse finally surrendered at the Red Cloud Agency in May (Crook had meanwhile deposed Red Cloud in favor of Spotted Tail, an even more amenable collaborator). In September Crook had Crazy Horse arrested and confined at Fort Robertson, where he was bayoneted to death "trying to escape." Red Cloud, looking on, shouted at the soldiers: "Shoot to kill!" Some of the Oglala escaped, leaderless, into Canada.

In the Pacific Northwest in the same year (1877) Chief Joseph, of the Nez Percés (who had been driven out of their hunting grounds as well as out of Oregon by the advance of the mining frontier), retreated eastward into Montana in a remarkable rearguard action with about six hundred of his people, only two hundred of whom were warriors. It was a forlorn trek, for they could go nowhere but into the lands from which the Sioux, the Cheyennes, and the Blackfoot had just been expelled. Pursued and harried by the U. S. soldiers, Joseph evaded them for nearly fifteen hundred miles and halted only when he (mistakenly) thought he had reached Canadian soil. Here, with only fifty of his braves still able to fight, he was forced to surrender and was sent with the survivors of his band into exile in the Indian Territory—instead of back to Idaho, as General Miles, his captor, had promised. That was the end of the Nez Percé nation also.

Apache resistance lasted a little longer, probably hardened as a result of General Carleton's harsh instruction in 1862: "All Indian men of that tribe are to be killed whenever and wherever you can

Chief Joseph. From Freeman Tilden: *Following the Frontier* (1964).

find them." The Apaches were also embittered by the fact that the Americans, when they came into the Southwest, continued the traditional Spanish and Mexican practice of making slaves of Apache women and children. As late as 1866 over 2,000 Indian slaves were held by white people in Arizona and New Mexico.[3]

3. Brandon: *American Heritage Book of Indians*, p. 384.

The Apaches had at first sought to make friends with the Americans, possibly because the "White Eyes" were thought to be the hereditary enemies of the hated Mexicans, but their overtures were repulsed. Red Sleeves (*Mangas Coloradas*) was brutally flogged by white gold miners in New Mexico; Cochise was shot and wounded while parleying with Army representatives under a flag of truce; both these men went on the war path against the Americans when the outbreak of the Civil War left the Arizona frontier ill-guarded. In 1863, when General Carleton arrived on his extermination campaign, Red Sleeves was tricked into peace talks, at which he was murdered. Even Colonel Kit Carson, no Indian lover, found Carleton's orders too extreme, and accepted Apache surrenders as previously he had those of the Navajos, letting his prisoners depart in peace. The Apache survivors retreated into the mountains after the all-out campaign against them in 1864. The war of extermination ended with the unsavory Camp Grant massacre at Tucson in 1871, when a civilian mob lynched eighty-five Apaches who had surrendered and were under Army protection there. The war had cost over $40 million and the Apaches were still unsubdued. Conciliation was then tried, under the guidance of that very experienced Indian fighter General George Crook.[4] Crook used Apache to catch Apache, his scouts being recruited from pacified sections of the tribe—which had many branches. By 1875 the Apaches who had not escaped across the border had been herded into reservations, pacified after a fashion. Cochise, now a moderating influence, had died on the reservation in 1874, and Crook was transferred the next year to the Black Hills to operate against the Sioux. By 1876 the Apaches were on the war path again (to remain so for another decade), led by Victorio (who was killed in 1880) and Geronimo. Arbitrary treatment contrary to Crook's promises, and at times almost a return to the old extermination policy, were the chief causes of this, and Crook was brought back in 1882 to pacify them once more. By 1886, Geronimo, having been pursued into Mexico

4. He was said to admire the Apaches—"No Indian has more virtues," claimed his adjutant, Capt. J. G. Bourke—and the Apaches to trust him. Only Geronimo, old, embittered, interned, and turned pious, contributed a sour note by saying of Crook: "I have suffered much from such unjust orders as those of Crook. Such acts have caused much distress to my people. I think that General Crook's death was sent by the Almighty as a punishment for the many evil deeds he committed" (according to S. M. Barratt, who set down Geronimo's autobiography from dictation).

by Crook, was talked into surrendering, but he escaped while being escorted back to the reservation. General Miles, Crook's replacement, received Geronimo's final surrender, saying (according to Geronimo's *Autobiography*): "While I live you will not be arrested." But Geronimo was almost immediately taken prisoner and sent off to exile in Florida. Miles even sent General Crook's loyal Apache scouts into exile as well, for the Army and people of the United States had by now acquired an almost pathological hatred

Geronimo (left) and Natchez on horseback, 1886. A posed picture before returning to the warpath.

of the Apache. It was about this time, too, that the gangsters of the Paris tenderloin districts began to be called Apaches, and a New World phobia thus transferred to the Old.

The Apaches were hardly prepossessing, either in their appearance or in their habits. No European or American could ever glamorize *them* into noble savages. They wore neither feathers nor buckskin, but loose-fitting smocks, shapeless trousers, and floppy hats, or head scarves that made them look like pirates or worse.

Even General Crook, who grew to respect them—and jeopardized his career by arguing their case for better treatment in Washington —never grew to like them. Geronimo lived on until 1909, having been transferred from Florida to Alabama and then to Fort Sill in Oklahoma and given his freedom. The old man made one last expedition into the white man's country in 1903, when he visited the Fair at St. Louis which commemorated the centennial of the Louisiana Purchase. Here he sold photographs of himself—kneeling with a rifle and scowling his "hatred"—for two bits each to

The end of the frontier. Geronimo (in top hat) and friends (in assorted peace bonnets), Fort Sill, Oklahoma, in latest model Buick, *c.* 1905.

gawking tourists, though by that time he was a harmless-looking old patriarch, all passion spent.

Chief Joseph, though a much gentler man than Geronimo, and handsomer by far, and who, according to General Sherman, "abstained from scalping, let captive women go free, and did not commit indiscriminate murder of peaceful families" during his famous retreat, was accorded very much the same treatment as the implacable Apache, and met very much the same fate. He was allowed to lead back the remnants of his people from internment in the Indian Territory to a new reservation in northern Washington in 1885, to eat his heart out, and there he died, in 1904, still far from his beloved Wallowa Valley.

Another resistance leader who at last made his peace with the white man fared somewhat better. Quanah Parker, who was a half-breed, son of a Comanche chief and a captive white woman named Cynthia Ann Parker, fought the intruder on his hunting grounds until 1874, but then settled down on a reservation in western Oklahoma, near Fort Sill, and collaborated with the Indian agents and Army officers in every possible way to keep his fellow Indians in order and out of trouble. On their side, the Whites recognized him as a chief and eventually made him a judge in the Court of Indian Offenses, a quasi-legal tribunal that existed from 1886 to 1901. Quanah and his fellow Indian judges dispersed "a rough and ready type of justice"[5] and performed a valuable function on the reservation, but a new rule, according to which a polygamist could not serve as a judge in one of the courts, deprived him of his seat on the bench in 1898. Meanwhile, he had increased the number of his wives from five to seven, and invited the Commissioner for Indian Affairs to select the wives he should discard. It is said that the commissioner was not equal to this task.[6] Quanah Parker continued loyally to serve the cause of good relations between red man and white until his death in 1911, and was honored in return: in 1905 he had ridden in Teddy Roosevelt's inaugural parade—a Western-type Roman triumph for that "Cowboy at the White House"—and in 1907 he was put on the telephone by a grateful agency at government expense.

Spotted Tail, once one of the most active of the Sioux war leaders, surrendered himself at Fort Laramie as one of those responsible for the Grattan massacre in 1855 and for an attack on a stagecoach a little earlier. Treated more humanely than the Minnesota Sioux in St. Paul were to be in 1862, Spotted Tail never again gave serious trouble to the white men. Indeed, like Red Cloud, he was regarded by many other Indians as far too supine. He went to Washington with Red Cloud, and, at the Spotted Tail Agency, received many favors from the Army and the agents, who were at last beginning to concede that a live Indian could also be a good

5. W. T. Hagan: "Quanah Parker Indian Judge," in *Probing the American West*, p. 75.

6. Hagan, p. 77.

Quanah Parker, as photographed by Hutchings in 1892.

one. It is ironical that Spotted Tail was to meet his death early in the eighties at the hands of a really "bad" Indian, Crow Dog, who murdered him (presumably for being a "collaborator") and who

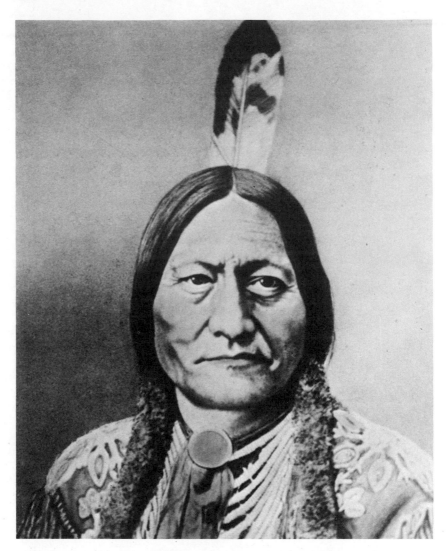

Sitting Bull. From Freeman Tilden: *Following the Frontier* (1964).

then, after conviction and being condemmed to death, went scot free: the Supreme Court decided that the jurisdiction of the federal courts did not extend to the reservations! The "pacified" Indians were therefore not left in peace, even in the eighties and nineties: if the white man did not starve them to death by failing to give them their promised meager rations, or by moving them on to even more barren reservations, the Indian resistance movement might "get" them. While he lived, Spotted Tail was only too conscious of the double jeopardy in which he had placed himself. An old-timer tells the story of how he was in Indian country where the "hostiles" were still active, and observed a group of Indians approaching. He and his companions readied their guns and waited. When the Indians were near enough, it was observed that they carried a long banner stretched out in front of them by two braves, bearing the inscription SPOTTED TAIL AND HIS BAND OF FRIENDLY SIOUX.[7]

A Sioux who never exactly became "friendly" but who did eventually bury the hatchet to the extent of returning (in 1881) from his self-imposed exile in Canada, and refighting his battles (it is hoped without rancor) for the benefit of the spectators at Buffalo Bill's Wild West Show (in 1885), was Sitting Bull. His status as an Indian leader may still be debatable, but the dignity with which he acted in his days of adversity, and while he was letting himself be exhibited to the public by his former enemies, is not in doubt. Though he never fought again after Little Big Horn, he suffered a fate as cruel as that of Crazy Horse, for he was shot and killed by Indian police in the service of the Standing Rock Agency (where he had been directed to take up his abode in 1883) while being placed under preventive arrest for suspected intention of participating in the Ghost Dance demonstrations that had broken out among the Sioux in 1890. It is obvious that an easy excuse was taken to get rid of a man who was a possible leader or organizer of another Sioux outbreak; but there is no evidence whatsoever that he had any renewed hostile intentions.[8] Buffalo Bill Cody, his old associate in war—and grease—paint, tried to meet him again at Standing Rock, a short time before Sitting Bull was shot in the back by agent McLoughlin's police, but was prevented by the agent from doing so! McLoughlin even tried to get Bill drunk in order to stop him, but finally had to call in the Army, because the Colonel had a very strong head. Had this meeting taken place,

7. William M. Breckenridge: *Helldorado: Bringing Law to the Mesquite* (Boston, 1928), p. 49.

8. See Utley: *Last Days of the Sioux Nation,* and Stanley Vestal: *Sitting Bull* (Norman, Okla., 1957), passim.

think Buffalo Bill's biographers,[9] Sitting Bull's life might have been
saved, for Bill would have protected him from victimization. At
least Bill could recruit some of the ex-ghost dancers for his Wild
West Show in 1891, and he used the "Peace Meeting at Pine
Ridge" for a poster illustration.[1]

The ghost-dance craze arose only after Indian resistance had
been broken; it was a gospel of despair. It was not a resistance
movement—not even one advocating passive resistance—so much
as belief in a miraculous deliverance from the white man and his
depredations. Dead Indian heroes would return to life and the
buffalo in their myriads come back to the plains. A golden age for
the red man would exist once more. The chief prophet of this
belief was Wovoka, a Piute in Nevada who had been brought up
by Christians and who proclaimed the second coming of a messiah
for early in 1891 in words that oddly jumbled Indian and Christian
ideas together. He has been called "Johnson Sides, the Peace-
maker . . . well known to all people living along the line of the
Central Pacific Railroad, in the vicinity of Reno and Winnemuca,
Nev."[2] Whatever he is called, and however improbable the stretch
of the Central Pacific between a latter-day Sodom and a new
Gomorrah as a site for the rise of a new religion, Wovoka's (or
Johnson Sides's) creed rapidly traveled eastward to influence tribes
as far away as Montana and the Dakotas. Smarting under the
forced purchase in 1889 by a congressional commission headed by
ex-Governor Foster of Ohio, and General George Crook, their old
enemy, of vast areas of their reservation, in return for additional
annuities and another million pounds of beef per year (which was
not forthcoming), the Sioux held a great council at Wounded
Knee Creek in the spring of 1890. Here Chief Two Lance presented to them the new creed "brought from the country of the
Utes." No weapons were to be used. "We are simply to pray and
trust in the Messiah and dance as he shall command." The ghost
dances went on all through the summer and autumn, embellish-
ments being added, like the wearing of the ghost shirt that was
guaranteed to make an Indian impervious to the white man's bul-

9. Victor Weybright and Henry B. Sell: *Buffalo Bill and the Wild West*
(New York and London, 1955), p. 190.

1. Weybright and Sell, p. 193.

2. *Wild Life on the Plains*, p. 533; see also Paul Bailey: *Wovoka, The
Indian Messiah* (Los Angeles, 1957).

lets, until the agency whites became thoroughly, though unjusti-
fiably, alarmed, and began to fear another Indian outbreak. Sitting
Bull's arrest and murder (for such it was) was an act of panic on
the part of the white agent McLoughlin, who even admitted that,
in conversation with him, Sitting Bull had expressed some skepti-
cism concerning the Messiah cult and a willingness to test its validity.[3]

The news of the death of Sitting Bull threw the Sioux in South
Dakota into a frenzy such as the ghost-dance craze could not of
itself have caused, and led to the tragic events at Wounded Knee at
the end of December 1890. At first hundreds of warriors made off
for the inaccessible Badlands, there to attempt to establish an impregnable fortress. After a ghost dance lasting thirty hours during
which "people went into trances by the dozen . . . several remained in trances as long as twelve hours . . . people were so
excited they trembled all over, their eyes rolled and the muscles of
their faces twitched,"[4] a council was held and General Brooke's
peace commission listened to. Then the ghost dance went on for
another two days. Two Strike and Crow Dog (the slayer of
Spotted Tail), told that "the Agent will forgive you if you will
return now, give you more rations, but not permit you to dance,"
accepted, but the band under Short Bull, after reluctantly following them for some distance, decided to return to the Badlands. The
7th Cavalry, under Colonel Forsythe, were ordered after them by
General Miles, from his headquarters in Chicago. Many more Indians subsequently came in peaceably to the Red Cloud Agency,
but a group led by Big Foot did not, and were caught up with on
December 27 at Wounded Knee. Here Big Foot came forward
alone and formally surrendered to Major Whiteside. There were
about 150 warriors, 250 squaws, and a large number of children
with him. The white troops numbered about 2,500. The next
morning, while the Indians were being disarmed, some of the
braves were alleged to have fired on the soldiers with weapons they
had concealed, but a great deal of contrary evidence exists as to
exactly where the provocation came from. Still, it was enough for
the trigger-happy 7th Cavalry, whose motto was "Remember
Custer," and they turned their newly acquired Hotchkiss quick-

3. *Wild Life on the Plains*, p. 567.

4. Louis Shargraux, a half-breed interpreter participating in the peace
parleys, quoted in *Wild Life on the Plains*, pp. 576-7.

firing machine guns on the unfortunate Sioux. Some thirty soldiers and nearly all the Indians, including their women and children, were killed. "It was the saddest, apparently the most senseless of all the tragedies connected with the dealings of this nation with its 'wards,'" concluded a by no means pro-Indian account published the following year.[5] It was also the last, for, aside from an Indian attack on a supply train (which was repulsed by the teamsters) at about the same time, Wounded Knee was "all the real fighting in that which has passed into history as the great Sioux outbreak."[6] It can hardly now be maintained, as was thought at the time, that "it promised to involve all the tribes of the northwest, and extend its devastating terrors from the Missouri to the Pacific" or that "the master mind of Sitting Bull had thought out the chance for the red man in such a conflict."[7]

The ghost dance cult was fundamentally harmless, perhaps even a good way of working off the frustrations of the by then almost helpless Indian tribes, if only the white man had not remembered Custer too vividly and discerned a scalp hunter inside every ghost shirt. Two Lance in his harangue had counseled peace and called for prayer; it was not so much another Little Big Horn that the ghost dancers longed for but the Big Rock Candy Mountain. Said Little Wound: "When I fell in the trance a great and grand eagle came and carried me over a great hill where there was a village such as we used to have before the Whites came into the country. The tepees were all of buffalo hides and we made use of the bow and arrow, there being nothing of White Man's manufacture in the beautiful land. Nor were any Whites permitted to live there. The broad and fertile lands stretched in every direction and were most pleasing to my eye," while Kicking Horse, a Sioux who claimed to have just returned from heaven, told the following curious story:

. . . that he entered heaven through a hole in the sky, and that he saw the Great Spirit, who told him that the Indians had suffered long enough, and that the time had come for their deliverance. They were to occupy the earth once more, which had been taken from them by the whites, but they were not to kill or molest them. The

5. *Wild Life on the Plains*, p. 585.
6. *Wild Life on the Plains*, p. 588.
7. Ibid., cf. attitude expressed in Utley: *Last Days of the Sioux Nation*.

Great Spirit told him that the earth was getting full of holes, and many places were rotten. He would gradually send a wave of earth 20 feet or more over the country, and that it would move slowly. The Indian must keep dancing so as to be on top, and when the wave passed all the pale-faces would be buried underneath and the Indians would be on top. All the dead Indians would be restored to life again, and the buffaloes, horses, game, and their old hunting grounds would be as they were hundreds of years ago, and the Indians would for all time in the future own and occupy the earth. All Indians who would not listen to the words of the prophet and keep dancing would be turned into fishes and dwell in the rivers and streams.

He said, that whilst talking to the Great Spirit the devil came to them. He describes the devil as being very tall, with immense knee-joints, a monster mouth and long teeth. He was covered all over with coarse hair. He asked for half of the people, meaning the Indians, but the Great Spirit refused to grant his request. He asked again, but the Great Spirit replied: "You can have none of my chosen Indian children, but you can have all the whites."[8]

Revenge is sweet, if only in words!

8. *Wild Life on the Plains*, pp. 536-7.

CHAPTER X

The Cowman's Frontier

WALTER PRESCOTT WEBB HAS CALLED THE GREAT PLAINS the "great obstacle," and it is true that until the days of the cattle drives of the 1860's, the American people didn't seem to know what to do with them. The Spaniards had been equally nonplussed by these vast areas of "cows and sky"—and deficient rainfall. Both peoples treated the Plains as a nasty experience to be got over as soon as possible so that they could press on to Quivira or El Dorado, or to gather the golden apples of the Willamette Valley. "They were in reality seeking the familiar and shunning the necessity of working out new ways in the Plains."[1]

The great obstacle was not easily overcome—Coronado, Castañeda, Pike, and Long had not so grossly exaggerated its uselessness to civilized man at the stage of technological development at their time—but when rangy herds of mean-looking Mexican longhorns began to be propelled up into Texas by even meaner-looking Mexican vaqueros and Texas "cowboys," a useful two-pronged weapon for dealing with its intransigeance had at last appeared. The Nueces Valley began to fill up with lean kine, which, finding there one blade of grass growing where none (in the deserts of Coahuila and other points South) had grown where they had been before, waxed fatter (but not yet fat), increased and multiplied, and began to low for a market. At about the same time, or even earlier, the cattle-ranching era had also begun for California. Here

1. Webb: *The Great Plains*, p. 149.

too came the Mexican cattle with their lariat-twirling, seraped vaqueros, about whose equestrian skills the Boston merchants and
young Harvard men serving before the mast wrote home with
bated breath. In California the age of hides and tallow, rather than
an age of iron or silver, preceded the age of gold. Hides became the
local currency, slightly more awkward to carry around shopping
than gold dust, but just as widely used as that commodity was later
to become in those same valleys. The easy-going Spanish Californians bought shoes at high prices, made in Massachusetts from
those very hides they had parted from to main-chancing Yankee
supercargoes for one to two dollars apiece, delivered at the cliff
edge, in creaking bullock wagons. When the British fleet, under

A California cattle drive, by James Walker.

Admiral Sir George Seymour, came cruising up from Mexico to
watch what Commodore Sloat was doing in July 1846 in Californian
waters, the enterprising Abel Stearns (out of Lunenburg, Massachusetts, by way of Valparaiso) wrote to an employee from the
pueblo of Los Angeles (his hide shed was then one of the two
buildings at the San Pedro anchorage down on the coast): "I
received yours of the first inst. in which you observe there is a
prospect of some English men of war arriving. I hope it may be the
case and that they may want a plenty of beef. . . . If you have a
chance, try and make something out of it. John Bull is a lusty old

fellow and has a stiff purse."[2] Nearly every other American in California at the time thought that Seymour had come to establish a British colony in, or a British protectorate over, California, but Stearns, faced with a surplus of *novillos*, thought only about supplying him with beef. Yet, California's surplus cattle, unlike those of Texas, did not long remain in search of a market. Some had been driven up into Oregon for the American settlers there (of whom there were many more until the late forties than in California)— and Ewing Young, it will be remembered,[3] had turned from fur trapping to ranching as early as the thirties—but even as long a drive as that soon became unnecessary, as beef-hungry miners began pouring into the pastoral solitudes of the now golden state in '48 and '49. Not for the last time did California thus solve a pressing economic problem in a unique way, and Abel Stearns's "Cattle on a Thousand Hills"[4] soon made him one of the richest men in the state, without benefit of gold mines.

It was a much longer trek from hoof to mouth for the Texas longhorns. The cattle trails they blazed had to go from south to north, against the grain of the westward movement. If the miners may be said to have pock-marked the map of the undeveloped West, the Texas cattlemen can be claimed to have cross-hatched it. It was the second major assault by man on the Great American Desert, and one it did not survive. While the cattle kingdom, dependent on the vast "open range" of government land for grazing the herds as they found their way north, was developing, "the frontier line was held practically stationary along the vicinity of the 98th meridian. During this period—which lasted, roughly, from 1840 to 1885—the agricultural frontier first jumped across the Plains, established itself on the Pacific slope, and then began to work backwards," Webb points out.[5] All this, while mighty convenient to the cattlemen (Webb might have added), badly knocked askew the as yet unformulated "Turner hypothesis,"[6]

2. Abel Stearns to James Johnson, July 3, 1846; printed from the Stearns Coll. in the Huntington Library, San Marino, Calif., in J. A. Hawgood, ed.: *First and Last Consul* (San Marino, Calif., 1962), p. 82.

3. See above, Ch. vi.

4. R. G. Cleland: *Cattle on a Thousand Hills* (San Marino, Calif., 1941) is the best account of the ranch cattle industry in California and of Stearns's part in it.

5. *The Great Plains*, p. 205.

6. See below, Ch. xii.

MONTANA

DAKOTA

Missouri R

TERRITORY

Yellowstone R

Bismarck

Grand R

TERRITORY

Big Cheyenne R

WYOMING

White R

Missouri R

Dakota R

Big Sioux R

TERRITORY

Ft Laramie

Niobrara R

NEBRASKA

100°W

Miles

0   100   200   300

Duluth

MINNESOTA

Minneapolis-
St Paul

Mississippi R

Des Moines R

IOWA

NORTHERN   PACIFIC   RR

Cheyenne

Denver

COLORADO

Pueblo

NEW

Santa Fé

MEXICO

TERRITORY

N.Platte

S.Platte

Ogallala

Republican R

Platte R

UNION   PACIFIC RR

R

Omaha

Lincoln

Hannibal

KANSAS

Abilene

KANSAS

Kansas
City

St.Joseph

MISSOURI PACIFIC
RR

Smoky Hill R

Ellsworth

PACIFIC RR

Arkansas R

Dodge City

SANTA   FE

Newton

RR

Sedalia

Cimarron R

Baxter
Springs

MISSOURI

Canadian R

INDIAN

TERRI-

TORY

ARKANSAS

Red R

Brazos R

T   E

Colorado R

FtWorth

Pecos R

Cross Timbers

X

A   S

Houston

Rio Grande

M E X I C O

San Antonio

Nueces R

Galveston

Gulf   of

M e x i c o

100°W

W.B.

GOODNIGHT—LOVING TRAIL

WESTERN TRAIL

CHISHOLM TRAIL

SEDALIA

TRAIL

PRINCIPAL NORTH-SOUTH
CATTLE TRAILS
1865~c.1885

Treeless Plains & Desert ☐

(3 1 3)

which was to see the orderly advance *westward* of civilization and settlement behind a "cutting edge" of frontiersmen.[7] One thing this grain-crossing did was to inject a way of life, hitherto southern—indeed, quasi-Mexican (especially in its vocabulary)—into the northern plains of Kansas, Nebraska, Colorado, Wyoming, and Montana, and even into Canada's prairie provinces. The "cowboy culture" of the cattle kingdom was to penetrate far beyond the Missouri and Kansas railheads, which were the first objectives of the trail herds. Soon the "Texas cowboy" was all over the Great Plains, sometimes appreciated, often resented; free-spending, painting the town red—and widely imitated. In the decades after the Civil War the spread of the "cow culture" up out of Texas helped to knit the divided country together again and keep the West "one society"—as it had always tended to be, even during the war. Men who had driven a herd of cattle all the way from the Rio Grande to the Blackfoot reservation in northern Montana—as had Andy Adams's outfit—could not but acquire a wide knowledge of their enormous country and an easy tolerance of sectional and local differences and idiosyncracies. These differences occasionally caused trouble, for many of the cowhands were Confederate veterans, but the long drive tended to be a melting pot rather than a tinder box.[8] The railhead cow towns (like the mining camps) contained elements from all over the country, some good, some bad, but very few of them indifferent to the fact that here—as on the long trails, and the new ranches that were being established all over the Great Plains—a new type of frontier history was being made, and a new type of American forged. Owen Wister's "ideal" cowboy was not a Texan in Texas but a Virginian in Wyoming; yet he and his fellow Virginians, New Yorkers, Vermonters, Kentuckians, and assorted Midwesterners and Northwesterners had to

7. Though even in 1893 F. J. Turner, in his famous essay, paid relatively little attention to the significance of the cattle kingdom, he did say (*Frontier in American History*, p. 16): "The ranges of the Great Plains, with ranch and cowboy and nomadic life, are things of yesterday and today. . . . The effect of these great ranches on the subsequent agrarian history of the localities in which they existed should be studied"; but he was obviously much more interested in the farmers' frontier.

8. Lovell, the owner of the herd, "had carried a musket in the ranks of the Union army," but young Tom "couldn't help feeling friendly toward him, Yankee that he was"—Adams: *Log of a Cowboy*, pp. 12, 23.

learn their craft (if not their manners) from the Texas cowboys up from the Rio Grande, the Nueces, and the Pecos.[9]

The word "cowboy" seems at first to have been almost synonymous with "cattle rustler." The Tory "cowboys" of Westchester county, New York, in the American Revolution, plundered the cattle of the patriot "skinners" and vice versa,[1] and in the Texas revolution a "cowboy" was one who ran Mexican-owned cattle across the Rio Grande in the general direction of Louisiana's mar-

Old-style Texan cowman, by Frederic Remington. From Theodore Roosevelt: *Ranch Life and the Hunting Trail* (New York and London, 1889).

kets. "The name 'cowboy' was even then—and still more emphatically later—one name for many crimes, since those engaged in it [*sic*] were mostly outlaws confessedly."[2] The name had to travel

9. "It was the Texas cowboy who taught his northern cousin the techniques of handling cattle in the vastnesses of the open range. . . . The Montana cowboy was a legitimate copy of the Texas cowboy, but he was just that, a copy of the original . . . the cattleman frontier was a Texas story from beginning to end"— Frantz and Choate: *The American Cowboy*, p. 35.

1. See *A Dictionary of American English*, ed. Craigie and Hurlbert, II, 658.

2. C. W. Webber: *Tales of the Southern Border* (Philadelphia, 1853), p. 124; quoted in Frantz and Choate, p. 74.

far and have many rough edges rubbed off it before it could sit becomingly on the lithe and graceful shoulders of that perfect gentle knight, *sans peur* and *sans reproche*, Owen Wister's "Virginian."

The first cattle king was of course a Texan, one Taylor White, who drove longhorn cattle to Louisiana long before the forties. When he moved to Texas in 1823, "his whole fortune was three cows and calves two small poneys a wife and three children, he now [1842] owns about 40,000 acres of land upwards of 90 negroes about thirty thousand head of cattle, has sixty thousand dollars in specie deposited in new orleans, marked and branded thirty seven hundred calves last spring and sold last fall in new orleans 11 hundred steers weighing about 1000 lbs each which he says cost him no more than 75 cents a head to drive them to market at orleans and what is extraordinary he cannot read or write and has made his fortune raising stock alone."[3] Similar modest fortunes continued to be made by Texas cowmen, both lettered and unlettered, up to the outbreak of the Civil War in 1861. After the Mexican War had ended any possibility of the Mexicans recovering their herds marooned north of the Rio Grande, the unbranded longhorns—and some branded ones—became public property and increased exceedingly, especially in the Nueces Valley. Various attempts were made to get these animals, almost valueless in Texas, to profitable markets. In addition to the drives to New Orleans, some were shipped out by sea from Galveston and other Texas ports and roadsteads, others driven up to Missouri, St. Louis, Chicago, and even New York. This last operation took two whole seasons (despite a train ride on the last leg, from Muncie, Indiana, to New York) in 1854. During the gold rush some were even driven to California, for a steer worth less than $5 in Texas at that time could fetch $160 on the booming Pacific Coast, where the inrush of population had overtaxed the supplies of "cattle on a thousand hills." But the way to California was long and hazardous, and the Midwestern farmers feared the Texas cattle fever, so they placed increasing obstacles in the way of the Texas drovers. In addition, Indian cattle thieves were a nuisance everywhere. From 1861 to 1865 the long-distance cattle drives were made impossible by war conditions, especially in border states like Kansas and Missouri. Most of the pre-war demand had been from

3. "A Letter Book of Joseph Eve," *Southwestern Historical Quarterly,* XLIII: 4 (April 1940), 488, quoted in Hogan: *Texas Republic,* p. 21.

the more populous North. An attempt to reopen the trade in 1866 proved disastrous; though over a quarter of a million Texas cattle were sent north and east that year, very few were sold at a profit;[4] Texas cattlemen—and their longhorns—were still not welcome there.

It required a stroke of genius to bring these Texas cattle into the packing stations, sleek, fat, and profitable, and this was provided by one Joseph McCoy—the authentic "Real McCoy"—out of Illinois. After an unsuccessful attempt to interest the short-sighted Missouri Pacific Railroad in his project, he made a deal with the Hannibal and St. Joseph and the Kansas Pacific for the transportation of cattle at preferential rates eastward to Chicago, and then set up his cattle barn, corrals, and scales at the end of the earth, or so it looked that summer of 1867, a place called Abilene—"a small dead place . . . of about one dozen log huts."[5] Aside from its good grass and plentiful water, Abilene's only merit was that it was about to be reached by the railroad from the East. Despite assiduous advertising, both in Texas and along the trails, McCoy attracted only some 25,000 cattle to Abilene in 1867; but it was the start of a movement that, lasting until 1872, was to bring hundreds of thousands of Texas longhorns into Abilene each year, and to see both the birth of a new industry and the crystallization of a new frontier type. "Abilene, more than four hundred miles north of the Red River and nearly a thousand miles from the Nueces country, was to become the commercial capital of Texas . . . to know in prosperity a lustiness and a greed which would make it legend wherever cattlemen stopped to talk. It would be superseded by other and better towns . . . but Abilene would be the first and most fondly remembered. . . . In Abilene the Texas cowboy was discovered and first became a distinct type, and here he first displayed for a national audience those extremes of temperament that make a hero."[6]

By 1872 Abilene had grown more or less respectable—in 1871 Wild Bill Hickok, its trigger-happy marshall, proved too tough for it, and his commission was allowed to lapse—and, besides, the

4. E. E. Dale: *The Range Cattle Industry* (Norman, Okla., 1930), p. 50.

5. J. C. McCoy: *Historical Sketches of the Cattle Trade of the West and South West*, ed. R. P. Bieber (Glendale, Calif., 1940), p. 116 ff. This book, first published in 1874, when the cattle trails were still warm, has become a classic.

6. Frantz and Choate, p. 32.

railroad had pushed out beyond it. Other cow-towns arose: Ells-worth, Newton, Jutesburg, Wichita, Hays City, Ogalalla, Cheyenne, Laramie, and others; Dodge City, a little west of where the Santa Fe Railroad reached the Great Bend of the Arkansas River and near Coronado's Quivira, was the last, the wildest, and the most notorious of them all. Dodge City received and trans-shipped more than a quarter-million head of Texas cattle a year during the boom of the late seventies and early eighties. "In its moment of glory Dodge City was better known than Denver or St. Paul or Kansas City."[7] Andy Adams's famous *Log of a Cowboy*,[8] in which he describes visits to both "Dodge" and Ogalalla, gives Dodge rather a good name, thanks to its formidable peace officers:

"I've been in Dodge every summer since '77," said the old cowman, "and I can give you boys some points. Dodge is one town where the average bad man of the West not only finds his equal, but finds himself badly handicapped. The bufflalo hunters and range men have protested against the iron rule of Dodge's peace officers, and nearly every protest has cost human life. Don't ever get the impression that you can ride your horses into a saloon, or shoot out the lights in Dodge; it may go somewhere else, but it don't go there. So I want to warn you to behave yourselves. You can wear your six-shooters into town, but you'd better leave them at the first place you stop, hotel, livery, or business house. And when you leave town, call for your pistols, but don't ride out shooting; omit that. Most cow-boys think it's an infringement on their rights to give up shooting in town, and if it is, it stands, for your six-shooters are no match for Winchesters and buckshot; and Dodge's officers are as game a set of men as ever faced danger."

Nearly a generation has passed since McNulta, the Texan cattle drover, gave our outfit this advice one June morning on the Mul-berry, and in setting down this record, I have only to scan the roster of the peace officials of Dodge City to admit its correctness. Among the names that graced the official roster, during the brief span of the trail days, were the brothers Ed, Jim, and "Bat" Masterson, Wyatt Earp, Jack Bridges, "Doc" Holliday, Charles Bassett, William Till-man, "Shotgun" Collins, Joshua Webb, Mayor A. B. Webster, and

7. Riegel: *America Moves West*, p. 521.

8. Boston and New York, 1903 and 1931. Cast in fictional form but based upon actual experience, this is regarded as one of the best accounts ever written of life on the old cattle trails of the west.

"Mysterious" Dave Mather. The puppets of no romance ever written can compare with these officers in fearlessness. And let it be understood, there were plenty to protest against their rule; almost daily during the range season some equally fearless individual defied them.[9]

To Adams, it is Ogalalla that is Gomorrah:

. . . below us in the valley of the South Platte, nestled Ogalalla, the Gomorrah of the cattle trail. From amongst its half hundred build-

A fight in the street, by Frederic Remington. From Theodore Roosevelt: *Ranch Life and the Hunting Trail* (1889).

ings, no church spire pointed upward, but instead three fourths of its business houses were dance halls, gambling houses, and saloons. We all knew the town by reputation, while the larger part of our outfit had been in it before. It was there that Joel Collins and his outfit rendezvoused when they robbed the Union Pacific train in October, '77. Collins had driven a herd of cattle for his father and brother, and after selling them in the Black Hills, gambled away the

9. *Log of a Cowboy*, pp. 191-2.

proceeds. Some five or six of his outfit returned to Ogalalla with him, and being moneyless, concluded to recoup their losses at the expense of the railway company. Going eighteen miles up the river to Big Springs, seven of them robbed the express and passengers, the former yielding sixty thousand dollars in gold. The next morning they were in Ogalalla, paying debts, and getting their horses shod. In Collin's outfit was Sam Bass, and under his leadership, until he met his death the following spring at the hands of Texas Rangers, the course of the outfit southward was marked by a series of daring bank and train robberies.

We reached the river late that evening, and after watering, grazed until dark and camped for the night. But it was not to be a night of rest and sleep, for the lights were twinkling across the river in town; and cook, horse wrangler, and all, with the exception of the first guard, rode across the river after the herd had been bedded. Flood had quit us while we were watering the herd and gone in ahead to get a draft cashed, for he was as moneyless as the rest of us. But his letter of credit was good anywhere on the trail where money was to be had, and on reaching town, he took us into a general outfitting store and paid us twenty-five dollars apiece. After warning us to be on hand at the wagon to stand our watches, he left us, and we scattered like lost sheep. Officer and I paid our loans to The Rebel, and the three of us wandered around for several hours in company with Nat Straw. When we were in Dodge, my bunkie had shown no inclination to gamble, but now he was the first one to suggest that we make up a "cow," and let him try his luck at monte. Straw and Officer were both willing, and though in rags, I willingly consented and contributed my five to the general fund.

Every gambling house ran from two to three monte layouts, as it was a favorite game of cowmen, especially when they were from the far southern country. Priest soon found a game to his liking, and after watching his play through several deals, Officer and I left him with the understanding that he would start for camp promptly at midnight. There was much to be seen, though it was a small place, for the ends of the earth's iniquity had gathered in Ogalalla. We wandered through the various gambling houses, drinking moderately, meeting an occasional acquaintance from Texas, and in the course of our rounds landed in the Dew-Drop-In dance hall. Here might be seen the frailty of women in every grade and condition. From girls in their teens, launching out on a life of shame, to the adventuress who had once had youth and beauty in her favor, but was now discarded and ready for the final dose of opium and the coroner's verdict—all were there in tinsel and paint, practicing a careless exposure of their charms. In a town which has no night, the hours pass rapidly and before we were aware, midnight was upon us. Returning to the gambling house where we had left Priest, we found

Painting the town red, by Frederic Remington. From Theodore Roosevelt: *Ranch Life and the Hunting Trail* (1889).

him over a hundred dollars winner, and, calling his attention to the hour, persuaded him to cash in and join us. We felt positively rich, as he counted out to each partner his share of the winnings! Straw was missing to receive his, but we knew he could be found on the morrow, and after a round of drinks, we forded the river.[1]

1. *Log of a Cowboy*, pp. 259–61.

Nevertheless, his outfit was better behaved in Ogalalla than in Dodge City. In Dodge they had to paint the town red on the $25 in gold advanced to each of them by the trail boss, but made such nuisances of themselves that they were shot up by peace officers (without material damage to man, but one of their horses was killed) on the way out. In Ogalalla, on a second visit after getting the balance of their pay, "Tom" and his two bunkies won $1,400 playing monte at The Black Elephant, and departed quietly after buying new outfits, including "cheap new suits the color of which we never knew until the next day."

> As we scaled the bluffs we halted for our last glimpse of the lights of Ogalalla. The Rebel remarked "Boys, I've traveled some in my life, but that little hole back there could give Natchez-under-the-hill cards and spades and then outhold her as a tough town."[2]

Not every outfit was five months on the way, as was that of foreman Jim Flood, which took Adams's alter ego young Tom along as a trail hand in the early spring of 1882, and, after receiving the herd from across the Rio Grande River in Old Mexico, delivered it intact on the Blackfoot reservation in the northwest corner of Montana at the end of August. When all was over, Don Lovell, the owner of the herd, took his cowboys to the railhead of the Northern Pacific at Silver Bow, Montana, and stood drinks all round while they waited for the train. "Turn to and help wait on these thirsty Texans," he said, "and remember that there is nothing too rich for our blood today. This outfit has made one of the longest cattle drives on record, and the best is none too good for them."[3]

Chief among the many trails followed by the cattle drives to the northern railheads were: the Sedalia Trail, opened up in 1866 but veering too far east into the wooded Ozarks to be followed in later years; the Chisholm Trail to Abilene via Fort Worth and the Indian Territory, resulting from McCoy's enterprising idea; the Goodnight-Loving Trail to the Pecos River and then north through New Mexico, Colorado, and beyond; and the Western Trail (which Andy Adams's heroes followed in 1882), up through

2. *Log of a Cowboy*, p. 274. I stayed the night in Ogalalla in 1952, seventy years after this, but the glory had departed. The little town was so dull that I went up to a motel in the Kingsley Dam resort area and spent the evening writing. I left at dawn without hearing even one shot.

3. *Log of a Cowboy*, p. 274.

the later notorious cow-towns of Dodge City, Kansas, and Ogalalla, Nebraska, and thence into Montana across northeastern Wyoming. The Goodnight-Loving Trail, named after two well-known cattlemen who used it, belied its cozy name, for it went through Comanche country and was perhaps the most hazardous of all. Every one of these trails had to cross a number of eastward flowing rivers, very few of them "two miles wide and half an inch deep," as the Platte was claimed to be, for many were swift-flowing, deep, and treacherous. In Andy Adams's book the trail boss (or foreman) of one herd loses his life at one such crossing, and, at another, a full day is spent in improvising a bridge of brushwood and logs and cajoling the unwilling longhorns across this makeshift causeway, using, as a last resort, a bellowing calf as a decoy, lugged on the end of a rope and followed by its anxious mother. The inquisitive steers found it impossible to resist investigating this intriguing situation, and crowded across in her wake.

Only in the earliest years after the Civil War were the Texas cattle driven North principally for shipment East by rail, though this remained an important trade well into the eighties. They were also used to stock the Northern Plains, there to be cross-bred with beef cattle of higher quality but lower stamina from the East, the expensive stud-bulls being worth importing all this way by rail. As the population of this area increased, Texas cattle were also used for local consumption, after a period of fattening at the end of their long, slenderizing drives. This would have been the fate of most of the herd driven up by Andy Adams's outfit in 1882 from the Mexican border to the Blackfoot reservation. The federal government had undertaken to deliver beef cattle to the Indian reservations regularly, and in most cases it fulfilled its obligations. The Indians, deprived of the now almost extinct buffalo herds and not yet acclimatized to subsistence farming or cattle ranching, might have starved without this "subsidy." Sometimes they did.

According to the U. S. Tenth Census Report,[4] up to 1880 nearly four and a quarter million head of Texas cattle were shipped eastward by rail. Of these, nearly a million and a half passed through Abilene between 1867 and 1871, over a million through Wichita and Ellesworth between 1872 and 1875, and over a million through Dodge City and Ellis between 1876 and 1879. The record year was 1871, when over 700,000 Texas cattle reached Kansas.

4. Vol. III (1883), "Statistics of Agriculture," p. 975.

There had still been over four million longhorns in Texas in 1870, about as many as in 1860, despite the size and number of the long drives of the second half of that decade.

The cattle boom in the Great Plains continued until the mid-eighties and in its later years attracted large amounts of foreign

A buffalo hunter's camp on the Southern Plains, in the
Texas Panhandle, 1874.

capital. Range cattle worth only $7 or $8 a head in 1878 were fetching the peak price of $30 to $35 in 1882, as a result of which the drives increased and the northern range became overstocked. In view of this glut, the Chicago packers slashed the prices they offered, and cattle were back to $8 a head by 1885. The severe winter of 1885–86 brought disaster to many cattlemen and bankrupted even some of the large corporations—like the Swan Company of Wyoming and the Niobra Company of Nebraska. Millions of cattle died that winter on the ranges and ranches.[5] "The winter of 1885–1886 was the sort of sharp punch calculated to puncture permanently an overblown speculative bubble,"[6] and by 1887 prime beef cattle were down to under $2 per hundred pounds on the Chicago market. A twelve-hundred-pound steer could net the owner as little as $5, after all shipping and other expenses had been met.[7] The wheel had thus come full circle to the almost valueless cattle that had roamed the Nueces valley a quarter-century earlier, threatening to become a pest.[8] An era in the history of the American frontier and in the development of the Great West was over, and within a generation! "To sum it all up, the collapse of 1885 converted ranching from an adventure into a business, which is today carried on with as much system as farming and manufacturing" says Webb.[9] But this transition and the necessary readjustments took time. "By 1892 the story of the frontier ranch and its cowboys had already been lived, and many cowboys were getting ready to reminisce in print and at cowboy reunions."[1] It was not until after 1900 that the Western "cattle business" began to take on its soulless modern form; not until around 1950 that the cowboy began to forsake his horse for a jeep and "learn his songs from the radio," and the cattle barons to "ride the range" in air-conditioned Cadillac ranch wagons, with built-in bars and telephones, or to "mend their fences" on stock markets of a different kind via their own executive aircraft. "Waiting for a Chinook"[2] took a long time, but when the warm winds began to blow again on the cattle industry, it was, in the twentieth century, to become bigger than ever before. But by then all the romance had gone—or had it?

There was no more romance about the cattlemen, the owners,

5. See E. S. Osgood: *Day of the Cattleman* (Minneapolis, 1929), pp. 220–1.

6. Frantz and Choate, p. 66.   7. Webb, p. 237.

8. Webb, p. 212.   9. Webb, p. 240.

1. Frantz and Choate, p. 67.

2. The title of Charles Russell's famous miniature (postcard size) watercolor of an emaciated steer "drifting" before a snowstorm on the Northern Plains. The original is in the Montana Historical Society Museum in Helena. Enlarged copies, by the original artist, can be found in several other collections.

the tycoons, "The Cattle Kings,"[3] than about the mine owners and entrepreneurs who waxed rich out of the mining boom. Collis P. Huntington was about as romantic as a bullfrog, and even the gifted turn-of-the-century novelist Frank Norris failed to make an exciting character out of him; John Mackay was almost ostentatiously unglamorous; Joseph McCoy was about as featureless as the Illinois prairies from which he hailed, and he obviously disapproved of the picturesque Texas cowboys out of whom he made his filthy lucre;[4] the most romantic thing about Charlie Goodnight was his name.[5] It is the hired hands, from the trail boss or foreman down to the wrangler (and even including the cook, usually an ex-cowboy grown too old or too heavy for the saddle, and nearly always an ornery "character,"[6] who have become the heroes of high romance, as imperishable as the knights of the Round Table and the paladins of Roncesvalles. The noble cowboy has followed the noble savage into literature, and has stayed in much more successfully. Eighty years after the frontier cowboy passed his apogee, three quarters of a century after the open range disappeared from the West, more is written, sung, "shot," or projected every year about the cowboy than about any other hero of the American frontier, old or new—perhaps about all of them together. Acres of this effluvia are sheer pulp, following well-worn grooves and repeating stereotypes, but every now and then the cowboy frontier still produces a classic, or the old-time cowboy evokes a bit of descriptive writing, a piece of sculpture, a painting or drawing, a poem, a song, a film script, a piece of acting, or a realistic reappraisal that has true inspiration. Nearly all of these (and we all have our favorites)—with the possible exception of the last category—tend to paint the cowboy larger than life and twice as handsome. But who cares! Owen Wister's "Virginian" at his

3. Lewis Atherton: *The Cattle Kings* (Chicago, 1961), passim.

4. *Sketches of the Cattle Trade*, p. 131 ff.

5. Though Charlie knew the rigors of the long drive at first hand, he forsook them as soon as he could for married bliss and the comforts of his "JA" Ranch, "a two-storey plank-and-log structure with water piped in . . . and a separate mess-house for the men"—Frantz and Choate, p. 55; see also J. E. Haley: *Charles Goodnight, Cowman and Plainsman* (Boston, 1936; repr. Norman, Okla., 1949), passim. Andy Adams: *Reed Anthony, Cowman* (Boston, 1907) attempted to make a hero out of Charlie Goodnight, but only succeeded in making him a worthy. His hired hands in *The Log of a Cowboy* are much more alive.

6. "As techy as a cook," the saying went.

Line riding in winter, by Frederic Remington. From Theodore Roosevelt: *Ranch Life and the Hunting Trail* (1889).

bright dawn, Gary Cooper at *High Noon*, or Ramon Adams in the campfire's evening glow have all depicted him as we would like him to have been, even if he was not quite like that. When Frederic Remington, illustrating young Theodore Roosevelt's *Ranch Life and the Hunting Trail* in 1888 with cowboys drawn from life, shows the cowboy (p. 72) as he really is *most* of the time, riding the range and mending barbed-wire fences in winter, blue with cold, muffled up to the eyebrows, sagging on an equally sorry-

7. See also Ramon Adams: *The Best of the American Cowboy* (Norman, Okla., 1957) for a ripe selection of twenty-seven items, beginning with the classic and anonymous "A Man Suited to His Times" (pp. 3–26).

looking pony, sombrero-less, scarfless, chapless, and bored, we turn eagerly to page 92, where he and his bunkies are painting the town red, or to page 40, where he is riding a bucking bronco, or to page 91, where he is scaring the daylights out of a city slicker. This is the cowboy as we *want* to remember him, but as he very rarely, and for only brief moments, was.[8] Ramon Adams, no cowboy himself and no kin to Andy (except under the skin), but a skilled chronicler and bibliographer of the cowboy era, came up to Denver in 1962 and told us members of the newly formed Western History

Making a tenderfoot dance, by Frederic Remington. From Theodore Roosevelt: *Ranch Life and the Hunting Trail* (1889).

Association what the "old-time cowhand" was really like. Though Paul Horgan[9] has produced a highly literary,[1] and greatly respected, evaluation of the cowboy, this writer prefers the saltier and more down-to-earth treatment—which really requires to be intoned aloud in a slow Texas drawl—given by Ramon Adams:

8. Remington drawings from *Ranch Life* are repr. on pp. 315, 319, 321, and 327-8.

9. *Great River*, 2 vols. (New York, 1954), II, 871-86.

1. Frantz and Choate call it "belletristic"!

I have been interested in the cowboy and his lingo for more than sixty years—way back, as the cowboy would say, since I was "fryin' size." My real interest probably started when Jim Houston, a typical Texas cowboy, told a group of other cowmen, into which I had poked my young ears, of the time he had a narrow escape from a cow on the prod while he was afoot in a branding pen:

"There's no love-light in that cow's eyes as she makes for me," said Jim. "I fogs it across that corral like I'm goin' to a dance, an' she's a-scratchin' the grease off my pants at ever' jump. Seein' I can't make the fence in time, Brazos Gowdy jumps down off the fence an' throws his hat in the old gal's face. Seein' a cowboy come apart in

Steer rider, by Charlie Russell.

pieces like that makes her hesitate till I climb the fence without losin' anything more'n some confidence, a lot o' wind, and a little dignity. You can take it from me, a cow with a fresh-branded calf might be a mother, but she shore ain't no *lady*." . . .

There is an underlying humor in nearly every utterance of the cowboy. The country he lived in was vast and vivid; the life he lived was hard and lonely. This loneliness, his lack of education, and a certain restrained lawlessness all had their influence. His natural dislike for rule and restraint, his hatred for all authority, his extravagant and often grotesque humor, his exceptional capacity for word pictures—all these attest the spirit of the West, and from such qualities its language is nourished.

Though he led a hard and dangerous life, he could usually see the funny side, even if the joke was on him. His humor grew out of what he knew and observed. It expressed itself in picturesque, full-flavored, fertile, and vigorous speech, in practical jokes and rough horseplay, and in the tall tales he spun around the campfire. His capacity for humor was largely due to the fact that he was a young man, full of prank and play. His kind rarely considered the problems of life seriously. His humor was not merely an occasional flash of mood; it was a way of living, a standard reaction to the problems of life. Even in his ordinary everyday speech, his humor was evident.

A typical example is Bud Puryear, an old cowhand of the Texas

Cowboy riding the fence line, by Charlie Russell.

Panhandle. The ranch had sent several cowboys to drive in a small bunch of cattle to the home ranch. They had to drive these cattle through a desert section nearly all day before reaching the ranch, and both cattle and men suffered extremely from thirst. By the time they reached the southern edge of the ranch where there was a surface tank, the cattle were frantic and the men's tongues were swollen. When the cattle smelled the water of the tank they made a run for it, and the men followed.

Bud rode right in among the cattle, lay down on his belly, and stuck his muzzle in the water. The other boys had ridden over to the other side where the water wasn't muddied.

"Hey, Bud!" one of them yelled over, "Why don't you come over here where the water's clear?"

"Hell," answered Bud, "what difference does it make? I'm goin' to drink it all anyway." . . .

The real cowhand's typical day was anything but romantic. There was no romance in getting up at four o'clock in the morning, eating dust behind a trail herd, swimming muddy and turbulent rivers, nor in doctoring screw worms, pulling stupid cows from bog holes, sweating in the heat of summer, and freezing in the cold of winter.

If, when he got to town, after long months out in the brush, on the lone prairie, or on the long, long trail, the cowboy "cut his wolf loose" and had a little fun, he could hardly be blamed. He was a robust animal, full of vinegar and pride, and generally came from venturesome ancestors.

The old-time cowhand lived in the saddle. He was strictly a riding man, and detested walking, even for short distances. A self-respecting cowhand would never be going far on foot. This is why he was mighty particular about a straight riding job. When he was out of work and rode to a new range seeking a job, he was careful to inquire about the outfit before he arrived. He didn't want to sign up with some little "three-up" outfit that didn't own enough beef to hold a barbecue. On such an outfit there would be chores to do that were beneath his dignity, such as feeding, digging post-holes, or cutting stove wood, and the only place a cowhand could cut wood and not hurt his pride was at a line camp where it was chop wood or "no eat."

When he "hit" a fenced ranch for a job, he hoped that all the fencing and cross fencing had been done and no more post-holes needed to be dug. He didn't want to be caught on the blister end of no damned shovel. High-heeled boots weren't made for foot work, and he wouldn't be caught in a low heeled shoe. But he didn't shirk any duty as long at it could be done from horseback. He worked without complaint long hours through flood and drought, heat and cold, and dust and blizzard, never once thinking of his own discomfort if the cattle and the welfare of his boss demanded his attention.

Fighting prairie fires, the dangers of stampedes, the loneliness of range riding, the discomforts of standing guard in the rain or sleet— none of these things seemed unusual if he could do them from the back of a horse. On the other hand, he didn't even want to open a gate unless he could lean over and do it from the saddle. His profession was born of necessity, and with it was born a tradition that he followed jealously until he became the most colorful and picturesque hired man ever known. About the only footwork he considered honorable was roping in the corral, or doing the branding.

A lot of sunshine put that squint in the old-timer's eyes, and a lot of prairie wind tanned his face. That ten-gallon hat and those fancy boots were not what made him look like a cowman. It was the elements, the corral dust, and horse smell, and the cow-camp chuck that branded him. He could go away from the cow country and dress in fancy society togs, and another cowman would still know him to be a cowman.

After the fences came, most of these old-timers were always bellyaching with a yearning to go somewhere where they could spread a loop without getting it caught on a fence post. Most of the real old-timers have now saddled a cloud and ridden into the Great Beyond, and their like will never be seen again. . . .[2]

Ramon Adams's cowhand might have been a "character," but he was hardly either a glamorous figure or a hero. But if his is the cowboy as he really was, then the cowboy of Western mythology is a man transformed—and made larger than life. The old time cowhand was no hero, not even to his horse (and quite a number of cow horses were reputed to be a sight more intelligent than their riders), yet look what has happened to his latter day image! Clifford Westermeier asks: "What is there about him that makes a halo of his stetson and a dragon-slaying sword of his six-shooter? The West had other heroes with traits just as admirable—the explorer, the trapper, the prospector, the homesteader . . ."[3] and goes on to say that the *mystique* is no doubt connected with the cowboy's horse—*pas de cheval, pas de cowboy*, as that Westernized Frenchman, Paul Coze, has aphorized—but, then, other frontiersmen have ridden horses. The Freudians, too, have pushed their way in, not to

2. Excerpted from "The Old-Time Cowhand," in *The American West: An Appraisal*, Papers from the Denver Conference on the History of Western America, ed. R. G. Ferris, pp. 15–24. This is a shortened "version" of the item of the same title Mr. Adams himself contributed to *The Best of the American Cowboy* (and is gratefully printed here with his express permission).

3. "The Modern Cowboy—An Image," in Ferris (ed.): *American West*, p. 34.

A bucking bronco, by Frederic Remington. From Theodore Roosevelt:
Ranch Life and the Hunting Trail (1889).

propound a centaur complex, but with the suggestion that "the
cowboy hero is the eternal son, repetitively and compulsively acting out an archetypal fantasy. . . . The villain represents the 'bad'
father, who deprives the narcissistic 'king of the nursery' of his

heart's desire, the good mother. In overwhelming the villain, the hero is simultaneously re-enacting the oedipal crime against the father, making restitution for it, and avenging both his father and himself. . . . The saloon and the 'hangout' are allusions to the primal scene . . . the gun-battles are threats and counter-threats of castration. . . . The Western story may be considered as a heroic myth in which are concealed themes of oedipal and other conflicts."[4] And so on. It is all so simple. If he could read Dr. Barker's psychoanalysis of the hired man on horseback, the bones of Eugene Manlove Rhodes[5] would buck in his grave at the summit of Rhodes Pass, in his beloved San Andrés Mountains of New Mexico.

No matter whose definition of the American cowboy we choose—Andy or Ramon Adams's, Eugene Manlove Rhodes's, Emerson Hough's, Charles Siringo's, Philip Rollins's,[6] Dr. Barker's, or Dr. Freud's—he is still with us a hundred years after he first came up from Texas to Baxter Springs and Sedalia. The myth and the reality, as Frantz and Choate have demonstrated, have become inextricably intermingled. What he was like in the great drives

4. Warren J. Barker, M.D. (Pittsburgh): "The Stereotyped Western Story," *The Psychoanalytic Quarterly*, XXIV:2 (1955), 270–80.

5. Eugene Manlove Rhodes (1869–1934)—whose name, had he not been born with it, might credibly have been invented for him by the editors of the *Saturday Evening Post*, which published so many of his stories—was a real cowboy who made his living (off and on) by writing about the cowboy as he really was, but weaving a web of romance around him by telescoping his real-life adventures and moving the scenic wonders around him in a little closer. In many ways the life of this "Hired Man on Horseback"—the title of his wife's happy and entirely uncloying biography of him (May D. Rhodes: *The Hired Man on Horseback*, Boston, 1938)—was more interesting than any of his stories, in which he drew copiously on his own memories of the old West of the last open range. "I came to Mexico the year that Billy the Kid was killed [1881]," he proudly proclaimed, and although he never met that sawed-off desperado, he knew Pat Garratt, the Kid's slayer, well, and once hid a couple of "wanted" men from this redoubtable sheriff, smuggling them into another county to secure them less summary justice. Forced by circumstances to live for many years in the home of his wife's parents, Rhodes once confessed: "I have been friendly with a number of outlaws. . . . Outlaws are more interesting than in-laws." See W. H. Hutchinson: *A Bar Cross Man: The Life and Personal Writings of Eugene Manlove Rhodes* (Norman, Okla., 1956). Few people today read Rhodes's books—*Good Men and True* (1910), *The Desire of the Moth* (1916), *Stepsons of Light* (1921), *The Trusty Knaves* (1934)—but they are better than their glossy titles suggest and do not deserve to die. See also J. Frank Dobie: *My Salute to Gene Rhodes* ("A Christmas Remembrance from Bertha and Frank Dobie," El Paso, Texas, 1947, 12 pages).

6. See Bibliographic Note, pp. 436–7.

MISSISSIPPI

MISSOURI

ARKANSAS
(STATE·1836)

LOUISIANA
(STATE·1812)

New Orleans

Gulf of Mexico

Arkansas R.

36°30'

66

80

90

Shreveport

67

INLAND PORT

Galveston

Sabine R.

ADAMS-ONIS
LINE 1819

MISSOURI COMPROMISE'
LINE OF 1820

OKLAHOMA
(STATE·1907)

Marshall

Neches R.

Houston

Beaumont

Matagorda Bay

Dallas

Trinity R.

75

Canadian R.

77

81

Oklahoma City

Red R.

Brazos R.

Waco

Austin

81

59

Corpus Christi

Kingsville

Brownsville

LINE OF 1845

Ft Worth

80

Abilene

Colorado R.

87

San Antonio

81

Nueces R.

281

Laredo

PAN-AMERICAN HIGHWAY

90

Amarillo

281

San Angelo

Big Spring

80

Eagle Pass

281

NEW MEXICO
(TERRITORY·1850-STATE·1912)

66

87

Pecos R.

Ft Stockton

Rio Grande

BIG BEND
NAT. PARK

Staked Plain

Sweetwater

66

Santa Fe

Albuquerque

Rio Grande

Guadalupe Mts.

Van Horn

Apache Mts.

El Paso

80

M E X I C O

Miles

200

0

MODERN
TEXAS

U.S. Highways
Southern Trail
(Old Spanish Trail)
Principal Oilfields
Timbered country

W.B.

(335)

between 1865 and 1885 we can now fairly clearly discern; but what he has since become is beyond history and is the stuff that dreams are made of. The Rodeo "cowboy" of today, always "on the road," is essentially a showman and more than a bit of an actor. He possesses great skill, takes great risks, and wins (if he is lucky) big prizes. His long drives are in 300-horsepower ranch wagons. He shuttles from Dallas to Cheyenne, to Pendleton, to Albuquerque; to Madison Square Garden, New York; to Calgary, to Denver. In 1955 alone there were 421 rodeos approved by the national Rodeo Cowboys' Association, and in 1961 there were 542, offering over $3 million in prize money. Cheyenne's Frontier Days Rodeo, called by its proud sponsors the "Daddy of them All," is worth $2 million to that city in business annually. One rodeo cowboy, Jim Shoulders, won over $43,000 in prize money in a year.[7]

The "cowboy" who "learned his songs on the *rad*-io" and makes his living playing in horse operas and the like, may never have been on the range at all. William S. Hart, Tom Mix, and Will Rogers were ranch fed, all right, but some of their singing, guitar-strumming successors have been less authentic, though most of them can at least ride a horse. The "cowboy" of the "Western" movies has had a long inning ever since Bronco Billy Anderson played in *The Great Train Robbery* in 1903, and television has given him a new lease of life. Even Japan now makes her own "Westerns," and, by way of retaliation, *The Seven Samurai* was remade in the "Western" idiom by Hollywood for distribution in the English-speaking world as *The Magnificent Seven*.

Westerners' Societies, or "Corrals," have been founded in many countries besides the United States and Canada, and have flourished, particularly in Great Britain and Germany. The president of the German "Westerners" is himself a prolific writer of Western paperbacks,[8] and those who sit at the feet of Karl May, "the German Fenimore Cooper," turn out by the thousands to attend an annual festival in which they can watch the cowboy hero "Old Shatterhand" worst his Apache foe.[9] The cowboy craze has

7. Westermeier: "The Modern Cowboy . . . ," in Ferris: *American West*, p. 30.

8. Robert Ullman: *Stolz der Vergessenen: Western* (Rastatt, Baden, 1964), the story of a "Grubline Rider."

9. And to be reported by *Time* as "*Schnell* on the Draw."

penetrated even behind the Iron Curtain, though "Corrals" do not as yet exist (above ground, at least) in Moscow or Peking.

As for rodeos, since the celebrated one at the British Empire Exhibition in London in 1924 (of which this writer has vivid adolescent memories) they have been organized as far afield as China, the South Pacific, Honolulu, Guam, and North Africa—and, of course, "Down Under."[1]

Though the big ranchers never acquired the literary glamour of the cowboys they hired in summer and (too often) turned loose in winter to forage for themselves, they were, of course, much more important factors in the cattle industry. To begin (and end) with, the hired hands on horseback rarely grew rich. Even as recently as 1962 David Brinkley[2] cited the instance of a twenty-three-year-old cowboy in Wyoming "who began work at a salary of $90 a month, plus room and board [and] is now earning $150. He spends fourteen hours a day in the saddle, riding approximately forty miles; his excursions to town include drinking beer, watching television and eating chicken." The typical cowboy works, according to Brinkley, a seven-day, hundred-hour week for wages "that would make a union business agent cry like a baby,"[3] and leaves the world as devoid of personal wealth as when he enters it. Walter Prescott Webb, more than thirty years earlier, wrote of: "cowboys at work, eighteen hours a day, for the herd left the bed ground by daybreak and kept it until dark; cowboys at work, riding, singing, nursing the cattle; yet it is difficult for those who now read of their hardships to realise that they worked at all."[4] Programs like "Brinkley's Hour" serve to keep the record straight and realistic and help to dispel the illusion that all the modern cowboy does is strum a guitar in an air-conditioned bunkhouse. Very few American teen-agers today, in all probability, want to run off and become cow-

---

1. Westermeier: "The Modern Cowboy . . . ," p. 228.

2. "David Brinkley's Hour," N.B.C. television program (July 1962) depicting in fifteen exciting but sobering minutes the life of the typical present-day cowboy on a Wyoming cattle ranch. I am indebted to Mr. Brinkley and to his producer, Ted Yates, for the loan of a "print" of this program, which I missed, but picked up via Clifford Westermeier's analysis of it at the Denver Conference on the History of Western America (Oct. 10–12, 1962). See Ferris: *American West* (which prints Westermeier's paper), p. 277.

3. "Brinkley's Hour," N.B.C., July 4, 1962.

4. *The Great Plains*, p. 268.

boys—at $90 a month for a hundred-hour week—though Andy Adams's hero had, in 1880, taken "to the range as a preacher's son takes to vice."[5]

But even in 1880 nobody wanted to become a sheepman. These despised rivals of the cowboys were nobody's ideal. Following their flocks alone and usually on foot, they were as much a prey to predatory and resentful humans, both white and red, as were their charges to the wolves and coyotes. "A cowboy might marry a squaw, but associate with a shepherd—never!"[6] The feuds of cattlemen and sheepmen sometimes almost reached the scale of pitched battles. On the Green River in Wyoming, 8,000 sheep were clubbed to death in one night; in the Tonto Basin of Central

Visiting a Colorado sheep ranch. From *Harper's Magazine*.

Arizona, twenty-six cattlemen and six sheepmen were killed in the Tewkesbury-Graham feud within five years.[7] There was only one thing the open-range cattleman hated more than sheep, and that was barbed wire.[8] But he had to learn to live with it. This he found as hard at first as he had the existence of the sheepman and their

5. *Log of a Cowboy*, p. 7.

6. Frantz and Choate, p. 112.

7. Frantz and Choate, p. 114. See further C. W. Towne and E. R. Wentworth: *Shepherds' Empire* (Norman, Okla., 1945), passim.

8. J. F. Glidden's U. S. Patent No. 157, 124, of November 24, 1874, and that of Jacob Haish a little earlier (June 17, 1874) revolutionized the appearance and changed the economy of the prairies and the Great Plains. W. P. Webb has sung the prosaic but penetrating saga of barbed wire (*The Great Plains*, pp. 295–318), making use of the Washburn Company's archives.

herds. During a few days in 1881, "fence-cutters" destroyed 500 miles of barbed wire in Coleman County, Texas, alone. But it was a losing battle, and W. S. James conceded in 1893 that "between barbed wire and the railroads the cowboys' days were numbered."[9] Yet, "though barbed wire revolutionized ranching it did not destroy it, and would not have threatened it seriously, had it not been for its effects on the farmer's frontier. . . . It was barbed wire and not the railroads or the homestead law that made it possible for the farmers to resume, or at least to accelerate, their march across the prairies and on to the Plains."[1]

9. *Cowboy Life in Texas* (Chicago, 1893), p. 116.
1. Webb, pp. 316–17.

CHAPTER XI

Land for the Farmer

I F THE MYTH (AND IN SOME PLACES THE REALITY) OF THE
Great American Desert held up the orderly westward
advance of the farming frontier of the United States and
Canada for a whole generation after the first tier of trans-
Mississippi states filled up, and until further technological advances
in agriculture, in fencing, and in the provision of water, had occurred, and the Indian menace had been removed from the Plains,
there was nevertheless a tremendous amount of agricultural "in-
filling" in those parts of the Far West which (like the Willamette
and San Joaquin valleys) were well watered or easily irrigated,
or which were reached earliest by railroads. It has already been seen
how easily certain areas (as in Colorado east of the Continental
Divide and central Montana) turned to farming after their mining
booms had first opened them up and then passed them by. The Far
West[1] was patched and striped with agricultural in-filling long
before the middle eighties saw the break-up of the open range
and the end of the great cattle drives up from Texas. The farmer
—or "nester"—was breathing down the neck of the stockman,
even in the High Plains, by the early seventies, and by the late
seventies he had been recognised as yet another of the cowman's
enemies—like cattle fever, sheepmen, rustlers, and barbed wire. But
the farmer had powerful allies, including the transcontinental-

1. See map, p. 356.

railroad promoters and the federal government itself. Such a combination was to prove irresistible!

The public-lands policy of the federal government—which also comprehended the railroad land grants not made by separate states—has played a dominant role in the settlement of the United States west of the Alleghenies. The greatest landmarks in this policy were the Ordinance of 1785 (passed by the Continental Congress), the Pre-emption Act of 1841, the Homestead Act of 1862, and the ending of all private purchase of public land in 1935. Up to 1841 the national land policy was conservative, favoring Eastern and monied interests; thereafter it tended to be radical, favoring the Western settlers and farmers; but at no period did it fully or even adequately achieve its ostensible objectives. When it failed openly to favor the land speculator (as did the Act of 1820, which ended the purchase of land on credit), the speculator found a way around its provisions. This applied particularly to the famous Homestead Act of 1862, passed by Lincoln's administration in the midst of the Civil War,[2] which, after nearly a century of agitation, at last provided (on paper) free land for the poor and land-hungry settler, but (in fact) poured many more millions of acres—and dollars—into the pockets of capitalists, speculators, railroad magnates, and other strictly non-agrarian interests. There is no doubt that Congress meant to make its legislation effective, and the administration its policy efficient, but, even in the agrarian West, opinions were often sharply divided as to how best, and most equitably, to distribute the public domain. Nor did the small farmer refrain from speculating himself. Some farming families moved on to new land seven or eight times in one lifetime, not through failure, but in order to benefit financially from either the improvements they had made or from the unearned increment that had accrued from the increased demand for land in the areas where they had settled.[3] When every small farmer was a land speculator

2. The public interest and enthusiasm aroused by this purely domestic measure, in the midst of great national peril and crisis, can be compared only with the reaction of the British public to the announcement of the Beveridge social security plan in 1942 and to its adoption as government policy in the White Paper of 1944. Lincoln, as a Westerner, was in favor of the Homestead Bill; whereas Churchill, concentrating on winning the war to the exclusion of all else, barely tolerated the Beveridge Report and obviously resented the attention it attracted.

3. Sometimes, it has to be admitted, a farming family moved on out of sheer restlessness, and did not necessarily improve its lot by doing so. The Garlands and

(or would-be land speculator), and individual gain was the guiding star, it was hard for a land system devised for the greatest good of the greatest number to remain valid.

The somewhat conservative Ordinance of May 20, 1785, applied to the Western lands handed over by seven of the original states to the Continental Congress and which now constituted the public domain of the United States. This land was to be surveyed, divided up into six-mile squares ("Townships"), and every alternate township divided into "sections," each a mile square (640 acres). Apart from the five sections in each township reserved by Congress for special purposes (the sixteenth was to provide common schools), each section could then be offered by public auction to the highest bidder at a minimum price of $1 per acre. Surveying fees, payable by the purchasers of the land, were fixed at $1 per section. This was a workmanlike system and had many merits, which were enhanced by the more comprehensive Northwestern Land Ordinance of 1787. The new federal government accepted these land ordinances of the Continental Congress and continued to apply them; unfortunately, the ordinary settler possessing little or no capital could not afford even the minimum cost of $640 for a section, plus the cost of transporting himself and his family to it. But he could start by picking up land, with ample credit facilities, at twenty cents per acre in western New York, for instance. For some years the separate states possessing unsettled public domains could sell easily below the federal minimum. It was the monied interests that moved into the national domain. By the year 1800 only about 50,000 acres of land had been sold to settlers under the terms of the Ordinance of 1785, and an act of May 10, 1800, attempted to make the acquisition of land easier for them. It provided liberal credit and reduced the minimum amount of land to be offered for sale; but the minimum, at $2 an acre for 320 acres, and the down payment of one fourth of the purchase price of the land at auction, were still too high. An effort to introduce the principle of "pre-emption" (or sale of land on specially favorable terms to

---

the McClintocks, their kinsmen, were a case in point. Hamlin Garland, in his vivid autobiography, *A Son of the Middle Border* (New York, 1925), tells how they moved in the 1840's from Maine to Ohio, then on to Wisconsin (where he was born in 1860), to Iowa, and to the Dakota Territory, where (in 1889), "after eight years of cultivation, father's farm possesses neither tree nor vine. . . . Doesn't the whole migration of the Garlands and the McClintocks seem a madness? After nearly a third of a century the Garlands were about to double on their trail."

the actual squatters who had settled on it and improved it, while it was still unsurveyed), was unsuccessful, and pre-emption had to wait for adoption until 1841.

With the Louisiana and Florida purchases, a liberal land policy became all the more urgent for the United States, and many settlers went into Mexican Texas in the 1820's and early 1830's, owing to its more liberal system, especially in the Austin colonies. In fact, a fresh outburst of land speculation accompanied these great national land purchases, and the speculators were also to get hold of most of the land made available by Indian removals in these years. The economic depression in the West which produced the Panic of 1819 was attributed by many (including Andrew Jackson) to the deficiencies of the national land system, although the pro-government *National Intelligencer* declared in 1819 that "so wise, beautiful and perfect a system was never before adopted by any government or nation on earth."[4] An act passed in 1820 made matters even worse by eliminating credit facilities in the purchase of the public domain altogether. A minimum of eighty acres could now be purchased for as little as $1.25 per acre—but only for cash. This played straight into the ever-ready hands of the speculator. "The land act of 1820 brought the whole population of the frontier to the brink of ruin."[5]

A halfway Pre-emption Act of 1830 gave the squatter some privilege in the purchase of 160 acres of the land he actually occupied; Senator Benton's plea for a "graduated price" for Western land, to accord with its fertility and accessibility, was met by the Eastern campaign (with which Henry Clay was associated, although a Westerner) for "distribution" of the public domain among the several states. Clay's distribution bill passed Congress, but Jackson subjected it to a "pocket veto." The limited pre-emption system of 1830 was continued in 1838 and again in 1840 on a temporary basis, with some modifications, but it was not until 1841 that the frontier interests at last triumphed in the shape of full-blooded pre-emption for squatters. The Panic of 1837 had served to bring this nearer as a measure of relief for the poor or impoverished farmer, driven by foreclosure from his farm further east, although some of these foreclosures had been prevented by the action of "Claim Clubs," or Settlers' Associations. In 1838 the

4. Quoted in Robbins: *Landed Heritage*, p. 33.
5. Ibid., p. 38.

CAN

49TH PARALLEL

CEDED TO GREAT
BRITAIN · 1818

CEDED BY GREAT
BRITAIN · 1818

OREGON
TERRITORY
1846
(CONDOMINIUM · 1818-1846)

Continental Divide

42ND PARALLEL

LOUISIA
PURCHA
1803

MEXICAN
CESSION
1848

Continental Divide

Arkansas R.

Claimed by TEXAS 1835
Ceded by MEXICO 1848

DISPUTED
1835-1846

37TH
PARALLEL

Gila R.

TEXAS
ANNEXED
1845
(INDEPENDENT
1835-1845)

GADSDEN
PURCHASE · 1853

Rio Grande

TERRITORIAL
GROWTH OF
The UNITED STATES
1776 — 1853

MEXICO

Nueces R.

Rio Grande

PACIFIC OCEAN

0   Miles   500

MAINE BOUNDARY
RECTIFICATION ·1842

A   D   A

Lake of
the Woods

L. Superior

Mississippi

L. Michigan

L. Huron

L. Ontario

L. Erie

N A
S E

U N I T E D
S T A T E S
1783

ORIGINAL THIRTEEN STATES

ATLANTIC OCEAN

36°30' PARALLEL

ed R.

Red R.

31ST PARALLEL

WEST

EAST

FLORIDA
CESSION
1810-1819

DISPUTED
1835-1846

Gulf of

Mexico

CUBA

W.B.

Territory of Wisconsin protected "sitting" settlers by law against the speculative buying up of land occupied and improved by them.

"The Battle between the Log Cabins and the Palaces" of 1840–50 produced Benton's "Log Cabin Bill," which Clay fiercely opposed. Clay then produced his own bill, which the Democrats proceeded to emasculate. Both distribution and pre-emption remained features of the bill, but distribution was not to take effect if the tariff were raised above a 20% level. Thus Clay was ultimately defeated and Benton was partially triumphant. Occupation prior to purchase by a "squatter" was no longer legally a trespass, and the pre-emption of 160 acres at $1.25 per acre was now open to heads of families and single men over twenty-one years of age who were citizens or who had taken out first papers. Lands reserved by the government for special purposes or granted to railroads, or for public improvements, were not subject to pre-emption. The frontier had triumphed—but at a price—though free homesteads for all were still a long way off.

The enormous accessions of land to the United States resulting from the Texas and Oregon settlements of 1846, and the cessions by Mexico in 1848, greatly increased the public domain (though it did not extend to Texas, which kept control over its own unsettled land) and also greatly complicated the situation. In California, in particular, the old Spanish and Mexican land grants were challenged in the courts, and many of them were subjected to the depredations of squatters who, knowing that the titles might be questioned, took a chance and settled upon land they knew to be claimed by others. This was a rather different and much more aggressive procedure than simply moving out ahead of the official U. S. land surveyors and hoping to retain land by the process of pre-emption, or priority right to purchase when it was put up for sale. The gold rush only added to the pressure on land in California. "Squatter trouble" harrassed not only those (like John Augustus Sutter) who held Mexican land grants, but also those (like John C. Frémont) who had bought land after the commencement of the American occupation and who had always been American citizens. Many Mexican grants had been obtained for less than value received and a few by outright fraud, but most were genuine and the land held had often been considerably improved. Most of these grants were overrun by squatters in the early 1850's, and it was the large landowners, like General Vallejo and Sutter (with his thirty-three square leagues), who suffered most. Even the eleven square leagues to which Sutter was given full title by the U. S. courts, although the twenty-two square leagues granted to him by Governor Micheltorena were taken away, became the happy hunting ground of squatters, who not only took his land but also destroyed his crops, slaughtered his cattle, and attacked his servants and field hands. This was the man who had shown so many kindnesses to the overland settlers from the United States in their time of need in the early and middle forties. Landowners who were "just Mexicans" suffered even greater indignities at the hands of the land-hungry and gold-greedy squatters, not all of whom, by any means, were from the United States.

Lawyers argued the cause of the California squatters with great ingenuity and skill through many courts, and much eloquence and special pleading was poured out on their behalf in the state legislature and in Congress. More lately, historians[6] have sought to explain, and in some cases justify, the squatters' actions as an outgrowth of their craving for land, and the wide extent, lack of development, and shaky titles of some of the Mexican land grants. But it remains a sordid story, one of the most disreputable in the history of the American frontier, as Josiah Royce long ago pointed out, and it left a legacy of bitterness which lasted for a whole generation between the Spanish-Mexican and American peoples in California.

While the advance of the American frontier of settlement (except in the gold and silver regions) was temporarily halted between 1842 and 1862 under the blighting influence of sectional rivalries and of an inadequate land-disposal system, reformers, both Northern and Southern, continued to be active. In 1843 Robert J. Walker, of Mississippi, initiated in Congress a new drive for Benton's old "graduation" of the price of public land. Horace Greely, still a distributionist at this time, claimed in the New York *Tribune* that "demagogues . . . are incessantly trying to squander the public lands by reducing their price."[7] Walker,[8] as President Polk's Secretary of the Treasury, continued to work for graduation and persuaded Polk to advocate it, with respect to swampy or sterile

6. See, e.g., Paul W. Gates: "California's Embattled Settlers," *California Historical Quarterly*, XLI: 2 (June 1962), 99–130.

7. New York *Weekly Tribune*, February 3, 1844.

8. See further *Dictionary of American Biography*, XIX, 355–8.

land at least, in his annual message in December 1845. The Whigs' opposition (and Henry Clay's in particular) to graduation brought them much unpopularity. Clay's opposition to pre-emption, said an opponent,[9] his "unjust and impolitic aspersions" upon "honest squatters," his advocacy of distribution, which led him into opposition to graduation, induced the people of the Western states to turn away from him "with odium and disgust." The advocates of completely free land for homesteaders on the public domain now began to press their case, led by such men as G. H. Evans. Evans's philosophy was a sort of advanced Fourierism applied specifically to the American public domain: land reform was to effect a social revolution and finally defeat the speculator. Even Horace Greeley, who as late as 1843 had claimed "Pre-emption is trespassing," was won over to this crusade and, by 1845, was being openly accused of being "a Fourierist, an Agrarian, and an Infidel." A national party was advocated, with the slogan "Vote Yourself a Farm" and the objective a free grant of a quarter-section (160 acres) from the public domain to every landless man. Greeley even went on to propose something akin to the French national workshops, set in the midst of rural areas—a crude foreshadowing of Henry Ford's celebrated idea of "industrial barns" nearly a century later. He urged the urban unemployed to migrate to rural areas, only to be told by his opponents: "We should soon have the whole contents of European poorhouses emptied down upon our fertile West." He replied by asking: "Whoever heard of a farmer starving *on his* land?" and proposed that the starving Irish be welcomed to "the untilled lands of the great West" to help create "a mighty empire resting upon the Great Lakes and the Northern Mississippi."[1] He then went West himself on a trip that reinforced his new stand on land reform.

The first true homestead bill was introduced into Congress by Representative McConnell, of Alabama, on March 9, 1846. Andrew Johnson, of Tennessee, produced another three days later. But homestead legislation was an early casualty of the Mexican War, which broke out that same spring, and none of the three parties—not even Martin Van Buren's Free Soil party—which fought the 1848 election could be persuaded to adopt land reform

9. Jacob Thompson, in the House of Representatives, July 9, 1846.
1. See Robbins: *Landed Heritage* (1942 edn.), pp. 100–2.

and homestead legislation as planks of its official platform. Greeley thought that "land reform" could have elected Van Buren, and when the latter would not advocate it, the mercurial editor threw in his lot with General Taylor and the Whigs. Greeley, when an interim member of Congress in 1848, introduced a homestead bill of his own, but could get only twenty members to support it. By 1849 both Sam Houston and Stephen A. Douglas were advocating homestead legislation. William H. Seward and Daniel Webster were also supporting land reform. A homestead bill that passed the House on May 12, 1852, by 107 votes to 56, failed even to get debated in the Senate. This bill, reintroduced in 1854, again failed to pass, and further homestead legislation was now to be smothered by the great Kansas-Nebraska debate, which absorbed everybody's attention. "Suddenly in 1853 and 1854," says Paul Gates, "the Kansas-Nebraska country beyond the Mississippi loomed up as a tremendously attractive area, and there erupted in Congress the press and the pulpit an ominous war of words. . . . For the next forty years Kansas was the focus of greater public attention than any other western community,"[2] and for that reason the fight for free homesteads and the fate of the homesteads on the sod-house frontier can be studied no better than on the wide expanses of the Sunflower State, where "In God We Trusted, in Kansas We Busted."

Kansas was in many ways an ideal testing ground for the system the United States had so laboriously worked out by the middle of the 1850's for the disposal of her public lands. If the system worked there, it would probably work anywhere. Kansas Territory was on the borders of the North and the South, lying as it did between 37° and 40° N., and while two thirds of it lay in the reasonably well-watered prairies east of the hundredth meridian, the other third stretched westward in the treeless and water-deficient High Plains, as far as the hundredth and second; an almost unbroken Indian barrier of tribal lands stretched from the southern to the northern border of eastern Kansas.[3] This meant that when the Kansas Territory was officially opened to settlers on May 30,

2. P. W. Gates: *Fifty Million Acres: Conflicts over Kansas Land Policy, 1854–1890* (Ithaca, 1954), pp. v–vi. He calls "the Kansas Story a grotesque composite of all the errors involved in the growth of the American West."

3. See Gates: *Fifty Million Acres*, map, p. 23.

1854, "not an acre of land was available for pre-emption of purchase."[4] Much Indian land was very soon afterward made available to settlers by the ratification of Indian treaties, but this easement was to be more than canceled out by the enormous extent of land grants to railroad companies (all of which land had to be withdrawn from public sale) in the later fifties and the sixties. These grants, in some cases, cut wide swathes right across the state.[5] Federal land grants to railroads in Kansas amounted to 8,346,603 acres, while nearly another 2 million acres were given by the State of Kansas to these railroads or purchased by them for nominal sums per acre from the Indians or the government. Only a very small proportion of these grants was subsequently voided or forfeited through non-compliance of the railroads with the conditions on which they had accepted them, though in many cases these conditions were either not met at all, or only after delays running sometimes into decades. While in some places the railroads were very enterprising in advertising and selling their lands (at considerably "improved" prices, in most cases) to settlers, in others they were most dilatory, especially as they did not have to pay taxes on any land they had not yet patented for sale. The Kansas and Pacific Railroad, which stretched right across the state from east to west, was a special offender in this respect. The "K.P." began land sales in 1869, completed its line in 1870, and finished surveying the adjacent land in 1875, but patented no land in Kansas before 1873 or in Colorado before 1875. As late as 1882 the K.P. had taken title to little more than one sixth of its land and therefore paid no tax on the other five sixths. The record of the Santa Fe Railroad was very much better.[6]

Thus, before the Homestead Act of 1862 gave settlers free land in Kansas and elsewhere on the public domain—provided they could locate themselves legally on it—such land was very hard to reach and find, and even after 1862, in Kansas at least, it still tended to be inaccessible and of poor quality, for the speculators and the railroads were there first and wanted money for their "improvements." Things also became worse before they got, even theoreti-

4. Gates, p. 22.
5. See Gates: *Fifty Million Acres*, map, p. 252. Alternate sections of these strips were granted to the railroads, and the others reserved.
6. See Waters: *Steel Trails to Santa Fe*, passim.

cally, better; the extremely conservative land policies of the Pierce and Buchanan administrations in the latter part of the fifties played—it would almost seem deliberately—into the hands of the speculators once again, just as had the legislation of the twenties. Eighteen Indian reserves in Kansas were barred from becoming part of the public land of the United States (including the Osage reserve of nearly 9 million acres) or subject to homestead or pre-emption laws. Instead they "became the booty of speculators, land companies and railroads, with substantial benefits accruing to helpful politicians."[7] In addition, the period of grace for pre-emption was cut back sharply to one year. This greatly contributed to the depression of 1857, for squatters who had expected up to four years in which to pay for their lands, under the pre-emption acts, now had to find the balance right away, or forfeit. It was this illiberal land policy that was largely responsible for the decisive defeat of the Democratic party in 1860. Kansas moved almost bodily into the Republican camp, as became even more evident in the presidential election of 1864, the first in which voters from that State participated.

A bill passed the House in May 1860 to restore the right of squatters, in frontier areas not yet surveyed, to purchase their claims over a period of four (in some cases even eight) years, but again failed to be debated in the Senate. Then an even more radical House bill, providing free homesteads, was amended by the Senate, giving squatters on public land two years more grace, and reducing the cost of land occupied for at least five years to twenty-five cents an acre. The Southern opponents of land reform let it pass thus "eviscerated," though Greeley called it "a miserable makeshift"; but President Buchanan, with incredible stupidity, vetoed it, giving as one of his reasons: "It is a boon exclusively confessed upon the cultivators of the soil."[8] It was only natural that the Republicans should now make full political capital out of the land-reform issue, which the Democrats had so woefully fumbled during the last two administrations, and their presidential-election platform of 1860 contained a strong plank favoring free homesteads. As most Western Democrats wanted this also, many left the party when neither of its wings came out in favor of the policy.

7. Gates: *Fifty Million Acres*, p. 6.

8. *Congressional Globe*, 36th Cong., 1st Sess., IV, 3263–4. This is a strong contender for the title of the crassest state paper in American history.

The bill vetoed by Buchanan in 1860 was reintroduced with some emendations in 1862 after Abraham Lincoln had become president, and with its Southern opponents now absent, it passed both houses of Congress without undue difficulty. The bill was signed by Lincoln, who had long been in favor of free homesteads, on May 20, 1862, almost exactly ten years after the House of Representatives had first accepted a homestead bill.[9]

Both by personal inclination and by his election pledges, Abraham Lincoln was bound to approve the passing of a free-homesteads bill. "I am in favor," he said on February 1, 1861, "of settling the wild lands into small parcels so that every poor man may have a home."[1] It is doubtful that he—or, for that matter, anyone else living at the time—was able to judge the effect this bill would have on the settlement of the West. Certainly Horace Greeley was not, for he called the bill "one of the most beneficient and vital reforms ever attempted in any age or clime";[2] indeed, in that year of great decisions, it was regarded as far more important than the Morrill bill[3] for land-grant colleges, or the first Pacific Railroad Act, and as equal in significance to the Emancipation Proclamation itself.[4] That the Homestead Act was to have far less beneficent results than its promotors and well-wishers hoped for was, to a large extent, owing to circumstances beyond both their control and their ken; it has in fact only gradually dawned upon economic and agricultural historians that the Homestead Act turned out to be a fiasco: some popular histories still speak of it in superlatives. That it was a landmark is undoubtedly true, but Walter Prescott Webb exaggerated somewhat when he claimed: "There is no question but

9. Horace Greeley, in the New York *Weekly Tribune* of June 30, 1860, in criticizing Buchanan's veto of the earlier homestead bill as typical of a man who "has no sympathy for the poor, and who regards only the interests of the speculators," had rightly prophesied that Abraham Lincoln would never veto such a bill. Greeley was probably the author of the homestead plank of the Republican platform of 1860.

1. *Works of Lincoln*, ed. Nicolay and Hay, I, 637.

2. New York *Semi-Weekly Tribune*, May 9, 1862.

3. Also passed in 1862.

4. A contemporary Canadian view of the Homestead Act of 1862 declared it to be "the complement of the prohibition of slavery" and commented: "The civil transactions of the last few months at Washington will make their impression upon ages to come, when the battles on the Potomac and Tennessee will be regarded as mere incidents in history"—Montreal *Herald*, quoted in the New York *Daily Tribune*, May 27, 1862. Robbins, p. 206.

that the Homestead Act gave a great impetus to the advancing frontier while it remained in the fertile prairie region";[5] he was nearer the truth in saying: "The Homestead Act had not solved the problem in the region where it had to do most of its work"—the arid regions of the United States beyond the hundredth meridian. The judgments of later critics, such as Robbins (1942), Shannon (1945), and Gates (1953), grew increasingly severe,[6] until the Homestead Act, instead of being one of the two "most important land acts in the history of the world,"[7] has nearly been demoted into a costly mistake.

What did the Homestead Act of 1862 really seek to do, and to what extent and for what reasons did it fail? Under the Act, any American citizen, or alien immigrant who had filed his first papers of intention to become a citizen, provided he was over twenty-one or the head of a family or had served for fourteen days in the armed services of the United States, could claim 160 acres of surveyed and unappropriated public land on paying $10 and, after occupying this land for five years, receive full title to it upon paying a further small fee. No charge per acre was payable unless the homesteader wished to accelerate the grant of the title, when he could secure the freehold after only six months residence by paying $1.25 per acre. These and other simple conditions appeared straightforward and easy to administer, but in fact the Act turned out to be full of holes. "In its operation," claims Shannon, "the Homestead Act could hardly have defeated the hopes of the enthusiasts of 1840–1860 more completely if the makers had actually drafted it with that purpose uppermost in mind."[8] Poor farm tenants or laborers, or city dwellers in the East, could afford neither the cost of travel to the trans-Mississippi West, where nearly all the remaining public domain was situated, nor even the modest claim and registration fees amounting to from $22 to $34 in all; they could not maintain themselves until their first year's crops were harvested and sold; they had no more wherewith to build houses or to fence their land. Such people were simply non-starters in the race for free homesteads. Most of the actual homesteaders—like the

5. *The Great Plains*, p. 411.

6. See Bibliographic Note, p. 437.

7. A. E. Sheldon: *Land Systems and Land Policies in Nebraska* (Lincoln, Neb., 1936), p. 75.

8. *Farmer's Last Frontier*, p. 54.

Garland family—were already farming in the Midwest, in states like Wisconsin and Illinois by 1862, and even at that, about two thirds of all homestead claimants up to 1890 failed to make successes of their farms. Not more than 2 million people settled on free government land up to the year 1900, although between 1860 and that year the population of the United States increased by 45 million. In the same period, by contrast, over 7 million additional people settled on farms which they either had to buy or rent or where the breadwinner was a hired laborer.

Besides bringing far too few of the people who most needed free land onto the homesteads, the Act gave inadequate protection against the speculator. The commutation clauses of the Act, and of amending legislation, permitted speculators and capitalists to secure large numbers of homesteads through nominees, and to obtain title after six months for $1.25 an acre. The title could then be transferred to the large landowners. These and the speculators could also purchase foreclosed or forfeited homesteaders' claims at public auction. After 1900 a speculator could double his money, for anybody who had already commuted one homestead was thenceforward permitted to claim and commute a second. This meant 320 acres, at $1.25 an acre, in his own name, plus all he could arrange to secure in addition through nominees, plus all he managed to buy cheaply at public auction out of the two thirds of all homesteads that had to be forfeited by their original claimants.

Finally, the size of the free homestead under the Act of 1862 was far too small to be economically viable in the arid lands beyond the hundredth meridian, where, after 1865, vast numbers of would-be homesteaders sought their fortunes and ended up, like the Lane County Bachelor,[9] starving to death on their government claims.

9. One verse of this famous folk-ballad, with its chorus is:

How happy am I on my government claim,
Where I've nothing to lose and nothing to gain,
Nothing to eat and nothing to wear,
Nothing from nothing is honest and square.
But here I am stuck, and here I must stay,
My money's all gone and I can't get away;
There's nothing will make a man hard and profane
Like starving to death on a government claim.

CHORUS

But, hurrah for Lane County, the land of the free,
The land of the grasshopper, bedbug and flea,
I'll sing loud her praises and boast of her fame,
While starving to death on my government claim.

Whereas eighty acres were as much as a farmer needed, or could manage, to start with, on the untilled lands of the well-watered and abundantly timbered East and Midwest, he required much more even than 160 acres to make a living for himself and his family on the High Plains of western Kansas, where "Lane County" was situated, even if he used dry-farming techniques. From 10,000 to 25,000 acres of grazing rights were the best economic unit in many areas further west,[1] of which (before 1890) 1,280 acres at most could be secured free by any one individual directly from the government by the use of every legal resource available. Larger holdings cost money (which most settlers did not have) and often involved the use of extralegal devices as well.

The plight of a homesteading family that had failed to make good in Kansas, and then had moved back further east as tenants of a run-down farm owned by a speculator (and when they sought to purchase the holding, they found they were being charged for the improvements they themselves had put into it), is poignantly told by Hamlin Garland in "Under the Lion's Paw":

"Sarah, this is Mr. Haskins, from Kansas. He's been eat up 'n drove out by grasshoppers. . . ."

"I didn't like the looks of the country, anyhow," Haskins said. . . . "I was ust t' Northern Ingayannie, where we have lots a timber 'n lots o' rain, 'n I didn't like the looks o' that dry prairie. What galled me the worst was goin s' far away acrosst so much fine land layin' all through here vacant."

"And the 'hoppers eat ye four years hard running, did they?"

"Eat! They wiped us out. They chawed everything that was green. They jest set around waiting f'r us to die t' eat us too."

"Waal, why didn't you stop and settle here? . . ."

"Fer the simple reason that you fellers wanted ten 'r fifteen dollars an acre, fer the bare land, and I hadn't no money fer that kind o' thing. . . ."[2]

The results of the Homestead Act were by no means all bad, even though it failed utterly in the primary object of its promoters. Its magic promise of "free land" for the land-hungry did draw people from all over the United States, and also many hundreds of

1. Shannon: *Farmer's Last Frontier*, p. 58.

2. *Main-Traveled Roads* (New York, 1891), pp. 223–4; 2nd edn., illus., 1899; rev. 3rd edn. 1922; paperback edn. Signet Classics (1962), pp. 144–5, cited here.

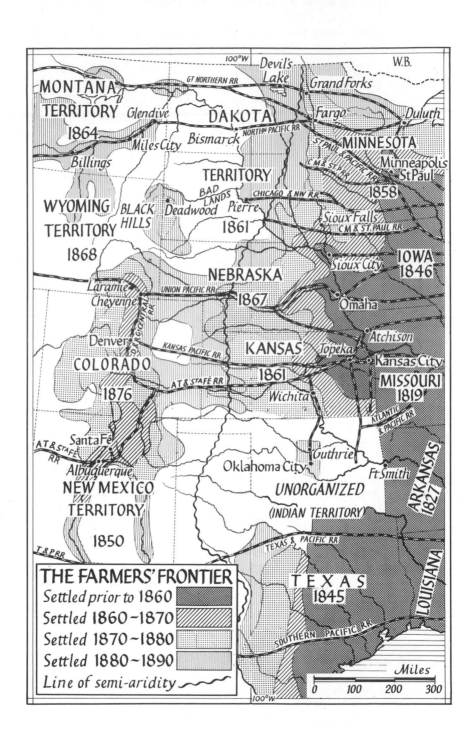

THE FARMERS' FRONTIER

Settled prior to 1860	
Settled 1860–1870	
Settled 1870–1880	
Settled 1880–1890	
Line of semi-aridity	

thousands from Europe,[3] into the underpopulated second tier of states—Kansas, Nebraska, and the Dakotas—of the trans-Mississippi West, and on into the arid regions of the Great Plains, which had so recently been designated the Great American Desert. It took the American farmer a whole generation to subdue these Plains and make them agriculturally profitable; but though this was done at a colossal expenditure and much waste of human effort, man could not have subdued the plains had he not been brought to them first. The Homestead Act may have been something of a will o' the wisp, but westward it made the land look bright. Its propaganda value was enormous.

Added, of course, to the shimmer and gleam (even if it sometimes turned out to be a mirage) of "free land for the settler" was the enormous promotional activity of railroads, land companies, and private speculators with land to sell, and of state and territorial governments with the desire for taxable population and (in many cases) with considerable amounts of public lands to dispose of themselves. All these combined to draw farmers and would-be farmers westward almost as compellingly as the gold and silver of the mining areas had worked on the previous generation of Americans and immigrants—but the population of the United States was now much larger, and the immigrant tide had resumed after 1862, to become greater than ever before. There was enormous hunger for the land—any land—and if this land was marginal or submarginal for purposes of agriculture, perhaps blood, sweat, and tears—and science—could make it productive. There were plenty who were ready to try.

There are two ways of judging the process whereby the undeveloped lands of the United States came into the hands of settlers. One is to emphasize the enterprise and initiative of the explorers, the railroad promoters, the speculators, the financiers, and the politicians who made them known, accessible, and purchasable. Another is to concentrate upon the hard life of the frontier farmer, the sacrifices made by his wife, the cultural deprivations of his family, the ways in which he was exploited and cheated by promoters, middlemen, and bankers, and the failure of the government to give him a square deal. It is hard to strike a balance between these two extremes, but at least one thing is clear: the agrarian ideal of such men as Greeley and Evans was not attained

3. For further references to "the Great Immigration" see Ch. xii, passim.

during the nineteenth century, even though the subsidized and feather-bedded American farmer of the second half of the twentieth century may indeed have attained that Nirvana.

Many attempts were subsequently made to put teeth into the ineffective Homestead Act of 1862 and to reduce the opportunities for speculation provided by its commutation clauses. The Timber Culture Act of 1873 was perhaps the most fruitful of these. A further 160 acres was made available to the homesteader provided he planted a quarter of it with trees within ten years.[4] By contrast with the Timber Culture Act,[5] which really did benefit some homesteaders (though far too few), the Desert Land Act of 1877 was lobbied through by the big cattle companies and was the monopolists' bonanza. In exchange for a first payment of twenty-five cents an acre (and a subsequent and final payment of another dollar per acre) and a promise to irrigate the land within three years,[6] each claimant could secure title to 640 acres of land within designated Western states (extending as far east as the Dakota Territories) which would grow crops only if irrigated. Much of this was, in fact, good grazing land, and the cattle kings managed to get hold of most of it. It is estimated that some 95 per cent of the patents granted under the Desert Land Act were obtained by fraud. The genuine homesteader benefited hardly at all. In 1891 the Act was extended to Colorado, very little of which state can be claimed to be "desert land" by any stretch of the imagination.[7] The Timber and Stone Act of 1878 also benefited the monopolist rather than the homesteader: a quarter-section of land "unfit for cultivation" in four of the most westerly states (extended in 1892 to all states with public lands) could be bought by any individual for $2.50 per acre. This was made by the great timber companies to include most of the unexploited timber-covered land of the United States, so that by 1901 "immense tracts of the most valuable timber

4. This was changed to one sixteenth within eight years by a law passed in 1878.

5. By 1904, when this legislation was finally repealed, only 65,292 grants had been made under it, involving under 10 million acres in all. Shannon, p. 59.

6. Placing one bucket of water on it appeared to be accepted as qualifying in some cases.

7. The maximum amount of land obtainable by one entrant under the Desert Land Act was reduced in 1890 to 320 acres, but this provision could be easily evaded.

land . . . have become the property of a few individuals and corporations," and in the year 1903 alone "nearly half as much timber land was monopolized as in the whole period from 1878 to 1900."[8] Some of these acquisitions were obtained by fraudulent means, but most of them were considered legal under the laxly drawn Timber and Stone Act and even more outrageous legislation subsequently passed.[9]

A new land-reform movement was bound to arise in reaction against the most glaring abuses and inadequacies of the policies initiated in 1862. By the early seventies this movement was in full swing. It found its apostle in Henry George, a San Franciso printer,[1] who gave early warning that the United States was rapidly becoming a land of tenant farmers and could easily deteriorate into a land of agricultural laborers working for big landlords. "Under present conditions the small American freeholder is doomed," he prophesied.[2] In Congress the most active land reformer was now Representative George Julian, of Indiana, who spearheaded the attack on railroad land grants which led to their discontinuance in 1871, and demanded (with less success) the forfeiture of existing ones when the conditions of the grants had not been met. The Democratic Party made forfeiture a plank of its platform in 1874, claiming that the Republicans had "squandered 200,000,000 acres on railroads." It was not until 1890 that all grants not utilized by railroads up to that date were declared forfeited, but probably only about 2 million acres were actually returned to the public domain under this legislation, so resourceful were the railroads in taking court action to avoid forfeiture[3] and, in some cases, meeting (even if belatedly) the terms of their grants. Though the

8. Public Lands Commission of the U.S.A. *Report* (1905), p. 186; Shannon, p. 62.

9. See S. A. D. Puter and H. Stevens: *Looters of the Public Domain* (Portland, Ore., 1908), and J. Ise: *The United States Forest Policy* (New Haven, Conn., 1920) for details of some of these transactions.

1. See *Dictionary of American Biography*.

2. These ideas, first presented in newspaper articles, were developed further in Henry George: *Our Land and Land Policy, National and State* (San Francisco, 1871).

3. See B. H. Hibbard: *History of Public Land Policies* (New York, 1924), p. 250.

railroads had, by their practices, made themselves vulnerable to attack by the land reformers, yet their exploitation of their own grants had not always operated against the interests of the home-steader, or of the would-be farmer possessing but little capital. Quite apart from the way in which they opened up otherwise inaccessible tracts of country to settlement and to markets, they were sometimes generous in the way in which they were prepared to sell land. It is true that they were never known actually to give it away in any quantity, but the price at which railroad land in the West was disposed of averaged no more than $5 an acre between 1862 and 1890,[4] and when a colony of German Mennonites from Russia came to Kansas in 1874, the Santa Fe Railroad sold them 60,000 acres for the $250,000 in gold that these 1900 immigrants brought with them. This averaged about $4 an acre, but the rail-road also built them temporary barracks and gave them a number of sections of land free to help them establish a poor fund. While this was all very profitable to the railroad, it was in no sense exploitation of the unfortunate, as is testified by the inscription on the historical monument set up beside U. S. Highway 56 by the Mennonites near the site of the first church to be built on their Kansas land. Here, we are told, the Mennonite community estab-lished itself "by the Graces of God and with the Aid and Assist-ance of the Acheson, Topeka and Santa Fe Railroad." Never did an American Western railroad approach nearer to a state of bliss! The Southern Pacific Railroad of California hardly emerged from the notorious Mussell Slough affair of 1880 with any similar halo. Here it attempted to sell railroad land at from $25 to $40 an acre instead of the basic $2.50, the government price, which they had expected to pay, to settlers it had earlier invited to take up leases on this land in Tulare County before it had been patented. The railroad sought to benefit exclusively from all the improvements its tenants had put into the land. Before the suit brought by the local Settlers' League in the federal courts could be appealed, a fracas occurred between the local U. S. marshal and two Southern Pacific "strong-arm men" on the one side, and a group of militant tenants on the other, which led to several deaths. The S.P. was subsequently to win its suit in

4. The Northern Pacific, for instance, charged only from $2.50 to $8.00 an acre, depending on the distance of the land from the line, and gave credit for seven years at 7 per cent. See J. B. Hedges: *Henry Villard and the Railways of the Northwest* (New Haven, Conn., 1930).

the state Supreme Court, but this and similar incidents brought it great unpopularity, especially with the press in the eighties and nineties—the three leading newspapers of San Francisco were at one time attacking it simultaneously—and inspired the title of Frank Norris's powerful novel *The Octopus*, published in 1901, which he based in part on the Mussell Slough incident. An interview which Norris had with Collis P. Huntington, president of the S.P., while the novel was in progress, and which he wrote into the

A Marsh self-binder drawn by oxen. From Freeman Tilden: *Following the Frontier* (1964).

book as the encounter between the poet-hero Presley and the tycoon Shelgrim, head of the "Pacific and South-Western Railroad," softened Norris's attitude somewhat toward "the Octopus," but it and its minions (especially the malevolent "S. Behrman," who, like Presley, is never given a Christian name throughout the novel) remain the villains of the piece, the despoilers and exploiters of honest farmers and mechanics, the bringers of misery and degradation to their families, though, "occupying the position of Greek gods, Huntington and his pals were immune, like the gods, to punishment."[5]

Despite the legislation of 1890, land reformers continued their attacks on the railroad grantees and the speculators. Senator William A. Peffer, of Kansas, speaking for the Populist party, said in 1891: "The farmer has been the victim of a gigantic scheme of spoliation. Never before was such a vast aggregation of brains and money brought to bear to force men into labor for the benefit of the few."[6] As early as 1880 a specially appointed Public Land Commission had proposed a comprehensive new land code, but this failed to pass, and the reforms advocated by A. J. Sparks, President Cleveland's General Land Commissioner, in 1886 were also not adopted; but, between 1889 and 1891, most forms of cash sale of land were terminated, the amount of land one individual could secure was limited to 320 acres, and the Pre-emption and Timber Culture acts were repealed, while the Desert Land Act was restricted in its application. This, says Fred Shannon sardonically, "locked other stables after the horses were stolen,"[7] but as late as the year 1902 Theodore Roosevelt's Secretary of the Interior was still asking for the final repeal of the Desert Land Act, the commutation clause, and other measures that had favored the speculator, so that the government could "preserve" the remaining public lands as homes for actual settlers.

Thus, even by the beginning of the new century, many of the demonstrable inadequacies of the homestead legislation had not been remedied, though some of the holes had been plugged. One sweeping criticism of the land laws of the United States as they existed in the year 1901 stated:

There is not a land law in effect which applies intelligently to the public agricultural domain as it is now to be found, and each and

5. According to Oscar Cargill, ed. of the Mentor Classics paperback edn. of *The Octopus* (New York, 1964), Norris was actually intimidated by Huntington much more than was Presley by Shelgrim in the novel. "Was he obsessed by his own metaphor and afraid that if he attacked the octopus a punishing tentacle would reach for him?" Collis P. Huntington had a reputation for neglecting nothing—not even literature. It was he who put up anonymously $750 for the best answer to Markham's "socialistic" poem "The Man with the Hoe," the influence of which he feared in California, points out Cargill (Afterword, pp. 464–9).

6. W. A. Peffer: *The Farmer's Side, His Troubles and His Remedies* (New York, 1891), p. 73.

7. *Farmer's Last Frontier*, pp. 73–4.

every law which is in force is used daily as a means for the fradulent segregation of land from the public domain by those whom the law does not contemplate as possible beneficiaries.[8]

In 1860 the line of agricultural settlement had barely advanced beyond the Missouri River, and places like Atcheson and Topeka, Lawrence and Omaha, St. Joseph and Kansas City, were still frontier towns. Aided by the building of east-west railroads (which were also to play so big a part in the development of the cattle kingdom), Kansas and Nebraska filled up with farmers to approximately the hundredth meridian by 1880, in which year the former had over 850,000 inhabitants and the latter over 450,000. Immigration into the Dakota Territory further north did not get into its stride before the middle seventies (aided by the driving out of the Sioux from the Black Hills and the discovery of gold there), but by 1885 the Dakotas had a population of 550,000, three out of every four of whom had arrived within the last five years. Two transcontinental railroads, the Northern Pacific and the Great Northern, were advancing across these territories bringing settlers, many of them freshly arrived from Europe in their hundreds of thousands. No wonder the city of Bismarck could consider itself to be a world metropolis of the future during these years.[9] By contrast, Wyoming and Montana, both in the arid belt well beyond the hundredth meridian, and still given over mainly to ranching (whereas wheat bonanza farming had come to Minnesota and North Dakota further east), still had only 62,000 and 132,000 inhabitants respectively by 1890. Nevertheless, Wyoming (along with Idaho) was made a State of the Union that year, following the admission of the two Dakotas, Montana, and Washington in 1889. Nebraska had achieved statehood in 1867 and Colorado in 1876, so now (in 1890) only the Arizona and New Mexico territories in the old Spanish Southwest, the "outlawed" territory of Utah (with its peculiar institutions), and the former Indian Territory, now called Oklahoma, had still to achieve statehood out of all the lands that had constituted the United States at the end of the Civil War.

As fertile, accessible, free (or at least cheap) agricultural land became less available, and as the terrible series of droughts in the

8. J. D. Whelpley: "The Nation as a Landowner," *Harper's Weekly*, November 30, December 7, and December 14, 1901; quoted in Shannon, p. 75.

9. See above, Ch. viii, pp. 244–5.

late 1880's made many "marginal" farms elsewhere unprofitable—
or, indeed, unworkable—the U. S. government was pressured to
open to the settler the one remaining extensive area east of the
hundredth meridian, which was good farm land. This area was the
Indian Territory, all that remained of the great Indian reserve that
had stretched from the Texan to the Canadian border half a century earlier. Kansas, Nebraska, and the Dakotas had already been
split off from this reserve and handed over to the white man. Now
it was the turn of all that was left, despite the fact that much of it
had been granted to the Five Civilized Tribes, and subsequently to

A sod house in the Cherokee Strip, c. 1894. Family group with three
Cherokee girls.

many other tribes, in perpetuity. In 1889 the floodgates were
opened, and a year later the Oklahoma Territory, as it was now
called, organized. Exploited by the white man with incredible
rapidity, Oklahoma became a state in 1907 even without benefit of
the great oil boom she was later to experience. The opening up of
Oklahoma presents a case study of the effects of land hunger and,
as a frontier experience, is comparable in some ways to the California gold rush itself. At the beginning of 1889 the Indian Territory
had not a single white man legally settled on it; by 1905 its population was already at the half-million mark; by 1920 it was to contain
over 2 million inhabitants, having outstripped both Kansas and

Nebraska and breathing down the necks of Minnesota and Iowa. Even by 1900 it had far outstripped the Dakotas, as well as every one of the Mountain and Pacific States except, of course, California.

The settlement of Oklahoma followed a decade of ceaseless agitation on the part of interested railroads, and of ceaseless illegal

An Oklahoma homesteader, his family and possessions. In front of their sod house, Oklahoma Territory; note McCormack reaper and wind-pump.

activity by the "Boomers," illegal immigrants who burst into "the Oklahoma District" prematurely. David Payne, the first leader of the "Boomers," died in 1883, but they remained as active as ever, and in 1885 Congress agreed to negotiate with the Indian tribes for the opening of the Oklahoma District and the Cherokee Strip, two as yet unsettled areas of the Indian Territory. Early in 1889 the tribes surrendered their rights to the Oklahoma District and it was declared open to homesteaders. On April 22, 1889, occurred the remarkable "land rush" which not only brought over 60,000[1] pioneers into the District in one day, but also conjured brand-new cities into

1. Billington: *Westward Expansion*, p. 721, says 100,000.

Guthrie, Oklahoma: The first day. Two armed men holding down their town lot claim, April 22, 1889.

Guthrie, Oklahoma: The first week. Three men on their claim shack, April 1889.

Guthrie, Oklahoma: The sign painter was the busiest man in town,
April 1889.

Guthrie, Oklahoma: End of the first week, April 29, 1889.

existence in an afternoon.[2] Similar scenes were witnessed as fresh areas of Oklahoma were added to the public domain between 1889 and 1893, thus providing, as Shannon points out, "eloquent testimony to the preference of farmers for land where there was sufficient rainfall to ensure crops."[3] In addition to many "busted" Kansans and Nebraskans, people also came down out of the Dakotas, driven by drought and hard winters, into the lush Indian Territory, which at that time was unimaginable as the future center of the dust bowl of the 1930's.[4] By contrast with Oklahoma, Kansas and Nebraska hardly increased in population at all during the 1890's.[5]

Oklahoma richly deserved her statehood in 1907; indeed, by then she had over sixteen times the population with which California had come into the Union in 1850 and over twenty times the population Nevada still possessed after half a century in the Union. Oklahoma was the United States' last great natural farming frontier and, as such, was opened up with an almost supersonic boom. Other farming frontiers have opened up since then, but nearly all of these have been man-made—by dams, as in eastern Oregon and Washington, and by the flooding of former deserts, as in southern California, for instance—and on a much smaller scale. Oklahoma was the last big agricultural bonanza, worthy of the way in which she has since been celebrated in song and story by such writers as Rogers and Hammerstein, Edna Ferber, and Marquis James.[6]

2. "In some respects the recent settlement of Oklahoma was the most remarkable thing of the present century. Unlike Rome the city of Guthrie was built in a day. To be strictly accurate in the matter it might be said that it was built in an afternoon . . . making a total population for the first day of about ten thousand"—W. W. Howard: "The Rush to Oklahoma," *Harper's Weekly*, May 18, 1889, pp. 391–2.

3. *Farmer's Last Frontier*, p. 219.

4. Oklahoma's decennial population figures over fifty years are instructive:

1890	—	258,657
1900	—	790,391
1910	—	1,657,155
1920	—	2,028,283
1930	—	2,396,040
1940	—	2,336,434

5. Kansas increased from 1,428,108 (1890) to 1,470,495 (1900), and Nebraska from 1,062,656 (1890) to 1,066,300 (1900). Kansas had grown from 107,206 in 1860 to 996,096 in 1880!

6. Rogers and Hammerstein's *Oklahoma* was a fabulously successful musical play on Broadway, and Edna Ferber's *Cimarron* a best-selling novel. Marquis James's *Cherokee Strip* (New York and London, 1947) tells of a boyhood spent in

All of Oklahoma but the western half of its panhandle, which forms part of the Cimarron Desert, has a rainfall of twenty inches or more in a normal year, so that part of the state which was not naturally forested (with the exception of the small area mentioned) was natural tall or prairie grassland, where grain also would grow "as high as an elephant's eye" once it was plowed. By contrast, very few areas of Utah (or, as the Mormons first called it, the State of Deseret), which was wholly west of the hundredth meridian, had as much as twenty inches of rain, while half the state had less than ten, and was by nature sagebrush desert. From the beginning, therefore, the practice of farming in Utah taxed human ingenuity to the limit, and could only have been started at all by a disciplined

The opening of the Cherokee Strip at noon on September 16, 1893, drawn on the spot by H. Worrall.

and dedicated body of settlers convinced not only that "this is the place," despite its obvious disadvantages, but also that no other place would do. The advance of the farming frontier into Utah, jumping a whole tier of territories further east, at the end of the 1840's, was a remarkable phenomenon, cutting right across the

the Oklahoma Territory and indicates that it possessed as many of the romantic attributes of frontierland as had the upper Mississippi Valley half a century earlier, in the days of Tom Sawyer and Huckleberry Finn. Marquis once proudly found himself introduced by his father to Temple Houston, son of the great Sam, as "the Strip's own Huck Finn" (*Cherokee Strip*, London edn., p. 29). But it was Dick Yeager, who died in Garfield County jail on September 7, 1895, who was Marquis' real hero and "any Cherokee Strip youngster's ideal of what an outlaw should be and do" (p. 30).

grain of the Turner hypothesis and, indeed, comparable in modern history only with the "Great Trek" of the Boer farmers in South Africa a decade earlier. Because the frontier history of Utah was so different from that of every other part of the American West in the nineteenth century, it deserves special attention. The Great Salt Lake Valley was most unpromising land and yet was made to blossom like the rose. Brigham Young spoke of "these barren valleys, these sterile mountains, this desolate waste, where none but Saints can or would live."[7]

The population of Utah did not grow spectacularly fast, as California's did between 1850 and 1860, or that of Kansas between 1860 and 1880, or Oklahoma's between 1890 and 1910. Uninhabited in 1846, the Territory contained 11,380 people in 1850, 40,273 in 1860, 86,786 in 1870, and 143,963 in 1880. By 1890 it had reached 207,905, though Utah was still denied statehood on account of the continued practice of polygamy there. But to sustain even 11,000 people in 1850, let alone well over a quarter million by 1900, meant not only backbreaking toil but also masterly planning and execution. Mormon methods of colonization (already worked out in other communities in the course of the migration of the Saints westward) plus extensive irrigation—the first time it had been attempted on a really large scale in North America—provided the answer.

Indians had dug irrigation ditches in the pre-Columbian Southwest, the mission Fathers and the Spanish soldiers had supervised the building of dams in the vicinity of their settlements, but the Anglo-American settlers had nowhere encountered a pressing need for irrigation until the first advance party of Mormons reached the Salt Lake Valley on July 22, 1847. Even before Brigham Young had caught up with them two days later, they had dammed a stream and irrigated a field for planting potatoes.[8] From this small beginning the Mormons spread a wide network of irrigation works over every part of Utah where sources of water could be tapped at all, and even into adjoining territories. "To the pioneer," says C. H. Brough, "water was not only the basis of wealth,

7. Brigham Young: *Journal of Discourses*, IV, 344; quoted in P. A. M. Taylor: *Expectations Westward* (Edinburgh and London, 1965).

8. Orson Pratt: "Extracts from the Private Journal of Orson Pratt," *Utah Genealogical and Historical Magazine*, XV (1924), xvii, 119, 209–12; quoted in Taylor, p. 51.

ADVANCE of POPULATION · 1790–1960

1790

1840

1890

1960

OREGON COUNTRY (U.S. + Br.)

UNORGANIZED TERRITORY

REPUBLIC OF MEXICO

LOUISIANA

NEW SPAIN

CANADA

MEXICO

W.B.

0   Miles   1000

● = over 6 per square mile

but of human existence; the irrigation canal was the first and highest of public utilities. . . . A destitute people having no resources save the genius of their leader and the labor of their own hands, resolved to associate and organize their efforts to bring the water on as the people of Holland were compelled to keep the water out."[9]

A more detailed history than has already been sketched of the Mormon church and its tribulations further east, an account of its doctrines or its organization, or even of its migration westward into

A first view of polygamy—a Mormon and his family. From Samuel Bowles: *Our New West* (1869).

Utah is not called for here, but the way in which the Mormons' faith and their organization contributed toward the establishment of their communities in an environment most men at that time believed to be uncultivable desert, is relevant to the theme of this chapter, and of this book.[1]

"Making the waste place blossom as the rose, and the earth to yield abundantly of its diverse fruits, was more than an economic necessity; it was a form of religious worship. As one early writer

9. *Irrigation in Utah* (Baltimore, 1898), p. 12.

1. See Bibliographic Note, pp. 437 ff., for general works on the Mormon church, its leaders and its history.

later wrote, the construction of water ditches was as much a part of the Mormon religion as water baptism," says Leonard Arrington,[2] and, indeed, the earliest irrigation dam built in the valley served a dual purpose, for many of the first arrivals in 1847 were rebaptized "in the dam" as a sign of dedication to their new life in Utah,[3] just before Brigham Young returned east to lead the 1848 migration. On December 2, 1847, Young was nominated for First President of the Church of Jesus Christ of Latter-day Saints, which nomination was confirmed or "sustained" the following year; he was to rule with an iron authority, assisted by his two Counselors, twelve Apostles, and a growing bureaucracy. Together they controlled not only the detailed settlement and exploitation of Utah but even the migration of converts from overseas and their conveyance to the Promised Land. All this was big business and was run in a thoroughly businesslike way; yet they followed a well-tried—indeed, what Arrington rightly calls an "Early American"—pattern:

It should be obvious that in establishing their institutions and in meeting their first problems in the Great Basin the Mormons relied primarily on their own early ideals and experiences. The careful planning which preceded the development of their great city, the patriarchal husbanding of resources and sharing of burdens, the pooling of productive efforts, the nature of their property institutions— all these might have been predicted long before the Mormons reached the Great Basin. The pattern had been foreshadowed in Jackson County, Kirtland, Far West, and Winter Quarters, and it had been formally incorporated in Mormon theology. Moreover, in acknowledging, as the first colonists in the Salt Lake Valley acknowledged, the social responsibility of government (in this case a theocracy) to arrange and supervise their economic life, the Mormons were recalling the policies and practices of early Americans in Massachusetts, where many of their ancestors were born; in Pennsylvania, where their first prophet was baptized and given the priesthood; and in Missouri, where their first economic experiments were tried. Far from being unique, the spirit and technique of Mormon colonization and organized activity were common, if not typical, in the age which produced Mormonism.

2. *Great Basin Kingdom: An Economic History of the Latter-day Saints, 1830–1900* (Cambridge, Mass., 1958). Quotations from this volume are used by permission of Harvard University Press.

3. Taylor, p. 52.

Yet, Mormon economic institutions *were* unique in the contemporary American West. To be sure, there was the same hunger, the same improvisation, the same struggle for success, as in all Western settlements. But the unity, homogeneity, joint action, and group planning all stamped the Mormon frontier as unique—as a contrast with the scattered, specialized, exploitative, "wide open" mining, cattle, lumber, and homestead frontiers with which historians have familiarized us. . . .

. . . the character of Mormon economic organization, as early as 1847–1849, and more certainly in the succeeding half-century, suggests the feasibility of regarding Mormon institutions as the more typically early American, and the individualistic institutions of other Westerners as the more divergent. The Mormon response to the problems imposed by the settlement of the Great Basin—a response which becomes ever clearer in succeeding decades—suggests that Mormon economic policies bore a greater resemblance to those of the ante-bellum northeast than did the economic policies of the West during the years when the West was won. Isolated as they were from American thought-currents after 1847, and under the necessity of continued group action to solve the many problems which plagued them, the Mormons were not affected by the growing accommodation to the private corporation, rugged individualism, Social Darwinism, and other concepts which account for the rise of laissez-faire after 1850. It may yet be conceded that the well-publicized conflicts and differences between the Mormons and other Westerners and Americans were not so much a matter of plural marriage and other reprehensible peculiarities and superstitions as of the conflicting economic patterns of two generations of Americans, one of which was fashioned after the communitarian concepts of the age of Jackson, and the other of which was shaped by the dream of bonanza and the individualistic sentiments of the age of laissez-faire.[4]

Less "Early American" was the decision that water for irrigation remain under public management and control even after the land through which it flowed had been parceled out as individually owned lots. The old doctrine of riparian rights adhered to in the better watered East was unworkable in the arid regions of the West; thus the Mormons worked out a new doctrine in 1847–49,

4. *Great Basin Kingdom*, pp. 62–3.

which was to be widely followed in other states and territories as well. In Utah, for example, it worked this way:

As expressed by Brigham Young, this policy was as follows: "There shall be no private ownership of the streams that come out of the canyons, nor the timber that grows on the hills. These belong to the people: all the people." The same principle was applied to mineral resources.

The decision with respect to water was particularly crucial. Although water was first turned on the land on July 23, 1847, it took the Mormons at least three years to learn the importance and effective use of irrigation. In this they had little precedent to guide them. Anglo-Saxon law, as adopted generally in the East, provided that water must not be taken from the streams unless it could be returned undiminished in volume. Known as the doctrine of riparian rights, this principle of law protected streams for use as sources of power and as channels of transportation. It also tended to restrict the establishment of homes to the banks of streams and gave privileged protection to the few who could profitably utilize the water.

The public ownership and management of water in the Great Basin prevented the application of this principle in curtailing irrigation, for obviously every use of water for irrigation robbed a stream of part of its water supply. Under the arrangement worked out by the Mormons in 1847–1849, dams and ditches were constructed on a community basis, rights to use the water were associated with the utilization of land, and a public authority was appointed to supervise the appropriation of water for culinary, industrial, and agricultural purposes. The avowed goal of this supervision was equitable division and maximum use of available water supplies. In 1847–1848, for example, a community ditch furnished water primarily for culinary purposes, and its distribution was under the control of a "watermaster" appointed by the high council.

It was during the next two years, however, when water matters were in the hands of the bishops of the various wards, that the Mormons developed the well-known principles by which canals and ditches were to be constructed and the waters divided. When a group of families found themselves in need of water (or additional water) to irrigate their farms and gardens, the bishop arranged for a survey and organized the men into a construction crew. Each man

was required to furnish labor in proportion to the amount of land
he had to water. Upon completion of the project the water would
be distributed by a ward watermaster in proportion to this labor.
The labor necessary to keep the canal in good repair was handled in
the same way, in accordance with assignments made in regular
Sunday services or priesthood meetings.

On this cooperative nonpecuniary basis, then, water was diverted from a natural source into a general canal, and from that into
"laterals" and ditches which carried the water to the individual plots
of ground needing it. "Corrugates" were dug next to each row to
carry water to the crops. "Waste ditches" carried the water from
one watered field to the next one below it.

When Utah became a territory this system of public ownership
was confirmed by the legislature and placed under the legal supervision of the county courts. The territorial government gave additional recognition to this system of cooperative construction and
ownership in 1865 by providing for the creation of irrigation districts, resembling Western mining districts, with a large degree of
local autonomy. Even today, farmer-owned "mutual" companies
control virtually all the irrigation canals in Mormon communities in
the West.[5]

Another authority has stated that the majority of Utah's canals
"were built by farmers, owned by farmers, and operated by the
farmers. In fact they constitute one of the greatest and most successful community or cooperative undertakings in the history of
America."[6] An even grander project of the Saints, to utilize systematically the water flowing from Utah Lake into Salt Lake via the
Jordan Valley through a Deseret Irrigation and Navigation Canal
Company—almost a "Jordan Valley Authority," though it was of
course before the days of hydroelectric power—was checkmated
by the veto of a gentile governor in the middle sixties. In words
almost worthy of a "barefoot boy from Wall Street" championing
private power and irrigation interests in the 1930's, Governor
Charles Durkee explained that, while the project "awakens my

5. *Great Basin Kingdom*, pp. 52–3.
6. G. Thomas: *Development of Institutions under Irrigation, with Special
Reference to Early Utah Conditions* (New York, 1920), p. 27; quoted in Arrington, p. 53.

admiration by its magnitude and boldness, it would exclude competition. . . ."⁷ No possible competition, in fact, existed.

Irrigation agriculture was expensive, both in labor and in maintenance cost, but while the Great Salt Lake Valley remained isolated, it had no reason to fear competition from the prairie states farther east, which produced their crops at far lass cost by other methods. With the completion of the transcontinental railroad through Utah in 1869, this competition became a serious threat, but Mormon enterprise and initiative, and the injunction to "grow your own or do without it" helped support the economy against the importation of manufactured goods from outside the territory. Joseph Smith's "Word of Wisdom" (a revelation dating back to 1833) was now strictly enforced with regard to the consumption of tea and coffee, liquor and tobacco, in a campaign launched by Brigham Young in 1867 and pursued by such organizations as the male School of the Prophets and the Womens' Relief Society. A boycott of gentile business establishments was also organized, and the School voted in 1868 that "those who dealt with outsiders should be cut off from the Church." The Zion Cooperative Mercantile Institution was founded, and cooperative retail stores opened in many communities.⁸ The School of the Prophets, also setting itself up as the guardian of the interests of Mormons who had settled on land that might be claimed by the Pacific railroads under their federal grants, seems to have helped resolve any such disputes with a minimum of friction.

The Womens' Relief Society took the battle into the homes of the Saints. Household manufacturers were encouraged and enjoined; imported fashions were to be spurned. Brigham Young himself took a hand in this campaign by pouring scorn on the Grecian Bend, which he said made a woman look like a camel, and on leg-of-mutton sleeves, which were sinfully wasteful, taking "seven yards for the sleeves, and three for the dress." Calling the female members of his by then not inconsiderable family together in the parlor of his multiplex office-cum-residence, the Lion House, in November 1869, he urged them to set an example and to "retrench from their extravagance in dress, in eating, and even in speech."⁹ As a result, Young Ladies' Retrenchment Societies were

7. *Great Basin Kingdom,* pp. 224–6.
8. *Great Basin Kingdom,* pp. 298–322.

set up all over the territory, to be followed by a Senior Department, concerned with the possible extravagances of older women. "Let the Sisters think of what they can wear that is Zion made," they were told, but the Relief Society tempered the wind to the shorn lamb (or mutton) by setting up a Deseret Silk Association. By 1877 there were 5 million silkworms in Zion.[1]

In addition to the silk industry, a number of others were established to meet the economic threat presented by the railroad. These included the making of wagons, carriages, and agricultural machinery, furniture, woolen and cotton goods, ink and matches. In July 1869 the First Presidency even decided to go on the offensive and initiate an export drive, now that the railroad had actually arrived at Ogden, only thirty-seven miles from Salt Lake City. The first step was an attempt to reduce local wages "in order that Utah might be able to compete with the manufactures of the States," and the second was to build the Utah Central Railroad, linking Salt Lake City with Ogden and the Union Pacific depot there. Wages were not brought down by anything like the one-third to one-half demanded, but the railroad was completed as a Mormon public enterprise, with Brigham Young as president of the line, by January 10, 1870. At its dedication Young indulged in a little very justifiable boasting:

"Since the day that we first trod the soil of these valleys, have we received any assistance from our neighbors? No, we have not. We

9. *Great Basin Kingdom*, p. 253. Brigham Young can hardly be said to have obeyed the last part of this injunction himself. His language remained flowery and, at times, violent to the end. He was, after all, a prophet in the Old Testament tradition. In a speech uttered in 1853 he had shouted: "I will unsheath my bowie knife and conquer or die"—John D. Lee: *A Mormon Chronicle*, ed. R. G. Cleland and Juanita Brooks, 2 vols. (San Marino, Calif., 1955), 1, 83. On another occasion Young warned food hoarders that their heads might be "found wallowing in the snow," and on yet another he said: "If you are not heartily on the Lord's side, you will be hewn down."

1. The spearhead and the battle-ax of these Women's Retrenchment Societies were wielded by the redoubtable Eliza Snow, once a wife of Joseph Smith and later an inmate of the Lion House. Sister Snow, as renowned for her poetry as much as for her piety, ran a number of campaigns both for the Prophet and for the First President. She managed at one and the same time to be a plural wife and an ardent feminist. It was perhaps too much to expect her also to be a good poet. See further Fawn M. Brodie: *No Man Knows My History* (New York, 1945; London, 1963), passim; this is the best life of Joseph Smith, by no means hostile to him, though highly critical of the divinity of his revelations. See also Kimball Young (a descendant of Brigham): *Isn't One Wife Enough?* (New York, 1954), a careful sociological analysis of Mormon polygamy, despite its catch-penny title.

have built our homes, our cities, have made our farms, have dug our canals and water ditches, have subdued this barren country, have fed the stranger, have clothed the naked, have immigrated the poor from foreign lands, have placed them in a condition to make all comfortable and have made some rich. We have fed the Indians to the amount of thousands of dollars yearly, have clothed them in part, and have sustained several Indian wars, and now we have built thirty-seven miles of railroad.

All this having been done, are not our cities, our counties and the Territory in debt? No, not the first dollar. But the question may be asked, is not the Utah Central Railroad in debt? Yes, but to none but our own people. . . .

We have felt somewhat to complain of the Union Pacific railroad company for not paying us for the work we did, in grading so many miles of their road. But let me say, if they had paid us according to agreement, this road would not have been graded, and this track would not have been laid today. It is all right. . . .

I also thank the brethren who have aided to build this, our first railroad. They have acted as Elders of Israel, and what higher praise can I accord to them, for they have worked on the road, they have graded the track, they have laid the rails, they have finished the line, and have done it cheerfully "without purse or scrip." An official of the Union Pacific attending the celebration followed the same theme. He said: "The Utah Central Railroad, although thirty-seven or thirty-eight miles long, is perhaps the only railroad west of the Missouri River that has been built entirely without Government subsidies; it has been built slowly with money wrung from the soil which, a few years ago, we used to consider a desert, by the strong arms of men and women who stand before me."

These and other speeches delivered on the occasion of the completion of the road manifested the pride felt by the Mormon people in building the road "without outside help."[2]

The city and territory of the Saints was now well and truly part of the great world from which they had fled more than two decades earlier. After the setbacks of the fifties, owing to the quarrel with the federal government and the abandonment of outlying settlements (such as San Bernardino) as well as the idea of a

2. The *Deseret News*, January 11, 1870; quoted in *Great Basin Kingdom,* pp. 272–3.

Mormon outlet to the Pacific, the territory had by 1861 been reduced to little more than the boundaries of Utah; a new self-sufficiency on more modest lines was sought in the sixties, so that Zion
would be impregnable and unassailable economically when the
transcontinental railroad finally came. Political isolation was now
known to be impossible, but economic isolation might still be
maintained, it was thought. "Even the approach of the transcontinental railroad in the late 1860's brought no relaxation in the drive
for independence from the economy of Babylon."[3] The result was
a drawn battle. The Mormons continued to trade with the gentile
world, and to benefit from this trade, but they did so to a large
extent on their own terms. Sir Richard Burton had somewhat
distorted the situation in 1860 when he wrote: "The Mormons
having lost all hopes of safety by isolation, now seek it in the
reverse: mail communication with the Eastern and Western states
is their present hobby: they look forward to markets for their
produce and to a greater facility and economy of importing."[4]
Agricultural progress in Utah had rather overimpressed him,
though he admitted that "Utah Territory is pronounced by Immigrants from the old country to be a 'mean land' hard, dry and fit
only for the steady, sober and hard-working Mormon. Scarcely
one-fiftieth part is fit for tillage."[5] During the sixties, Arrington
points out, "The group struggle for self-sufficiency manifested
itself in immigration, public works, communications, colonization,
industry, transportation, and in the church's investment policy
generally. In each case one sees an attempt to develop an economy
with few entangling alliances, and yet with a capacity for growth
and expansion through superior organization. If group achievement
was somewhat less than expected, it was due to the failure of Great
Basin agriculture to produce bounteous harvests."[6] Yet the population of Utah doubled (rising from 40,000 to 80,000) between 1858
and 1869. The ninety Mormon settlements in the territory of 1857
rose to 200 by the end of 1867, and to 300 or more by 1877.[7] Long

3. *Great Basin Kingdom*, p. 195.
4. *City of the Saints*, p. 319.
5. *City of the Saints*, p. 312.
6. *Great Basin Kingdom*, p. 205.
7. M. R. Hunter: *Brigham Young the Colonizer* (Salt Lake City, 1940);
Hunter's figures are critically appraised in Taylor, pp. 95–6.

before 1877 (the year Brigham Young died) the easily irrigable areas of Utah were nearly all under cultivation, and, to increase the productive acreage further, resort had to be made to dry farming. As with large-scale irrigation, "It was in Utah that the first considerable success was achieved in dry farming."[8] After several failures in the fifties, it appears that a Scandinavian settlement at Bear River City was the site of the first successful experiment in Utah, about 1863.[9]

Dry farming, or "dry-land farming," the use of the stored capillary water in the soil just under the growing crops, which without proper and constant cultivation (especially after rain has fallen) would be lost, was known and practised even in antiquity, but it was not widely resorted to in the United States outside northern Utah before the end of the nineteenth century. By 1909 more land was being tilled in Utah by dry-farming methods than by irrigation, though in 1900 there had already been about 6 million acres under irrigation. Dry farming was not practicable where the rainfall was less than ten inches a year on the average,[1] so not much of Utah could benefit from it, but it was very suitable for Kansas and Nebraska, west of the hundreth meridian and for many other areas with between ten and thirty inches of rain a year. The practice pioneered in Utah (and, on a very local scale, in parts of California, under the stimulus of the ideas of the soil scientist F. W. Hilgard) nevertheless spread only slowly into other states and territories. There was some dry farming in Edwards County, Kansas, in the eighties, but it required the evangelical zeal of Hardy W. Campbell to bring dry farming into Nebraska at the turn of the century.[2] Colorado was equally slow in making use of the technique to which, it had been estimated, fully three hundred million acres of the United States were suited, compared with three hundred and fifty million cultivable without special techniques, and only eighty thousand irrigated or irrigable.[3]

8. Webb: *Great Plains*, p. 368.

9. Webb quotes J. A. Widsoe: *Dry Farming* (New York, 1913), and W. MacDonald: *Dry Farming: Its Principles and Practice* (New York, 1911), as his authorities for this statement.

1. Webb's figure; Shannon (*Farmer's Last Frontier*) says fifteen.

2. See MacDonald: *Dry Farming*, pp. 18–19; Webb: *Great Plains*, p. 369.

3. Webb, p. 366.

By the year, 1900, irrigation as the result of federal or state action (against which the formidable Major Powell[4] had set his face so resolutely in 1878) was still in its infancy in the United States. The "bungling"[5] Carey Act had only been passed in 1894, a timid first step into the shallow end of the problem; barely 4 million acres had been irrigated by the turn of the century, and under 9 million by 1902. Shannon estimates that only about a quarter-million acres of this irrigation resulted from the Carey Act, instead of the 17 million allowed for!

Bonanza agriculture. Harrow team on the Grandin Farm, Red River Valley, as photographed by F. J. Haynes. From Freeman Tilden: *Following the Frontier* (1964).

If the year 1890 saw the end of an era for American agriculture through the breakup into "islands" of the hitherto unbroken belt of free uncultivated land westward of the settlements, a new era had hardly commenced by 1900, and the 380,000,000 acres of the United States capable of cultivation by means of irrigation and dry farming (more than the total area cultivable or under cultiva-

4. J. W. Powell: *Report on the Lands of the Arid Region of the United States* (Washington, D. C., 1878); and W. Stegner: *Beyond the Hundredth Meridian* (Boston, 1954), which contains the best appraisal of Powell's importance.

5. So called in Shannon: *The Farmer's Last Frontier*, p. 216.

tion without such aids) remained to a large extent unexploited. American agriculture stood to benefit immensely from the new techniques pioneered by the Saints in Utah, but they were being only very slowly learned and adopted elsewhere. So: "The end of the century came with the farmer on his last frontier, always hopeful that the next year would reverse his luck but never sure that he could 'keep his belt buckle from chafing his backbone' till the next crop was raised."[6]

6. Shannon, p. 220. Fred Shannon, in his commendable effort not to appear a pollyanna, has painted a somewhat too somber picture of the plight of the American farmer during the last third of the nineteenth century. Reading his volume in the *Agricultural History of the United States,* it is sometimes hard to remember that not all farmers were ruined and that some of them even made fortunes. Shannon, a professional iconoclast, was an academic curmudgeon who, while infinitely kind and helpful to younger scholars, much enjoyed quarreling with his contemporaries. When he took on men of the caliber of Frederick Jackson Turner, Walter Prescott Webb, and Avery Craven (see Bibliographic Note, pp. 437 ff.), the battle tended to be royal and sparks, fur, and dirt to fly. He gave no quarter and to him no holds (even with the teeth) were barred. But there was no malice in him.

CHAPTER XII

The End of the West?

Twentieth-Century

Frontiers

N THE REMOTER WEST, THE RESTLESS RUSHING WAVE OF settlement has broken with a shock against the arid plains. The free lands are gone, the continent is crossed, and all this push and energy is turning into channels of agitation. Failures in one area can no longer be made good by taking up land on a new frontier; the conditions of a settled society are being reached with suddenness and with confusion." Thus wrote Frederick Jackson Turner,[1] the Wisconsin historian, in *The Atlantic* in September 1896, in an attempt to popularize a conclusion that had first been stated in the U. S. Census Bureau's bulletin in 1890, and which he himself had presented to a scholarly audience in his famous essay on "The Significance of the Frontier in American History" in 1893.

This unpalatable truth, if truth it was, that the free lands of the United States were running out, was soon also to be trumpeted abroad by the politicians and the leaders of business. From Theodore Roosevelt's fear that the nation's population would soon outstrip its food supply (although at the time the population of the United States was still under one hundred million), and James J. Hill's warning of a nationwide famine, to Franklin D. Roosevelt's famous remark thirty years later (when the population of the

1. "The Problem of the West," *The Atlantic*, LXXVII (Sept. 1896), 289; repr. in *The Frontier in American History* (New York, 1920 and 1947; paperback edn., 1962), pp. 205–21.

country had risen above 125 million, with still no famine, and indeed a vast overproduction of foodstuffs): "We can no longer escape into virgin territory; we must master our environment," the note of alarm continued to be sounded. Only after the legislation of the New Deal had been applied to this problem, and the coming of the Second World War had ushered in another era of farm prosperity, did scholars and economists begin to express a different sort of alarm. Then, in the 1950's, the United States was told that it contained a "people of plenty" whose high standard of living and tendency to overproduce was a danger to the well-being of the nation, and whose "affluent society" was arousing the envy and hatred of the whole outside world, no matter how high a proportion of their superabundance the Americans were prepared to give away. Such public philosophies could only create as much confusion in the mind of the citizen as when he had been told some sixty years earlier that the great safety valve of "free land" was now closed and that the consequences were bound to be dire.

Whatever economic ups and downs the future may hold in store for this "people of plenty," this "affluent society" of the 1950's and 1960's, the prophesies of doom uttered in the 1890's by those who viewed with alarm the census figures of 1890 turned out to be oddly at sixes and sevens with reality. The early nineties (like the late eighties) were indeed a period of falling prices and rural distress. The Populist Party of the nineties, dedicated to raising "less corn and more hell," sought by various panacea—including the bimetallism, which found its apostle in William Jennings Bryan in 1896—to solve the problem. Ironically, however, from 1897 on, after the electoral defeat of Bryan and the Populist cause and in an era of continued Republican ascendancy, prosperity suddenly and somewhat unaccountably reappeared. The price of farm land skyrocketed, having risen, on an average, over 100 per cent by 1910 (and in the Dakotas, from which there had been a serious rural exodus in the early nineties, over 300 per cent), and the general price index for produce rose from 100 to nearly 190 during 1899–1910. This boom was achieved without bimetallism, without Bryan at the helm of affairs, and without the safety valve of free land. To Professor Turner and the Superintendent of the Census Bureau, and even to Theodore Roosevelt, it must all have appeared very mysterious. It was not until 1920 that a new agricultural depression began to set in, and once again the pundits were taken by surprise.

It was when this agricultural depression was followed by the stock-market crash of 1929 and the industrial depression of the thirties that critics began to turn savagely on Turner's "safety-valve theory," claiming that there was no longer a safety-valve in free or cheap farm land farther west for the economic and social ills of settled American communities in the East and Midwest, if in fact there had ever been one. It was pointed out that during depression years—after the panic of 1837 and those of 1857, 1873, and 1893—migration westward, as well as immigration from overseas, had slowed down rather than accelerated. It was in years of relative prosperity or of boom that the westward movement was greatest, as, also, was immigration. The immigration from Germany was at its peak in 1854 and 1882, and the all-time record year for immigration from all sources was 1907. The American ego received a severe shock in 1931 when the tide of immigration reversed for the first time since records had been accurately kept in 1820, and three times as many emigrants departed from the United States as immigrants reached its shores. Fred Shannon's mordant "Post-Mortem on the Labor Safety Valve Theory"[2] came only at the end of a decade of attacks on the theory, which left it pretty effectively shredded to pieces.

The discrediting of the safety-valve theory did not, of course, automatically invalidate the remainder of the Turner hypothesis, though it did bring out the jackals and the buzzards in considerable numbers. Every aspect of the hypothesis now came under close scrutiny, and budding historians (as well as others well past the budding stage, like Charles A. Beard) seemed to consider it their professional duty to get themselves blooded in the attack on it. Not every attack was as clinical as Shannon's, as vicious as Beard's, or as doctrinaire as Hacker's. The most effective criticisms, such as those of George Pierson, Carlton Hayes, and David Potter, tended to be those that conceded much validity to the Turner hypothesis yet pinpointed its shortcomings; the most successful defenders of Turner tended to be those, like Avery Craven, Frederick Paxson, or Ray Billington, who did not demand a 100 per cent adherence to every opinion that Turner had ever expressed. An all-out apologia, such as Joseph Schafer's attempt to justify the safety-valve theory, tended to play into the hands of the enemy.

2. *Agricultural History*, XIX (Jan. 1945), 31–7; adapted for, and incorporated in, his *Farmer's Last Frontier*; already quoted in Ch. xi.

It began to be realized that Turner, in 1893, had been generalizing about an American agrarian society that had already passed its apogee; that he had not given sufficient weight to the effect of the technical advances of the Industrial Revolution; and that, "by failing to recognize that the frontier was only one form in which America offered abundance, he cut himself off from an insight into the fact that other forms of abundance had superseded the frontier even before the supply of free land had been exhausted, with the result that it was not really the end of free land but rather the substitution of new forms of economic activity which terminated the frontier phase in our history."[3] This still left the Turner hypothesis a valuable asset to the historian, as was demonstrated most strikingly in 1952 by one of his leading disciples, Walter Prescott Webb, who sought, not without success, to expand the Turner hypothesis from America to the whole world. In *The Great Frontier*, Webb may, with characteristic Texan verve, have at times overstated his case, but he did "bring Turner up to date" by giving adequate weight to the exploitation of the mineral wealth of the soil (whereas Turner had concentrated too exclusively on the products of its tillage) in the modern world (and thereby "clarifying a vital factor which remained obscure in Turner");[4] and he also stressed the importance of commerce in "that form of wealth classed as Things or commodities," and of the accumulation of surplus wealth in forms other than that of the abundance of the soil. His simplified version of a Keynesian *obiter dictum* that the loot of the *Golden Hind* had been parlayed into the wealth of Britain—the Britain of joint stock banks and the national debt—within little more than a century has at least pointed to the fact that there were alternative ways for men and nations to become rich, even prior to the eighteenth century, to pursuing the agrarian ideal. Turner, it is true, recognized the existence of "the trader's frontier, the rancher's frontier and the miner's frontier,"[5] as well as the farmer's frontier, but the frontier speculator, the frontier town builder, and the frontier technologist and inventor get short shrift from him. In *The Great Frontier* (and, on a narrower stage, in *The*

3. D. Potter: *People of Plenty* (Chicago, 1954), p. 156.
4. Ibid., p. 160.
5. Turner: *Frontier in American History* (1920 and 1947; paperback edn. 1962), p. 12; and *Frontier and Section: Selected Essays of F. J. Turner*, ed. R. A. Billington (New York, 1961), p. 44.

Great Plains and *The Texas Rangers*), Webb filled in (indeed, sometimes overfilled) the gaps. Glidden and his barbed wire, Colt and his revolver, Halladay and his self-regulations wind pump, play no part in the Turner story, but they are major characters and properties in Webb's. It is true that Webb, like Turner, concluded on a note of gloom: 400 years of abundance on the Great Frontier of the New World and the Old had ended, just as free land—even to the west—no longer existed for North America, and man faced an uncertain and more restricted future. "Science can do much but it is not likely to find a new world or make the one we have much better than it is," wrote Webb in 1952.[6] Even two years later, David Potter was questioning this assertion,[7] and today, with Mars and Venus probes in the news and a landing by man on the moon quite likely in the near future, it already seems to have been a very dangerous one.

Webb may be said not so much to have exposed the inadequacies of the Turner hypothesis as to have disclosed its wider possibilities.[8] Turner was anything but a prolific writer: in over forty years of history teaching and research, he produced only twenty-six short, seminal essays and one book.[9] Had he published more, he might have presented a more rounded and less assailable philosophy of history, and the famous hypothesis might not have been left so full of holes. His posthumous publications display an interest in many themes he did not fully develop, such as the significance of the "section" (a major geographical area comprising a number of states or territories) in American history and the influence of increasing urbanization upon American life.[1] Billington's mature judgment is that

6. W. P. Webb: *The Great Frontier* (Boston, 1952).

7. Potter: *People of Plenty*, p. 164.

8. Some of which will be discussed in the Epilogue.

9. See R. A. Billington: "Why Some Historians Rarely Write History: A Case Study of Frederick Jackson Turner." *Mississippi Valley Historical Review*, L: 1 (June 1963), 3-27. The one book was *The Rise of the New West, 1819–1829*, "American Nation" series, ed. A. B. Hart (New York, 1906; paperback edn. ed. R. A. Billington, New York, 1962). "It ought to be carved on my tombstone," wrote A. B. Hart, "that I was the only man in the world that secured what might be called an adequate volume from Turner."

1. Since Turner's death other scholars have begun to pursue these topics further: for instance, Roy F. Nichols: "The Territories: Seedbeds of Democracy," *Nebraska History*, XXXV (Sept. 1954), 159–72; Richard C. Wade: *The Urban Frontier* (Cambridge, Mass., 1959); B. McKelvey: *The Urbanization of America (1860–1915)* (New Brunswick, N. J., 1963).

Most modern scholars, then, would agree with Turner that the frontiersman did develop certain traits and that these have been perpetuated to form the principal distinguishing characteristics of the American people today. Americans display a restless energy, a versatility, a practical ingenuity, an earthy practicality to a degree unknown among Englishmen and other Europeans. They do squander their natural resources with an abandon unknown elsewhere; they have developed a mobility both socially and physically that marks them as a people apart. In few other lands is democracy worshipped so intensely, or nationalism carried to such extremes of isolationism or international arrogance. Rarely do other peoples display such indifference toward intellectualism or aesthetic values; seldom in comparable cultural areas do they cling so tenaciously to the shibboleth of rugged individualism. Nor do residents of non-frontier lands experience the same degree of heady optimism, the blind faith in the future, the belief in the inevitability of progress, that is part of the American creed. These were pioneer traits, and they have become part of the national heritage.[2]

These traits so frankly stated by an American historian have been noticed with varying degrees of sympathy and understanding by foreign observers from Crèvecoeur to the Chinese "Silent Traveler";[3] by Tocqueville, Dickens, Frederika Bremer, James Bryce, Rudyard Kipling, André Siegfried, Halvan Koht, Louis Adamič, Karel Čapek, Denis Brogan, and Nikita Khrushchev. Khrushchev was happiest, during his visit to the United States, when on an Iowa farm, unhappiest when, in California, he was taken to a Hollywood Studio but prevented from going to Walt Disney's "Frontierland." Bryce praised the exuberance of the "Western Parts of America," already living in the future, with today only half finished and yesterday already forgotten. Brogan noted (as early as 1935) "The Rise and Decline of the American Agricultural Interest," which had bulked so large in the United States from Jefferson to Turner and had remained important, though on the defensive, in the shape of the "farm bloc" even thereafter. Not all

2. Billington: *The American Frontier*, American Historical Association pamphlet (Washington, D. C. 1958), p. 22.

3. Chiang Yee: *The Silent Traveler in San Francisco* (New York and London, 1964), pp. 364–5. "How fortunate it is for the United States to possess not one but two lasting spirits, the *Pilgrim's* and the *Pioneer's*. . . . The *Pioneer's spirit* remains alive to spur her into taking *chances*. . . ."

GRAND
COULEE
DAM

FORT
PECK
DAM

BONNEVILLE
DAM

Columbia R.

C A N A

A

Yellowstone R.

Snake R.

G R E

Great
Salt
Lake

U T A H   P L A I

Arkansas R.

BOULDER
DAM

A R I Z O N A

NEW

DUST

SALTON
SEA

ROOSEVELT
DAM

Colorado R.

Gila R.

M E X I C O

BOWL

Pecos R.

Rio Grande

FALCO
DAM

FRONTIERS SINCE TURNER
States created { UTAH • NEW MEXICO
since 1890   { ARIZONA • OKLAHOMA
Major Reclamation & ROOSEVELT
Irrigation Projects } DAM
Oilfields ◉ Atomic Energy Centres Ⓐ
Uranium (Veins yielding over 100 tons of ore) **U**
Wooded country ▓ Desert ▨ Semi-desert ▨

100

of these commentators could agree on what exactly constituted the American creed and why it was different from the national heritage of the peoples of Europe, but they all admitted that it *was* different.

Turner, in one of his most celebrated and poetic passages, wrote: "American democracy was born of no theorist's dream; it was not carried in the *Susan Constant* to Virginia nor in the *Mayflower* to Plymouth. It came stark and strong and full of life out of the American forest, and it gained strength each time it touched a new frontier."[4] In this resounding and often quoted passage, Turner issued a challenge, not only to the "germ theory"[5] of G. B. Adams, but also to those who think that free institutions, hard won in seventeenth- and eighteenth-century political struggles in England, may possibly have been brought to America by the emigrants in their little ships, and that the thirst for liberty, even if unslaked (but intensified on countless barricades) in France, Spain, Italy, Germany, the Habsburg realms, and even Russia, may have been carried across the Atlantic in cabin and steerage alike, all through the Great Immigration of the nineteenth century. Tom Paine and Robert Owen, Carl Schurz and Lajos Kossuth, Wilhelm Weitling and Karl Heinzen, needed no refresher course in the American backwoods on the meaning of freedom or the pursuit of democracy, according to their lights. Had Tocqueville ever met Davy Crockett (and how we wish that this could have happened!), he would have found him a very crude practitioner indeed of "Democracy in America," though he might have discovered how to buy a man's vote with a swig of brandy and a quid of tobacco. Even indigenous American apostles of democracy could do without the inspiration of trees. George Norris came from the treeless plains of Nebraska; if William Alan White wanted a tree to grow in Emporia, Kansas, he had to plant it himself and keep it watered; Fiorello La Guardia took his inspiration from the asphalt jungle of New York;[6] the men who owned most of the Big Trees in Califor-

4. F. J. Turner: "The West and American Ideals," *Washington Historical Quarterly*, V (Oct. 1914), 245; slightly modified repr. in *The Frontier in American History* (1920 and 1931), p. 293.

5. The "germ theory" postulated that the "germs" of democratic principles originated among the primitive Anglo-Saxon tribes and were carried by them both to Britain and to America. G. B. Adams, Europe-trained, taught it at The Johns Hopkins University, which Turner attended and where he took his Ph.D.

6. The "Little Flower" was born in New York all right, but he also went to

nia were not the biggest democrats in that state, or in any other:
their beliefs (if they had any) ran to feudalism rather than
radicalism; but even the radicals who established their temporary
"Utopian Colonies" among the Giant Sequoias administered the
unkindest cut of all to the "democracy-comes-out-of-the-Amer-
ican-forest" theory by naming the largest of them all (now re-
consecrated and christened "General Sherman") the "Karl Marx
Tree."[7]

It is perhaps too easy to make fun of one of Frederick Jackson
Turner's very rare naïveties and to forget his many words of
wisdom, and the inspiration he gave to others. Though he himself
may not have fully acknowledged the ideological value of what the
European immigrants brought over with them to plant in the
American forest, he did nurture the genius of Marcus Lee Hansen,
whose pioneering, and, unhappily, uncompleted studies of *The
Atlantic Migration 1607–1860* (1940) and of *The Immigrant in
American History*,[8] gave due weight, perhaps for the first time, to
a number of factors that Turner had failed to stress. "Unlike most

---

school in Arizona, served for three years (1907–10) as an interpreter on Ellis
Island (so he knew all about bare-foot immigrants), and commanded a United
States Army Air Corps base in northern Italy in World War I. This all happened
before he went into Congress and on to even greater glory (and national fame) as
mayor of New York. It may with confidence be said that New York has never
been the same since La Guardia read the "comics" to the kids (now grown-ups)
over the radio during one of that city's endemic newspaper strikes.

7. Robert V. Hine: *California's Utopian Colonies* (San Marino, Calif.,
1953; repr. New Haven, 1966), p. 90.

8. M. H. Hansen (1892–1928) was, according to Oscar Handlin, "the first
serious student of the history of American immigration." Though the judgment
ignores the by no means valueless works (even today) of John R. Commons:
Races and Immigrants in America (New York and London, 1907), and of N. W.
Stephenson: *A History of American Immigration* (Boston, 1926), it has a good
deal of truth in it. The native-born son of Scandinavian immigrants, Hansen went
from the University of Iowa to Harvard in 1917 to work under the master. There
"Turner directed the young man's attention to the opportunities for creative
scholarship on the history of immigration" (Handlin). Twenty years of arduous
research were overtaken by his premature death in 1938, before he had published
any of his main conclusions; but Professor H. Hale Bellot had persuaded him to
give a course of public lectures on "The Immigrant in American History" at
University College, London, in 1935 (which the present writer attended, to his
very great benefit), and these were published as the posthumous book *The
Immigrant in American History* (New York and London, 1941). Hansen in his
turn had influenced a whole new generation of writers on immigration problems,
including Oscar Handlin, Charlotte Ericson, Maldwyn Jones, Theodore Saloutas,

historians of Immigration," Arthur M. Schlesinger, Sr., has written,[9] Hansen "takes his stand in Europe rather than in America."

> As the story grows under the author's pen, no reader can fail to perceive its epic character. Less familiar than the advance of the pioneers into the American West, the long continuous migration across the ocean forms the necessary background for that movement. To the courage and determination of these humble folks from Europe historians ascribe some of the finest traits of the national character.

The author of *New Viewpoints in American History*[1] had already, in that seminal book, pointed out the importance of immigration in the making of America and the opening up of the West. By presenting the fruits of Hansen's researches to the world he underlined this importance.

Much of the story of the Great Atlantic Migration from Europe to the United States—and, in a lesser degree, to Canada—is irrelevant to a history of the American West and will not be considered here, but some of it is very relevant indeed. It is not without significance that the really huge immigration did not commence until easily available free land in the West was no longer to be had. The record of 790,000 immigrants in 1882 stood for over twenty years and during the depression of the nineties the annual figures dropped to 216,000 in 1897. Then they rapidly climbed to a million a year and stayed above the million mark (with no fewer than 1,285,000 in 1907 alone) until the middle of 1914. The impact of these new millions, most of them crowding into the cities,

---

and myself, for in 1935 he read through the typescript of my *Tragedy of German-America* (New York, 1940) and made many very valuable suggestions, though we agreed to differ on a number of points regarding the hyphen in German-Americanism. *The Atlantic Migration, 1607–1860*, which was prepared for publication from Hansen's manuscripts and notes by Arthur M. Schlesinger, Sr., deservedly won the Pulitzer Prize for History in 1941. It has since been reissued as a paperback (New York, 1961) with Schlesinger's original foreword and a new, somewhat supernumerary, introduction by Handlin. Hansen had intended to write two more volumes, taking the story of *The Atlantic Migration* up to 1914, but his published volume, edited by Schlesinger, contains enough signposts to how the rest should be written to have enabled other scholars to complete the story, not perhaps quite as he would have done it, but adequately enough.

9. *Atlantic Migration*, p. xix.

1. Arthur M. Schlesinger: *New Viewpoints in American History* (Cambridge, Mass., 1921).

alarmed not only politicians, publicists, trade-union leaders, women's clubs, and all red-blooded 200 per cent Americans—however recent their own arrival—but even scared Frederick Jackson Turner: "Where Braddock and his men, 'carving a cross on the wilderness rim,' were struck by the painted savages in the primeval woods, huge furnaces belch forth perpetual fires and Huns and Bulgars, Poles and Sicilians struggle for a chance to earn their daily bread, and live a brutal and degraded life."[2] How unlike the home life of our own dear Daniel Boone! But Marcus Lee Hansen and

Immigrant-landing in New York, by W. J. Hennessy. From *Harper's Weekly*, June 26, 1858.

his school have discovered why these Huns and Bulgars, Poles and Sicilians chose to emigrate to America and how they succeeded in doing so, often against incredible odds. The young girl from off a Galician (or Bessarabian or Calabrian) farm who walked barefoot[3] down the gangplank onto Ellis Island around the year 1907 could well have become, by 1965, another Helena Rubenstein.[4]

It is Hansen's contention that the statistically "greatest" mi-

2. "The West and American Ideals" (1914), as repr. in *Frontier and Section*, ed. R. A. Billington (New York, 1961), pp. 105–6.

3. See illus., p. 396; from J. R. Commons: *Races and Immigrants*, p. 230. She also appears in the photograph facing p. 78 of that book.

4. Helena Rubenstein, the famous manufacturer of cosmetics, was born near Cracow, in Austrian Poland, around 1875. She died an American citizen and a multimillionaire in 1965.

gration into the United States (1898–1914) was less "great" in its effects upon American life than that between 1850 and 1860, when "something like 2,600,000 aliens poured into the country and the foreign-born inhabitants increased from 2,244,600 to well over 4,000,000. . . . This migration was great in comparison with the native American population, great in the trails of settlement it broke, great in the cultural foundations it laid. Subsequent decades were to see a larger volume of arrivals, but no later migration paid richer dividends to American civilization."[5] This view is perhaps

Immigrants awaiting admission at Ellis Island. From J. R. Commons: *Races and Immigrants in America* (New York, 1907). Note peasant girl standing barefoot.

open to argument, and what Hansen does not point out (as he might have done, had he completed a sequel to this volume) is that the later migrations may well have paid richer dividends in happiness and well-being to the migrants than this earlier one. While the earlier did bring relief from the consequences of the potato famine in Ireland and help to assuage land hunger among Germans and Scandinavians, a relatively small proportion of the middle nineteenth century emigrants from Europe were seeking to escape religious and political persecution in addition to adverse economic conditions. A much higher proportion of the emigrants from 1881

5. Hansen: *Atlantic Migration* (paperback edn., New York, 1961), p. 281.

onwards had these additional incentives. This applied less to the Italians, whose motives remained mainly economic,[6] but after 1881 the active and systematic persecution of the Jews in European Russia commenced. This began a great exodus to America, hastened by occasional pogroms and rumors of more to come. The Great and White Russian peasant did not emigrate, and 98 per cent of the emigration from the Russian Empire to the United States came from its "subject" peoples or races. Of these, in the year 1906, 125,000 were Jews, 46,000 Poles, 14,000 Lithuanians, 13,000 Finns, and 10,000 Germans. Five sixths of all the Jewish emigration from Europe to the United States in that year came from Russia, and the remaining one-sixth almost entirely from Austria-Hungary and Rumania.[7] As, naturally, most of the Russian Jews were German-speaking, the U. S. Census Bureau (which, after 1900, ceased to record the religion of an immigrant) classified them as Russian-Germans. Their *lingua franca* was the hybrid Yiddish tongue, though a proportion of the Orthodox Jews also understood Hebrew. While many of these persecuted people came from rural areas in Russia (where, however, they were not permitted to farm the land) Austria-Hungary, and Rumania, they almost invariably stayed in the larger cities in America, where the skills they possessed were in more demand and where their abject poverty on arrival was less of a bar to getting a new start in life. As it was, many of them had to be supported by relatives and relief organizations at first. While they helped to relieve the urban labor shortage in the "boom" years after 1897, they aroused resentment among the native born, and the earlier immigrant groups, for being willing to accept low wages and inferior living conditions, just as had the Irish peasants who had fled the famine half a century earlier.

Even more people (265,000) emigrated from Austria-Hungary to the United States in 1906 than from Russia. As opposed to the eighties and nineties, when most emigration was from the more northerly parts of the Empire, the southern Slavs—Croatians and Slovenians—now led the emigration with 43,000 in that one year.

---

6. This view is close to, but does not accord entirely with, that expressed in the forthcoming study by Andrew Rolle (with intro. by R. A. Billington) of the successful migration of Italians to western America, to be entitled "The Upraised," which will examine this subject in its wider implications and present an alternative interpretation to that of Handlin's *The Uprooted*.

7. Commons: *Races and Immigrants*, p. 88.

There were also 16,000 Ruthenians—a large number from so small an area—and 11,000 Rumanians. German-speaking subjects of the Hapsburgs emigrating numbered 35,000. There were fewer Magyars than before, owing to the measures taken by the Hungarian government toward discouraging their emigration. Wrote Commons in 1907:[8]

> Practically the entire migration of the Slavic element at the present time is that of peasants. In Croatia the forests have been depleted, and thousands of immigrant wood-choppers have sought the forests of our South and the railway construction of the West. . . . So it is with the Slovak peasants of the Northern mountains and foothills. With agricultural wages only eighteen cents a day, they find employment in the American mines, rolling mills, stockyards and railroad construction at $1.50 a day.

Before very long, some of them would be receiving Henry Ford's $2-a-day minimum. Many of those who worked on the early Model-T assembly lines were Middle Europeans.

Italy sent 273,000—or more than a quarter of all immigrants received by the United States—in 1906; in 1876 she had sent only 3,000! Italian emigration, principally from the south and Sicily, was mainly for economic reasons, for there was little political oppression in the easy-going kingdom of those days, though a large number of young men left to escape military conscription. Many of them were only "temporary emigrants," aiming to make a little money and then return home (as did fully 150,000 in 1906 from various countries abroad); but of those who did not return, a large proportion sent back remittances to their families, or sent for their wives and sweethearts. "It is said that already there are several small country towns in Southern Italy which have risen from squalor to something of prosperity through the money and influence of those who have come home," wrote Commons in 1907.[9] These returned emigrants swaggered through the dusty little piazzas, criticizing everything; unmortgaged or purchased the family farm, extending its miserably small holding to a decent size; built garish villas complete with victrolas and running water; loaned money at high interest to the hard-up local squire and sometimes even married his daughter as an alternative to foreclosure. They introduced machin-

8. Commons, p. 84.
9. Commons, p. 77.

ery and know-how and the *Saturday Evening Post;* they told
incredible tales (all of them believed—some of them true) of the
sinful and salubrious city of Columbus, Ohio, or of Wilkes-Barre,
Pennsylvania, or of Fresno, California. They were the *Americani,*
back from Eldorado, their pockets full of gold and "you becha's"
on their lips. Up and down the Dalmatian Coast and in the broad
uplands of Croatia and Slovenia, on Greek Islands and mainland
valleys, these *Amerikanĉi*—or whatever they were called locally—
also appeared. They tended to be the ones who had succeeded only
moderately well in the United States, for those who failed in the
New World rarely returned home (even if they had the passage
money) to explain their shame, and those who became really well
heeled usually stayed in America, resolved to make even more
money and bring up their children as real Americans, which they
knew they themselves could never quite become. The successful
tended to get themselves Americanized with almost indecent haste.
The movie magnate Carl Laemmle, reminiscing in 1934 on the
fiftieth anniversary of his emigration to America from Germany (a
signed photograph of Franklin D. Roosevelt on the wall behind his
desk), confessed that he had turned his back on Germany from the
beginning, had allowed only English-language newspapers in his
home, and had forbidden the use of the German language in his
family circle.[1] This may be an extreme example, but if a Jewish
emigrant from Germany in 1884—when anti-Semitism was in its
infancy there and pogroms unknown—felt this way, how much
greater was the incentive to the refugee from the ghettoes of
Warsaw and Lodz and Lublin—who could have no hope of, or
incentive for, returning, and whose remittances might well never
reach their destination—to forget the old-world ties completely
amid the stresses and excitements of the new.

What have the recent immigrant "hordes" contributed to the
development of the trans-Mississippi West? By the very nature of
things they appear superficially to have contributed less than the
Germans and the Irish in the Old and the New Northwest between
the Ohio and the Mississippi. Although the Scandinavians have set
an unmistakable stamp on Minnesota and Iowa, western Kansas and

---

1. In an interview granted to me at Universal City, Calif., in 1934; Mr.
Laemmle's life story had been told after a fashion in John Drinkwater: *Carl
Laemmle* (New York and London, 1931), a book written between scenario
assignments at Universal City.

Nebraska, and the Dakotas, no city there has ever been as "Scandinavian" as once were (in their turn) Cincinnati, St. Louis, and Milwaukee concentration points of German settlement and social, cultural and business centers for a much more wide-spread German-born population in the small towns and villages and on the farms of Ohio, Illinois, Missouri, and Wisconsin. The eastern, southeastern, and southern Europeans, arriving even later than the Scandinavians, have never succeeded in "taking over" any large city or state or section of the country, even for a short period. The Poles in the Connecticut Valley have not de-Yankeefied it; the Italians in the Napa Valley and the Valley of the Moon of California have trodden and pressed (and now presumably atomize) its grapes without eradicating its old-time Spanish atmosphere; the French-Canadians have rescued neither Massachusetts' politics from the Irish nor its culture from the Puritans. Nevertheless the Poles and the French-Canadians have put back into cultivation derelict fields and farms deserted by their earlier, more improvident, more foot-loose Yankee exploiters; and the Italians, assisted by smaller numbers of other European immigrants, have provided the inherited skill, the patience, and the acceptance of rural standards of living (such as could not be found in sufficient quantity among Americans, of either Anglo-Saxon or Spanish descent) that the specialized agriculture of the Napa and other Californian valleys needed. These peoples were not the first to break the soil in such areas, and they did not even (except here and there) come to own it outright; the place names were not of their coinage, but they have contributed mightily to the prosperity of these regions. No incorporated place in Minnesota has a recognizably Welsh or Cornish name, despite the Welsh and Cornish contribution to the exploitation of the iron mines of that state; and the same state even has only two names that are unquestionably Scandinavian. While Wisconsin had a Cambria, her largest city still bears an Indian name. "Kohler of Kohler" (the German-American bathtub king) had to create and incorporate a company town to get out from under the wing of nearby Sheboygan, named after another forgotten Indian worthy; neither Anheuser nor Busch—nor even Jefferson—has been able to push a saintly king of France off his pedestal down at St. Louis; Pittsburgh, the birthplace of Czechoslovakia,[2]

2. The Pittsburgh Proclamation of 1918 is recognized as Czechoslovakia's "Declaration of Independence."

despite this association and the very large number of Bohemians, Slovaks, and Ruthenians who settled there in the age of steel, is still named after an English eighteenth-century statesman who never crossed the Atlantic; New York, the world's largest Jewish community, still bears the name of a seventeenth-century British King who was certainly, among his other unpleasant traits, anti-Semitic.[3] The engaging habit of changing all the place names when you take over a region or a settlement has not yet spread from the Polish People's Republic and other European "succession states," or from the new nations of Africa and Asia to the United States, where "first come, longest preserved" seems to be the rule.

It is impossible to say what proportion of the post-1890 immigrants became and remained city dwellers in the United States. That this proportion was far higher than that of those who arrived before 1890, and particularly before 1860, only follows from the whole population trend of the United States into the cities. With the end of free or cheap land, with increasing farm mechanization —meaning fewer farm jobs even on larger acreages—with a larger demand for workers in steel mills, coal mines, automobile factories, and industry generally, the trend was an inevitable one. Only the most resolute, and the most fortunate, of the millions of European peasants who crowded into the United States after the 1880's managed to become farmers there; only a very small proportion were able to contemplate owning their farms someday—unless they were prepared to accept abandoned or marginal land that the native-born stock and earlier immigrants had scorned or given up. They had to acquire some skill or craft by hard work and unusual enterprise or go into the towns as ordinary unskilled workers. This was in most cases neither their fault nor their inclination. It was the terms on which American society in the machine age was prepared to absorb them.

Thus an ingrowing urban frontier had replaced an ever ad-

---

3. James Stuart, duke of York, afterwards James II. New York also, in 1900, near the peak of the Great Immigration, had two and a half times the number of Jews as Warsaw, nearly as many Germans as Hamburg, twice as many Irishmen as Dublin, and half as many Italians as Naples, Bohemians as Prague, and Swedes as Stockholm. "New York excels Babel," wrote Commons in 1907 (*Races and Immigrants*, p. 165), with "sixty-six languages spoken, forty-nine newspapers published in foreign languages, and one school . . . with children of twenty-nine nationalities." The Negroes, the Mexicans, and the Puerto Ricans had not yet arrived in any numbers.

vancing rural frontier before the turn of the century. No more
Oklahomas existed, and reclamation on a large scale was in its
infancy. Between 1900 and 1914 the big cities grew great and
many small cities grew big. All of them, by the outbreak of the first
world war, had a polyglot population, often concentrated in "Little Italys," "Little Polands," Lithuanian belts, Greek quarters,
Jewish ghettos, and the like. This would have astounded Benjamin
Franklin—who resented even a few thousand "Palatine Boors" in
Pennsylvania—or Jefferson—who envisaged the population of the
United States doubling itself every twenty-six years without
the aid of immigration—for in 1790 only three per cent of the
population of the United States lived in cities, whereas by 1900
more than 33 per cent lived in places of 8,000 inhabitants and
more, and was soon to rise to over 50 per cent.[4] In 1900, two
fifths of the foreign-born population lived in cities of 100,000
inhabitants or more, while the average for the entire population
was only one fifth.[5] This great transformation in a hundred years
completely changed the face of America. It now had an urban
civilization, in which the "American farmer" of Crèvecoeur and
Dickenson was rapidly becoming a minor figure, and in the big
cities every other person was now an immigrant or the son or
daughter of an immigrant. It was the opportunities for jobs in the
cities, not the availability of free or cheap land, which now dominated the relative rate of growth of the different states and sections.
The frontier in the Jeffersonian or Turnerian sense had indeed
gone.

Immigration as a stimulus to phenomenal urban growth in the
United States was not to be a continuing phenomenon. By 1930 the
"Great Immigration" was over, and the increase in the percentage
of urban population in the United States between 1930 and 1940
was only three tenths of one per cent.[6] As one expert[7] sums it up:

Immigration has largely ceased, except for a relatively few refugees
and some displaced persons, who are being afforded a haven in

4. Taking the U. S. census criterion of places with 2,500 or more inhabitants
being classed as "urban," the urban percentage of the population rose from 5.1 in
1790 to 58.7 in 1950. By this computation the urban percentage in 1900 was 39.7.

5. Commons, pp. 160–1.

6. By contrast it was 5 per cent between 1920 and 1930, 5.5 per cent between
1910 and 1920, and 6 per cent between 1900 and 1910.

7. W. C. Hallenbeck: *American Urban Communities* (New York, 1951),
pp. 64–5.

America; so the immediate past and probabilities in the future make this source practically insignificant. There have been some periods in the past, however, when this source has been a large factor. The twentieth century immigration tended to settle disproportionately in the cities. The first decade was an all-time peak of immigration to the United States—in four of these years the number exceeded one million. The total for ten years was a little over 8,750,000, the equivalent of more than half the total increase of population during that decade and three quarters as much as the increase in urban population. From 1911 to 1920, with only two years over one million and a big decrease with the coming of World War I, the total dropped to just under 5,750,000 but still represented 42 per cent of total population growth and 47 per cent of urban increase. In the decade 1921–30 the total was a little more than 4,000,000 and the percentages 24 and 28 respectively. In the 1931–1940 decade there were just over half a million immigrants, which represented 6 per cent of the total population increase, and a little less than 10 per cent of the urban population growth. Since 1940 even smaller numbers have entered America.

Again, were this a history of American Immigration rather than of the American West (and principally of the trans-Mississippi West, at that), much further attention would need to be paid to this change in the rural-urban balance of population and to the opening up of "new frontiers" in the streets, suburbs, and metropolitan and "exurban" areas of cities. As it is, all we need to ask is to what extent this was a Western phenomenon rather than a national one. Up to the year 1930 it was not. The great immigration flooded into the Eastern cities because it reached them first, and then favored the more easily accessible of the Midwestern ones to those across the wide Missouri and in the Far West. Direct immigration by sea into California and the Pacific Northwest was no longer a common practice after the 1860's, when the transcontinental railroad was opened. Even as inveterate a seafarer as Robert Louis Stevenson went "across the plains"[8] in an immigrant train to California in the year 1879. Between 1910 and 1930 the cities growing fastest in the United States were scattered all over the country, but in 1930–40 they were nearly all in three states—California, Texas, and Florida—two of which are in the West. This tendency con-

8. R. L. Stevenson: *Across The Plains* (New York and London, 1893).

tinued during the 1940's, when half of the cities in the country increasing in size by 50 per cent or more were in these same three states. Florida's growth was of course a special phenomenon connected with the real-estate booms there, the increasing popularity of the state for purposes of retirement, and the expansion of winter-resort facilities there, with the increase in the American's leisure time and the vogue for "two holidays a year." The wartime decade of the 1940's was atypical in many ways, but it sent vast numbers of people into certain far western cities from other parts of the United States to work in industries such as aircraft manufacturing and shipbuilding. The San Francisco–Oakland area gained a phenomenal 39 per cent in population between 1940 and 1947, the Los Angeles metropolitan area increased by 35 per cent, Seattle by 33 per cent and Portland by 31 per cent.[9] At the end of the war, this urban increase in population continued, in the California cities especially; by the middle fifties, 70 per cent of the immigrants from outside California settled in the southern part of the state, and between 1950 and 1960 the state's population as a whole increased by 48.5 per cent to 15,717,204, and was estimated as probably reaching over 25,000,000 by 1975. The metropolitan area of Los Angeles alone is expected to contain fully 11 million people in that year. In 1890 Los Angeles had barely 50,000 inhabitants; in 1950, just on 2 million; and, during the next three years alone,[1] an increase of 6.8 per cent, or 134,305, of whom nearly a quarter were Negroes. It was said at this time that an average of over 600 persons *a day* were arriving by train at the Union Station in Los Angeles from other states with the intention of taking up permanent residence in Southern California (This is larger than the whole population of the pueblo of Los Angeles in 1846, when American rule commenced.) Vast areas of farm land and even of citrus groves disappeared in Los Angeles and the adjoining counties during the 1950's and 1960's under the subdivider's hand, and enormous stretches of "tract" housing appeared on the old Spanish and Mexican ranchos. To get these people to and from their work and to and

9. U. S. Bureau of the Census: *Current Population Reports*, Series P-21, No. 35 (Washington, D. C., 1947), passim. These West Coast cities were only matched by Washington, D. C., with 33 per cent and San Antonio, Texas, with 31 per cent, due mainly to increase in civil service personnel and armed forces establishments respectively.

1. Up to the special census of September 23, 1953. See, also, W. S. Thompson: *Changes in California's Population* (Los Angeles, 1955).

from the nearby beaches and mountains a colossal network of superhighways, or "freeways," had to be built.[2] One completely sober prophet[3] had discerned in his crystal ball that "one day a solid city will stretch northward from San Diego to Los Angeles, then to Santa Barbara and perhaps even to San Luis Obispo. Its east-west line will probably run from the Sierra Madre Mountains to the ocean. In northern California a second decentralized, sprawling urban complex is being formed. This may become a continuous metropolis around San Francisco Bay—with offshoots into the valleys northward, southward and inland from the bay." The population of the San Francisco Bay area in 1950 was two and one quarter millions, and it was confidently expected to be five and a half millions by 1975.

In case it should be thought that the foreign-born have continued to cling to the eastern and mid-western states and cities since 1930, leaving the subsequent great domestic migration entirely to the native-born, it should be noted that in 1950 California had nearly one million foreign-born citizens,[4] second only to New York (with two and a half million),[5] while the state of Washington had 191,000 and Oregon 83,000. Colorado had 58,000 and Montana 43,000; Texas had 276,000—of whom 196,000 came from Mexico. Of the European-born immigrants, more Danes and Swiss were living in California than in any other state in 1950, more Belgians, Dutch, and Finns in Michigan, more Lithuanians and Swedes in Illinois, more Norwegians in Minnesota, more Czechs in Pennsylvania, more Yugoslavs in Ohio, and more Portuguese in Massachusetts. New York State had the largest numbers of the remaining European-born groups. Thus although the foreign-born Europeans have continued to participate in the twentieth-century movement into the Far West, the native-born have dominated it, just as they

---

2. The California freeways really are "free," and no tolls are payable on public highways (though there are many bridge tolls) because by state law the entire revenue of the state's gasoline tax has to be devoted to highway improvement. This tax amounts to seven cents a gallon, and California has over nine million automobiles currently in use.

3. Andrew F. Rolle: *California: A History* (New York, 1963; rev. ed. 1964), p. 1612.

4. 104,000 from Great Britain, 104,000 from Italy, 70,000 from Germany, and 28,000 from the Republic of Ireland; though 110,000 came from Canada and no fewer than 162,000 from Mexico.

5. Illinois came third with 783,000.

dominated the nineteenth-century migrations westward across the United States.

In the early and middle thirties there was a new rural migration westward out of the "dust-bowl" states of the plains.[6] This stream of destitute or near-destitute farming families—so vividly described by John Steinbeck in his *Grapes of Wrath*[7]—sought to resettle mainly in California, where they were most unwelcome, and many of them ended up there living in shanty-towns, as migrant workers, with little hope of ever becoming landowners or tenant farmers or even sharecroppers again. The huge demand for labor in California during the war emergency years from 1939 onward absorbed most of these people into other than farming occupations and solved for California's relief and employment agencies a problem which might otherwise have continued to exist for a generation. The "Arkies" and "Okies" continued to migrate westward through the 1940's, but by this time they were no longer unwelcome; nor were the Negroes from the Old South,[8] who were beginning to rival them in numbers.

The industrialization of the Far West, and of California in particular, during the twentieth century has made further large-scale westward migration across the United States possible, and continued to encourage it. This is a story in itself, of which only the principal landmarks can be noticed. Before the end of the nineteenth century the mining boom had long since been succeeded by the farming and lumbering boom in the Rocky Mountain and Pacific Coast states. The canning and food-processing industries arose naturally out of the former. Citrus fruit growing in Southern California, in particular, was put on an industrial basis, and the famous SunKist trademark and guarantee of quality established. The motion-picture industry was another one that, though

6. See map pp. 390–1 for the approximate location of the "dust bowl," and, also, P. Lauber: *The Dust Bowl* (New York, 1958).

7. New York, 1936.

8. The states which declined in population between 1930 and 1940 were Kansas, Nebraska, Oklahoma, and North and South Dakota. In the 1940's Arkansas also had a net loss in population, and so did Mississippi. North Dakota and Oklahoma continued to decline, but there was a slight net increase in Kansas, Nebraska, and South Dakota. All other states increased in population during both decades, except for little Vermont, which remained static during the thirties. During these two decades California increased in population from 5,677,000 to 10,586,000. There were nearly half a million Negroes in California by 1950.

born in the East, had firmly established its center in Southern California, with all its climatic advantages, by the beginning of the twenties. A cultural exodus from the New York stage and literary scene was to follow; it included all three of the famous Barrymores,

An early Oklahoma oil well. Note wooden derrick and steam engine.

writers of the caliber of F. Scott Fitzgerald, and producers, musicians, and stage designers without number. Europe sent such "names" as Lang, Lubitsch, Garbo, Hitchcock, Dietrich, and Laughton. Improvised studios on vacant lots out among the oil rigs

near Santa Monica, or up Cahuenga Pass, suddenly blossomed into
"cities"—such as Culver City and Universal City—and became big
business. The new movie tycoons came from the ends of the earth
—Louis B. Mayer from Minsk, Russia (by way of New Brunswick, Canada), Carl Laemmle from Laupheim, Germany (by way
of Oshkosh, Wisconsin), and Sam Goldwyn (né Goldfisch) from
Warsaw, Poland. But Jesse L. Lasky (by the way of exception)

The resources of Wyoming: cattle and oil.

was a native son, born in San Francisco, who had been in the
Alaska gold rush and in show business in Hawaii before taking up
an option on the foot of the rainbow.

Oil was another new industry of the West, for not only was it
found there, but its refining required a complicated industrial process before it could pass into the thirsty tanks of America's automobiles and trucks, which increased in numbers from 8,000 in 1900 to
10 million in 1921, to nearly 20 million by 1925, and to over 40

million by 1948.[9] Oil was found in Pennsylvania in the 1850's, in Kansas as early as 1860, and in Texas in 1866 (though the first boom there was not until the eighties); and the famous Spindletop gusher, at Beaumont on the Gulf Coast, did not come in until 1901. The enormous East Texas oil field became a big producer only in the 1920's, and the West Texas field beyond the Pecos later still. Wyoming and Montana oil-field exploitation dates from 1908. California oil was also late on the scene but soon made up for that. Santa Maria and Coalinga were early developments around 1910, and then came Long Beach and the forest of derricks on Signal Hill, one of the greatest oil fields in the world. Offshore oil discoveries have latterly become important along the California coast (as along those of Texas and Louisiana), and when the Eisenhower government handed over offshore oil to the separate states in the 1950's, its exploitation was stimulated, though much revenue was lost to the federal government. Oil was also found in many inland areas of California, the Bakersfield region proving one of the richest. In Oklahoma, oil was discovered in the 1890's, and by 1907, the year of statehood, she produced over 43½ million barrels of crude. Gushers on the Osage Indian reservation made rich men of some of the hitherto indigent braves, and they squandered their new-found wealth right royally.[1] Arkansas also saw important oil discoveries, and more was found in Kansas.

Every one of the major oil fields opened up in the twentieth century was in the trans-Mississippi West, half of them beyond the hundredth meridian. Texas and California became, and have remained, the greatest producers. The opening of each new oil field tended to produce "frontier conditions" once again, with lawlessness, honky-tonks, wide-open towns, and hangers-on of every kind, in addition to the solid oil engineers and the wide-eyed oil lessors, some of whom found oil rigs in their back yards and among their flower beds and had to learn to live with a sickly smell than which only the smell of the lessee's money was stronger. Texas benefited even more than California from the oil boom. Houston, a city and inland port of 44,000 inhabitants in 1900, had reached

9. In 1963 there were over 82 million of them; nine million in California alone; over three million of these were registered in Los Angeles County! *Automobile Facts and Figures*, 1964 edn. (Detroit, 1964), pp. 18–19.

1. A modern counterpart to the "squaw man" of the fur trapping era now appeared, in the shape of *Anglo* women, some of them from Eastern cities, who married these oil-rich Indians.

nearly 600,000 by 1950 and was pushing one million by 1965. Dallas grew with almost equal rapidity from 42,000 in 1900 to 434,000 in 1950; she and her twin and rival city, Fort Worth, together now come above the million mark. San Antonio, without benefit of a nearby oil field, grew more slowly until 1940, but then jumped up by 50 per cent in one decade to 408,000, and, with defense establishments all around and a splendid climate for the oil-rich to retire to or recuperate in, is now well over the half-million. Rural Texas[2] did not increase in population so spectacularly as her well-oiled cities in the twentieth century, for, with twice California's population in 1900, she had only three-quarters as many people as the Golden State in 1950.

Oil continued to be of great importance, but new sources of industrial energy and employment arose to challenge it, and once again it was mainly in the West that these were developed. The great atomic plants started up during the second world war had to be near to abundant water and hydroelectric power. The Columbia River Valley was one of the greatest available sources of both. The atomic proving-grounds needed to be in uninhabited areas, and the deserts of the West provided these. Defense projects like Hanford in Washington and Los Alamos in New Mexico had to be created out of nothing, and the thousands of scientists, technicians, craftsmen, and others needed to create new communities out of the wilderness were drawn to them from all parts of the United States and also from abroad. Once again new frontiers were opened up, but with this difference: these were orderly, balanced societies, unlike the old unruly, unsophisticated frontiers of the past; but in the early days of Hanford, Los Alamos, and the like, the excitement of living on a frontier certainly existed, even if some of its traditional discomforts were never experienced. The Coca-Cola bottling plant was usually in production before the reactor, the supermarket opened up before the saloon, and the school marm arrived even before the stripper.

The atomic frontier also created the need for new raw materials, such as uranium ores, which caused some of the remotest wildernesses of the United States to be re-explored, re-prospected, and sometimes even settled. Such new developments occurred in parts of southeastern Utah where only hunters and Indians had

2. But she produced two presidents: Dwight D. Eisenhower, born in Denison in 1890 and Lyndon B. Johnson, born in Johnson City in 1908.

penetrated before, and on the Navajo Reservation of northern Arizona. The Navajo, from being one of the poorest of the tribes of the Southwest, subsisting miserably from their herds of sheep and from sporadic craftsmanship in silver, pottery, and rug-making for the tourist trade, suddenly found themselves, when they leased their uranium-bearing soil, one of the richest. The Tribal Council, profiting from the knowledge of how the Osage had squandered their oil-lease money, had used these funds for social services and education, and to start up profitable community enterprises. The

Buffalo Bill brings it in—Colonel William F. Cody (fourth from right) and friends at oil strike near Cody, Wyoming, 1909. Governor George T. Beck is third from left.

high school and the hospital at Window Rock, the tribal capital, have become showplaces, and the tourist may stay at a Navajo-owned and -run luxury motel there. Since Kit Carson "pacified" the Navajo and corralled them on their desolated and barren reservation just a century ago, the wheel has truly come full circle; well-armed Navajo mobile police now keep overinquisitive *Anglos* off restricted areas of their reservation! New frontiers can open up for the first Americans as well as for the newest ones, even in the second half of the twentieth century.

From Columbus to the launching pads of Cape Kennedy and Jet Propulsion Laboratories of Pasadena, from Coronado to the proving grounds of Los Alamos and the slaughterhouses of Wichita, from Jedediah Smith to that air-conditioned nightmare which is Las Vegas, from Marcus Whitman to the Grand Coulee Dam, from the cliff houses of Mesa Verde to the City of the Saints, from Cabeza de Vaca to Lyndon Baines Johnson, from Drake to Disney, is a long haul, but all are part of the never ending story that is the history of the American West. "What the Mediterranean Sea was to the Greeks, breaking the bond of custom, offering new experiences, calling out new institutions and activities, that, and more, the ever-retreating frontier has been to the United States directly and to the nations of Europe more remotely."[3]

3. Turner: *Frontier in American History* (1962 edn.), p. 38.

Other Peoples' Far Wests

THE HISTORY OF THE AMERICAN WEST HAS A NUMBER OF unique features; others it shares with formerly unexplored and undeveloped parts of the world in which similar conditions existed—in South America, Australia, Siberia, and Africa in modern times; in eastern and southeastern Europe in medieval times; in the Mediterranean basin and in northern and northwestern Europe in ancient times. The great Chinese Empire, growing eventually to eighteen provinces and spilling over even from these into areas such as Manchuria and Mongolia, Turkestan and Tibet, must have seen, during its long period of expansion, the creation of many sets of "frontier conditions" resembling phases in the history of the American West. Some of these were described, with wide-eyed wonder, by the European traveler Marco Polo in the thirteenth century A.D. The western world still awaits a full exposition of Chinese history in terms of this great expansion, relatively too much attention having been paid to the process of contraction and decay of the last century and a half. More has been published in the West on the peopling of Australia and Siberia. Here perhaps (pending the twentieth-century filling-in of the vast undeveloped plains and rain forests of Brazil) the closest parallels to the conditions of the American West may be said to have existed: vast empty lands, large areas of them within the temperate zones, inhabited by only a scattering of nomads, apart from a few sedentary agricultural settlements in the richer river valleys, or colonies of fishermen around the coasts; great mineral wealth only belatedly discovered, and that mostly in the more inaccessible regions; poor or nonexistent communications; and remoteness from the existing centers of world population. Both the Americas and Australia required long sea voyages before they could be reached; Siberia, though approachable by land (over high mountain chains, from Europe and Southern Asia), was almost equally inaccessible. Neither the Americas nor Siberia could expect to be heavily populated until railroads had traversed them, and this happened only toward the end of the nineteenth century. In the year 1800 the United States had as few as 5 million inhabitants, and Siberia under a million. Today the United States has nearly 200 million; Siberia over 40 million; Brazil over 80 million, Australia (saddled with a virtually uninhabitable central desert) 11 million. Aircraft have helped to annihilate distances in these great countries for administrators, tourists, and—to a certain extent —settlers and ordinary citizens, but bulky produce and machinery still has to be transported by land. Air-conditioning may have made desert living bearable, but it cannot render it attractive for large populations until science has made whole communities air-conditioned, both outdoors and in.

Africa and Central America tend to fall outside the patterns of frontier development in the larger countries of North and South America and in Siberia and Australia. Both of these areas possessed in places large indigenous populations before the white man came, and in a few regions a high (though very different) cultural standard had been reached. The Ashanti kings in no way considered themselves inferior to the Portuguese; nor did the Aztecs and the Incas to the Spaniards. An area containing an indigenous population far larger than the number of white settlers presents problems that are quite different from those existing in most parts of North America or in Australia. In Siberia the numbers of immigrants from European Russia have grown[1] since the late nineteenth century greatly to outnumber the indigenous population, except in a few areas; in South Africa this has not been the case, and the "Great Trek" of the Boers, now over a century ago, remains their one striking parallel with the frontier experiences of North and South America and of Australia. In all of these other areas the settlers, very early, came to outnumber the indigenes.

1. See D. Treadgold: *The Great Siberian Migration* (Princeton, 1957), passim.

It would require a further volume to make a proper comparison of these different "Westward" movements and of the frontier experiences that accompanied them; the literature of the subject, although still patchy, is already extensive.[2] For similar reasons, the "frontier experiences" of the ancient world cannot here be brought into detailed comparison with the history of the American West, illuminating as that might be.[3]

No attempt has been made in this book to separate frontier experiences of Canadian history from that of the United States, for they are inseparable. The 49th parallel, from the Lake of the Woods to Puget Sound, though politically and psychologically of great significance, has no physical, climatic, zoological, or anthropological existence. The Indian and the buffalo did not recognize that border; neither did the corn plant or the salmon, the elk, the moose, or the bear. The scenery is similar as you journey up from the Great Falls to Calgary, or from Bellingham to Vancouver, and this is also true further east, between Bismarck and Regina, Duluth and Port Arthur, Detroit and Windsor, Buffalo and Hamilton, Montpelier and Montreal. Glacier and Waterton, split by the border, constitute one great mountain National Park area.

But, although they are inseparable, they have, paradoxically, tended to grow apart as time has gone on. In the age of exploration and in the Mountain Man era they cannot be disentangled: Mackenzie and Ogden have been given equal billing in this book with Lewis and Clark and Jedediah Smith. While the condominium lasted there, the Oregon Country was both No Man's Land and Everyman's. Smith was up at Fort Vancouver, and Ogden down on the Colorado and the San Joaquin. Dr. McLoughlin succored Americans (even when he suspected their motives) on the Columbia, and the Hudson's Bay Company opened up a trading post on San Francisco Bay. The Reverend Samuel Parker (a Yankee Methodist) was far better received by the Roman Catholic Canadian Dr. McLoughlin than was the Reverend Herbert Beaver (a British Anglican); Thomas Oliver Larkin loathed his fellow Yankee, Hall Jackson Kelley, and gave him short shrift at Monterey in 1834, but he did all he could for his trading rival, the unfortunate John

2. See Bibliographic Note.

3. This is being attempted in *The Frontiers of Rome and America* by Donald R. Dudley (a professor of classics) and myself, to be published as a Mentor Book by the New American Library.

McRae, representative of the Hudson's Bay Company at Yerba Buena and McLoughlin's son-in-law. McLoughlin and George Simpson were also, themselves, well received at Yerba Buena and Monterey when they visited the California coast in 1841. Camaraderie on those remote frontiers seemed not only to go with, but also to extend far beyond, joint occupancy.

After 1846, lines were drawn more tightly, and the new Canadian colony of British Columbia blossomed (in and after the Fraser River gold rush of 1858) into a bulwark and outpost of Canadian nationalism in the Far West. The organization of the Oregon and Washington territories, and Oregon's statehood, served to crystallize American sentiment on the other side of the border. The Canadian federal Act of 1867 made it clear that the northern nation would not fall like a ripe pear before a new onward march of Manifest Destiny. Indian troubles in the border regions in the sixties and seventies, especially after the Canadian opening up of the Red River Valley area and the American penetration of the Sioux hunting-grounds in the Black Hills, found the two countries pursuing rather different policies toward the tribes that bestrode or tried to cross the 49th parallel. The Great White Queen in London appeared more tolerant at times toward the cause of the red man than did the Great White Father in Washington. Both Sitting Bull and Chief Joseph sought refuge in Canada. The Mounties sometimes fed and protected the very same Indians that the Seventh U. S. Cavalry had hoped to starve and exterminate. No events quite so ugly as the Chivington Massacre or Wounded Knee occurred north of the border,[4] but on the Indian side there was nothing comparable there to the Whitman or Fetterman massacres, no Lava Beds affair, no crushing and embittering defeat of the white man comparable to Little Big Horn.

Canada's Indian policy may be said to have learned, from some of the mistakes made by the Americans. On the whole, it was more humane and more even-handed; no jurisdictional conflict comparable to that between the Department of the Interior and the Department of the Army of the United States bedeviled Indian relations in Ottawa or in the provincial capitals. The Indians were exploited and had their lands taken away from them on the Canadian side, all right, but rather less crudely. As a result, perhaps,

---

4. But there was the savage repression of the half-breeds' rebellions in the Red River Valley in Canada and the execution of their leaders.

Canada's Indians produced no last-ditchers like Chief Joseph and Geronimo.

Canada's mining frontiers were also less lawless than those of the United States. The system of licensing on the Fraser River, though greatly resented by the miners, made the rush there more orderly—and also more directly profitable to the government. When the great rush into the Yukon came at the end of the century, the Canadians could profit from the lessons learned on many more American mining frontiers, as well as on several of their own, and the Mounties were there almost from the beginning. The rush over the high pass to Dawson City was not exactly a Sunday School outing, but it was more orderly and safer for all concerned than the early days in, say, western Nevada, Colorado, Montana, and South Dakota. It was also far less picturesque.

Canadian and American frontier experience, then, was linked at the 49th parallel, but not inflexibly so. A. L. Burt has convincingly and wittily applied the Turner touchstone to Canada: "If Turner had looked at Canada,"[5] he would have found, even in colonial New France "a surprising confirmation of the thesis he was propounding"—that frontier conditions produce and nurture democracy.[6] "If Turner had looked North," Burt continued,[7] "he could not have failed to see that the frontier movement crossed and

---

5. A. L. Burt: "If Turner had Looked at Canada, Australia, and New Zealand when he Wrote about the West" in *The Frontier in Perspective*, ed. Wyman and Kroeber (Madison, Wisc., 1957), pp. 59–77. This illuminating little essay is one of the best in an excellent collection, based upon lectures delivered in the summer session of 1954 at the University of Wisconsin in honor of the memory of Lyman Copeland Draper, father of the State Historical Society, who, coming there as unpaid corresponding secretary in 1854, parlayed a collection of fifty books into the magnificent library it had become by the time of his death in 1891, since when it has become far more magnificent. It was Draper who provided men like Turner with the tools of their trade, ready to hand. See further W. B. Hesseltine: *Pioneer's Mission* (Madison, 1954), a biography of Draper.

6. Burt takes to task B. J. Wright for the superficiality of his remarks on New France in "American Democracy and the Frontier," *Yale Review*, XX (1931), 350, one of the earliest and least effective attacks upon Turner and his school. Different conditions in the New World made it impossible to transplant French feudalism to Canada and also impossible for the Roman Catholic Church to collect tithes there, except to a token extent. *Lods et ventes, banalités* and all the other burdens imposed upon the peasant in France were shrugged off by the *habitant*, who always had the safety valve of becoming even freer as a *coureur des bois*. The *habitant*, according to the Jesuit writer Charlevoix, "breathed from his birth the air of liberty."

7. Ibid., p. 68.

recrossed the international border." Before the Revolution, New
Englanders had for two decades been migrating into Nova Scotia;
after Independence, this migration was resumed, but now it consisted of refugees—the dispossessed Loyalists. A smaller number of
United Empire Loyalists founded Upper Canada, further west.
"The Upper Canada Loyalists put the American frontier north
into British territory," where there were no Indian troubles, the
land was fertile, and 200 acres were to be had free (or almost free)
for the asking. This exodus went on until the outbreak of the War
of 1812. After the war, Upper Canada's population came to be
reinforced by a new immigration from the Old Country, and there
too Disraeli's "two nations" fought it out until a more democratic
governmental system and a broader franchise was achieved by the
reforms of the forties.

Meanwhile, westward advance north of the border had been
checked by the barren "Laurentian Shield" of virtually unusable
pre-Cambrian rock-strewn soil, and back the frontier of settlement
went across the border into the United States. Canada suffered a
severe drain on her still meager population (amounting to about
one third of its total) during the middle years of the nineteenth
century in the direction of the free—or believed-to-be free—lands
of the new midwestern and Prairie territories of the United States.
Gold discoveries in the extreme west of Canada in 1858, and the
stimulus to national development by the formation of the Do-
minion out of a group of separate colonies in 1867, began the
reversal of this southward tide (which the California gold rush had
of course only served to stimulate), but not until it was prematurely noised abroad in the nineties that "free land" was no longer
available in the United States did Canada's own prairie provinces
beyond the infertile Laurentian Shield begin to fill up. The building of railroads across that barrier had to precede this development.
The first transcontinental line, the Canadian Pacific, (after innumerable political and financial hitches) was completed in 1885, but the
Canadian Trunk, which was the second, not until 1911. Canada's
total population was still only 4,300,000 (barely more than that of
the U. S. A. in 1790) in 1881, and had increased by only one million
in 1901. Spectacular increases had to wait until the twentieth century. By 1911 it was over 7 million (twice the 1871 figure), and by
1931 over 10 million. Immigration had been very small (compared

with that into the United States) before the turn of the century, having reached only 21,716 in the year 1897; but by 1904 it was 146,000 in that one year, and in 1912 it was over 400,000, a figure that still stands as the record influx for any single year. Only 2,000 people emigrated from the United States to Canada in 1897, compared with over 43,000 in 1904 and nearly 140,000 in 1912. This last total represented almost as many people as reached Canada from the United Kingdom that year (150,000) and more than the 112,000 who came from all other countries combined. Over 860,-000 people emigrated from the United States to Canada in the ten years 1904–1913 inclusive. Canada's frontier certainly had not "gone," for a good proportion of these went to her western provinces, and two new ones, Saskatchewan and Alberta, were created in 1905. Immigration failed to recover to its pre-war size after 1918, despite the fact that restrictions similar to those obtaining in the United States were not imposed by Canada. The highest post-war figure was 167,000 in 1929, but by 1932 it was down to 25,000, and by 1937 to 15,000. By then Canada, also, had temporarily ceased to be a "land of opportunity" and, like the United States, was re-exporting to Europe more people than she received each year. Not until 1931 did she have a larger urban than rural population, and even in 1941 only eight of her cities contained more than a hundred thousand inhabitants each. She was still predominantly a farming country—and a producer of basic raw materials, such as wood pulp—rather than a manufacturing one, even by the middle of the twentieth century. This made her very different from the United States. Her untapped mineral resources still remained enormous, though by 1945 she was already the world's greatest producer of nickel, radium, platinum, and asbestos, and its second greatest of gold, aluminum, uranium, molybdenum, and wood pulp. As each new mining area was opened up, frontier conditions continued to break out all over Canada, and they will continue to do so. The Great Bear Lake area, just below the Arctic Circle, in the Northwest Territories, has been a true "frontier" in the classic tradition during the last thirty years since large deposits of pitchblende were found there in 1936. The vastly increased strategic importance of uranium since that date has made these deposits of primary importance in a new nuclear age.

When Frederick Paxson claimed in 1930 that "the West is

gone,"[8] "he wore a blinker on his north eye," says Burt,[9] and failed
to notice that it was still in full flower in Canada, especially in the
"Whoop-up Country," about which Paul Sharp has written[1] so
vividly. Since then the Great Bear Lake mines have opened up, and
enormous hydroelectric projects, like the Kootenay in British Columbia, have been initiated. In 1958 Vancouver celebrated its centennial with every manifestation of "Western" enthusiasm, even if
Victoria (a few years older) may have rattled its teacups in mild
disapproval. In the Canadian far North the climate, the remoteness,
the sparse population, and the barrenness of the soil have retarded
development, but surely the fuller exploitation of this great area
will open up yet another set of frontiers. The building of the Alcan
Highway as a war measure in the 1940's, and the coming of the air
age, have brought this nearer to realization.

Alaska, purchased from imperial Russia in 1867, was to remain
in its frontier stage for a hundred years—but as a frontier with a
difference. Characterized at first as "Seward's Folly," this new and
huge territory of the United States remained in the doldrums until
near the end of the nineteenth century. American influence had to
come by sea, for Alaska possessed neither highway nor railroad
links with the rest of the Union.

The first ten years (1867–77) constituted a period of military
occupation; the second ten years (1877–87) saw the beginnings of
economic prosperity with the foundation of the fish canning and
tourist industries. "By the century's closing decade the Far North
frontier displayed not only a modicum of internal vigor, but its
society boasted a reassuring amount of law, order and public civil-
ity." But the world did not really become aware of Alaska until
the Klondike rush across the Territory occurred in 1897.

In 1882 Ed. Schieffelin, discoverer of the "Lucky Cuss" mine
at Tombstone, Arizona, in 1879, brought prospectors for gold up
the Yukon River by steamboat; but this time his luck was out.
Miners continued to go to the Yukon across Alaska each summer
until 1893, when about two hundred of them actually wintered
there. By 1895 about fifteen hundred men were working at placers

8. *When the West is Gone* (New York, 1930).

9. Op. cit., p. 72.

1. Paul Sharp: *The Agrarian Revolt in Western Canada* (Minneapolis,
1948); "When our West Moved North," *American History Review*, LV (1950);
and *Whoop-up Country* (New York, 1955).

along the Yukon valley. By May 1896 over two thousand of these latter-day Argonauts had arrived, though only one man in twenty found any gold. Then Rabbit Creek was discovered (by a Californian miner, George Washington Carmack) to be rich in gold, and was renamed "Bonanza." Thus began the Klondike gold rush; and Alaska, as the only way into the new Eldorado, appeared to be made. A railroad was projected—to connect up with Siberia across the Bering Strait, no less—by her energetic boosters as the stampede to Dawson began. Tens of thousands of Canadians and Americans, and thousands of foreigners, poured in. Alaska boomed and her hitherto anaemic settlements of Juneau and Sitka at last became firmly established. The Klondike gold rush was to peter out, but Alaska was now indubitably "on the map," though she still had to wait another sixty years for statehood.[2]

2. Alaska, a state of the Union at last, is, on the American side of the border, the true "new frontier" of the 1960's. It should be remembered that the last American frontier of the nineteenth century was also a shared experience with Canada. In the Yukon gold rush of 1897–99, Skagway in Alaska was the chief supply point for the mines around Dawson City, 570 miles inland. As a last frontier Skagway had everything: "Dodge and Deadwood had nothing on Skagway in its first two years. Before the summer of 1898 was gone some 70 saloons were in business despite territorial prohibition," writes William Bronson in a vividly illustrated short article, "Rush to the Yukon," *American West*, II:2 (Spring 1965), 66–80. The great Smith family once again distinguished itself on this last and furthest frontier. Says Mr. Bronson (ibid. p. 71): "Jefferson Randolph Smith, better known as Soapy Smith, was a Georgia-born, Leadville-Denver trained bunco man who ran Skagway from late summer 1897 until he was shot and killed by a vigilante on July 8, 1898." Gold once again had got its man! Its lure was even too strong for the morale of some of the Canadian Mounties at Fort Cudahy, who left their post to join the rush.

BIBLIOGRAPHIC

NOTE

THIS IS IN NO SENSE TO BE REGARDED AS A COMPREHENSIVE bibliography. It does not include many of the specialist accounts and monographs referred to or cited in the footnotes to this book. It is intended as a guide to further reading on the subject matter of each succeeding chapter or section, and it is highly selective. Where the same field is covered in a number of different books, as is often the case with different aspects of the history of the American West, only one or two of such books are listed; others at least as good are omitted. For these a comprehensive scholarly bibliography of the history of the Westward Movement, such as that in Ray Allen Billington's *Westward Expansion,* 3rd edition (New York, 1966), should be used. His bibliography extends to over a hundred closely printed two-column pages, and includes articles as well as monographs, and books printing contemporary accounts and other source material. A number of regional or topical bibliographies also exist, which, in their more limited fields, are even more comprehensive than is Billington's. That very learned bibliographer Henry R. Wagner was responsible for a number of these, including *A Bibliography of Printed Works in Spanish relating to those parts of the United States which formerly belonged to Mexico* (Santiago de Chile, 1917; suppl., Berkeley, Calif., n.d.), *The Spanish Southwest: A Bibliography* (Berkeley, 1924; rev. edn., Albuquerque, N. M., 1937), and *The Plains and the Rockies, 1800–1865: A Contribution to the Bibliography of Original Narratives of Travel and Adventure* (San Francisco, 1921; rev. by C. L. Camp, San Francisco, 1937; 3rd edn., Columbus, Ohio, 1953). Most students will find Billington's "Bibliographical Note" more than adequate, and it possesses the great advantage of being thoroughly up-to-date. In smaller compass Nelson Close's *A Concise*

Study Guide to the American Frontier (Lincoln, Neb., 1964) lists over six hundred titles, topically arranged, in his "Bibliography of Frontier History." For periodicals O. O. Winther's *A Classified Bibliography of the Periodical Literature of the Trans-Mississippi West, 1811–1957* (Bloomington, Ind., 1961) is indispensable. This lists over nine thousand articles, no fewer than fifty-five hundred of them published since 1938.

The Pre-Columbian West

While *Handbook of American Indians North of Mexico*, ed. Frederick W. Hodge, 2 vols. (Washington, D. C., 1912), and Clark Wissler's *The American Indian* (New York, 1922) and *Indians of the United States* (New York, 1940) remain standard works, they have now been supplemented by more recent treatments. These include Harold E. Driver's *Indians of North America* (Chicago, 1961) and William Brandon's eloquent and lavishly illustrated *The American Heritage Book of Indians* (New York, 1961; text repr., New York, 1964). Helen M. Wormington's *Prehistoric Indians of North America* (4th printing, Denver, 1959) is a valuable short handbook by a leading authority in her field. George E. Hyde is equally authoritative on the Plains Indians in *The Indians of the High Plains* (Norman, Okla., 1959) and other works dealing with specific tribes, both in the pre-Columbian period and since. The terrain of the pre-Columbian West is discussed by Eugene W. Hollon in *The Great American Desert: Then and Now* (New York, 1966) as well as by Walter P. Webb in his older, classic treatment, *The Great Plains* (Boston, 1931). An even older work, Ellen C. Semple's *American History in its Geographic Conditions* (Boston, 1903, 1933) still has value. For the geographical background the standard work is Nevin M. Fenneman's *Physiography of Western United States* (New York, 1931), and an excellent recent textbook is J. Wreford Watson's *North America* (London, 1963); for historical geography, including facsimile reproductions of many early maps, both pre- and post-Columbian, see *The Atlas of the Historical Geography of the United States*, ed. C. O. Paullin and J. K. Wright (Washington, D. C., 1932). The introductory sections in Brandon's book and in the companion volume by David Lavender, *The American Heritage History of the Great West* (New York, 1965), deal with the pre-Columbian period, and both contain excellent simplified maps. By no means to be despised, even by adults, is *Indians of the Plains* by Eugene Rachlis in consultation with John C. Ewers (New York, 1960), in the American Heritage Junior Library. It, like the other volumes in the same series, is superbly illustrated.

Overland Exploration of North America (to 1800)

Two reasonably short and still valuable general surveys are John B. Brebner's *The Explorers of North America, 1492–1806* (New York and London, 1933; repr. 1955) and Herbert E. Bolton's *The Spanish Borderlands*, "Chronicles of America Series" (New Haven, 1921). Bolton's important paper on "The Mission as a Frontier Institution in the Spanish-American Colonies," in *American Historical Review*, XXIII (1917), has been reprinted together with fifteen other of his essays in *Bolton and the Spanish Borderlands*, ed John F. Bannon, S.J. (Norman, 1964). Bolton's *The Rim of Christendom* (Cleveland, 1936), on Father Kino and the Spanish colonization of Sonora and southern Arizona, and his short biography of Kino, *The Padre on Horseback* (San Francisco, 1932; repr. Chicago, 1963), as well as his *Coronado, Knight of Pueblos and Plains* (New York, 1950) are standard monographs. A popular and detailed account of the colonization of New Mexico—and of much besides—is Paul Horgan's *Great River*, 2 vols. (New York, 1954). Less "literary" in their approach are Eugene W. Hollon's *The Southwest: Old and New* (New York, 1961); Stephen Clissold's *The Seven Cities of Cibola* (London and New York, 1961), shorter and also very readable; and Warren A. Beck's *New Mexico: A History of Four Centuries* (Norman, Okla., 1962). For specific periods in the history of Spanish Texas there are Herbert E. Bolton's essay "The Spanish Occupation of Texas, 1519–1690," in *Southwestern Historical Quarterly*, XVI (1912), which has been reprinted in the book edited by Father Bannon; Henry Folmer's *Franco-Spanish Rivalry in North America, 1542–1763* (Glendale, Calif., 1953), which tells of Florida and the Mississippi River valley as well; and Odie B. Faulk's *The Last Years of Spanish Texas, 1778–1821* (The Hague, 1964). Robert S. Weddle's *The San Saba Mission: Spanish Pivot in Texas* (Austin, 1964) is a new specialist survey in the best Bolton tradition, which some scholars had thought (and a few had hoped) was dead.

Imperialism on the Pacific (to 1800)

There is a vast and growing literature on Spanish California. Henry R. Wagner's *Sir Francis Drake's Voyage around the World: Its Aims and Achievements* (San Francisco, 1926) is dogmatic but massively documented on the subject of Nova Albion. The earlier portions of Robert Glass Cleland's *From Wilderness to Empire* (New York, 1933; repr. 1959), a general history of California, contain one of the most readable accounts; and the inevitable Herbert E. Bolton's *Outpost of Empire* (New York, 1921) tells the story of the founding of the mission and presidio of San Francisco. A recent scholarly history of one of the most important of the Franciscan missions in Alta California is Maynard Geiger, O.F.M.: *Mission Santa Barbara* (Santa Barbara, 1965); an exhaustive treatment of the histories of all the missions is Zephyrin Engelhardt: *The Missions and Missionaries of California*, 4 vols. (San Francisco, 1908–15). The best biography of Father Serra is Maynard Geiger's *The Life and Times of Fray Junípero Serra, O.F.M.*, 2 vols. (Washington, D. C. 1959). The editions by Herbert E. Bolton of the various accounts and diaries of secular and missionary explorers in Spanish California are detailed above, page 424, and therefore need not be listed again in this bibliography; the results of some of these are summarized in Herbert I. Priestley's *Franciscan Explorations in California* (Glendale, Calif., 1947). Charles E. Chapman's *A History of California: The Spanish Period* (New York, 1921) is still one of the most useful and readable surveys available, but for further general histories of California, during as well as after that period, see also the bibliographic note "By Land and Sea to El Dorado" which follows. Foreign visits to Spanish California are narrated by George Vancouver in his *A Voyage of Discovery in the North Pacific Ocean*, Vol. II (London, 1798), by Jean François Gallup de la Pérouse in his *Voyage autour du Monde*, Vol. I (Paris, 1797; Eng. tr. London, 1798), in *The Rezanov Voyage to Nueva California in 1806*, ed. T. C. Russell (San Francisco, 1926) and in *Langsdorff's Narrative of the Rezanov Voyage*, ed. Russell (San Francisco, 1927), by Otto von Kotzebue in his *A Voyage of Discovery in the South Sea* (Eng. tr. from the Ger., London, 1821), and (with interesting illustrations by the author, who was Kotzebue's artist) by L. Choris, *Voyage pittoresque autour du monde* (Paris, 1822).

Exploring and Exploiting the Louisiana Purchase

Walter P. Webb's *The Great Plains* is again useful for background. Richard Van Alstyne's *The Rising American Empire* (Oxford and New York, 1960) presents an unorthodox and anti-nativist viewpoint and does not hesitate to call Thomas Jefferson an imperialist. For the centennial of the Louisiana Purchase the documentation was usefully collected in a government publication by Binder Hermann, *The Louisiana Purchase* (Washington, 1898), of which the documents and maps are more useful than the commentary. The Lewis and Clark expedition is put into its historical perspective by E. W. Gilbert: *Exploration of Western America, 1800–1850* (London, 1933), and this book also usefully summarizes other explorations of the period it covers. Lewis and Clark's own account of their expedition, written up by Nicholas Biddle and edited by P. Allen, was not printed until 1814; it was reprinted, and edited, by Elliott Coues as *The History of the Expedition of Lewis and Clark*, 4 vols. (New York, 1893), with notes and additional material and is now available in three paperbound vols. (New York, 1965). Lewis and Clark were, however, anticipated by their own Sergeant, Patrick Gass, whose *Journal* (for full title see above, p. 89) came out first in 1807 in Pittsburgh and in a French translation in Paris in 1809. It is quaint but not very reliable. The recent discovery of the actual field notes from which Clark wrote up his story is leading to a new series of publications, of which *The Field Notes of Captain William Clark, 1803–05*, ed. Ernest S. Osgood (New Haven, 1964), lavishly illustrated with facsimile documents, was the first. We can now look over the shoulders, as it were, of the two explorers as they wrote their day-by-day accounts. Most students not engaged in fundamental research will prefer to use one of the several excellent abridged versions of the Lewis and Clark journals, such as Bernard de Voto: *The Journals of Lewis and Clark* (Boston, 1953; London, 1954), or John Bakeless: *The Journals of Lewis and Clark* (New York, 1964), each in one volume. Both of these have excellent introductions and notes giving continuity to the journals. The best scholar's edition remains that of Reuben G. Thwaites: *The Original Journals of the Lewis and Clark Expedition . . . printed from the original manuscripts in the American Philosophical Society*, 8 vols. (New York, 1904–5), to which the texts of the journals of Floyd and Whitehouse and facsimiles of many of Clark's own maps are added; but for more recently discovered material now see Osgood's edition of the field notes and *The William Clark Papers: A Description of the Notes of Captain William Clark in the Papers of General John H. Hammond* (Charlottesville, Va., 1953). A useful joint biography of the two explorers is John Bakeless: *Lewis and Clark, Partners in Discovery* (New York, 1947); books on them for popular and juvenile consumption abound, but authoritative full-length biographies of each, using the new material, remain to be written. The best edition of Washington Irving's *Astorians*, first published in 1846, is that by Edgeley Todd (Norman, Okla., 1963). Zebulon Montgomery Pike's own published *Journal* (New York, 1810; London, 1811) should be supplemented by *The Expeditions of Z. M. Pike*, ed. Elliott Coues 3 vols. (New York, 1895), and a useful biography is Eugene W. Hollon: *The Lost Pathfinder* (Norman, 1949). *The Journals of Zebulon Montgomery Pike*, ed. Donald Jackson, 2 vols. (Norman, 1965), is definitive. See also Hollon's *Great American Desert Then and Now* for both Pike and Long. Reuben G. Thwaites has edited *Edwin James's Account of an Expedition from Pittsburgh to the Rocky Mountains* in his invaluable "Early Western Travel" series (Vol. XVII). Any library which possesses this magnificent and now rare *Early Western Travels, 1748–1846 . . . A series of annotated reprints*, 32 vols. (Cleveland, 1904–6), is indeed fortunate. For the history of the West in the period covered, it is invaluable. It has now been reprinted.

Fur Traders and Trappers of the Far West

This chapter was extensively annotated and much bibliographical information concerning individual traders and Mountain Men will be found in its footnotes. With a few exceptions only works of a more general and comprehensive nature will be listed here.

The first serious attempt to write a complete history of the fur trade, Hiram M. Chittenden's *The American Fur Trade of the Far West*, 3 vols. (New York, 1902; repr., 1935), remains valuable. It needs to be complemented by Harold D. Innis: *The Fur Trade in Canada* (New Haven, 1930; rev. edn., 1962). Robert Glass Cleland's *This Reckless Breed of Men: The Trappers and Fur Traders of the Southwest* (New York, 1950), both scholarly and absorbingly readable, deals more specifically with the trappers than with the traders, as does also Ray Allen Billington's *The American Frontiersman . . . An inaugural lecture . . .* (Oxford, 1954), although the chapter based on this in his *Far Western Frontier, 1830–50*, "New American Nation" series (New York, 1956), is more comprehensive and has a good bibliography. Grant Foreman: *Pioneer Days in the Old Southwest* (Cleveland, 1926), is a general survey of the trade between 1800 and 1840; William H. Goetzmann: *Army Exploration in the American West, 1803–63* (New Haven, 1960), deals with Mountain Men's trails as well and reproduces one of the few Mountain Man maps (that of Jim Baker) to have survived. Goetzmann also reproduces the important central section of Preuss's Second Frémont Expedition map. Carl L. Wheat's "Mapping the American West, 1540–1857," in *Proceedings of the American Antiquarian Society*, LXIV (1954), 19–194, is a useful guide; more specialized are Dale L. Morgan and Carl L. Wheat: *Jedediah Smith and his Maps of the American West* (San Francisco, 1954). Dale Morgan's model biography of the most important of the Mountain Men, *Jedediah Smith and the Opening of the West* (Indianapolis, 1953; Lincoln, Neb., 1962), with full bibliography, is also an account of the fur trade in wider perspective up to 1831; while his *The West of William H. Ashley: The International Struggle for the Fur Trade of the Missouri, the Rocky Mountains and the Columbia, 1822–1838* (Denver, 1964) is as broad in scope as its title is long. Earlier works of Dale Morgan, *The Great Salt Lake* (Indianapolis, 1947) and *The Humboldt: Highroad of the West* (New York, 1943), gave the historical geography of the Great Basin area. The activities of the Hudson's Bay Company in this period are best summarized by Frederick Merk in his introduction to *Fur Trade and Empire, George Simpson's Journal,*

1824–25 (Cambridge, Mass., 1931) and by E. E. Rich in his edition of
The Letters of John McLoughlin . . . First Series, 1825–38 (Toronto
and London, 1941). Rich has acted as general editor of the important
series of records of the Hudson's Bay Company, including the absorbing *Peter Skene Ogden's Snake Country Journals, 1824–25 and 1825–26*
(London, 1950), an epic story comparable to Harrison Dale's *The
Ashley Smith Explorations and the Discovery of the Central Route to
the Pacific, 1822–29* (Cleveland, 1918), which included the diary of
Smith's ebullient but unfortunate clerk, Harrison Rogers. Life in two
important bases for the fur trade is described in LeRoy R. Hafen and
Francis M. Young: *Fort Laramie and the Pageant of the West, 1834–
1890* (Glendale, 1938), and in David Lavender's somewhat more popu-
larly presented *Bent's Fort* (Garden City, N.Y., 1954), both of which
are also relevant to the following chapter. New editions of J. Cecil
Alter's *Jim Bridger* (Norman, 1962) and J. T. Kelly's *Old Greenwood*
(Georgetown, Calif., 1965), with the collaboration of Dale L. Morgan,
are vast improvements on earlier editions, which should no longer be
used; while LeRoy R. Hafen's monumental *The Mountain Men and the
Fur Trade of the West: Biographical Sketches by Scholars of the
Subject with Introductions by the Editor* (Glendale, 1963–), in progress, with two volumes so far published, bids fair to tell us, when
completed, all that we need and perhaps more than we ought to know
about these rugged and picturesque characters. But a broadly based,
scholarly, and up-to-date history of the fur trade of the Far West,
within reasonable compass and with a critical bibliography, is still
required and impatiently awaited.

Breaking the Wagon Trails West

Goetzmann's *Army Exploration* continues valuable for this topic,
to be supplemented by W. Turrentine Jackson: *Wagon Roads West: A
Study of Federal Road Survey and Construction in the Trans-Mississippi West, 1846–1869* (Berkeley, 1952; new edn., New Haven, 1965)
for the later, government road-building phases of establishing the
wagon trails. While awaiting William Brandon's new book on the
Santa Fe Trail, one can still use Henry Inman's *The Santa Fé Trail:
The Story of a Great Highway* (New York, 1898) and R. L. Duffus's
The Santa Fé Trail (New York, 1930). But the classic contemporary
account is Josiah Gregg: *Commerce of the Prairies*, 2 vols. (New
York, 1844); it has been many times reprinted, the Dallas (1933) and
Norman (1954) editions are among the best. This should be supple-
mented by James J. Webb: *Adventures on the Santa Fe Trail, 1844–47*
(Glendale, 1931), and Philip St. George Cooke: *Scenes and Adven-
tures in the Army* (New York, 1857); Cooke had been on the Trail

both in 1829 and in 1843. Eugene C. Barker wrote the standard biography *Stephen F. Austin, Founder of Texas* (Nashville, 1925); and also *Mexico and Texas, 1821–36* (Dallas, 1928); and William Hogan's *The Texas Republic* (Norman, 1946) is the best general history. William C. Binkley's *Expansionist Movement in Texas, 1836–50* (Berkeley, Calif., 1935) portrays the Lone Star State's overweening ambitions. Marquis James: *The Raven* (Indianapolis, 1929), is a satisfactory life of Sam Houston. For the opening up of the Oregon country O. O. Winther's *The Great Northwest: A History* (New York, 1947) is a good scholarly account. More popular accounts are W. J. Ghent: *The Road to Oregon* (New York, 1929), which is very readable; Jay Monaghan: *The Overland Trail* (Indianapolis, 1937), dealing with other trails as well; and David Lavender: *Westward Vision* (New York, 1962). More detailed treatments are to be found in LeRoy R. and Anne Hafen: *To the Rockies and Oregon, 1832–1842* (Glendale, 1955), and Clifford Drury: *Marcus Whitman, M.D., Prophet and Martyr* (Caldwell, Idaho, 1937), *H. H. Spaulding* (Caldwell, 1936), *Elkanah and Mary Walker* (Caldwell, 1940), and *First White Women over the Rockies*, 3 vols. (Glendale, 1963, 1966). The Hafen and Drury books contain skilfully edited diaries and letters of major importance, some never previously published. The diary of Narcissa Prentice Whitman has literary as well as historical value. William N. Bischoff, S.J., has written *The Jesuits in Old Oregon* (Caldwell, 1945), a survey of that order's local activities, and a definitive biography of Pierre-Jean De Smet is eagerly awaited from the pen of Father W. L. Davis. James C. Bell: *Opening of a Highway to the Pacific, 1838–46* (New York, 1921), dealt with both the Oregon and the California trails, but George R. Stewart: *The California Trail* (New York, 1962), treats the latter in much greater detail, while his *Opening of the California Trail* (Berkeley, 1953) and his *Ordeal by Hunger* (New York, 1936; rev. edn., Berkeley and London, 1961) prints original diaries and letters of the Stevens-Murphy and the Donner parties, respectively, as well as telling their stories. Norman A. Graebner: *Empire on the Pacific* (New York, 1955), and Frederick Merk: *Manifest Destiny and Mission* (New York, 1960), present interesting if not entirely convincing new interpretations of the Americanization of the Pacific slopes. The Mormon trek to Utah is discussed by Nels Anderson in his *Desert Saints: The Mormon Frontier in Utah* (Chicago, 1942), by Andrew L. Neff in his *History of Utah, 1847–60* (Salt Lake City, 1949), and by Leonard Arrington in his monumental *Great Basin Kingdom* (Cambridge, Mass., 1958). Says Wallace Stegner in his skilfully written and carefully researched *The Gathering of Zion: The Story of the Mormon Trail* (New York, 1964; London, 1965): "The literature on the Mormons is enormous, repetitious, contradictory and embattled," and his "Word of Bibliography" (pp. 313–19) offers the handiest guide, to date, to that battlefield. He points out that a comprehensive Mormon Trail bibliography yet remains to be compiled, not by himself but, preferably, by "someone who is in the confidence of the Church Historian" (p. 315).

By Land and Sea to El Dorado

The American take-over of Mexican Alta California, before and after the conquest, is discussed in R. G. Cleland: *The Early Sentiment for the Annexation of California . . . 1835–1846* (Austin, Tex., 1915), in the introduction by J. A. Hawgood to *First and Last Consul: Thomas Oliver Larkin and the Americanization of California—A Selection of Letters* (San Marino, Calif., 1962; repr. Palo Alto, Calif., 1967), by Josiah Royce in *California . . . 1846–1856* (New York, 1885; repr. with a valuable intro. by R. G. Cleland, New York, 1948), and in Cleland's *From Wilderness to Empire*, Rolle's *California: A History*, and Graebner's *Empire on the Pacific*. An excellent contemporary account is Walter Colton: *Three Years in California* (New York, 1850), covering the period 1846–9 and thus including the American occupation, the early stages of the Gold Rush, and the framing of California's first constitution (which is reproduced in an appendix) as well. See also T. Grivas's *Military Government in California* (Glendale, 1960). William Tecumseh Sherman's *Memoirs*, Vol. I (New York, 1890), covers the occupation and the Gold Rush while he was adjutant to the military governor, Colonel Mason; but the memoirs of John Charles Frémont do not, only the first volume (New York, 1887), which breaks off in 1845, ever having been published. His *Geographical Memoir on California* (Washington, D. C., 1849; repr. with an intro. by Allan Nevins, San Francisco, 1965) was a compilation of material from a number of sources, rushed out to meet public demand. Mrs. Jessie B. Frémont's *A Year of American Travel* (New York, 1878; repr. San Francisco, 1960) contains a vivid account of the journey to California via the Isthmus of Panama and up the Pacific coast in 1849, and of the riches of the "Mariposa Grant." Women, despite their scarcity in California at the time, have written some of the best first-hand description of the early mining camps, among them Louise Clappe's ("Dame Shirley") in *The Shirley Letters from the California Mines* (best edn. with notes by Carl Wheat, New York, 1949), and Sarah Royce (mother of Josiah Royce), whose letters were edited by Ralph H. Gabriel as *A Frontier Lady* (New Haven, 1932). Mrs. Clappe includes a good account of mining methods, and so does the Swiss traveler Carl Meyer in *Nach dem Sacramento* (Aarau, 1856), tr. Ruth Axe and ed.

Henry Wagner under the title *Bound for Sacramento* (Claremont, 1938). Rodman W. Paul: *California Gold: The Beginning of Mining in the Far West* (Cambridge, Mass., 1947), is a useful modern summary of mining developments, and he has edited *The Miner's Own Book: Containing correct Illustrations and Descriptions of the Various Modes of California Mining* (San Francisco, 1949: orig. pub. San Francisco, 1858) and an anthology, *The Discovery of Gold in California* (Georgetown, Calif., 1966). Published memoirs and diaries of participants in the California Gold Rush are legion and grow more numerous yearly. Carl Wheat, in *Books of the California Gold Rush* (San Francisco, 1949), critically appraises many of these. A handy anthology, containing long extracts from a number of the best first-hand accounts, is *Pictures of Gold Rush California*, ed. M. M. Quaife (Chicago, 1949), illustrated with contemporary drawings. Perhaps the most renowned book to come out of the California Gold Rush was Bayard Taylor's *Eldorado*, 2 vols. (New York, 1850); the best modern edition is that by R. G. Cleland in one volume (New York, 1949). Less polished but more spontaneous are *The Journals, Drawings and other Papers of J. Goldsborough Bruff*, ed. Georgia W. Read and Ruth Gaines, 2 vols. (New York, 1944), with his own delightful if crude illustrations. San Francisco's remarkable history up to the end of 1855 was chronicled in detail by Frank Soulé, John H. Gihon, and James Nisbet in *Annals of San Francisco* (New York, 1855), copiously illustrated. Less detailed but more comprehensive is John S. Hittell: *History of the City of San Francisco and Incidentally of the State of California* (San Francisco, 1878)—a revealing title. His *Resources of California* (San Francisco, 1863) is valuable for statistics of early growth, to be compared with the more impressionistic word-picture of San Francisco and California in 1859 written by R. H. Dana for the revised edition of his *Two Years before the Mast* (see above, p. 164).

The Mining Boom Moves Inland

The "Essay on Bibliography" (pp. 217–230) in Rodman W. Paul's *Mining Frontiers of the Far West, 1848–1880* (New York, 1963) is most valuable; the book itself is a useful introductory guide to the various mining frontiers and especially to the evolution of mining techniques. W. P. Morrell: *The Gold Rushes* (London, 1940; New York, 1941), broadens the canvas and sets the American gold strikes in their world perspective. Mark Twain's *Roughing It* (Hartford, 1872; many subsequent eds.) is important both for the literature and for the history of the Nevada silver frontier, but factually "Dan de Quille" (William Wright): *History of the Big Bonanza* (Hartford, 1876; repr.

with orig. illus., New York, 1947), and Grant H. Smith: *History of the Comstock Lode, 1850–1920* (Reno, Nev., 1943), are more dependable. Eliot Lord: *Comstock Mining and Miners*, U. S. Geological Survey Monograph (Washington, D. C., 1883), should be used in the modern edition by David F. Myrick (Berkeley, 1959). Samuel Bowles: *Our New West* (Hartford, 1869), describes the Nevada and Colorado mining districts as he saw them in the course of two official trips as a member of the entourage of Vice-President Schuyler Carfax, one by stage coach and one by train. Other well-known journalists who took and wrote up this grand tour of the diggings were Horace Greeley (*An Overland Journey*, New York, 1860), A. D. Richardson (*Beyond the Mississippi*, Hartford, 1867), and Henry Villard (*Past and Present of the Pikes Peak Gold Region*, St. Louis, 1860). Specialist and technical material on the Colorado mines is listed by Rodman Paul in his bibliography (*Mining Frontiers*, pp. 223–5). A selection of contemporary Colorado material was presented by LeRoy R. Hafen in *Colorado Gold Rush: Contemporary Letters and Reports, 1858–1859* (Glendale, Calif., 1941). M. G. Burlingame and K. Ross Toole: *A History of Montana*, 3 vols. (New York, 1957), gives the not always sober truth about the Montana Gold Rush; and T. J. Dimsdale: *The Vigilantes in Montana* (Virginia City, Mont., 1866; repr. Norman, Okla., 1953), and N. P. Langford: *Vigilante Days and Ways*, 2 vols. (Boston, 1890), mix truth with a certain amount of fiction. Two of the best accounts by participants are Granville Stuart: *Journals and Reminiscences*, 2 vols. (Cleveland, 1925), and the diary of James K. P. Miller ("J. Sidney Osborn"), edited by Andrew F. Rolle as *The Road to Virginia City* (Norman, Okla., 1960). William J. Trimble: *The Mining Advance into the Inland Empire: A Comparative Study of the Beginnings of the Mining Industry in Idaho and Montana, Eastern Washington and Oregon, and the Southern Interior of British Columbia* . . . (Madison, Wis., 1914), is as useful and comprehensive as its portmanteau title indicates, and it is still not "dated." Richard B. Hills: *Pioneer Years in the Black Hills* was edited by Agnes Wright Spring (Glendale, 1957). Mrs. Spring's own *The Cheyenne and Black Hills Stage and Express Routes* (Glendale, 1949; repr. Lincoln, Neb., 1964), while even more relevant for the succeeding chapter, is also useful here, for these routes served the mining frontier primarily. A good scholarly history of mining in the Black Hills is still needed, though the amount of trash written about bad men and bad women in Deadwood Gulch has been voluminous. Estelline Bennett's reminiscences, *Old Deadwood Days* (New York, 1928), are, by way of exception, authentic as well as colorful. The publication of Moses Manuel's "Forty-Eight Years in the West," an incomplete typescript of which is in the possession of the

Homestake Mining Company of South Dakota, would seem to be overdue, judging by the samples of it quoted by Rodman Paul. The Southern Arizona mining region has also suffered badly from the pulp merchants, from whom the eagerly awaited book by John Gilchriese, of Tucson, on the Earps at Tombstone (and points north, east, and west) may rescue it. Meanwhile one has to be content with the semi-scholarly works of Stuart N. Lake (*Wyatt Earp*, Boston, 1931), Walter Noble Burns (*Tombstone*, Garden City, N. Y., 1927), and similar offerings—good reading but not definitive history. Meanwhile see also *It Happened in Tombstone*, ed. J. Gilchriese (Tucson, 1965). Some useful articles on the Arizona and other mining frontiers are listed in Winther's *Classified Bibliography of Periodical Literature*. John M. Myers: *The Last Chance: Tombstone's Early Years* (New York, 1950), breaks off in the middle of a good story but is useful as far as it goes. Historians of the copper frontier in Montana have met with certain frustrations, but Joseph Kinsey Howard's charmingly written *Montana: High, Wide and Handsome* (New Haven, 1943; repr. New Haven, 1966) and K. Ross Toole's *Montana: An Uncommon Land* (Norman, 1959) both took courageous bites at that cherry. The true history of the Anaconda Company (a useless "company history" already exists) is anticipated one day from the pen of Dr. Toole—if he doesn't get shot in the back first.

The Revolution in Western Transportation

Another Winther bibliography, that to his *The Transportation Frontier: Trans-Mississippi West, 1865–1890* (New York, 1964), pp. 198–210, is valuable here, and the book itself is indispensable. We are also indebted to Oscar Osburn Winther for *Express and Stagecoach Days in California* (Stanford, 1936), while Chapter xviii of his *Old Oregon Country: A History of Trade, Transportation and Travel* (Stanford, 1950) performs a similar service for the Pacific Northwest. The works, all already cited, of W. Turrentine Jackson, William Goetzmann—his *Exploration and Empire* (New York, 1966) should now be added to his *Army Exploration*—Agnes Wright Spring, and James K. P. Miller (edited by Andrew Rolle) continue relevant here, as do the contemporary descriptions of western stagecoach travel by Samuel Bowles, Horace Greeley, and—of course—Mark Twain. Sir Richard Burton, in his celebrated *City of the Saints* (London, 1861; repr. with intro. by Fawn Brodie, New York and London, 1963), gives a detailed itinerary of his stagecoach travel to the Great Salt Lake and California, making illuminating comparisons with the rigors of Old World travel. Lyle H. Wright and Josephine M. Bynum have edited W. L. Ormsby's sprightly diary of the first westward run of the

Butterfield Overland Mail (San Marino, 1942; repr. 1955) over the southern route in 1858; and Roscoe P. and Mary B. Conkling have written its history, exhaustively, in three volumes, *The Butterfield Overland Mail, 1857–1860* (Glendale, 1947). LeRoy R. Hafen: *The Overland Mail, 1849–1869* (Cleveland, 1926) is a comprehensive account, while the Russell, Majors, and Waddell enterprises are covered in *Empire on Wheels* by Ramond W. and Mary L. Settle (Stanford, 1949; rev. edn. 1965) and those of Holladay in J. V. Frederick: *Ben Holladay: The Stagecoach King* (Glendale, 1940). Oscar Winther's *Via Western Express and Stagecoach* (Stanford, 1945) is a useful and readable introduction to a vast subject. Railroad history, also, can only be dealt with here most selectively. Robert E. Riegel: *The Story of the Western Railroads* (New York, 1926) is a still useful, general account; but Ira G. Clark: *Then Came the Railroad: The Century from Steam to Diesel in the Southwest* (Norman, 1958) is more up-to-date, though geographically more restricted in its scope. John F. Stover's *American Railroads* (Chicago, 1961) covers the whole country, including the West. Professional engineers' accounts of transcontinental railroad building include Granville M. Dodge: *Romantic Realities: The Story of the Pacific Roads* (Omaha, 1889) and John D. Galloway: *The First Trans-Continental Railroad* (New York, 1950). Robert L. Fulton's stopgap *Epic of the Overland* (San Francisco, 1924) still leaves the saga of the Central Pacific only partially recited. Later scholarly histories of individual western railroads include Leslie L. Waters: *Steel Trails to Santa Fe* (Lawrence, Kansas, 1950); Robert Athearn: *Rebel of the Rockies* (New Haven, 1962), the story of the Denver and Rio Grande Western Railroad; Richard C. Overton: *Burlington West* (Cambridge, Mass., 1941), and his *Burlington Route* (New York, 1965); while James B. Hedges in *Henry Villard and the Railways of the Northwest* (New Haven, 1930) has perhaps produced the best book on the career of one of the great railroad building and promoting tycoons. George T. Clark's *Leland Stanford* (Palo Alto, 1931) deals in detail with Stanford's connection with the Central Pacific; Oscar Lewis's *The Big Four: The Story of Huntington, Stanford, Hopkins and Crocker, and of the Building of the Central Pacific* (New York, 1938) is a more readable but somewhat popular account—and a good introduction to the subject—but adequate biographies of Collis P. and Henry E. Huntington remain to be written when pious descendants and trustees come to realize that there is really nothing left that is worth hiding and that the truth is the best way of scotching ugly rumors. They should recollect how Collis himself dealt with Frank Norris (see above, p. 361). James J. Hill and E. H. Harriman also await definitive and all-revealing biographies. It will probably be just as difficult to produce scholarly biographies of the airline tycoons of America when the time comes to sum up men like Howard Hughes, Juan Trippe, Cyrus Smith Eddie Rickenbaker, and "Bud" Maytag.

The Indian Problem and Its Solution

William Brandon: *The American Heritage Book of Indians*, illustrated (New York, 1961; repr. 1964), is by far the best general account of a nontechnical nature. It is better than either Oliver La Farge's *A Pictorial History of the American Indian* (New York, 1956), which nevertheless possesses many virtues, or the National Geographic Society's publication *Indians of the Americas—A Color-illustrated Record*, ed. Matthew W. Stirling (Washington, D. C., 1955), which is most uneven in the quality of its contributions and illustrations, though some are very good indeed. Both these books remain useful, but Brandon's is outstanding, though it does not, unfortunately, contain a bibliography. For this one must use Harold E. Driver's *Indians of North America* (Chicago, 1961), the approach of which is mainly anthropological, and other and older works of a similar nature already cited in the first section of this bibliographical essay. Books varying in quality on almost every important Indian tribal group exist, and many of these have been published by the enterprising University of Oklahoma Press, whose catalogue itself constitutes a valuable bibliography. A more general work, also published by that press, is Edward E. Dale: *The Indians of the Southwest: A Century of Development under the United States* (Norman, 1949); while Carl C. Rister: *The Southwestern Frontier, 1865–1881* (Cleveland, 1928), dealing more specifically with Indian warfare, is still useful. A classic treatment of the Indian wars is Jacob P. Dunn: *Massacres of the Mountains* (New York, 1886; repr. with orig. illus., ed. J. A. Hawgood, London, 1962). Less satisfactory is Alvin M. Josephy: *The Patriot Chiefs* (New Haven, 1961; London, 1963), comprising nine biographical sketches of Indian resistance leaders, from the semimythical Hiawatha to Chief Joseph; but the same author's *The Nez Percé Indians and the Opening of the West* (New Haven, 1965) is somewhat better. A bibliography of Indian battles, army frontier reminiscences and of biographies of army generals in the West would fill a volume in itself, and one of Custer and his Last Stand would alone occupy many pages. Robert Utley's *The Custer Legend* (New Haven, 1962) contains a critical appraisal of much Custer literature. George Custer's own reminiscences, *My Life on the Plains* (St. Louis, 1876), still remains more readable—and revealing—than most other books about him, while its anonymous continuation in *Wild Life on the Plains* (Minneapolis, 1891) is an interesting period piece displaying White Man attitudes at about the time of the Ghost Dance crisis.

Official Indian policy is discussed more systematically and dispassionately in Loring B. Priest: *Uncle Sam's Stepchildren: The Reformation of United States Indian Policy, 1865–1887* (New Brunswick, N. J., 1942), and in Flora W. Seymour: *Indian Agents of the Old Frontier* (New York, 1941); while Roy L. Robbins: *Our Landed Heritage* (Princeton, N. J., 1942; repr. Lincoln, Neb., 1961) is invaluable on the policy toward Indian-owned lands. Helen Hunt Jackson's shrill though timely protest, *A Century of Dishonor* (New York, 1881), has recently been twice reprinted (see above, p. 283). Richard H. Pratt's *Battlefield and Classroom: Four Decades with the American Indians* has been re-edited by Robert M. Utley (New Haven, 1964).

The Cowman's Frontier

The Ranching Frontier has perhaps inspired more good writing, and it has certainly spawned more bad writing than any other. The following works stand in the first class: Ernest S. Osgood: *The Day of the Cattlemen* (Minneapolis, 1929); Edward E. Dale: *The Range Cattle Industry* (Norman, 1930); Louis Pelzer: *The Cattlemen's Frontier* (Glendale, 1936); and Lewis Atherton: *The Cattle Kings* (Chicago, 1961), to mention only general surveys. More specialized studies of high quality are Wayne Gard: *The Chisholm Trail* (Norman, 1954), and Robert Glass Cleland: *Cattle on a Thousand Hills* (San Marino, 1947) and *The Irvine Ranch* (San Marino, 1952; rev. by Robert V. Hine, San Marino, 1962)—the last two dealing with the cattle industry in Southern California. Out of the vast array of cowman and cowboy reminiscences only a few can be mentioned, but every short list should include Joseph G. McCoy: *Historic Sketches of the Cattle Trade of the West and Southwest* (1874; repr. Washington, D. C., 1932, and Glendale, 1940); Charles A. Siringo: *A Texas Cowboy, or Fifteen Years on the Hurricane Deck of a Spanish Pony* (New York, 1885; repr. 1950); W. S. James: *Cow-Boy Life in Texas* (Chicago, 1893); and—best of all, though recounted in fictional form—Andy Adams: *The Log of a Cowboy* (Boston, 1903; New York, 1931; also available paperbound). Andy Adams also attempted with far less success to write a fictionalized life of Charlie Goodnight, *Reed Anthony, Cowman* (Boston, 1907), but the biography by J. Evetts Haley, *Charles Goodnight: Cowman and Plainsman* (Boston, 1936; repr. Norman, 1949), is more dependable. W. H. Hutchinson: *A Bar Cross Man: The Life and Personal Writings of Eugene Manlove Rhodes* (Norman, 1956), tells the engaging story of another literary cowboy, while May D. Rhodes's tribute to her husband, *The Hired Man on Horseback* (Boston, 1938), is altogether delightful (see above, p. 334). The best analysis of the cowboy cult is Joe B. Frantz and Julian E. Choate: *The*

American Cowboy: The Myth and the Reality (Norman, 1955), and it has an excellent bibliography, which now could do with a little updating. Another useful bibliography is Ramon Adams: *Six Guns and Saddle Leather: A Bibliography of Books and Pamphlets on Western Outlaws and Gunmen* (Norman, 1954), for those who find bad men and outlaws "more interesting" than good men and true. J. Frank Dobie's salty *Guide to Life and Literature of the Southwest* (Dallas, 1943; rev. edn., Dallas, 1952) is literature in itself and disposes of *My Reminiscences as a Cowboy* (by that archphony Frank Harris) in one well-barbed line as "a blatant farrago of lies, included in this list because of its supreme worthlessness" (p. 64). Frantz and Choate have runners-up as analysts of the ethos of the cowboy in Douglas Branch: *The Cowboy and his Interpreters* (New York, 1926); Paul Horgan: *Great River: The Rio Grande in North American History* (New York, 1954; rev. edn. 1960); and Ramon Adams: *The Best of the American Cowboy* (Norman, 1957) and *The Old-Time Cowhand* (New York, 1961), the last two being part analysis and part anthology. (For a ripe piece of Ramon Adams, see above, pp. 329–32.) Walter Prescott Webb, once again, in *The Great Plains* and *The Texas Rangers* (Boston, 1935) has much to say—and all of it worth reading and rereading—on the cowman's frontier. His somewhat dated references to the barbed-wire frontier can now be supplemented from F. T. and H. D. McCallum: *The Wire That Fenced the Plains* (Norman, 1965). Clifford P. Westermeier's *Trailing the Cowboy: His Life and Lore as told by Frontier Journalists* (Caldwell, Idaho, 1955) is another valuable anthology. Westermeier is also one of the best interpreters of the contemporary cowhand, as in his "The Modern Cowboy—An Image," in *The American West*, ed. R. G. Ferris (Santa Fe, 1963), pp. 34 ff. The despised sheepman has been dealt with by Charles W. Towne and Edward N. Wentworth in *Shepherd's Empire* (Norman, 1945).

Land for the Farmer

Webb's *Great Plains* and Robbins's *Landed Heritage* remain most useful, while Fred A. Shannon's *The Farmer's Last Frontier: Agriculture, 1860–1897* (New York, 1945), one of the best volumes so far published in the series "The Economic History of the United States," is not only the standard work on the subject but devotes a whole chapter (pp. 379–414) to its "literature." For works published before 1945 this is comprehensive, and titles of books it mentions need not be repeated here. Since 1945 Paul W. Gates has given further dimension to the study of the American agricultural frontier in books like *Fifty Million Acres: Conflicts over Kansas Land Policy, 1854–90*. (Ithaca,

N. Y., 1954) and *Agriculture and the Civil War* (New York, 1965) to supplement his articles in periodicals and his earlier book on *The Illinois Central Railroad and its Colonization Work* (Cambridge, Mass., 1934). His volume on American agriculture between 1815 and 1860 (New York, 1962) in "The Economic History of the United States" series is also valuable and an essential background to much of Shannon's story. Shannon was a feuding historian, tilting not only at the windbags but also at some of the "national monuments" of the profession. He even took on Webb in "An Appraisal of Walter Prescott Webb's *The Great Plains:* A Study in Institutions and Environment," in *Critiques of Research in the Social Sciences* (New York, 1940), and Turner in "A Post-Mortem on the Labor-Safety-Valve Theory," *Agricultural History*, SIX (1945), 31–7 (see above, p. 386). The crusade against inadequate land policies was blasted off by Henry George in *Our Land and Land Policy, National and Federal* (San Francisco, 1871); Hamlin Garland's *Main Traveled Roads* appeared in 1891, and so did W. A. Peffer's *The Farmer's Side, His Troubles and his Remedies;* Frank Norris's *The Octopus* (see above, p. 362) was first published in 1901. All these constitute landmarks in the literary expression of agrarian unrest. The life and writings of Hamlin Garland provide revealing commentary on two generations of American agrarian history, and his autobiographical novel, *A Son of the Middle Border* (New York, 1917), sketches many of its ecstasies and agonies. One of the best recent accounts of the whole process of agrarian political protest since the Civil War is Russell B. Nye: *Midwestern Progressive Politics: A Historical Study of its Origins and Development, 1870–1950* (Lansing, Mich., 1951). This fills in details which the inevitably more impressionistic literary contributions to the subject tend to omit. The dramatic opening up of Oklahoma to agricultural settlement in and after 1889 is recounted in Edward E. Dale's and Morris L. Wardell's *History of Oklahoma* (New York, 1948) and in Grant Forman's *A History of Oklahoma* (Norman, 1942). The birth of cities overnight is told in *Guthrie: Oklahoma's First Capital* (Norman, 1938) by Gerald Forbes and in *The First Eight Months of Oklahoma City* (Norman, 1939) by Irving Geffs. Marquis James, in *Cherokee Strip* (New York and London, 1947), retails with delightful touches his boyhood and adolescence in the Oklahoma Territory and the new State before taking off (in 1911) for Kansas City and the great world. The best brief account of the farming frontier in Utah is to be found in Leonard J. Arrington's *Great Basin Kingdom: An Economic History of the Latter Day Saints, 1830–1890* (Cambridge, Mass., 1958); and an early but still useful account, *Irrigation in Utah* (Baltimore, 1898), was written by C. H. Brough. Mormon colonization policy and techniques in Utah are described by M. R. Hunter in *Brigham Young the Colonizer* (Salt Lake City, 1940) and by P. A. M. Taylor in *Expectations Westward: The Mormons and the Emigration of their British Converts in the Nineteenth Century* (Edinburgh and London, 1965). This has an excellent classified bibliography, comprehending far more than the emigration of British converts to Utah. Dry-farming techniques, with special reference to Utah, are discussed by W. MacDonald in *Dry Farming: Its Principles and Practice* (New York, 1911) and by John A. Widtsoe in *Dry Farming* (New York, 1914), as well as by W. P. Webb in *The Great Plains*. J. Wesley Powell's highly influential *Report on the Lands of the Arid Region of the United States* (Washington, D. C., 1878) has been discussed and appraised by Wallace Stegner in *Beyond the Hundredth Meridian: John Wesley Powell and the Second Opening of the West* (New York, 1954; also available paperbound), a brilliant study. Brigham Young's most important pronouncements have been edited by John A. Widtsoe in *Discourses of Brigham Young* (Salt Lake City, 1946). The farming frontier as it was in 1876 is well displayed in *Rand McNally's Pioneer Atlas of the American West (The Business Atlas of the Great Mississippi Valley and the Pacific Slope)*, first edition (Chicago, 1876; repr. and ed. Dale L. Morgan, Chicago, 1956). Gilbert Fite: *The Farmer's Frontier, 1865–1900* (New York 1966) has now appeared to supplement Shannon and update his bibliography.

The End of the West? Twentieth-Century Frontiers

The latest appraisal of Frederick Jackson Turner and his influence is Ray A. Billington: *The Frontier Heritage* (New York, 1966), with comprehensive bibliographical notes. Dr. Billington's biography of Turner is eagerly awaited by the whole Western Americanist fraternity, bouquets and long knives poised. Wilbur R. Jacobs has already edited (San Marino, 1965) *Frederick Jackson Turner's Legacy*, containing the master's unpublished writings in American history. Lonewolf Fred A. Shannon's attack upon Turner in "A Post-Mortem on the Labor Safety Theory"—also reprinted with other attacks upon and defences of Turner in *The Turner Thesis*, ed. George R. Taylor, in "Problems in American Civilization" Series (Boston, 1949), and in R. A. Billington's *The Frontier Thesis: Valid Interpretation of American History?* in "American Problem Studies" (New York, 1966)—attracted a number of jackals in his wake, but the controversy surrounding the validity of the Turner Frontier Hypothesis has also helped to produce such excellent and thoughtful books as Henry Nash Smith's *Virgin Land* (New York, 1949), David Potter's *People of Plenty* (Chicago, 1954), and Carl F. Kraenzel's *The Great Plains in Transition* (Norman, 1955). The counterattack on the anti-Turner reaction has now commenced, as in Ellen von Nardroff: "The American Frontier as a Safety Valve—The Life, Death, Reincarnation, and Justification of a Theory," *Agricultural History*, XXXVI (1962), 123–42. Some effects of the ending of the frontier phase in American history are discussed by John C. Parish in his *The Persistence of the Westward Movement and other Essays* (Berkeley, 1943) and in the series of papers contributed to a University of Wisconsin symposium in 1954 and edited by Walker D. Wyman and Clifton B. Kroeber as *The Frontier in Perspective* (Madison, 1957). On immigration a useful general survey is Maldwyn Jones: *American Immigration* (Chicago, 1960). The standard treatments include John R. Commons: *Races and Immigrants in America* (New York and London, 1907); N. W. Stephenson: *A History of American Immigration* (Boston, 1926); Marcus W. Hansen: *The Immigrant in American History* (New York and London, 1941) and *The Atlantic Migration, 1607–1860* (Cambridge, Mass., 1940; repr. New York, 1961); and Oscar Handlin: *The Uprooted* (New York, 1951). Handlin's main thesis is about to be challenged in "The Upraised" by Andrew F. Rolle (with an introduction by Ray A. Billington). Rolle's *California: A History* contains useful statistics and forecasts concerning the population explosion in the Golden State during the twentieth century. Earl S. Pomeroy in his *The Pacific Slope* (New York, 1964) broadens the survey to the whole West Coast region, while his *In Search of the Golden West: The Tourist in Western America* (New York, 1957) and Glenn S. Dumke's *The Boom of the Eighties in Southern California* (San Marino, 1944) discuss earlier periods of prosperity and promotion in the Far West. What may be called the ultimate odd-ball frontier is beautifully dissected by Robert V. Hine in his *California's Utopian Colonies, 1850–1950* (San Marino, 1953; repr. New Haven, 1966). The urbanization of western America is discussed by Richard C. Wade in *The Urban Frontier* (Cambridge, Mass., 1959) and by Wilbur C. Hallenbeck in *American Urban Communities* (New York, 1951). For the early oil frontier see Harold F. Williamson and Arnold Daum: *The American Petroleum Industry—The Age of Illumination, 1859–1899* (Evanston, Illinois, 1959). See also J. S. Clark's *The Oil Century* (Norman, 1958).

INDEX

(i)

A NOTE ABOUT THE AUTHOR

JOHN A. HAWGOOD was born in Sussex, England, in 1905. After taking his B.A. (1926) and M.A. (1928) at University College, London, and his Ph.D. (1928) at Heidelberg, he studied American history at Yale University and the University of Wisconsin. His research into the history of the American West has continued in most of the major research libraries in this country. He has been research associate at the Hoover Institute of Stanford University and research fellow in the social sciences of the Rockefeller Foundation in both Europe and the United States. During the war he served in the British Foreign Office—in the Political Intelligence Department from 1940 to 1943 and with the Political Warfare Executive from 1943 to 1945. Since the war he has been a consultant to the Library of Congress and a resident fellow of the Newberry Library in Chicago.

Much of his research for *America's Western Frontiers* was done at the Huntington Library, San Marino, California, and at the Bancroft Library in Berkeley. Mr. Hawgood, who is also an authority on the history of Germany, was led to his American studies as a result of his research here on mid-nineteenth-century emigration of Germans to the United States. He is married, the father of five grown children, and is presently professor of American history at the University of Birmingham, England. In 1944 the University of London conferred on him its coveted D.Lit. for his first three published works: *Political and Economic Relations between the U. S. A. and the German Provisional Central Government . . . 1848–1849*; *Modern Constitutions since 1787*; and *The Tragedy of German-America. America's Western Frontiers* is his seventh book.

A Note on the Type

The text of this book was set on the Linotype in Janson, a re-cutting made direct from type cast from matrices long thought to have been made by the Dutchman Anton Janson, who was a practicing type founder in Leipzig during the years 1668–87. However, it has been conclusively demonstrated that these types are actually the work of Nicholas Kis (1650–1702), a Hungarian, who most probably learned his trade from the master Dutch type founder Kirk Voskens. The type is an excellent example of the influential and sturdy Dutch types that prevailed in England up to the time William Caslon developed his own incomparable designs from these Dutch faces.

Composed, printed, and bound by

Kingsport Press, Inc., Kingsport, Tenn.

Typography and binding by

GUY FLEMING